COMIC SUPPORT

COMIC SUPPORT

Second Bananas
in the Movies

by Ronald L. Smith

A Citadel Press Book
Published by Carol Publishing Group

A Citadel Press Book
Published by Carol Publishing Group
Citadel Press is a registered trademark of Carol Communications, Inc.
Editorial Offices: 600 Madison Avenue, New York, N.Y. 10022
Sales and Distribution Offices: 120 Enterprise Avenue, Secaucus, N.J. 07094
In Canada: Canadian Manda Group, P.O. Box 920, Station U, Toronto, Ontario M8Z 5P9

Queries regarding rights and permissions should be addressed to
Carol Publishing Group, 600 Madison Avenue, New York, N.Y. 10022

Carol Publishing Group books are available at special discounts for bulk purchases, for sales promotion, fund-raising, or educational purposes. Special editions can be created to specifications. For details, contact: Special Sales Department, Carol Publishing Group, 120 Enterprise Avenue, Secaucus, N.J. 07094

Manufactured in the United States of America

10 9 8 7 6 5 4 3 2 1

Library of Congress Cataloging-in-Publication Data

Smith, Ronald L., 1952–
    Comic support: second bananas in the movies / by Ronald L. Smith
        p. cm.
    "A Citadel Press book."
    ISBN 0-8065-1399-3
    1. Motion picture actors and actresses. 2. Comedians. I. Title.
PN1998.2.S59 1993
791.43'028'092273—dc20   92-37559
                                                              CIP

Cast of Characters

Iris Adrian
Luis Alberni   Frank Albertson   Mabel Albertson
Eddie "Rochester" Anderson   Edward Andrews
Henry Armetta   Roscoe Ates   Mischa Auer

Baby LeRoy
Carl Ballantine   John Banner   Billy Barty
Bea Benaderet   Joe Besser   Willie Best
Herman Bing   Eric Blore   Ben Blue
Walter Brennan   Felix Bressart   Helen Broderick
Nigel Bruce   Edgar Buchanan   Billie Burke
Smiley Burnette   Mae Busch   Charles Butterworth
Pat Buttram

Eric Campbell
Ron Carey   Leo Carrillo
Walter Catlett   Fred Clark   Andy Clyde
Charles Coburn   James Coco   Jerry Colonna
Hans Conreid   Scatman Crothers

Cass Daley
Richard Deacon   Kenny Delmar
Vernon Dent   Andy Devine   Billy DeWolfe
Dudley Dickerson   Fifi D'Orsay   Margaret Dumont

Cliff Edwards
Leon Errol   Stuart Erwin   Tom Ewell

Herbie Faye
Fritz Feld   Norman Fell   Parker Fennelly
Stepin Fetchit   James Finlayson   Joe Flynn
Frank Fontaine   Paul Ford   William Frawley

Vincent Gardenia
Anita Garvin   Alice Ghostley
Billy Gilbert   George Givot   James Gleason
Bert Gordon   Gale Gordon   Charlotte Greenwood

Alan Hale, Jr.
Charles Hall   Thurston Hall
Margaret Hamilton   Richard Haydn
George "Gabby" Hayes   Hugh Herbert
Sterling Holloway   Edward Everett Horton
Arthur Housman   Shemp Howard

Marty Ingels

Lou Jacobi
Bud Jamison   Allen Jenkins   Gordon Jones

Carol Kane
Marvin Kaplan   Stubby Kaye
Larry Keating   Patsy Kelly   Pert Kelton
Edgar Kennedy   Guy Kibbee   Percy Kilbride
Leonid Kinsky   Fuzzy Knight

Elsa Lanchester
Harvey Lembeck   Sheldon Leonard   Sam Levene
Richard Libertini   George Lindsey   Marion Lorne

Donald MacBride
Gavin MacLeod   Marjorie Main
Chuck McCann   Hattie McDaniel   John McGiver
Frank McHugh   Howard McNear   Kay Medford
Victor Moore   Polly Moran   Mantan Moreland
Pat Morita   Burt Mustin

Jack Norton

Dave O'Brien
Virginia O'Brien   Una O'Connor
Edna May Oliver   J. Pat O'Malley

Eugene Pallette
Franklin Pangborn   Lee Patrick   Alice Pearce
Jack Pearl   Nat Pendleton   ZaSu Pitts

Mae Questel   Eddie Quillan

Charlotte Rae
Rags Ragland   Erik Rhodes
Lyda Roberti   Blossom Rock
"Slapsie" Maxie Rosenbloom   Benny Rubin
Charlie Ruggles   Sig Ruman   Irene Ryan

Al St. John
S. Z. "Cuddles" Sakall   Natalie Schafer
Vito Scotti   Reta Shaw   Alison Skipworth
Arnold Stang   Larry Storch   Robert Strauss
Grady Sutton   Mack Swain

George Tobias
Arthur Treacher   Mary Treen

Vera Vague   Joyce Van Patten

Raymond Walburn
Nancy Walker   Ray Walston
Carol Wayne   Jack Weston   Jesse White
Mary Wickes   Marie Wilson   Monty Woolley

COMIC SUPPORT

INTRODUCTION

"Comedy is a red rubber ball," Mel Brooks once said. "If you throw it against a soft, funny wall, it will not come back. But if you throw it against the hard wall of ultimate reality, it will bounce back and be very lively."

That's what "comic support" is all about.

Many of the film world's great supporting players made themselves into unyielding walls of authority. Then they braced themselves for the comic attack.

These "comic support" performers played cops (Edgar Kennedy) and detectives (Eugene Pallette), society dowagers (Margaret Dumont) and bluenoses (Franklin Pangborn), crusty butlers (Eric Blore), and cranky professors (James Finlayson).

They built their walls with care, including every implacable brick of thick-skulled propriety, every well-polished stone of hypocrisy, every ornate niche of pomposity. But they also built into their walls just enough of their own rubbery, likable comic resilience so that when the attack came, satiric or slapstick, the audience could guiltlessly enjoy the resulting devastation.

Mel Brooks mentioned that comedians battle against "the ultimate wall of hard reality." Sometimes, that reality is so tough it requires a different kind of "comic support": the sidekick.

That's why there's Nigel Bruce playing a lovably bumbling Dr. Watson during a grim and suspenseful Sherlock Holmes mystery. There's Una O'Connor with her exaggerated screams that let us take a laugh break from a Universal horror movie. There's Allen Jenkins with a comically glum look that takes the edge off a tense Warners gangster film. There's Jack Norton, the specialist at playing drunks, ready to stagger into a nightclub scene in a drama, get a quick laugh, and totter away.

Some of the best supporting players could play both sides of the wall. They would frustrate the star comedian with dizziness (ZaSu Pitts), eccentricity (Richard Libertini), dull apathy (Norman Fell), and other flaws of human nature. They created their little moments of chaos whether they were cast as foe or friend.

When it's time to assemble most any type of film, from comedy to drama, the casting call goes out for "comic support." Over the years, many stars have made careers out of playing the wisecracking pal, the long-winded associate, the befuddled uncle, the finicky aunt, and a host of odd and endearing others.

In the case of the great support players, such as Edward Everett Horton, Arthur Treacher, Fritz Feld, and the humorous colleagues featured in this book, they spent years perfecting their craft and brought to their roles the same dedication, professionalism, timing, and comic instincts as the performers who received top billing.

Here is a celebration of "comic support," and the memorable stars who have not only brought us smiles and laughter in countless films, but set themselves up for a fall so that others could get even more laughs.

The "red rubber ball" of comedy has always needed that "hard wall of reality." Without the comic supporting players and their "support walls," many a movie would fall flat.

IRIS ADRIAN
Iris Adrian Hostetter, May 29, 1913

IRIS ADRIAN, perennial wisecracking chorus girl.

*I*n playing a brassy, wisecracking blond, Iris Adrian was good for a laugh or two in dozens of B movies. She and actress Lona Andre played a pair of flirts having a good time with Laurel and Hardy in *Our Relations*. When the boys' wives show up, Iris complains, "I don't think much of your taste—ditchin' us for a couple of old frumps like these!"

Born in California, Iris was a beauty contest winner. The judges were stuck on the pretty blonde and so was a knife thrower who used her as his target in a vaudeville act. She moved on to dance in Broadway shows, including the 1931 *Ziegfeld Follies*. The dancer was soon given acting roles as well. She told author Leonard Maltin that her part in *The Fabulous Invalid* (1938) required both acting and very special dancing. At the time, "they had closed all the burlesque houses, but I did a striptease that George Kaufman taught me in *Fabulous Invalid*, and I was the only one doing a striptease on Broadway, at $4.80 top. That was a big deal."

Through the thirties and forties, Adrian turned up in films as a tough showgirl, gum-chewing waitress, or smart-mouthed best friend of the leading lady. She was a favorite with a number of comedians who gave her roles in their films. Iris was in *Go West* with the Marx Brothers (as a dance-hall singer), Milton Berle's *Always Leave Them Laughing* (playing Ruth Roman's sister in a vaudeville act), Abbott and Costello's *Wistful Widow of Wagon Gap* (as a saloon girl), and Jerry Lewis's *The Errand Boy* (as a movie star treated to slapstick indignities).

She was often seen in sitcoms, playing Dottie on *The Ted Knight Show* and a crabby neighbor of Don Adams on *Get Smart*. In one episode, Adams thinks she has a broken ankle. He comes to her door late at night only to be treated to sarcasm:

Iris: "Do you know what time it is, Mr. Smart?"
Adams: "Yes, but I knew you'd still be up with your ankle."
Iris: "I'm rarely up without it."
Adams: "I hope you didn't have to walk [to the door]."
Iris: "No, I took a bus from the living room!"

In films she was still playing the same tough roles. As a landlady in Disney's *That Darn Cat* she makes sure that everyone knows she's wise: "I didn't come in from Stupidsville on last night's bus!"

SELECTED FILM APPEARANCES:
Paramount on Parade (1930), *Gold Diggers of 1937* (1936), *Our Relations* (1936), *Go West* (1940), *Road to Zanzibar* (1941), *Meet the Chump* (1941), *Roxie Hart* (1942), *Taxi Mister* (1943), *Lady of Burlesque* (1943), *Swing Hostess* (1944), *Stork Club* (1945), *Wistful Widow of Wagon Gap* (1947), *The Paleface* (1948), *Miss Mink of 1949* (1949), *Mighty Joe Young* (1949), *Always Leave Them Laughing* (1949), *Blondie's Hero* (1950), *My Favorite Spy* (1951), *Carnival Rock* (1957), *The Errand Boy* (1961), *That Darn Cat* (1965), *The Odd Couple* (1968), *The Love Bug* (1968), *Scandalous John* (1971), *Gus* (1976), *Freaky Friday* (1977), *Murder Can Hurt You* (1980), *Paternity* (1981)

TELEVISION SERIES:
The Ted Knight Show (1978)

LUIS ALBERNI (right), white gloves, bewildered look and all, here with Gerald Oliver-Smith and Catherine Doucet in *When You're in Love.*

LUIS ALBERNI
October 4, 1886–
December 23, 1962

Known for playing a variety of excitable ethnic characters, Luis Alberni was at one time a calm young scholar, a graduate of the University of Barcelona.

He came to America and worked on Broadway throughout the twenties. Then he was recruited by Hollywood to support a variety of stars including John Barrymore (*Svengali*) and Eddie Cantor (*The Kid From Spain*). Before long he was getting a few moments to establish his own character and get a few laughs. He's the owner of a hotel in *Easy Living*, a film written by Preston Sturges. Alberni is not about to tolerate any insults or chaos in his fine establishment. And so he declares seriously, "What kind of a dump do you think this is?"

Alberni continued to find interesting supporting roles through the years including the mayor in *A Bell for Adano*. Married for a third time, with three sons, he died at the Motion Picture Home in Woodland Hills after a long illness.

4

FRANK ALBERTSON

February 2, 1909–
February 29, 1964

FRANK ALBERTSON, trying his best to "get it" as Clark Gable and Keenan Wynn explain matters to Douglas Fowley (left) in *The Hucksters.*

Despite a long career, Frank Albertson is best remembered as the naive would-be playwright Leo Davis, one minute conned, the next a willing confederate of the Marx Brothers in *Room Service.* As Davis, he gamely joins the Marx madness in trying to get his play *Hail and Farewell* produced. He's ready to fake a contagious disease or even suicide. As he enthusiastically puts it, "I'll give you the best performance you've ever seen in a hotel bedroom!" As this film's "fourth Marx Brother," Albertson was effective and sympathetic alternating between righteous anger and sudden bewilderment.

Youthful openness and a blameless sense of fun sparked Albertson's roles as the hero's best friend or the inexperienced-but-confident small-town boy trying to make good. He had a way with a corny line. In *Just Imagine* a dour woman comes to the door and announces, "I'm the census taker." Albertson drawls out a thoughtful "Sorry," then brightens, adding, "We're out of our census today!" He's clearly pleased with himself for such a bon mot. In *The Ghost Comes Home* boastful Nat Pendleton declares, "The Democrats want me to run!" Says Frank:

"As a Republican!" Albertson, like Tom Smothers years later, was a master at endearing himself by presenting a low-wattage joke with a high degree of pride and delight.

Born in Fergus Falls, Minnesota, Albertson worked in silent films and was already established in sound pictures when he came to Broadway to play brash Billy Randolph in *Brother Rat*. In addition to stage and film work, he had his own vaudeville act. In 1939 *Variety* favorably reviewed his eight minutes of "small talk and song and dance hokum." The same year, unhappy with the script, he left the cast of *Yokel Boy* and was replaced by Buddy Ebsen.

One role Frank Albertson coveted, and nearly won, was Dagwood Bumstead in the *Blondie* film series. He missed out mostly due to Arthur Lake's studio connections and was never connected with another big hit film. In 1947, too old to play enthusiastic cadets, wide-eyed rubes, or earnest young playwrights, Albertson accepted an unusual job from director Leo McCarey. For $650 a week Albertson coached an actor in the film *Good Sam* in all the mannerisms needed for being "a young Frankie Albertson."

In the fifties, Albertson and his wife had their own daytime *Frank and Grace Albertson Show*. On a blisteringly hot day in July of 1956, Grace was driving up toward Westchester in a Volkswagen bus with her three young daughters and her father-in-law. The roof of the car was opened to admit a breeze. When the car swerved off to the side of the road and hit a soft shoulder, it overturned, flinging the entire family out like dolls. Their youngest daughter was crushed under the car and Frank's father was killed. A month later, Frank and Grace bravely continued their work, performing in live commercials during coverage of the Republican and Democratic conventions.

Over the years, Albertson aged into a comic character actor barely recognizable from his Leo Davis days. In *Psycho* a smiling, tipsy rich man tells Janet Leigh, "Do you know what I do about unhappiness? I buy it off..." The man with the white mustache gives her $40,000 in cash to put in the office safe. Instead, she runs off with it. That was Frank Albertson, playing someone older and heavier, but perhaps just as naive as the young man who lost his typewriter and life savings to the Marx Brothers years before.

SELECTED BROADWAY APPEARANCES:
Brother Rat (1937), *The More the Merrier* (1941), *The Walrus and the Carpenter* (1941), *Mr. Adam* (1949), *Seventeen* (1951), *Late Love* (1953), *Champagne Complex* (1954)

SELECTED FILM APPEARANCES:
Happy Days (1930), *A Connecticut Yankee* (1931), *Big Business Girl* (1931), *The Brat* (1931), *The Cohens and Kellys in Hollywood* (1932), *The Cohens and Kellys in Trouble* (1933), *Alice Adams* (1935), *Ah, Wilderness* (1936), *The Farmer in the Dell* (1936), *Spring Madness* (1938), *Mother Carey's Chickens* (1938), *Room Service* (1938), *The Ghost Comes Home* (1940), *Ellery Queen's Penthouse Mystery* (1941), *Man-Made Monster* (1941), *Louisiana Purchase* (1942), *Here Comes Elmer* (1943), *How Do You Do* (1945), *It's a Wonderful Life* (1946), *The Last Hurrah* (1958), *Psycho* (1960), *Man Trap* (1962), *Don't Knock the Twist* (1963), *Bye Bye Birdie* (1963)

TELEVISION SERIES:
Date With Judy (1951), *Frank and Grace Albertson Show* (1955)

MABEL ALBERTSON
1901–September 28, 1982

A vaudeville actress and piano player Mabel Albertson had a long film career from *Mutiny on the Blackhawk* in 1939 to *Barefoot in the Park* in 1967. Like her brother Jack Albertson (who achieved national fame on TV with *Chico and the Man* after many years of fine comic and dramatic film roles), Mabel found that her most popular roles came late in life. She aged into a satiric "annoying mother-in-law" character that she played again and again.

Not the stereotyped fussbudget or busybody, she was far more realistic, a "non-joy-giver" who by her silence, her downturned mouth, and sadly disapproving gaze signals that her boy Rob Petrie is too good for Laura (*The Dick Van Dyke Show*) or that her boy Donald Hollinger is too good for Ann-Marie (*That Girl*) or that her boy Darrin Stevens is too good for Samantha (*Bewitched*).

Albertson began playing these types of parts in the early days of television. She was the mother-in-law to Tom Ewell on *The Tom Ewell Show*. But it didn't matter who the hapless son or daughter was. When the audience saw Mabel Albertson, they knew it meant trouble.

Mabel began her career in nightclubs and vaudeville. She recalled, "People were willing to pay me three hundred dollars a

MABEL ALBERTSON, Listening to Lew Parker's alibi on TV's *That Girl*.

week to sing a few silly songs at the piano." In 1933 Phil Baker booked her on his radio show as a stooge. After she made some good script suggestions, Baker hired her as a writer, but she left him in 1935 to write free-lance and to work on her own radio show, *Dress Rehearsal*.

As one of broadcasting's few women gag writers, Mabel was interviewed by the *New York Post* in November 1936 and admitted it was tough being funny and female. Men were put off by her gags: "When a fellow says to me, 'You've got a pretty foot,' I automatically come back with, 'Ah, a dog-fancier!' When he says, 'Your teeth are like pearls,' I ask, 'When were you out with Pearl?' If he admires my new smart daring evening gown, I say, 'It's a biblical dress—low and behold.' You see, I know all the answers…all the cards in my joke files keep turning over and over in my head.... They detest it and I don't blame them."

The quirky writer added that her work habits were a little different from most: "I never have any clothes on when I write."

In her film roles as a mother-in-law, she was always well clothed and quite disapproving of any sign of friskiness in others. Divorced from her second husband, screenwriter Ken Englund, Albertson was invited to live with her friend Cloris Leachman in the seventies. She continued to amuse television audiences, but her guest appearances became fewer and fewer following the diagnosis of Alzeheimer's disease.

EDDIE "ROCHESTER" ANDERSON
September 18, 1905–February 28, 1977

Unlike most of the black comedians of his day, Eddie Anderson did not fit the stereotypes. As with the rest of the cast on Jack Benny's radio and television shows, Eddie usually got the better of the boss and often made salty wisecracks at Benny's expense. True, he played Benny's chauffeur and valet, Rochester, but there was never any doubt that the two respected each other. Or that Rochester was usually the man in control. In their routines together, it was hard to tell who really was the comic support. Rochester was the one who was getting the laughs. And it was Benny who seemed to be doing the work:

Jack: "Rochester, answer the door."

Rochester: "Boss, you're nearer to it than I am!"

As with the rest of the cast, comedy about Jack's aging was fair game for Rochester:

Rochester: "Your dentist and your barber called."

Jack: "What did they say?"

Rochester: "Both gave me the same message. You can pick 'em up tomorrow!"

Benny had the utmost respect for Anderson as a person and as a professional: "He was a master of the slow take. His timing became as sharp as a razor." The role of Benny's butler didn't have to be played by a black actor. The star recalled, "I hired him because he was good. He was the best man for the part of my butler and he got better and funnier and funnier as the years went by." Benny admitted that some early episodes contained a few questionable lines now and then, but that changed very quickly: "When the black man's fight for equal rights and fair play became an issue after the war, I would no longer allow Rochester to say or do anything that an audience would consider degrading…"

Anderson had been in show business most of his life. His father was a vaudevillian and his mother a circus aerialist. After several revues, appearances at the Apollo Theater in Harlem, and membership in a musical trio called The Three Black Aces, Eddie went west

EDDIE "ROCHESTER" ANDERSON, pixilated by the reappearance of now dead Joan Blondell and Roland Young in the ghost comedy *Topper Returns*.

for his 1932 film debut in *What Price Hollywood*. Five years later he played a Pullman porter named Rochester Van Jones in an episode of Jack Benny's show. Anderson's gravel voice was well suited to radio and a perfect contrast to the mild, smooth Benny. From that $75 guest spot, Anderson was soon making $1,600 a week on radio. Benny's radio butler had a ten-room house, a yacht, and not one but two servants of his own.

Despite being so identified with his work as part of Benny's radio family that he became known as Eddie "Rochester" Anderson, there were many occasions for him to display his many talents elsewhere. He was Roland Young's chauffeur in *Topper Returns*, worked opposite W. C. Fields in *You Can't Cheat an Honest Man*, sang with Lena Horne in *Cabin in the Sky*, and, in addition to recording several novelty songs in the forties, performed his own musical number in the film *Star Spangled Rhythm*.

In the fifties Anderson was a regular on Jack Benny's television show and still very much his own man. Since he controlled the Benny household, the place was technically his. And his best gags were as pointed as those of white servants such as Arthur Treacher in the forties, or the independent and feisty black stars who would arrive in the following decade, like Redd Foxx and Sherman Hemsley:

Jack: "Rochester, be sure to come home at a reasonable hour."

Rochester: "Yes, sir. Your reasonable or my reasonable?"

SELECTED FILM APPEARANCES:
You Can't Take It With You (1938), *Gone With the Wind* (1939), *You Can't Cheat an Honest Man* (1939), *Man About Town* (1939), *Buck Benny Rides Again* (1940), *Topper Returns* (1941), *Tales of Manhattan* (1942), *Meanest Man in the World* (1943), *Cabin in the Sky* (1943), *It's a Mad, Mad, Mad, Mad World* (1963).

TELEVISION:
The Jack Benny Show (1953–65)

EDWARD ANDREWS
October 9, 1914–
March 8, 1985

EDWARD ANDREWS, holding the phone as Dick Martin (of Rowan and...) and Paul Lynde ponder who's the answer in *The Glass Bottom Boat.*

*U*sually playing a fussy, exasperated, somewhat shifty or lecherous businessman, heavy-set and white-haired Edward Andrews was a familiar figure in sixties movies and on TV. He had bright eyes behind his black-rimmed glasses and a slightly naughty smile which could turn into pouting dismay whenever sitcom disaster struck.

The son of an Episcopal minister, the moon-faced Georgia-born actor grew up in Pittsburgh and Cleveland and graduated from the University of Virginia in 1934. After understudying Broderick Crawford as Lenny in *Of Mice and Men*, Andrews got his first solid stage role in *The Time of Your Life*. Following service in the army during World War II, he returned to Broadway, appearing in over thirty roles, many of them as malicious, scheming weasels: "My specialty is the Babbitt villain, the country-club crook with a smile." One of his favorite roles was Babbitt in *Elmer Gantry*.

Andrews aged into a reliable, realistic comedy character actor. He recalled, "I'll be at an airport and some fellow will come up and pump my hand. 'Well, how are things back in Nashville?' he'll ask. Or Albany. Or Minneapolis. I just say, 'Fine, fine,' and go on. They always think I'm a businessman they met at a convention. Who am I to spoil it?"

He played the standard not-in-control commander on *Broadside* (a sort of female *McHale's Navy*), worked in several Doris Day films, and was a regular on her television series. His alternately imperious and conciliatory nature got a workout when he played Don Rickles's boss on the comedian's 1971 sitcom. Andrews admitted "I love comedy. It's the hardest thing to play, the most challenging…a dramatic role is apt to be down an emotional straight line. But a comedy has to be larger than life. It has to be life so they can believe it, but then it has to be larger than life. But not too big or you go into burlesque or caricature. And the joy of the thing is in timing it so it's funny."

Andrews starred in a stock production of *Never Too Late*, and was still working up to the end, playing the conductor on *Supertrain* in 1979 and taking parts in films like *Gremlins* and *Sixteen Candles*. In the latter, he altered lines to suit his character—changing his grandfatherly "I can't stand that rock and roll crap!" to "that rock and roll rubbish." Director John Hughes had to admit that Andrews's way was funnier. Said Andrews, "I'm cocky enough, still, to say that the things I do best, there isn't anyone in the business that can do them better than I…It seems awfully immodest, but I have no doubt in the world."

SELECTED BROADWAY APPEARANCES:
How Beautiful With Shoes (1935), *So Proudly We Hail* (1936), *The Time of Your Life* (1939), *They Knew What They Wanted* (1949), *I Am a Camera* (1951), *Three by Thurber* (1955), *The Gazebo* (1958), *The Child Buyer* (1962)

SELECTED FILM APPEARANCES:
The Phenix City Story (1955), *Tea and Sympathy* (1956), *The Fiend Who Walked the West* (1958), *Elmer Gantry* (1960), *The Absent-Minded Professor* (1961), *Love in a Goldfish Bowl* (1961), *Forty Pounds of Trouble* (1962), *Son of Flubber* (1963), *Kisses for My President* (1964), *Send Me No Flowers* (1964), *Good Neighbor Sam* (1964), *The Glass Bottom Boat* (1966), *Birds Do It* (1966), *The Trouble With Girls* (1970), *Charley and the Angel* (1972), *Now You See Him, Now You Don't* (1972), *Gremlins* (1984), *Sixteen Candles* (1984)

TELEVISION SERIES:
Broadside (1964–65), *The Doris Day Show* (1968), *The Don Rickles Show* (1971), *Supertrain* (1979)

HENRY ARMETTA
July 4, 1888–October 21, 1945

A chubby, compact Italian, Armetta had a determined gaze and huffy, excitable personality that made him a stock comic character in dozens of films. Born in Italy, he came to New York as a teenage stowaway and found work as an assistant to the barber at the Lambs Club. Armetta was discovered there by comedian Raymond Hitchcock, who gave him work in several stage productions.

In Hollywood, Armetta was used chiefly as comic relief in both lighter films as well as dramas. In *The Black Cat* he is a police officer who arrives briefly at a demonic castle, struts his ludicrously squat body around, offers a few words of warning and concern, salutes, and leaves, to the mutual confusion of both Bela Lugosi and Boris Karloff. In *The Big Store* he has trouble with all three Marx Brothers. He duels Italian accents with Chico Marx until Chico wins him over by remem-

bering they used to stomp grapes together back in Italy. Then he confronts department store detective Groucho when six of his dozen children were suddenly lost in a Murphy bed. Finally he has to get after lecherous Harpo, shouting, "Pressa the grapes, no pressa my wife!"

Armetta got a chance to star in some films as well, playing the head of the Gambino family in a series of Fox comedies that included *Speed to Burn* and *Winner Take All*. He paused between films to make a 78-rpm single, then took local stage roles. A critic for the *San Diego Union* noted that Armetta seemed to "struggle" through his performance of the 1945 play *Opening Night*. By the time the paper hit the streets, Armetta wasn't concerned with the review. He had collapsed back stage and died of a heart attack.

SELECTED FILM APPEARANCES:
The Silent Command (1943), *Love, Live and Laugh* (1929), *Ladies Love Brutes* (1930), *Lovin' the Ladies* (1930), *Laughing Sinners* (1931), *Hat-Check Girl* (1932), *Scarface* (1932), *The Passionate Plumber* (1932), *Central Park* (1932), *The Cohens and the Kellys in Trouble* (1933), *Laughing at Life* (1933), *What! No Beer?* (1933), *The Man Who Reclaimed His Head* (1934), *The Black Cat* (1934), *Embarrassing Moments* (1934), *The Gift of Gab* (1934), *Dinky* (1935), *Poor Little Rich Girl* (1936), *Manhattan Merry-Go-Round* (1937), *Make a Wish* (1937), *Everybody Sing* (1938), *Three Cheers for the Irish* (1940), *The Big Store* (1941), *The Ghost Catchers* (1944), *Anchors Aweigh* (1945)

ROSCOE ATES
January 20, 1895–March 1, 1962

A stuttering little comic with a small head, pasty face, big ears, and large eyes, Roscoe Ates often had brief roles in movies in which he could relieve the tension with his special brand of clowning. Since audiences only saw him in perhaps one film a month, and for only a few minutes, it took decades for the novelty to wear off. Occasionally he starred in a novelty short, such as Vitaphone's *So You Won't T-T-Talk*.

Born in Mississippi, Ates graduated from the Ohio Conservatory and had intentions of becoming a violinist but got sidetracked into vaudeville and comedy. He recalled how his comic trademark began. The year was 1920 and he was on stage in vaudeville: "I forgot a line and in trying to remember it I started stuttering. The audience thought

it was a gag, so I decided to keep it."
Ironically, in real life Ates had been
a stammerer in his youth, curing
himself at eighteen.

Some thought Ates's stammering routine cruel. Ates disagreed:
"When I was in England in 1935, I
received more than four thousand
letters from stammerers in the
British Isles asking for advice on
how to cure themselves. I hired a
stenographer and answered all the
letters... before I knew it I was
directing a speech clinic. I honestly
think I helped a lot of people."

During World War II, Ates bris-
tled when the Army Air Corps officers insisted there was no place for
a stutterer. He smooth-talked his
way in, and toughed his way to the
rank of major. After the war, he
returned to show business, and
eventually became a Western side-
kick, playing Soapy in a batch of Eddie Dean movies in the late forties.

ROSCOE ATES, obviously playing with less than a full
deck, here doing the sidekick bit to star Eddie Dean in
one of their many films together.

Over the years, he made more headlines for his topsy turvy love
life than his stuttering. He married many times, one ex-wife returning
for an encore. In 1955 the sixty-year-old comic was engaged to a
woman named Sandy Reeves—until they got into a fight and she beat
him up with the heel of her spiked shoe. She triumphantly posed holding it for newspaper photographers. Three years later, twenty-four-year-
old blond model Reba Sanborn took an overdose of sleeping pills while
in Roscoe's apartment. And three years later, he was arrested on a
drunk charge after arguing with his new twenty-seven-year-old bride,
Beatrice. His line to reporters and printed verbatim, sounded like something out of one of his old movies: "I w-w-walked into a w-w-wildcat!"

He died of lung cancer at age seventy.

SELECTED FILM APPEARANCES:
From Soup to Nuts (1930), *Cracked Nuts* (1931), *The Champ* (1931), *The Big Shot*
(1931), *Freaks* (1932), *Hold 'Em Jail!* (1932), *What! No Beer?* (1933), *Alice in Wonderland* (1933), *She Made Her Bed* (1934), *The People's Enemy* (1935), *Gone With the
Wind* (1939), *I Want a Divorce* (1940), *Sullivan's Travels* (1941), *Palm Beach Story*
(1942), *Stars Over Texas* (1946), *Down Missouri Way* (1946), *Tumbleweed Trail*
(1946), *Shadow Valley* (1947), *Tornado Range* (1948), *Abbott and Costello Meet the
Keystone Kops* (1955), *The Birds and the Bees* (1956), *The Big Caper* (1957), *The
Sheepman* (1958), *The Errand Boy* (1961)

TELEVISION SERIES:
Marshal of Gunsight Pass (1950)

MISCHA AUER, in his usual state of lust and confusion, checking out the compromising position of Joy Hodges and Charlie Ruggles in *Service De Luxe*.

MISCHA AUER

Mischa Ounskowsky,
November 17, 1905–
March 5, 1967

Unmistakable, thanks to his large eyes, angular head, pencil mustache, scrawny frame, and excitable ways, Mischa Auer was a Russian immigrant adept at playing semisuave playboys, bored European actors, saucy butlers, and a variety of impossible ethnics. He enlivened many movies with a well-timed, well-accented remark. One of the most memorable lines in *You Can't Take It With You* was Auer's. It was his simple Russian appraisal of a ballerina: "Confidentially—she steenks!"

Auer was stripped of his pants playing poker with Marlene Dietrich in *Destry Rides Again* and received an Academy Award nomination for his work as Carlo, a freeloading pianist-protégé of wealthy Alice Brady in *My Man Godfrey*. For her amusement he not only played the piano but mussed his hair and climbed on the furniture imitating a gorilla. Auer got his biggest laugh with a simple bit of melancholy histrionics. Pressing his hands over his face, the "sensitive" fellow who only lives to sponge off rich ladies mutters with grand sincerity: "Money, money, money! The Frankenstein monster that destroys souls!"

Auer's early years were less than funny. He was born in St. Petersburg, his father was killed during the Russo-Japanese War, and his mother died of typhus when Mischa was just thirteen. Auer sold what little he could find to finance his escape to Italy. From there, the teenager made connections with his grandfather, a New York-based violinist. Mischa came to America, but the scars of his childhood remained. He couldn't concentrate in school, telling one of his teachers, "After seeing death and torture, suppose I don't do algebra?"

In films, Auer was initially cast in sinister roles: "I was usually a leering villain, killed in the first reel. Fortunately, in 1936 Gregory La Cava decided I might do as a phony artist, something between a gigolo and a dilettante in *My Man Godfrey*. That's when I hit the Hollywood mother lode. That one role made a comedian out of me. I haven't been anything else since. It's paid off very well. Do you wonder that I'm flattered when people say I'm mad?"

Auer was an authentic madcap. David Niven told the story of Humphrey Bogart's 1938 wedding to Mayo Methot—and how mischievous Mischa jumped nude out of the wedding cake.

In the fifties, Auer utilized his fluency in Russian, German, Spanish, and French to secure work in European films, still playing his usual array of comically wide-eyed domestics, high-strung foreigners, suave but see-through playboys, and overly fastidious officers. A heart attack ended his life at age sixty-one, shortly after making a brief but always memorable appearance in the Tony Curtis movie *Arrivederci, Baby*.

SELECTED BROADWAY APPEARANCES:
Morals (1925), *Dope* (1926), *The Lady Comes Across* (1942), *Lovely Me* (1946), *Tovarich* (1953), *The Merry Widow* (1964)

SELECTED FILM APPEARANCES:
Something Always Happens (1928), *The Benson Murder Case* (1930), *Women Love Once* (1931), *Beauty Parlor* (1932), *Sucker Money* (1933), *Bulldog Drummond Strikes Back* (1934), *Biography of a Bachelor Girl* (1935), *I Dream Too Much* (1935), *My Man Godfrey* (1936), *Pick a Star* (1937), *One Hundred Men and a Girl* (1937), *Top of the Town* (1937), *Vogues of 1938* (1937), *You Can't Take It With You* (1938), *Destry Rides Again* (1939), *Public Deb Number One* (1940), *Hellzapoppin* (1941), *Hold That Ghost* (1941), *Lady in the Dark* (1944), *Up in Mabel's Room* (1944), *Brewster's Millions* (1945), *And Then There Were None* (1945), *Sentimental Journey* (1946), *Confidential Report* (1953), *Frou Frou* (1955), *Mamzelle Pigalle* (1958), *A Dog, a Mouse and a Sputnik* (1960), *We Joined the Navy* (1962), *Arrivederci, Baby* (1966)

BABY LEROY

Ronald LeRoy Overacker, May 12, 1932

The youngest star ever to receive star billing in a film, Baby LeRoy had his name up in lights when he costarred opposite Maurice Chevalier in *A Bedtime Story*. Baby LeRoy was just six months old.

He is probably the only comic support player who literally had no idea he was funny. In fact, he had no idea what he was doing.

By June of 1933 the parents of the cute, blue-eyed babe had signed a seven-year contract with Paramount. The country was mad for Baby LeRoy, and photos of him appeared in all the major magazines. Writing pieces on a one-year-old didn't tax the imagination of veteran columnists like Sidney Skolsky, who in October of 1933 wrote of Baby LeRoy, "He has a habit of whispering into your ear when you are holding him. What he whispers can't be printed here, but if you believe him you'll rush him to where he should go."

The child's last name was given as Weinbrenner—which was variously spelled Weinbrener, Weinebrunner, and Winebrenner in newspapers of the day. The child made film after film, barely uttering a gurgle. The *New York Evening Post* headlined an article on January 5, 1935: "He Talks!" The occasion was *It's a Gift*, with W. C. Fields. Fields and Baby

W.C. FIELDS
ALISON SKIPWORTH
and BABY LeROY

BABY LeROY, star though he once was, doesn't quite get the billing accorded his two fellow players.

LeRoy met up four times. In this first encounter, the youngster uncorks a keg of molasses that floods W.C.'s store. In *The Old Fashioned Way*, the child grabs hold of his costar's prodigious nose and later cheerfully dumps Field's watch in molasses. The Great Man's revenge was a famous if rather soft kick to Baby LeRoy's rump, sending him tumbling forward. LeRoy's reaction: an admiring smile as if to say, "Well, you got even! Good for you!"

It was good publicity for Fields to claim a chagrined feud with the scene-stealing Baby LeRoy. Fields wrote a piece called "The Treatment of Babies," describing apocryphal comic villainy: "When Baby LeRoy would scream and sing his cute little toothums…I would pour a noggin of gin into his porridge…it would calm him down." Some biographers took this as fact, but in a rare interview, LeRoy reported that Fields was always nice to him, even sending cards on his birthday.

Baby LeRoy "retired" from show business before he was eight. In 1951 he worked at his stepfather's deli. In 1954 he was a quartermaster third class in the navy. He shunned publicity, moved often, and has rarely talked about his film career. The exact reason why his real name was given as Weinbrenner instead of Overacker is also unknown but evidently reflects a difference between father and stepfather.

In 1965 a photo of him appeared in a syndicated article by Dave Smith, who found him in California working as a lifeguard. Baby LeRoy (now answering to Ron) said he was divorced and had three kids, and had little else to say. "I've never thought about going back to acting," he admitted. "I don't remember any of it…When I see the old movies, it's interesting to see myself as a baby, but it could just as well be anybody, not me."

SELECTED FILM APPEARANCES:
A Bedtime Story (1933), *Alice in Wonderland* (1933), *Tillie and Gus* (1933), *Miss Fane's Baby Is Stolen* (1934), *Torch Singer* (1934), *It's a Gift* (1934), *The Old Fashioned Way* (1934).

CARL BALLANTINE
September 27, 1922

A cheerful second banana (notably in *McHale's Navy*), six-foot-two, white-haired, putty-nosed Carl Ballantine usually played an average working guy, but with a vaudevillian streak. He was the one guy in the mob prone to muttering a wisecracking aside as he went about his job.

The vaudevillian streak was a legacy of his offbeat stand-up pseudo magic act in which he called himself "The Amazing Ballantine." Through the years, and periodically resurrecting it for TV variety shows, he offered intentionally terrible magic tricks. With furrowed brow and the worried smile of cheerful desperation, he'd nervously tell jokes to cover up the hilarious mistakes. He'd "accidentally" expose how a trick was done and mutter a disgusted "Who put *that* there?"

He played a failed magician on an episode of television's *Night Court* in the eighties, declaring, "I lost my touch...I reached in my pocket and pulled out a little pigeon. It bit my finger. I produced a rabbit out of a top hat—it bit my nose. That night I had 'em both for dinner...I threw my trunk into the East River. It sank. Now *that's* magic."

Carl practiced magic in his hometown, Chicago, and performed in high school. In vaudeville, his comedy act was met with silence: "The audience just thought I was an awkward magician. I bombed in Atlanta, then Holyoke, then Des Moines." Fortunately, back in Chicago in 1942, "it was the same act, but the audience knew what I was driving at this time and loved it."

"The Amazing Ballantine" performed all over the country, and in 1952 he married Ceil Cabot, a luminary in Julius Monk's New York comedy revues. After many supporting roles, he was a prominent costar in *McHale's Navy* as the good-natured shipmate Gruber. "I'd never last on submarine duty," he admitted in one episode, "I like to sleep with the windows open!" Following his exposure on the television sitcom, Ballantine found more film work. He also returned to the stage, costarring with Phil Silvers in an early seventies West Coast production

CARL BALLANTINE, the most inept magician in show biz, finds himself nose to nose with Fritz Feld in *The World's Greatest Lover.*

of *A Funny Thing Happened on the Way to the Forum*. In the eighties he continued in films and television while maintaining his "Amazing" stand-up act.

JOHN BANNER
January 28, 1910–January 28, 1973

A character actor who rose to belated fame playing the bulky and benign Sergeant Schultz on *Hogan's Heroes*, John Banner began his career in his native Germany in the days when he was thin enough to star as a romantic lead.

He fled the Nazis in the late thirties, found acting work in Switzerland, and in 1939 was fortunate to find some Broadway shows that needed his ethnic qualifications. One of them was *From Vienna*. After several stage productions he came to Hollywood for film work and TV roles, finally getting his big break as P.O.W. camp guard Schultz, whose catchphrase was a strained gasp of "I see nothing! Nothing!" while Colonel Hogan's gang of captive soldiers plotted their sitcom mischief, and "I know nothing! Nothing!" after it was over.

His good nature and bumbling reluctance to enforce camp rules made him a sympathetic character—the average man dragged into the army and just biding his time to get out again. He said, "There is no such thing as a cuddly Nazi. I do not see Schultz as a Nazi at all: to me he represents some kind of goodness in any generation." He admitted in a 1966 letter to the author, "I, who am a Jew, would never be involved in anything that excuses or idealizes the German regime at that time. We are making fun of them. As proof we are shown in

JOHN BANNER "sees nothing, knows nothing" as Bob Crane and Ivan Dixon pull a weekly *Hogan's Heroes* scam.

SELECTED BROADWAY APPEARANCES:
From Vienna (1939), *Pastoral* (1939), *The Big Two* (1947)

SELECTED FILM APPEARANCES:
Once Upon a Honeymoon (1942), *The Fallen Sparrow* (1944), *Black Angel* (1947), *My Girl Tisa* (1948), *The Juggler* (1953), *The Blue Angel* (1959), *The Story of Ruth* (1960), *The Interns* (1962), *Hitler* (1963), *Thirty-Six Hours* (1964), *The Wicked Dreams of Paula Schultz* (1968)

TELEVISION SERIES:
Hogan's Heroes (1965–71), *The Chicago Teddy Bears* (1971)

thirty-nine countries all over the world, except in Germany."

The gray-haired teddy bear of a man with the little mustache later became one of *The Chicago Teddy Bears*, playing Uncle Latzi to a gang of comic hoods. A few years later, on his birthday, he suffered an abdominal hemorrhage and died while on a trip to Vienna.

BILLY BARTY
October 24, 1924

Arguably the most famous "Little Person" in the entertainment world, Billy Barty (under four feet tall) tried to find humor beyond the easy laughs of little encounters with bigger people.

Barty and his sisters worked in vaudeville through the thirties and early forties. At first, some of his screen cameos were rather stereotypical. Whether he was dressed as a baby or a little boy, his grimacing adult expressions brought shock laughs to audiences watching him in *Alice in Wonderland* and *Golddiggers of 1933*.

Barty was with the Spike Jones band from 1952 to 1960, scoring his biggest hit with the 1954 recording "I'm in the Mood for Love," a deliciously oily parody of Liberace. Though his size added a certain bizarre bonus to the hilarity, on stage and television Barty was as funny as any mimic of his generation when he did Jimmy Cagney, Jimmy Durante, Johnny Ray, and others.

BILLY BARTY, the screen's veteran little person, rampaging in *Rumpelstiltskin*.

After hosting a children's show in Los Angeles in the sixties, Barty resumed his film work. Rather than submit to quick gag appearances that might call for the surprise laugh of a small man in an unlikely set-

19

ting, Barty created a specific identity for himself that led to more substantial supporting roles.

Making the most of his weatherbeaten features, Barty played comically aggressive and feisty types. He was downright dangerous in *Foul Play*, a toughie in *Under the Rainbow*, and a garrulous police captain in *Night Patrol* (shouting his catchphrase throughout the film, "Are you calling me a liar?"). He was a master at working himself into comic expressions of rage. The capable performer appeared in stage productions (including musicals) and sometimes took dramatic roles, notably in *The Day of the Locust*.

Barty founded "The Little People of America" in 1957, perhaps his most enduring legacy. The organization has done much, not only in aiding and counseling little people in need, but also in helping to change the public's perception of people who are never too small to make a large and meaningful contribution to the world.

SELECTED FILM APPEARANCES:
Alice in Wonderland (1933), *Golddiggers of 1933* (1933), *A Midsummer Night's Dream* (1935), *Bride of Frankenstein* (1935), *The Day of the Locust* (1975), *W. C. Fields and Me* (1976), *Foul Play* (1978), *Under the Rainbow* (1981), *Night Patrol* (1985), *Legend* (1985), *Willow* (1988), *UHF* (1989), *Life Stinks* (1991)

COLLECTIBLES:
Barty is on several videos (*Best of Spike Jones Vols. I, II, III*) as well as two record albums, *Best of Spike Jones, Vol. 2* (RCA) and *The Little Mouse That Roared* (Arrow)

BEA BENADERET
April 4, 1906–October 13, 1968

Bea Benaderet's voice was lilting, comical, and delightfully unique. She first made an impression on radio, playing Gertrude Gearshift, the switchboard operator on *The Jack Benny Show*, Eve Goodwin on *The Great Gildersleeve*, Mrs. Carstairs on *Fibber McGee and Molly*, and Gloria, the maid, on *The Adventures of Ozzie and Harriet*.

Television audiences first saw her as Gracie Allen's friend and foil, Blanche Morton, on *The George Burns and Gracie Allen Show*, a role she played for eight years. The show gave her a few chances to slip in a ruefully amusing quip. On one episode her suspicious and dour husband wonders if she may be thinking of having an affair. Says Bea: "Since the day I married you thirteen years ago, there's *never* been a man in my life!"

Long after her radio days, Bea was called on to play the voice of Betty Rubble on *The Flintstones* cartoon series. Then she tried out for the part of Granny on *The Beverly Hillbillies*. She evidently came pretty close. By way of concession she got the part of Pearl Bodine, mother of main character Jethro (Max Baer, Jr.). Since she didn't play a stereotypical hillbilly, the charm of the real Bea showed through. Producer Paul Henning quickly cast her as Kate Bradley in his next series, *Petticoat Junction*. With plenty of warmth and a light, giggling laugh, she guided the show through several seasons before being sidelined by illness.

She attempted a return to the series but had to leave again for lung cancer surgery and radiation treatments. June Lockhart filled in as Dr. Janet Craig, but the show was not the same and folded the year after Bea's death. She had enjoyed a long run on the show—a starring vehicle that served as a fitting goodbye to a woman who had appeared in so many bright supporting roles for thirty years.

BEA BENADERET, everybody's best friend, plays peacemaker for quarreling young married Robert Cummings and Barbara Hale in *The First Time*.

SELECTED FILM APPEARANCES:
Notorious (1946), *On the Town* (1949), *For the First Time* (1952), *Plunderers of Painted Flats* (1959), *Tender Is the Night* (1962)

TELEVISION SERIES:
The George Burns and Gracie Allen Show (1950–58), *The George Burns Show* (1958–59), *Peter Loves Mary* (1960–61), *The Flintstones* (voice) (1960–63), *The Beverly Hillbillies* (1962–63), *Petticoat Junction* (1963–68)

JOE BESSER
August 12, 1907–March 1, 1988

Chubby Joe Besser's sassy sissy character made him a star beginning with vaudeville. He toured with an army sketch and played an effeminate recruit. When the drill sergeant shouted, "Count off! Are you one?" The bright-eyed comic would make a fey, mincing gesture and insist, "No, are youuuuuuuu?"

The contrast between the short, balding, heavyset man and his childlike mannerisms was a sure laugh-getter. He moved on to Broadway and supported Olsen and Johnson in the 1940 *Sons o' Fun*. A versatile, underrated performer, Besser was able to adapt this character to radio, television, and film. As a foil for Milton Berle on radio, he was both puckish and silly:

Berle: "Besser, don't tell me that you are the world's greatest

JOE BESSER, with his classic impish expression, lends a hand to pals Lou Costello and Bud Abbott.

authority on income tax."

Besser: "Why, certainly, you crazy, you! You're such a crazy! Last year I myself paid an income tax of $50,000."

Berle: "Besser, you never worked a day in your life, how did you ever arrive at an amount like that?"

Besser: "I copied off of the man in front of me!"

Berle: "Besser, do you know what tangibles are?"

Besser: "Yes! Little oranges!"

After appearing in a variety of feature films, sometimes just to play off the lead comic for a few moments (virtually anyone from Jackie Gleason to Lou Costello looked brave and in control by comparison), Besser developed his big kid character on television on *The Alan Young Show* and later *The Abbott and Costello Show*. He recalled in his autobiography *Not Just a Stooge*, "To add to the effect, I donned a Little Lord Fauntleroy outfit, complete with napkin collar and short pants. I also wore a saucer-shaped hat with a ribbon. I'll admit the idea of a forty-year-old man playing a little kid each week was bizarre…but it was a living!"

One minute he was grinning and cheery, the next huffing, puffing, and pinching, crying, "Ewww, I'll harm you!" or if someone else was doing the pinching, "Not so haaaaard!" Besser was constantly paired with Lou Costello in comedy scenes, which was an interesting concept considering how childlike Lou's character was. In kiddie drag as Stinky, Besser was outrageously regressing even beyond Costello and audiences howled at Lou's frustration in having to act grown-up by comparison.

In 1955, following the death of Shemp Howard, Besser was brought in by Moe Howard and Larry Fine to join the Three Stooges. Oddly enough, there wasn't much chemistry between Besser's brand of childishness and the juvenile mentality of Moe and Larry. Besser recalled, "We were more like 'The Two Stooges, plus Joe Besser' at times, but that's because I wanted it that way…I had a special provision written into my contract which withheld Moe or Larry from causing me serious bodily harm in our scenes together." Even so, Besser's association with the Stooges solidified his standing as a star of comic support, and endeared him further to youngsters who laughed at the way he harmlessly fussed about and uttered his mildly stinging catchphrases.

In 1958 Joe chose to stay home with his wife rather than tour with

SELECTED BROADWAY APPEARANCES:
Sons o' Fun (1941), *If the Shoe FIts* (1946)

SELECTED FILM APPEARANCES:
Hey, Rookie (1944), *Eadie Was a Lady* (1945), *Talk About a Lady* (1946), *Feudin', Fussin' and A-Fightin'* (1948), *Africa Screams* (1949), *The Desert Hawk* (1950), *Sins of Jezebel* (1953), *Abbott and Costello Meet the Keystone Kops* (1955), *Say One for Me* (1959), *The Rookie* (1959), *Three Stooges Fun-a-Rama Compilation* (1959), *Let's Make Love* (1960), *The Errand Boy* (1961), *With Six You Get Eggroll* (1968), *Which Way to the Front* (1970)

TELEVISION SERIES:
The Ken Murray Show (1950–51), *The Abbott and Costello Show* (1951–52), *The Joey Bishop Show* (1962–65), *The Houndcats* (voice) (1972–73), *Jeannie* (voice) (1973–75), *Yogi's Space Race* (voice) (1978–79)

COLLECTIBLE:
Best of Spike Jones, Vol. 2 video and autobiography *Not Just a Stooge*

the boys. He played a comic handyman on *The Joey Bishop Show*, used his comic voice for various Saturday morning television cartoon characters, and was the only member of the Three Stooges well enough to attend the 1983 unveiling of the team's star on the Hollywood Walk of Fame.

Besser once analyzed the appeal of his unusual comic character: "Everybody has always had a secret yearning to forget their age and responsibilities and act like a kid again. I've done it for them, so that's probably why I've always been so well-liked by fans of all ages…"

WILLIE BEST
May 27, 1913–February 27, 1962

Originally dubbed "Sleep 'n' Eat" in films from 1930 to 1935, Willie Best outlived his stereotypical nickname but not roles calling for a humorously "slow-moving Negro." He's probably best known for playing "Chattanooga" Brown in a few Charlie Chan films. Not from Chattanooga at all, Best was born in Sunflower, Mississippi. Of course, had the film studios known that at the time, he probably would have been saddled with his birthplace as an even more demeaning nickname.

In a scene in the Charlie Chan epic *The Shanghai Chest*, Best finds himself locked up in jail. His pal, Mantan Moreland, tries to help: "Maybe I can get you out. I got an in around here." "I don't need no *in*, I'm already in. I want to get out!" "What are you in for?" "Oh, just loitering." "Where?" "In a bank…around midnight."

The slow-talking comedian sometimes had a few fairly neutral gags. He had some malaprop humor in *The Ghost Breakers* with Bob Hope, declaring, "I'm Alex, the old family detainer." But in the film he

WILLIE BEST, looking as always as though he's seen a ghost, actually does here, as do Helen Westley, Alexis Smith, and Roland Drew in *The Smiling Ghost*.

endured wisecracks from Hope like: "You look like a blackout in a blackout!"

In other films, he was merely an amiable dimwit. In *Murder on a Bridal Path*, he's interrogated by amateur detective Helen Broderick: "Have you been working regularly?" "All except the week I was in jail." "What were you doing in jail?" "Shootin' craps." "No, what were you in jail for?" "Shootin' craps." Later, more interrogation, this time from detective Jimmy Gleason: "How long's he been gone? Three quarters of an hour maybe?" "No sir, not that long. About an hour or two, maybe."

Willie Best continued to take character roles in films and came to television with his practiced looks of wariness and comical confusion. He appeared in several sitcoms and played Willie on *The Stu Erwin Show* and Charlie on *My Little Margie*, both handymen.

SELECTED FILM APPEARANCES:
Feet First (1930), *Kentucky Kernals* (1934), *Little Miss Marker* (1934), *Murder on a Honeymoon* (1935), *The Nitwits* (1935), *The Bride Walks Out* (1936), *Thank You, Jeeves* (1936), *General Spanky* (1936), *Gold Is Where You Find It* (1938), *Blondie* (1938), *Nancy Drew, Trouble Shooter* (1939), *At the Circus* (1939), *The Ghost Breakers* (1940), *Scattergood Baines* (1941), *The Body Disappears* (1941), *The Smiling Ghost* (1941), *A-Haunting We Will Go* (1942), *Whispering Ghosts* (1942), *Maisie Gets Her Man* (1942), *Thank Your Lucky Stars* (1943), *The Adventures of Mark Twain* (1944), *Hold That Blonde* (1945), *Dangerous Money* (1946), *Half-Past Midnight* (1948), *The Shanghai Chest* (1948), *Jiggs and Maggie in Jackpot Jitters* (1949), *South of Caliente* (1951)

TELEVISION SERIES:
The Stu Erwin Show (1950–55), *My Little Margie* (1952–55), *Waterfront* (1953–56).

HERMAN BING
March 30, 1889–January 10, 1947

H erman Bing came to Hollywood from Germany along with his friend F. W. Murnau. A former circus clown, Bing was content to work behind the scenes as Murnau's assistant. It wasn't until after the director's death that he began to find acting assignments. In the sound era, his trilling Gerrrrrrman accent and frrrractured English led the portly actor into a lot of comedy relief roles in serious films and musicals, as in *The Merry Widow*, playing the manager of Maxime's. He was dependable as a jolly father, flustered diplomat, excitable shopkeeper, or, in the case of his juicy role in the MacDonald and Eddy musical *Bitter Sweet*, a very agitated butcher. In *Maytime*, he managed to tell Nelson Eddy, somewhat incongruously, "I have known people to have died to be shouting at when sleeping."

Styles changed drastically in the forties, and World War II made it more and more difficult to laugh at kindly-looking German humorists. Along with other old-fashioned dialect comics, like Jack "Baron Munchausen" Pearl, the lovable Bing had trouble finding movie parts. "It wasn't that he needed the money so much," his daughter recalled. "He just couldn't stand not working. He had to act, and when he couldn't get any parts he became unhappy and nervous."

Bing came to live with his daughter and son-in-law. One morning, the breakfast ready on the table, the family heard a gunshot from Her-

HERMAN BING, in droopy-socks repose, was popular comic support in musicals during the late thirties.

man Bing's bedroom. He had put a bullet in his heart. He left behind two notes. The first one read: "Dear Ellen, Such insomnia. I had to commit suicide. Your Daddy." The second, along with a check for $1,000, was in an envelope. The note read: "My beloved Ellen, please forgive me. My nerves. Eternal love, Daddy." On the envelope, Herman Bing had written: "I tried so hard to make a comeback."

SELECTED FILM APPEARANCES:
The Guardsman (1932), *Dinner at Eight* (1933), *Footlight Parade* (1933), *The Bowery* (1933), *Twentieth Century* (1934), *The Black Cat* (1934), *Rose Marie* (1936), *The King Steps Out* (1936), *Bluebeard's Eighth Wife* (1938), *Bitter Sweet* (1940), *The Devil With Hitler* (1942), *Where Do We Go From Here?* (1945), *Night and Day* (1946)

ERIC BLORE, the drollest of screen butlers with his veddy best "veddy good, thar" look.

ERIC BLORE
December 23, 1887– March 1, 1959

Eric Blore was a grand comic butler, livening up many a film with his par excellence version of propriety. He looked down his nose at virtually everyone—and then looked heavenward, his large eyes hinting at his grievous irritation.

In Blore's London household, the acting profession was not as noble as butlering. He recalled, "My father loathed the theater. He called it 'that ladylike profession.' We did have theatrical talent in the family, though. I had a grandmother who would recite on the slightest provocation, 'In Texas Down by the Rio Grande.' Once she got her mind on it there was no stopping her."

Blore wrote a sketch called "The Disorderly Room" which ran for seven years and appeared in London revues including *All the Winners*. He wrote lyrics for shows as well. Once he followed Scottish entertainer Harry Lauder on a bill at the Paragon. The trouble was that the crowd wanted more Lauder. Blore recalled hearing a voice from the upper seats shout, "Are you going to get out of there or shall I have to come down and throw you out?"

A lieutenant in the infantry during World War I, Blore came to Broadway in 1923 for *Little Miss Bluebeard*. He arrived in Hollywood to play a role in the first version of *The Great Gatsby* and then went back to Broadway where he was the waiter in *The Gay Divorce*. Later he did the film version (retitled *The Gay Divorcée*, one of his many Astaire-Rogers supports).

The screen's archetypal gentleman's gentleman, he used his effete and lisping "Yes-sah, veddy good sah," catchphrase in his role as William Powell's valet in *The Ex-Mrs. Bradford*. He played Jamison the bumptious butler in Warren William's *Lone Wolf* films and had a big role as the butler to Edward Everett Horton in *Top Hat*. In that one he made humorous use of the plural: "We take all the blame, myself" and "How's our lumbago this evening, sah?"

Ginger Rogers remembered, "Eric Blore's deadpan expressions were worth their weight in gold." Off-camera Blore was not quite the condescending lackey. He recalled his encounters with director Josef von Sternberg on the set of *The Shanghai Gesture*, saying, "I got on very well with him. My hobby is bully-baiting, and we understood each other immediately."

Blore could invariably be depended on to give a scene a lift, making the most of any throwaway line. As Hugh Herbert's faithful servant in *To Beat the Band* (1935), he is asked, "Have you ever been in love?" Blore responds, "Oh, no sir, but I've been married."

The golden era of sophisticated comedy ended, but Eric Blore managed to find film work now and then in movies requiring a comic touch of class. He played a valet to Joel McCrea in *Sullivan's Travels*. In the forties he was billed as "the screen's funniest butler" for personal appearance tours. According to *Variety*, his act included a comic interview (Jackie Gleason and Jack Albertson both played a straight to Blore) and a closing song parody of "Pistol Packin' Mama" dubbed "Lugar Lugging Mater."

He suffered a stroke in 1956 and died a few years later, survived by his second wife, Clara Macklin.

In a 1938 memoir for the *New York Journal-American*, Blore reflected on how he played valets and waiters, but that fans knew him best one way only: "It is as a butler that I am remembered. Certainly that must prove something. Perhaps that we are all social climbers at heart and thus place the autocrat of the pantry on a plane above the dispenser of viands and the guardian of cravats." He did add, a bit wistfully, "I should say that the tendency to type actors and actresses in the films is carried rather a bit too far."

SELECTED BROADWAY APPEARANCES:
Little Miss Bluebeard (1923), *Mixed Doubles* (1927), *Here's Howe* (1928), *Meet the Prince* (1929), *Here Goes the Bride* (1931), *The Gay Divorce* (1932)

SELECTED FILM APPEARANCES:
The Great Gatsby (1926), *The Gay Divorcée* (1934), *Limehouse Blues* (1934), *Diamond Jim* (1935), *Top Hat* (1935), *The Good Fairy* (1935), *The Ex-Mrs. Bradford* (1936), *Sons o' Guns* (1936), *Swing Time* (1936), *Shall We Dance* (1937), *Swiss Miss* (1938), *The Lone Wolf Strikes* (1940), *The Boys From Syracuse* (1940), *Road to Zanzibar* (1941), *The Lady Eve* (1941), *Sullivan's Travels* (1941), *Secrets of the Lone Wolf* (1941), *The Sky's the Limit* (1943), *Abie's Irish Rose* (1946), *The Lone Wolf in London* (1947), *Love Happy* (1949), *Fancy Pants* (1950), *Bowery to Bagdad* (1955)

BEN BLUE, joined in mid gavotte by Gracie Allen and George Burns in *College Holiday*.

BEN BLUE

Benjamin Bernstein,
September 12, 1901–
March 7, 1975

Born in Canada and raised in New York, comic dancer and pantomimist Ben Blue began his career doing Chaplin imitations at thirteen to get people into the local movie house. He came to Broadway as a dancer in the shows *Irene* (1919) and *Mary* (1920) and owned a dancing school for a while. He moved on to vaudeville with a sketch called "Death of a Swan." His trademark was a strawhat perched above his long, sadly surprised face. Blue made his screen debut in 1927 in a series of Warners shorts.

"As a kid I didn't talk very well," he recalled. "It was difficult to understand me because I talked too fast and ran my words into each other. So I had to use my face and body to make people understand what I meant." Briefly teamed with Billy Gilbert as "The Taxi Boys" for Hal Roach Studios, Blue was mostly used for brief sight gags in films. A shot of his sad face was often enough for a quick chuckle. In fact, a running gag in *Where Were You When the Lights Went Out?* was nothing but poor Ben trying to shave. In *Easy to Wed* a stewardess has this exchange with the doleful comedian: "Sir, are you all right? Do you need oxygen?" "I always look this way."

In the late fifties Blue opened his own nightclub in Santa Monica, but by 1967 the club was gone and the government was busy trying to collect $40,000 in back taxes. Ultimately, Blue was fined $1,000 in 1969. By then, Blue's prospects for owning another business were slim and there was little hope of revitalizing his film career.

SELECTED FILM APPEARANCES:
College Rhythm (1933), *College Holiday* (1936), *High, Wide and Handsome* (1937), *Paris Honeymoon* (1939), *For Me and My Gal* (1942), *Panama Hattie* (1942), *Thousands Cheer* (1943), *Easy to Wed* (1946), *One Sunday Afternoon* (1948), *It's a Mad, Mad, Mad, Mad World* (1967), *The Russians Are Coming! The Russians Are Coming!* (1966), *A Guide for the Married Man* (1957), *The Busy Body* (1967), *Where Were You When the Lights Went Out?* (1968)

WALTER BRENNAN
July 25, 1894–September 21, 1974

An actor who played an endless variety of colorful characters and curmudgeonly old cusses (even when he was young), Walter Brennan finally had a starring role as cantankerous Grandpa Amos McCoy on television's *The Real McCoys*. The role made him popular with both a national audience and nightclub impressionists. Brennan's distinctive rasp could sink gulpingly low in moments of contrition, then, like a pelican trying to fly, awkwardly swoop high in agitation. His speech pattern blended the rural West with his native Boston. Brennan's excitability, which raised his voice an octave in moments of stress, was matched by his trademark of clenched fists and flapping elbows.

Brennan worked in vaudeville before becoming a stuntman in silent films. He lost a few teeth in that occupation, and after serving in World War I, he had even fewer. He appeared in a few early shorts with the Three Stooges, taking bit parts in *Womanhaters* and *Restless Knights*, and merely played a button-eyed simpleton in W. C. Fields's *The Man on the Flying Trapeze*. A few years later and Brennan had found his niche in supporting roles. In fact, he won three supporting Academy Awards (*Come and Get It* in 1936, *Kentucky* in 1938, and *The Westerner* in 1940).

Though most agree that one of his best performances was as the ornery, mean-spirited head of the Clanton clan in *My Darling Clementine* (battling Henry Fonda as Wyatt Earp), comedy parts began to dominate through the forties. Brennan was memorable as the booze-soaked pal of Humphrey Bogart in *To Have and Have Not* (asking the immortal question, "Was you ever bit by a dead bee?"). He was bizarrely amusing as Featherhead, the cackling, self-admitted "half-wit" who became Bob Hope's sidekick in *The Princess and the Pirate*, letting go with at least a half dozen insanely high-pitched squeals of laughter throughout the film.

WALTER BRENNAN late in his career in his best down-home pose.

Brennan was beloved for *The*

Real McCoys, for which he promised and delivered wholesome entertainment. "Boy, let me tell you," he said at the time, "there's no risqué stuff in my show. No sir, I won't allow it. In a TV series, you're going right into the living room and families are watching you. It sure burns me up to see some of the stuff they let get by on other shows." Capitalizing on his fame from the show, Brennan recorded several albums and issued singles ranging from sentimental narratives ("Old Rivers") to comical monologues set to music ("I Wanna Go Back to the Farm").

Though his archconservatism and borderline anti-Semitism (he referred to Jews as "Hebes" in a *TV Guide* interview) did not make him popular with many of Hollywood's greats, he always had the admiration of the fans who knew him for the lovable old codgers he portrayed. He followed *The Real McCoys* with a dramatic series *The Guns of Will Sonnett* and quite a few codgers in family-oriented Disney comedies of the late sixties.

SELECTED FILM APPEARANCES:
Tearin' Into Trouble (1925), *Man on the Flying Trapeze* (1935), *Wedding Night* (1935), *Bride of Frankenstein* (1935), *These Three* (1936), *Come and Get It* (1936), *Adventures of Tom Sawyer* (1938), *Kentucky* (1938), *The Westerner* (1940), *Meet John Doe* (1941), *Sergeant York* (1941), *The Pride of the Yankees* (1942), *To Have and Have Not* (1944), *The Princess and the Pirate* (1944), *My Darling Clementine* (1946), *Red River* (1947), *The Far Country* (1955), *Bad Day at Black Rock* (1955), *Tammy and the Bachelor* (1957), *Who's Minding the Mint?* (1967), *Support Your Local Sheriff* (1969), *The Over-the-Hill Gang* (1969), *The Over-the-Hill Gang Rides Again* (1970), *Home for the Holidays* (1972)

TELEVISION SERIES:
The Real McCoys (1957–63), *The Tycoon* (1964–65), *The Guns of Will Sonnett* (1967–69), *To Rome With Love* (1970–71)

COLLECTIBLES:
Among Brennan's record albums: *Mark Twain Stories* (Caedmon), *Old Rivers* (Liberty), *Wonderful World of Walter Brennan* (Liberty), *Dutchman's Gold* (Dot)

FELIX BRESSART
March 2, 1892–March 17, 1949

Felix Bressart was a leading star in Germany, appearing in dozens of films. Though he came to America only a few times in the early thirties to star in some Broadway productions, his German films often played in the United States to good reviews. In 1932 the *New York Herald-Tribune* reviewed *Der Schrecken der Garnison*, declaring, "Felix Bressart, the German clown, is back in town and cutting merry capers." In 1934, the *New York Times* hailed his part in *Der Glueckszylinder* as "one of his best roles." But soon the Prussian-born Bressart was sailing for England to escape Hitler, and from there, he came back to America to stay. He recalled in a 1940 interview:

"I had just completed a picture in London. It was summer and I had a few weeks ahead for a vacation, and so we secured our passage and sailed. I have never been back. In fact I am now an American citizen. I fell in love with America the minute I got off the boat, and while I didn't have a sign of a job in Hollywood, I had friends there."

Bressart was a hit joining Sig Ruman and Alexander Granach as the commissars in *Ninotchka*. In a Paris hotel he and his Russian comrades try to get a room. "I'm afraid our rates our too high," says the clerk. Bressart asks, "Why should you be afraid?"

FELIX BRESSART, one of the screen's beloved "foreigners" of the thirties and forties, gives encouragement to musicians Ann Sothern and Lee Bowman in *Three Hearts for Julia*.

Bressart often played foreigners in roles that called for bewilderment, irony, and a certain touch of sadness. He looked like he had been downtrodden by the powers that be, resuscitated by his own individuality. He had wild stringy hair, arched eyebrows, a long nose, and a receding chin that gave him a glum, questioning look.

Bressart was partnered with little Curt Bois for the comedy relief in *Bitter Sweet* and had one of his best roles as Greenberg in Jack Benny's classic *To Be or Not to Be*. In the film he played a gentle actor who seemed to appreciate the humor in most any scene being performed. As he said in all seriousness, "A laugh is nothing to be sneezed at." Even his insults were gentle. To a ham actor he remarks almost apologetically, "What you are, I wouldn't eat."

In the film, Bressart's character serves to symbolize Jewish suffering, the long days of accepting frustration and indignity, and the quiet, ironic humor that makes life bearable. The running gag is his desire to play the role of Shylock; in an acting company where the hams get the good parts and he's just a spear carrier. But when it's time for him to put on a rousing performance and distract the Nazis long enough for an escape, his speech as Shylock is by turns funny, touching, and glorious.

Another highlight role for Bressart was a defector in *Comrade X*. Attending a baseball game, he's bewildered by a sudden roar from the crowd. "What happened?" he asks. Hedy Lamarr shouts, "The Dodgers are murdering the Reds!" "Aha!" says Bressart. "The counterrevolution!"

After appearing in *Portrait of Jennie* and *A Song Is Born*, Bressart was signed for a role in the 1949 comedy *My Friend Irma* but died of leukemia before filming began.

SELECTED BROADWAY APPEARANCES:
The Royal Family (1931), *Die Journalisten* (1932), *Auslandreise* (1932), *The Big Two* (1947)

SELECTED AMERICAN FILM APPEARANCES:
Three Smart Girls Grow Up (1939), *Ninotchka* (1939), *The Shop Around the Corner* (1940), *Swanee River* (1940), *Edison the Man* (1940), *Comrade X* (1940), *Bitter Sweet* (1940), *Third Finger Left Hand* (1940), *Ziegfeld Girl* (1941), *Married Bachelor* (1941), *Mr. and Mrs. North* (1941), *To Be or Not to Be* (1942), *Above Suspicion* (1943), *Song of Russia* (1944), *The Seventh Cross* (1944), *Greenwich Village* (1944), *Without Love* (1945), *I've Always Loved You* (1946), *A Song is Born* (1948), *Portrait of Jennie* (1948), *Take One False Step* (1949)

HELEN BRODERICK, sophisticated but slightly dazed.

HELEN BRODERICK
August 11, 1891–September 25, 1959

The team of "Broderick and Crawford" produced a lot of laughs in vaudeville, and eventually a son (the gruff star of TV's *Highway Patrol*, Broderick Crawford). But in her long solo career, Philadelphia-born Helen Broderick was known primarily for her droll wit and airy charm in film roles.

After working in 1907 in the very first *Ziegfeld Follies*, she costarred on Broadway in *Fifty Million Frenchmen* and *The Band Wagon* with Fred and Adele Astaire. She came to Hollywood specializing in roles calling for satiric sophistication. (In *Top Hat*, she was Edward Everett Horton's matchmaking wife.) She was paired with pained, bumbling actor Victor Moore in a few films (*We're on the Jury*, *Swing Time*, and *Meet the Missus*).

In *We're on the Jury*, one of her best films, Broderick plays a breezy, eccentric woman who ruptures the decorum of the proceedings. "I'm afraid I sat on your hat!" she says to Moore, who wistfully replies, "Don't be afraid; you did." She both charms and aggravates the jury with her inquisitiveness and deductions, but always demonstrates a certain sense of logic. During the proceedings she interrupts: "May I ask a question…may I ask if the lawyers are also under oath to tell the truth?"

She and Moore starred in their own radio show in the thirties, *Twin Stars*. Broderick and Moore had become far more popular than the early vaudeville team of Helen and her husband, Lester Crawford.

Broderick's wit wasn't confined to lines supplied to her by the script writers. In *Picturegoer Weekly* (February 5, 1938), she wrote a piece on moving into her new home: "Saturday night I leave the studio in high expectations. Saturday is always a lovely day, I'm told. The sun shines, although I'm inside a sound stage and can't see it. But the Chamber of Commerce is satisfied, so why shouldn't I be? Sunday dawns…. The birds are singing insistently. I suppose they figure that since they can't sleep nobody else is going to. I scamper from my warm bed into the garden, which isn't a garden yet, and start pulling weeds and wondering about a black cloud that is obscuring most of the sky of sunny California…I had turned on the heat before I went out. A push of the button does it. Or does it? Anyway, the house is nice and cold. It seems that the boys from the gas company slipped up on the job. Apparently they expected to, because they've left a little sign telling me how to reach them in case anything goes wrong…"

SELECTED BROADWAY APPEARANCES:
Nifties of 1923 (1923), *The Wild Westcotts* (1923), *Mama Loves Papa* (1926), *Oh, Please!* (1926), *Fifty Million Frenchmen* (1929), *The Band Wagon* (1931), *Vanities* (1932), *As Thousands Cheer* (1933)

SELECTED FILM APPEARANCES:
Fifty Million Frenchmen (1931), *Top Hat* (1935), *Love on a Bet* (1936), *Swing Time* (1936), *We're on the Jury* (1936), *Meet the Missus* (1937), *Life of the Party* (1937), *Radio City Revels* (1938), *Rage of Paris* (1938), *Rolling Stones* (1938), *My Love for Yours* (1939), *Naughty But Nice* (1939), *No No Nanette* (1940), *Three Is a Family* (1944), *Love, Honor and Goodbye* (1945), *Because of Him* (1946)

NIGEL BRUCE
William Nigel Bruce, February 4, 1895–October 8, 1953

I f he wasn't saying something silly, he looked like he was about to. As comic relief in dramas, Nigel Bruce turned up in everything from Hitchcock movies (like *Rebecca* and *Suspicion*) to Sherlock Holmes films. He was adept at playing a stereotyped jolly, good-natured fool or a stuffy and staid Englishman whose bumbling, mumbling sense of decorum and amiable incompetence were laughable.

Though Bruce was not prone to deliberate catchphrases or trademark funny faces, he did have one little comic trick he used from time to time. He liked to "make a noise like a duck." This was his attempt to deliberately amuse someone, such as the depressed Joan Fontaine in *Suspicion* or a frightened child in the Holmes film *Dressed to Kill*. Of course neither found it funny, which greatly amused viewers.

"Good old Watson," Sherlock Holmes says of him, "The one fixed point in a changing age." The combination of good egg Nigel Bruce and tasteful ham Basil Rathbone yielded both a film and radio series of Holmes adventures. Along the way, Bruce's harumphing Dr. Watson

NIGEL BRUCE, often baffled by Sherlock Holmes, is stunned at George Brent's discovery in *Adventure in Diamonds*.

leaned increasingly toward comic relief. His Watson admired Holmes but couldn't resist competing with him and making (wrong, of course) deductions. He often tried to impress strangers by intimating that he was practically the detective's partner on important cases. He was comfortably human compared to the computer-brained detective, whether grumbling about a rabbit's foot ("Very poor taste. Fancy going about with a dead animal's foot dangling from your pocket.") or conducting a graveyard conversation not realizing that he's talking to an owl, "I never did trust that woman."

"Hooo." "Why, Mrs. Montieth, of course."

Glenhall Taylor, who directed the Holmes radio series, reports that in the recording studio Bruce and Rathbone were hardly staid Englishmen: "They would stop at a market on the way over and pick up a couple of cartons of milk and some Danish. When they finished, they would throw the leftover pastry at me…[the program] was a serious show on the air, but Rathbone and Bruce were two of the most humorous men I ever worked with." The duo burlesqued their characters in Olsen and Johnson's *Crazy House*, with Rathbone insisting, "I am Sherlock Holmes! I know everything!"

The fact that Watson didn't, delighted most fans. An exception was Sir Arthur Conan Doyle's daughter who said in 1991, "I couldn't abide Nigel Bruce as Dr. Watson. Dr. Watson was never meant to be a buffoon." Bruce fans would counter that in several films, Watson was handy with a gun or provided great moral support for Holmes, and that in general his whimsical mumblings were merely eccentric, as in *Sherlock Holmes Goes to Washington*, where he recalls, "We had a carrier pigeon in the last war. Belonged to the Brigade Signal Corps. The poor bird kept flying around in circles all day long. Found out later it was cross-eyed. Tragic thing!"

Nigel Bruce's brand of Englishman (though he was born in Ensenada, Mexico) was something of a stereotype, but he was a welcome member of the "British Colony" in Hollywood, friends who got together for cricket matches and parties. Others included Rathbone, David Niven, and Boris Karloff. Sometimes they got to talking about the old days, or their experiences in World War I. Nigel Bruce could recount stories that belied his identity as Dr. Watson. Bruce was in the thick of the battle and in a machine-gun blitz sustained eleven bullet wounds.

Rathbone recalled Bruce's "great joy in Elizabethan humor" in private life, and a Watsonian bluster. Rathbone urged Bruce to come to the ballet with several other friends: "He spluttered and grunted and mumbled his unqualified refusal in that form of speech indigenous to himself alone, and which was often quite untranslatable! At last, pouring himself another drink (like Falstaff, all drinks were disposed of by him in one enormous gulp—bottoms up!) he finally refused to accompany us, giving as his reason that... 'I will not spend good money to watch buggers jump!'"

SELECTED BROADWAY APPEARANCES:
This Was a Man (1926), *The Letter* (1927), *Dishonored Lady* (1930), *Springtime for Henry* (1931), *Virginia* (1937), *We Were Dancing* (1940)

SELECTED FILM APPEARANCES:
Red Aces (1929), *The Squeaker* (1931), *Springtime for Henry* (1934), *Stand Up and Cheer* (1934), *The Lady Is Willing* (1934), *Treasure Island* (1934), *The Scarlet Pimpernel* (1935), *The Man Who Broke the Bank at Monte Carlo* (1935), *Becky Sharp* (1935), *She* (1935), *Make Way for a Lady* (1936), *The Charge of the Light Brigade* (1936), *Kidnapped* (1938), *The Hound of the Baskervilles* (1939), *The Adventures of Sherlock Holmes* (1939), *Rebecca* (1940), *The Bluebird* (1940), *Suspicion* (1941), *Sherlock Holmes and the Voice of Terror* (1942), *Sherlock Holmes and the Secret Weapon* (1942), *Sherlock Holmes in Washington* (1943), *Sherlock Holmes Faces Death* (1943), *Crazy House* (1943), *Follow the Boys* (1944), *The Pearl of Death* (1944), *The Scarlet Claw* (1944), *House of Fear* (1945), *Woman in Green* (1945), *Pursuit to Algiers* (1945), *Dressed to Kill* (1946), *Terror by Night* (1946), *The Two Mrs. Carrolls* (1947), *Hong Kong* (1951), *Bwana Devil* (1952), *Limelight* (1952), *World for Ransom* (1954)

EDGAR BUCHANAN
March 21, 1903–April 4, 1979

T he right man for playing small-town windbags, cheesy wise guys, less-than-honorable judges, and dubiously effective sheriffs, Edgar Buchanan was a fixture in dozens of Westerns. A sort of a scruffy wild west W. C. Fields, he was always on the lookout for some easy money—and usually prone to grumbling when the deal didn't pan out.

Buchanan was born in Humansville, Missouri. His childhood nickname was "Beans," from the time he stole a can of beans and ate every last one—getting terribly sick in the process. Buchanan's father was a dentist and Edgar became one as well. He even married a dentist, Dr. Mildred Spence, and the two had offices together in Eugene, Oregon. After appearing in amateur theatricals in Eugene, the couple moved to Southern California and Edgar tried getting assignments at the Pasadena Community Theater. One woman there informed him, "You're not for the theater. You have glotal shock and no ear for sound." She was

EDGAR BUCHANAN, querulous old rascal.

surprised when a talent scout from Columbia signed him for a role in *Arizona*.

The scratchy-voiced, wily actor aged into a wary-eyed rascal and loved it: "I love playing an old coot," he once said. "Fact is, I feel kind of naked without those false whiskers…. Dentistry is the hardest work in the world. I'd be dead right now if I'd stayed with it." After a stint as Hopalong Cassidy's TV sidekick, Buchanan starred in his own television show as *Judge Roy Bean*. His lasting TV fame would come from his role as old codger Uncle Joe on *Petticoat Junction*. Like Fields, who always showed such devotion to his young film daughters, Buchanan was seemingly benign and well-mannered to the three beauties who costarred as his granddaughters on the show. Had he lived to play the same part in the eighties, he probably would've taken binoculars with him to watch the show's opening scene—the girls bathing in a water tower, their petticoats draped over the side of the huge tub. Buchanan said of the role, "I'm pretty much the same type of guy myself—I'm lazy and ignorant."

SELECTED FILM APPEARANCES:
Arizona (1940), *When the Daltons Rode* (1940), *The Sea Hawk* (1940), *Three Cheers for the Irish* (1940), *Penny Serenade* (1941), *The Richest Man in Town* (1941), *The Talk of the Town* (1942), *Buffalo Bill* (1944), *If I'm Lucky* (1946), *Best Man Wins* (1948), *The Big Hangover* (1950), *Rawhide* (1951), *Toughest Man in Arizona* (1952), *Shane* (1953), *It Happens Every Thursday* (1953), *She Couldn't Say No* (1954), *Destry* (1954), *The Sheepman* (1958), *Chartroose Caboose* (1960), *Cimarron* (1960), *Tammy Tell Me True* (1961), *A Ticklish Affair* (1963), *Move Over Darling* (1963), *The Rounders* (1965), *The Over-the-Hill Gang* (1969), *Benji* (1974)

TELEVISION SERIES:
Hopalong Cassidy (1951–52), *Judge Roy Bean* (1959), *Petticoat Junction* (1963–69), *Cade's County* (1971)

BILLIE BURKE

Mary William Ethelbert Appleton
Burke, August 6, 1884–
May 14, 1970

BILLIE BURKE, the queen of ditz in Hollywood's Golden Age.

Schooled by her father, a red-headed clown who had his own touring circus, Billie Burke was in show business almost all her life. While her father toured the world, the Washington-born actress was schooled in England, appearing there in musical comedies. One of her big hits was *The School Girl* (1903). Brought to Broadway to star opposite John Drew in the comedy *My Wife*, Burke proved a sensation. The stylish performer's taste in perfume and clothing set fashion trends. Her habits of wearing baby blue, decorating herself in lace and ruffles, and pausing to powder her nose were oft-imitated. Women were amazed to read how she poured champagne over her red hair before her shampoos and advocated walking five miles a day.

In her day, Billie had famous admirers including Enrico Caruso, Mark Twain, and Somerset Maugham. Of Caruso she remarked, "He made love and ate spaghetti with equal skill and no inhibitions. He would propose marriage several times each evening." She met Florenz Ziegfeld in 1913 and they were married the next year. The actress who had done so well with Broadway farces found herself working even harder in films—after she and her husband were wiped out by the 1929 stock market crash.

As she aged, she accented her coquettish behavior, delightful singsong speech pattern, and fluttery, dithery mannerisms for a variety of costarring roles in film comedies. She recalled moving from funny ingenue and leading lady of the stage into character comedy parts, "That sad and bewildering moment when you are no longer the cherished darling but must turn the corner and try to be funny!" She was a success, The *New York Times* raving over her "addlepated, scatterbrained, twittery, jittery or skittish" comedy style.

Burke was well-known for playing Mrs. Topper to Roland Young's *Topper*. She appeared in the sequels as well, always huffy and ditsy. Typically impatient and distracted, she tells her maid, "It's chilly isn't it?

SELECTED BROADWAY APPEARANCES:
My Wife (1907), *Love Watches* (1908), *Mrs. Dot* (1910), *The Amazons* (1913), *The Land of Promise* (1914), *A Marriage of Convenience* (1918), *Caesar's Wife* (1919), *The Intimate Strangers* (1921), *Annie Dear* (1924), *Pardon My Glove* (1926), *The Happy Husband* (1928), *The Mad Hopes* (1932), *Mrs. January and Mr. Ex* (1944)

SELECTED FILM APPEARANCES:
(Many silent films dating back to 1916), *A Bill of Divorcement* (1932), *Dinner at Eight* (1933), *Becky Sharp* (1935), *A Feather in Her Hat* (1935), *Piccadilly Jim* (1936), *Topper* (1937), *Merrily We Live* (1938), *Topper Takes a Trip* (1938), *Young at Heart* (1938), *The Wizard of Oz* (1939), *Zenobia* (1939), *Eternally Yours* (1939), *Topper Returns* (1941), *The Man Who Came to Dinner* (1941), *What's Cookin'?* (1942), *The Barkleys of Broadway* (1949), *Father of the Bride* (1950), *Three Husbands* (1951), *The Young Philadelphians* (1959), *Pepe* (1960)

TELEVISION SERIES:
Doc Corkle (1952)

COLLECTIBLES:
Two autobiographies, *With a Feather on My Nose* and *With Powder on My Nose*

Emily, remind me to send this coat back! It doesn't keep me warm at all!" "Mrs. Topper, you haven't got it on." "Oh. How silly of me."

In 1939 Burke achieved a certain screen immortality for playing, with a dash of flighty, tongue-in-cheek humor, the role of the Good Witch in *The Wizard of Oz*. In 1936, Myrna Loy played Billie in *The Great Ziegfeld*, the film biography of her late husband. (Samantha Eggar played Billie Burke in the TV Ziegfeld biography in 1978.) In 1949 Burke published her first autobiography, *With a Feather on My Nose*. Burke continued to make films through the fifties, including shorts for Columbia. She never fought against her image, insisting, "I am not always saner than I seem."

Billie Burke's fame endured for more than three decades. Her 1952 attempt at a sitcom, *Doc Corkle*, lasted only three weeks. It was immediately forgotten, and time has dimmed the lustre of her Broadway years, but her films of the thirties and forties remain as a bright reminder of a shining—and whimsically fluttering—star.

SMILEY BURNETTE
Lester Alvin Burnette, March 18, 1911–February 16, 1967

The heavy-set, gentle, tall-tale-telling Smiley Burnette was one of the most beloved sidekicks in film Westerns. Originally a musician, Burnette performed while attending the Astoria (Illinois) High School. He worked as a singer for a local radio station in Tuscola, Illinois, when he was discovered by Gene Autry. Autry needed an accordion player in a hurry and signed up Burnette for $50 a week. Burnette had been making $18 at the station. Autry and Burnette ended up in Chicago where they appeared on the WLS "National Barn Dance," and later brought their music and comedy act to Hollywood.

As Gene Autry's sidekick in a series of films in the thirties, playing Frog Millhouse, Burnette could handle a novelty tune (he wrote over three hundred songs) and lighten up the action with a story or just some genial goofing around. His trademarks were his smile and his big cowboy hat with the upturned brim. He lived up to his nickname, raising at least a smile if not belly laughs. After making fifty-six pictures with Autry, the partnership began to erode and Burnette moved on to be partnered with another Western favorite, Charles Starrett. This combination lasted even longer: fifty-seven pictures. Burnette also worked with Rocky Lane and Roy Rogers.

When an injury sidelined Pat Buttram, Smiley Burnette returned to work with Gene Autry in the 1951 film *Whirlwind* and several subsequent quickies. There was no longer much of a market for B Westerns and before long Autry and Burnette both hung up their spurs. Smiley was in semire-

SMILEY BURNETTE, always billed as "The West's No. 1 Comic," here serenading pal Charles Starrett and cowgal Eve Miller.

tirement when he got the assignment to play a train engineer on TV's *Petticoat Junction*. He didn't have much to do but his smiling, pleasant personality did add to the comfortable, folksy feel of the show. He was still working on the show when he died of leukemia. Gene Autry recalled in his autobiography, "It pleased me that he had a few good years on television, near the end, so he could relax and travel less."

SELECTED FILM APPEARANCES:
Melody Trail (1935), *Tumbling Tumbleweeds* (1935), *Red River Valley* (1936), *Comin' Round the Mountain* (1936), *The Singing Cowboy* (1936), *Ride Ranger Ride* (1936), *The Big Show* (1936), *South of the Border* (1939), *Back in the Saddle* (1941), *King of the Cowboys* (1943), *Terror Trail* (1947), *Laramie* (1949), *Smoky Canyon* (1952), *Winning of the West* (1953)

TELEVISION SERIES:
Petticoat Junction (1963–67)

MAE BUSCH, the "ever-popular" one according to Jackie Gleason, prepares to brush off suitor Stan Laurel in *Chickens Come Home*.

MAE BUSCH
January 20, 1897–
April 19, 1946

On television Jackie Gleason occasionally extolled the memory of the woman he called "the Ever Popular" Mae Busch. Though the tribute to a dimly remembered film comedienne was tongue in cheek, there was once a time when Busch was a serious rival to the silent era's reigning comedy queen Mabel Normand. Unfortunately the rivalry was more in the boudoir than on the screen.

Busch had been one of Normand's closest friends and had Mabel to thank for getting an audition at Keystone Studios. But the actress couldn't keep away from Mabel's boyfriend, director Mack Sennett.

One night Mabel caught Mack and Mae together. The naked Busch smashed Normand over the head with a vase and the force of the blow sent the dazed, bloodied actress staggering back out the door.

A short time later Mabel won Mack back and Mae Busch was through. She drifted through some minor film comedies, not making much of an impression on anyone until years later when she joined up with Sennett's prospering rival, Hal Roach.

Ironically, her best work at the Roach Studios was generally playing a home wrecker in Laurel and Hardy shorts. She played Ollie's blackmailing ex-lover in *Chickens Come Home*, while in *Come Clean* she was a woman of questionable virtue who decided to jump into the river and end her life. Laurel passes by, waving a friendly "Good-bye!" But Hardy dives in and saves her—only to discover that she now expects him to take care of her. Occasionally Mae actually played Hardy's wife, as in *Their First Mistake*, but the role called for comical nastiness. In that one she walked out on him after slapping Laurel with a lawsuit "for the alienation of Mr. Hardy's affections." She was similarly antagonistic as Hardy's wife in *Sons of the Desert*.

The more appealing and charming side of Busch could be seen in *Them Thar Hills* and *Tit for Tat*, where she played someone else's wife—flirting with Oliver Hardy! The Australian-born (she grew up in America and was educated in a convent in New Jersey) costar so often "married" to Hardy actually married three times. Her husbands were silent star Francis McDonald in 1924, John Cassell in 1926, and Thomas Tate in 1936. Not surprisingly, Mae Busch's lifestyle led to exhaustion. She checked into the San Fernando Valley Sanitarium in 1945, and died there five months later, only forty-four years old.

SELECTED FILM APPEARANCES:
The Agitator (1912), *A One-Night Stand* (1915), *The Rent Jumpers* (1915), *A Rascal of Wolfish Ways* (1915), *The Best of Enemies* (1915), *A Bath House Blunder* (1916), *Foolish Wives* (1921), *Nellie the Beautiful Cloak Model* (1924), *The Unholy Three* (1925), *While the City Sleeps* (1928), *Come Clean* (1931), *Chickens Come Home* (1931), *Their First Mistake* (1932), *Sons of the Desert* (1933), *The Bohemian Girl* (1936), *Prison Farm* (1938), *Women Without Names* (1940), *Ziegfeld Girl* (1940), *Masquerade in Mexico* (1946)

COLLECTIBLES:
Keystone Comedies, Volume 6; Keystone Comedies, Volume 7, (Video Film Classics)

CHARLES BUTTERWORTH
July 28, 1896–June 13, 1946

CHARLES BUTTERWORTH thinks he's got straight what light-suited Walter Catlett is telling him in *Give Out, Sisters.*

A dryly understated deadpan comedian, the elderly Charles Butterworth had a downturned mouth, knit brows, and long, thin nose. The mannerly actor often played a solemn milquetoast; flustered, preoccupied and tentative. In *Baby Face Harrington*, a timid bank teller begins counting out money and asks "How do you want it?" Customer Charles absent-mindedly mumbles, "Oh, very badly. I mean…in cash." Later in the film, a burglar invades his room shouting, "Put 'em up!" Charles murmurs, "This is a surprise. This is rather unusual, isn't it?"

The humor was all in Butterworth's mild and mournful characterization. "I'm selling a personality," he once said, "and to do this I have to be careful it doesn't go out of character—but I can't tell you how I do it. I've never been able to reduce myself to a formula. A story on what makes me funny to most people would be very unfunny." He rarely was given conspicuously funny lines but saved many a mild movie just by his costarring presence. "Things get so bad—then they get worse," was a typical line for him, and typical of many of the support characters he played.

Butterworth, a Notre Dame graduate, worked as a columnist for the *Chicago American* and as city editor for his hometown newspaper, the *South Bend News-Times*. He first performed humor in speech form at Rotary Club meetings and banquets. His eventual film success came when he was in his late thirties. He was perfectly cast as a timid bachelor or dull husband (his 1932 marriage ended in divorce in 1939). Butterworth always seemed like the kind of fellow nothing would happen to, but in his sitcom-oriented films (and his brief radio series in the late thirties) something always did.

Something happened just a few hours before dawn one day in June of 1946. At 3:30 A.M., en route home from Palm Springs, Butterworth's car reached about sixty-miles an hour, skidded one hundred eighty feet, jumped a curb, struck a light pole, and slammed into a building. Over the years, the accident has been given a new theory. According to *Hollywood Babylon* author Kenneth Anger, "He did, in point of fact, kill himself." Anger cited director Jean Negulesco's wife Dusty, with supplying this information. She claimed to be a close friend of both Butterworth and Robert Benchley—and that after Benchley's death, "the actor was inconsolable."

SELECTED BROADWAY APPEARANCES:
Americana (1926), *Allez-Oop!* (1927), *Sweet Adeline* (1929), *Flying Colors* (1932), *Count Me In* (1942), *Brighten the Corner* (1945)

SELECTED FILM APPEARANCES:
The Life of the Party (1930), *Love Me Tonight* (1932), *My Weakness* (1933), *Hollywood Party* (1934), *Orchids to You* (1935), *Baby Face Harrington* (1935), *Rainbow on the River* (1936), *Swing High, Swing Low* (1937), *Every Day's a Holiday* (1937), *Thanks for the Memory* (1938), *The Boys From Syracuse* (1940), *A Night in New Orleans* (1942), *This Is the Army* (1943), *Follow the Boys* (1944)

PAT BUTTRAM
June 19, 1917

With his cracking, yodeling voice in contrast to his heavy build and poker face, Pat Buttram was welcome comic relief in many movie Westerns. He became Gene Autry's sidekick both in films and on radio. In the late fifties Buttram had his own radio show on KNX in California at the same time as young disc jockey (and later sitcom star) Robert Crane and was a sought-after speaker. One of his comedy albums, *Off His Rocker*, is loaded with down-home humor: "Ralph Hunker's daddy made the first baseball glove in history. Made it out of genuine cowhide. Of course he cheated a little, he made it out of the part of the cow that already had the fingers in it."

The years with Gene Autry and his popularity in California helped Buttram keep his name out and about, leading to his role of bucolic con man Mr. Haney on the sixties sitcom *Green Acres*. Of all his supporting roles, this would prove to be his most popular. Haney was always working some kind of deal on unsuspecting city dude Oliver Wendell Douglas (Eddie Albert). Once Haney tried to push a new line of fertilizer: "I'll put you down for a hundred bags." "I'll take *one* bag just to experiment with." "Why don't we round it off to an even number. Say twenty-three bags?" "Uh uh, an even number would be twenty bags." "Sold!"

Buttram continued his after-dinner speaking and made a 1970 album, *We Wuz Poor*, featuring liner notes from Richard Nixon. Through the decades, Buttram remained a reliable performer at banquets

PAT BUTTRAM, the yodel-voiced sidekick to Gene Autry and others before doing TV's *Green Acres*.

and roasts. At one event he knocked off everyone on the dais from Johnny Carson ("He's an Episcopalian—that's an Off-Broadway Catholic") to Roy Rogers and Dale Evans ("The Lunt and Fontanne of the fertilizer set") to Yogi Berra ("He's got the kind of face that could make a train take a dirt road!").

Buttram continued to find sitcom and film work whenever a doleful rustic or a comical Western old-timer was needed, and with his unique voice, he sometimes found behind-the-scenes work in cartoons. He was the Sheriff of Nottingham in Disney's *Robin Hood* and had a cameo in *Who Framed Roger Rabbit*. He played a bullet.

While he continued to enjoy the recognition that *Green Acres* reruns gave him, Buttram retained a special fondness for his early days with Gene Autry. He said at a testimonial for his multimillionaire friend, "No matter what Autry touches he comes out fine. The other day he found a squid, squeezed it, and sold it as a ballpoint fish."

SELECTED FILM APPEARANCES:
National Barn Dance (1944), *Riders in the Sky* (1949), *Mule Train* (1950), *Wagon Team* (1952), *The Old West* (1952), *Twilight of Honor* (1963), *Roustabout* (1964), *Sgt. Deadhead* (1965), *The Sweet Ride* (1968), *Robin Hood* (voice) (1973), *Who Framed Roger Rabbit* (voice) (1989), *Return to Green Acres* (1990), *Back to the Future III* (1990)

TELEVISION SERIES:
The Gene Autry Show (1950–56), *Green Acres* (1965–71)

COLLECTIBLES:
The Gene Autry Show (Radiola), *Laffter Sweet and Profane* (KNX), *Off His Rocker* (Warner), *We Wuz Poor* (Ovation), *As I Look Into Your Faces* (Dore)

ERIC CAMPBELL putting his usual evil eye on Charlie Chaplin in *Easy Street*.

ERIC CAMPBELL
1870–December 20, 1917

Charles Chaplin literally bounced jokes off the most comically fearsome villain in silent films, Eric Campbell. He had a build like a pro wrestler; two-hundred fifty pounds of muscle and belly. His body was topped off with a small skull shaved almost to the bone. His face was smeared into exaggeration by heavy eyebrows that rose demonically above his scowling, darkened eyes.

Born in Scotland, Campbell was a member of Fred Karno's British vaudeville troupe. He was invited to make movies by ex-Karno alumni, Charles Chaplin.

In *Easy Street* he is the outrageously menacing bully who actually invites Charlie the Cop to pound his crew-cutted skull with a billy club (to no effect, of course). He and Chaplin were sort of a Mutt and Jeff combo in *Behind the Screen*, with Campbell playing the burly boss and Chaplin the little assistant forced to do all the work. In that one, the six-foot-four heavy got laughs on his own mincing about in a bit of gay parody thinking there is something peculiar about Charlie for kissing a fellow workman (Edna Purviance in disguise). Sometimes Campbell merely had to hulk around as a figure of imposing pomposity and gluttony, as in *The Cure* where he sports a bandaged, gouty foot and gets it whacked by poor thin Charlie.

1917 was the year of some of Campbell's best work, but also his greatest tragedies. On July 9, his wife died suddenly of a heart attack after eating in a local restaurant. His daughter went out to buy a black dress for the funeral and was nearly killed by a passing car. Less than a month after his wife's death, Campbell married again, but by November, his new wife sued for divorce. The rough year ended a little early. On December 20, Campbell was driving at an estimated sixty miles an hour when his car overturned twice and pinned him in the wreckage, killing the giant actor almost instantly.

SELECTED FILM APPEARANCES:
The Floorwalker (1916), *The Fireman* (1916), *The Vagabond* (1916), *The Count* (1916), *The Pawnshop* (1916), *Behind the Screen* (1916), *The Rink* (1916), *Easy Street* (1917), *The Cure* (1917), *The Immigrant* (1917), *The Adventurer* (1917).

RON CAREY
Ronald Cicenia,
December 11, 1935

RON CAREY, in the throes of terror as Madeline Kahn breaks some disturbing news to Howard Morris, Mel Brooks, and him in *High Anxiety*.

In films and on television, Ron Carey became typed as the swaggering little man trying to act big. Born in Newark, New Jersey, he graduated from Seton Hall in 1958 and began his career as an offbeat stand-up comic. He appeared on *The Tonight Show* in 1961 and recalled. "I was sensational. I killed them. I was so good Paar gave me a sign to keep going. I did twelve minutes. He liked me so much I came back two weeks later. And I bombed."

Carey had gotten some writers to create material for him and it didn't work. But over the next few years he began drawing most of his humor from his Catholic upbringing. Along with David Steinberg, Carey became one of the few who dared to perform religious comedy in the mid-sixties. His *Slightly Irreverent* album in 1967 included a sketch about a monk giving a tough, army sergeant-styled speech to the new recruits: "I'm gonna make real men out of ya. Tough men. Strong men. Now take off your shirts, your pants and your jackets and put on your little brown dresses…line up, you guys, chins in, heads bowed, and stand meek!"

Carey appeared in *Lovers and Other Strangers* on Broadway in 1968 and toured with the show. The five-foot-six actor said he made up to forty commercials a year between 1967 and 1971, but had some lean years until he landed the role of Officer Carl Levitt on the series *Barney Miller*. Costar Steve Landesberg said, "He's one of the most giving of performers. Ron's very quick to tell people what a great job they've done." The role itself was rather thankless; he played a man who hoped the chip on his shoulder made him look taller. Viewers could easily relate to him; he was every brown-nosing office weasel always ready to insinuate himself into a situation that could win him a promotion. As with another cocky little man, Don Adams, the sadistic fun was in watching Carey's inflated bravado get punctured, leaving his shrunken back to reality.

In Mel Brooks's *High Anxiety*, this part of Carey's comic persona was explored in one memorable running gag. With a macho smirk on his face, Carey would pick up huge, heavy packages with an easy, "I got it. I got it." Then…struggling under the weight and about to fall over: "I don't got it!"

SELECTED FILM APPEARANCES:
The Out-of-Towners (1970), *Silent Movie* (1976), *High Anxiety* (1977), *Fatso* (1980), *History of the World—Part I* (1981)

TELEVISION SERIES:
Melba Moore-Clifton Davis Show (1972), *Corner Bar* (1973), *The Montefuscos* (1975), *Barney Miller* (1976–82)

COLLECTIBLES:
The Irreverent Ron Carey (RSVP)

LEO CARRILLO, perennial, good-natured sidekick to the Cisco Kid.

LEO CARRILLO
August 6, 1881–September 10, 1961

"An unpretentious star, with fine diction, intelligence, and artistry." That was Leo Carrillo, according to a 1923 *Toledo Blade* review of his touring show, *Magnolia*. But that's not what fans remember. They remember Carrillo as the stereotypically jovial Pancho, sidekick to the Cisco Kid in films and on television.

Leo, whose father was the first mayor of Santa Monica, attended Loyola University and embarked upon a comedy career as a cartoonist for the *San Francisco Examiner*. His friends loved his mimicry, so he worked out a vaudeville act. Early supporters of his dialect comedy (he favored Oriental characters, not Hispanic ones) were Will Rogers and Walter C. Kelly, "The Virginian Judge."

Acting in early stage productions, Carrillo often put the comedy aside for romantic roles. He took top billing in such early films as *The Bad Man* (billed as a "colorful comedy drama of Mexico") and *Hell Bound* ("He made love with his lips—and committed murder with his hands!").

Carrillo's ability to handle dialect made him a valuable supporting player, and as was often the case in thirties movies, anyone who spoke in a dialect had to have a touch of humor to him. For example, in *The Gay Bride* he played a suave and dangerous Greek gangster, but one with limited speaking abilities and brains. Pointing to his head: "If there's one thing I got it, is brims!"

Carrillo was often a costar in screen comedies, mangling the English language in Abbott and Costello's *One Night in the Tropics* and two Olsen and Johnson films, *Crazy House* and *The Ghost Catchers*.

Initially he refused to take the role of Pancho, calling it "the part of a buffoon." Costar Duncan Renaldo assured him the part was in the same spirit as Sancho Panza in *Don Quixote*. After all the grumblings and misgivings, Carrillo ended up doing the part as a raucous stereotype with a lot of cheerful giggling. Fortunately the good cheer was infectious. "He overdid it," Renaldo recalled, "but everyone liked him. His accent was so exaggerated that when we finished a picture no one in the cast or crew could talk normal English."

After five *Cisco Kid* movies and the TV series, Carrillo was in a position to be even more independent. In the late fifties he toured with a show called *Leo Carrillo and Company*, emceeing an evening of Hispanic pianists and flamenco guitarists. In 1961 he wrote a book about California.

Though ridiculous, Carrillo's Pancho remains lovable, very much in the spirit of the fun-loving actor himself. In 1944 he said, "I'm happy—because it interferes with my pleasure to be unhappy!"

SELECTED BROADWAY APPEARANCES:
The Love Chef (1921), *Mike Angelo* (1923), *Magnolia* (1923), *Gypsy Jim* (1924), *The Saint* (1924), *Lambs Gambol* (1932)

SELECTED FILM APPEARANCES:
The Bad Man (1929), *Hell Bound* (1931), *The Guilty Generation* (1931), *Men Are Such Fools* (1932), *Parachute Jumper* (1933), *Viva Villa* (1934), *The Gay Bride* (1934), *The Band Plays On* (1934), *In Caliente* (1935), *Gay Desperado* (1936), *History Is Made at Night* (1937), *Manhattan Merry-Go-Round* (1937), *Too Hot to Handle* (1938), *Fisherman's Wharf* (1939), *Chicken Wagon Family* (1939), *Twenty Mule Team* (1940), *One Night in the Tropics* (1940), *What's Cookin'?* (1942), *Crazy House* (1943), *Larceny With Music* (1943), *Phantom of the Opera* (1943), *Follow the Band* (1943), *The Ghost Catchers* (1944), *Bowery to Broadway* (1944), *Valiant Hombre* (1948), *The Gay Amigo* (1949), *Satan's Cradle* (1949), *Girl From San Lorenzo* (1950), *Pancho Villa Returns* (1952).

TELEVISION SERIES:
The Cisco Kid (1950–56)

COLLECTIBLES:
Carrillo wrote *The California I Love*

WALTER CATLETT, one of moviedom's grand, wide-eyed eccentrics.

WALTER CATLETT
February 4, 1889–November 14, 1960

Tall, balding, and slightly goofy-looking, Walter Catlett specialized in playing plodding civil servants, flustered dignitaries with limited vision and a variety of mild eccentrics. His best roles were in *The Front Page, Bringing Up Baby*, and (as the drunken poet Morrow) *Mr. Deeds Goes to Town*.

Born in San Francisco, Catlett was a child actor and appeared in many Gilbert and Sullivan operettas. Then his voice changed, which wrecked his singing career. He tried boxing for a while, but took one too many beatings. His eyesight worsened, which caused his dismissal from the Marines. Following this run of bad luck, Catlett discovered a corpse while on a fishing trip.

As it turned out, there was a reward for any information on the missing man. And so while the unfortunate cadaver ended up in a morgue, Catlett took the reward money and journeyed to New York with enough of a stake to begin his Broadway career. He made his Broadway debut in 1911. His first major hit was *So Long Letty*, opposite Charlotte Greenwood.

In 1918 he costarred in *Baby Bunting* in London. A critic wrote: "He is like none of our low comedians. Instead of their conventional florid makeup, Catlett wears tortoise-shell spectacles and his own hair. All his fun is made by facial expressions and wonderfully agile dancing."

Catlett recorded a few discs in 1919 ("Married Life," "After the Ball," and "Tally Ho"), and enjoyed more stage success in America in the twenties. He got married, something he would do another two times. While he began developing an offstage reputation as a drinker and bon vivant, critics were noticing his crisply eccentric comedy style, one that he had worked at with great seriousness.

In 1927 he told an interviewer for the *New York Telegraph* that it was important to establish a physical comedy style. "Suppose you do have a good gag, and you treasure it because you know it is good for a laugh any time you use it. Well, the next week after you start it you read it in a newspaper…two weeks later half the vaudeville people in the country are pulling it and the radio has it…" But nobody could do the same faces and gestures as Catlett. And so he worked in one stage production after another, building his unique character. He remembered how evocative the characters were in his favorite books by Dickens: "Those characters are so full and rich. The truest comedy."

During his film career, Catlett worked with a variety of comedians, costarring with Raymond Walburn in Monogram's short-lived *Henry* comedy series, supporting Olsen and Johnson in *The Ghost Catchers*, Danny Kaye in *The Inspector General*, and Bob Hope in *Beau James*, playing Governor Al Smith to Hope's Jimmy Walker. Catlett extended his career into television, appearing in a few sitcoms. He played a bird watcher on an episode of *The Abbott and Costello Show*.

While Catlett tended to play harmless and amusing people on screen, his personal life was a bit more colorful. A much repeated story about him is the time he played roulette at Agua Caliente and ran out of money. He took out his false teeth and bet them on the red. He won and insisted on getting back $350, the price of the dentures.

He was a legendary drinker, and when someone boasted of being able to drink a quart of liquor a day, Catlett replied, "Why, I spill that much!" He and fellow actor Louis Calhern loved to carouse and spend money. Calhern remembered how others at New York's Lambs Club disapproved of their lifestyle. But when the stock market crashed, Calhern recalled that he and Catlett "laughed for hours. They were now as broke as we were without having had any of our fun!" Raymond Walburn agreed, but recalled that not all of Catlett's money was frittered away on himself: "His big trouble in life was his improvidence...he had been one of the highest paid people in the theater...but you couldn't stop Walter from giving his money away to some charity or some poor soul somewhere...he was a proud, grand and funny man."

SELECTED BROADWAY APPEARANCES:
Sally (1921), *Lady Be Good* (1924), *Lambs Gambol* (1925), *Lucky* (1927), *Treasure Girl* (1928)

SELECTED FILM APPEARANCES:
Second Youth (1924), *Summer Bachelors* (1926), *The Floradora Girl* (1930), *The Front Page* (1931), *The Captain Hates the Sea* (1934), *A Tale of Two Cities* (1935), *Mr. Deeds Goes to Town* (1936), *On the Avenue* (1937), *Bringing Up Baby* (1938), *Pop Always Pays* (1940), *Li'l Abner* (1940), *It Started With Eve* (1941), *Million Dollar Baby* (1941), *Hello, Sucker* (1941), *My Gal Sal* (1942), *They Got Me Covered* (1943), *How's About It?* (1943), *The Ghost Catchers* (1944), *Her Primitive Man* (1944), *Henry the Rainmaker* (1949), *The Inspector General* (1949), *Leave It to Henry* (1949), *Look for the Silver Lining* (1949), *Father's Wild Game* (1950), *Father Makes Good* (1950), *Father Takes the Air* (1951), *Here Comes the Groom* (1951), *Friendly Persuasion* (1956), *Beau James* (1957)

FRED CLARK, slow burner extraordinaire.

FRED CLARK
March 9, 1914–December 5, 1968

S low burns and smoldering looks of exasperated anger characterized Fred Clark, the tall, bald-headed, mustached nemesis of Bob Hope, Jerry Lewis, Judy Holliday, Abbott and Costello, and many others. Playing everything from ulcer-prone executives to abrasive film directors, Clark always seemed dead serious in his comic frustrations. Unlike past masters Edgar Kennedy or James Finlayson, Clark had to be realistic; his reactions were quick. A few moments of rising gall, a sudden barking command, and his temper tantrum was over.

Clark earned his A.B. at Stanford University and was set for a career in medicine until he began appearing in college plays. He won a scholarship to study acting and appeared in productions at a Laguna Beach theater where he was spotted by director Michael Curtiz in the forties and was cast as a detective in *The Unsuspected*. Clark recalled, "The picture that really made it for me was *Ride the Pink Horse*. I played a villain with a hearing aid." Clark grew to enjoy playing nasty characters, especially comedic ones. He said, "If the heel in the plot doesn't have you pulling for him, too, half the suspense is missing."

He had a small role in Gloria Swanson's *Sunset Boulevard* and starred opposite her two years later in *Three for Bedroom C*.

Clark returned to stage roles throughout his career. His first Broadway role was a 1938 walk-on in *Schoolhouse on the Lot*. He appeared in West Coast productions in the forties, meeting his soon-to-be wife, actress Benay Venuta in a production of *Light Up the Sky*. Oddly enough, Venuta played on Broadway in *Hazel Flagg* and Fred played the role (with a gender change, of course) when it was brought to the screen as *Living It Up*, starring Martin and Lewis. In 1956 he returned to New York for a stage revival of *Mister Roberts*, playing Doc opposite Charlton Heston. He had the lead, complete with beard, in the offbeat 1964 production *Absence of a Cello* and starred in both a New York and London production of *Never Too Late*.

On TV sitcoms the curmudgeonly Clark played George Burns's acerbic friend Harry Morton during the early days of *The George Burns and Gracie Allen Show*. He later played Granny's nemesis, the headshaking, sour Dr. Clyburn, in episodes of *The Beverly Hillbillies* and Red Buttons's irritated superior in *The Double Life of Henry Phyfe*.

ANDY CLYDE
March 25, 1892–May 18, 1967

ANDY CLYDE, Hopalong Cassidy's comic sidekick, getting a sample of Western cuisine from William Boyd.

Four generations remember Andy Clyde in four different ways. Born in Blairgowrie, Scotland, brought to films by his countryman, actor Jimmy Finlayson, Clyde had a first career as a supporting player to silent comedian Billy Bevan. A makeup master, Andy was behind many a bizarre beard, ultimately deciding on a grizzled model (and bushy) mustache for his character of a shy, bespectacled old country rube.

In the second phase of his career, Clyde was the star of minor short comedies. He played Pop Martin in a series of Sennett quickies, but left the studio in 1932 after a dispute over a dog that took its bit parts literally. Clyde was adamant about not working with the animal, but Sennett refused to part with what he considered one of the most talented stars on the lot. Andy moved

51

on to Columbia, making shorts there for over twenty-five years. He wore his trademark glasses but shaved his beard, leaving just his bushy mustache. His genial comedy series, which included supporting players from Shirley Temple and (screen wife) Vivien Oakland to Shemp Howard and Bud Jamison, combined character comedy and clever sight gags reworked from his early days. He made nearly 150 short comedies between 1930 and 1956.

Meanwhile, he had a third career. The average Western film fan knew Andy Clyde as the salty comic sidekick California Carlson in several Hopalong Cassidy films.

By the time the video generation arrived, Andy Clyde had spent over thirty years playing "old man" roles. Now, he really was old. Far from retiring, he enjoyed new popularity supporting Walter Brennan on *The Real McCoys* playing the spunky, cantankerous neighbor George MacMichael. This fourth phase of Clyde's career continued through two more series. He played a folksier and more lovable old fellow in *Lassie* and returned to the more spry mode for *No Time for Sergeants*. Most fans of those shows had no idea that Clyde's comic support had spanned several previous generations. The durable Andy Clyde was one of the few who managed to amuse new audiences with fresh comedy from the twenties consistently through to the sixties.

SELECTED FILM APPEARANCES:
Should a Girl Marry? (1928), *Midnight Daddies* (1930), *Million Dollar Legs* (1932), *McFadden's Flats* (1935), *Annie Oakley* (1935), *It's a Wonderful World* (1939), *In Old Colorado* (1941), *Stick to Your Guns* (1941), *Lost Canyon* (1943), *Song of the Prairie* (1945), *Throw a Saddle on a Star* (1946), *Strange Gamble* (1948), *Haunted Trail* (1949), *Outlaws of Texas* (1950), *Carolina Cannonball* (1955), *The Road to Denver* (1955)

TELEVISION SERIES:
The Real McCoys (1957–63), *Lassie* (1958–64), *No Time for Sergeants* (1964–65)

CHARLES COBURN
James 19, 1877–August 30, 1961

An Academy Award winner for his performance supporting Jean Arthur in *The More the Merrier*, Charles Coburn was a favorite in "old rascal" roles, always a dignified gent (his most notable prop was his monocle) with just a touch of larceny.

Born in Macon, Georgia, Coburn began his career in show business at sixteen when he became the manager of the Savannah Theatre. At nineteen he came to New York to try Broadway. He returned to Georgia a year later, but was not discouraged. He worked in touring companies and met his wife Ivah Wills in 1905, when they both appeared in *As You Like It*. In private they always referred to themselves by their character parts: Orlando and Rosalind. They had their own touring company specializing in Shakespeare and in 1910 performed Shakespeare for President William Howard Taft.

Billed as "Mr. and Mrs. Charles Coburn" for their shows, they appeared often on Broadway and in 1918 had a hit with the comedy *The Better 'Ole*. By now Coburn was popular enough not to be confused with British Music Hall star Charles Coburn, who had novelty hits with "Two Lovely Black Eyes" and "The Man Who Broke the Bank at Monte Carlo."

Coburn opened his own Coburn Theatre in New York in 1928, but went bankrupt in 1932 during the Depression. It was after his wife's death in 1937 that Coburn came to Hollywood to make films. Aside from the Oscar-winning role as the millionaire meddler Benjamin Dingle in *The More the Merrier*, he was also nominated for *The Devil and Miss Jones* (also supporting Jean Arthur) masquerading as a clerk in the department store he owns. Coburn got a lot of mileage out of a mild scowl or a moment of perplexed surprise that caused his monocle to drop.

Coburn was sometimes cast in dramas (he amputated Ronald Reagan's leg in *King's Row* and was the jowly but good-natured old detective trying to help out suspected murderer Brian Donlevy in *Impact*), but fans preferred him to play a lovable old codger in comedies. It was a role he played in real life, becoming a popular figure around Hollywood for his lively and social nature.

He played codger comedy roles through the decades, and in 1952

CHARLES COBURN and the monocle that invariably popped out in moments of surprise.

SELECTED BROADWAY APPEARANCES:
French Leave (1920), *The Imaginary Invalid* (1922), *The Right Age to Marry* (1926), *The Better 'Ole* (1927), *Diplomacy* (1928), *Yellow Jack* (1928), *Peter Ibbetson* (1931), *Kultur* (1933), *Rip Van Winkle* (1935), *Master of the Revels* (1935), *Three Wise Fools* (1936), *Around the Corner* (1936), *Sun Kissed* (1937)

SELECTED FILM APPEARANCES:
The People's Enemy (1935), *Yellow Jack* (1938), *Vivacious Lady* (1938), *Idiot's Delight* (1939), *The Story of Alexander Graham Bell* (1939), *Made for Each Other* (1939), *In Name Only* (1939), *The Captain Is a Lady* (1940), *The Lady Eve* (1941), *The Devil and Miss Jones* (1941), *George Washington Slept Here* (1942), *The More the Merrier* (1943), *Constant Nymph* (1943), *Heaven Can Wait* (1943), *Knickerbocker Holiday* (1944), *The Impatient Years* (1944), *Over 21* (1945), *A Royal Scandal* (1945), *Rhapsody in Blue* (1945), *Colonel Effingham's Raid* (1946), *The Paradine Case* (1947), *Impact* (1949), *Everybody Does It* (1949), *Mr. Music* (1951), *Monkey Business* (1952), *Gentlemen Prefer Blondes* (1953), *How to Be Very Very Popular* (1955), *The Story of Mankind* (1957), *How to Murder a Rich Uncle* (1957), *The Remarkable Mr. Pennypacker* (1959), *Pepe* (1960)

was the old boss lusting after his secretary, Marilyn Monroe, in *Monkey Business*. She was so beautiful it didn't matter if she could even type. "Anybody can type," he declared, allowing her to give such work to someone else. True to his image, in 1959 Coburn remarried. He was eighty-two, his bride forty-one. He told reporters, "I've burned the candle at both ends, but the darn thing keeps right on burning!"

In 1961, Coburn (age eighty-four) was still on the boards, working in a summer stock production of *You Can't Take It With You*. On August 28, he underwent throat surgery and died of heart failure three days later.

JAMES COCO, pudgy and lovable, here with *Last of the Red Hot Lovers* Broadway costar Doris Roberts.

JAMES COCO
March 21, 1928–
February 25, 1987

A chubby comedian who lent realistic touches to his portrayals of stocky stock characters, James Coco starred in two TV sitcoms and appeared in many classic film comedies and Broadway shows.

Raised in the Bronx, Coco first found work in the local Clare Tree Major Children's Theater. In his early days, he looked tough and rather lean (he was a sailor in *Ensign Pulver*). He played in many productions before winning an Obie for his role in the 1959 drama *The Moon in the Yellow River*. In 1967 he won another for *Fragments*. Over the years, the increasingly round actor, balding with a horseshoe of black hair around the sides of his head, became known for comedy, often playing well-intentioned, slightly flustered neurotics. Unlike some other roly-poly comedians of his generation, Coco wasn't zany, jolly, or prone to smiles. The mournful pout on his lips and the large baleful eyes gained him the sympathy of his audience even as he made them laugh with his agitation and desperation.

He won wide recognition for his starring role on Broadway in *Last of the Red Hot Lovers* in 1969, but national TV audiences knew him mainly as "Willie the Plumber" in 1960s Drano commercials. Two attempts at television stardom failed. His 1973 ensemble-cast show

Calucci's Department won good notices but low ratings. His 1976 *The Dumplings* didn't even win the good notices. Three-hundred-pound Coco was given nothing but fat jokes and dubious sight gags (Coco and his chubby wife on the series bouncing their bottoms together). When the show was cancelled, he said, "I've been in eight hundred flops that closed in New Haven. So thirteen weeks in a TV series is a long run, baby."

The television exposure did help secure more film work, and Coco appeared in many more comedies. He was a standout amid the all-star cast of *Murder by Death*, playing a parody of Hercule Poirot, here portrayed as a fussy fop who takes himself too seriously. In 1972, he was arguably the only one correctly cast (as Sancho Panza) in the critically lambasted film version of Broadway's *Man of La Mancha*. In 1975 he starred in *The Wild Party*, based on the Moncure March narrative poem. He received an Emmy for a 1983 episode of *St. Elsewhere*, and his career took a new direction the following year when he published *The James Coco Diet Book*. He had successfully lost a great deal of weight, but evidently it was too much too soon. Just two weeks after taping an episode of *Who's the Boss*, James Coco died of a heart attack.

Coco's first love was the theater. He lived in a modest Greenwich Village apartment and always put stage roles before movie and TV work. It was appropriate that Broadway honored him with a tribute. At the event, Colleen Dewhurst described her friend: "He was a joy. He was a love. Knowing Jimmy was to be alive." Linda Lavin added, "He was a treasure. He had no guile, no bitterness. When he was there, everything was okay."

SELECTED BROADWAY APPEARANCES:
Hotel Paradiso (1957), *Everybody Loves Opal* (1961), *Squat Betty* (1964), *The Sponge Room* (1964), *The Astrakhan Coat* (1967), *Here's Where I Belong* (1968), *Next* (1969), *Last of the Red Hot Lovers* (1969)

SELECTED FILM APPEARANCES:
Ensign Pulver (1964), *Generation* (1969), *A New Leaf* (1971), *Such Good Friends* (1971), *Man of La Mancha* (1972), *The Wild Party* (1975), *Murder by Death* (1976), *The Cheap Detective* (1978), *Charleston* (1978), *Scavenger Hunt* (1979), *Wholly Moses* (1980), *Only When I Laugh* (1981), *The Muppets Take Manhattan* (1984), *The Hunk* (1987)

TELEVISION SERIES:
Calucci's Department (1973), *The Dumplings* (1976)

COLLECTIBLES:
The James Coco Diet Book

JERRY COLONNA with his manic expression as he blasts out a tune, to the consternation of Johnny Arthur, in *Road to Singapore*.

JERRY COLONNA

Gerardo Luigi Colonna,
October 17, 1904–
November 21, 1986

His face was a living caricature: a walrus mustache springing out over a fiercely toothy smile, thick eyebrows flexing over bulgingly wide eyes. His manic expression seemed to flash "eccentric!" the moment he walked on stage. When he spoke, his clipped, ingratiating delivery got laughs for the mildest of jokes. When he sang, he didn't need jokes at all. His trademark was holding notes for insanely long intervals. On his histrionic version of "You're My Everything," there were about twenty or thirty seconds of "You," an outrageous trill over the "ɪ," and a swooping slide into "my everything" that never ceased to amaze and amuse.

A musician with Ozzie Nelson, Benny Goodman, and Artie Shaw, Colonna played trombone for the CBS orchestra, including classical pieces conducted by Eugene Ormandy. He was in the orchestra for Bing Crosby's 1937 radio show, but was soon up front as a supporting comic not only for Crosby but Fred Allen and others. He played a quack psychiatrist in Fred Allen's *It's in the Bag* and was Bob Hope's second banana from 1938 through the sixties not only for radio shows but also for overseas treks to entertain the troops.

The glib, eye-rolling purveyor of nonsense regularly bewildered the normally implacable Bob Hope, as in this radio sequence, with Colonna calling him from a pay phone: "Hope, hello! Colonna is this!" "Colonna, why are you talking backwards?" "Put the nickel in upside down." "That wouldn't have anything to do with it, Colonna." (After hearing the sound of an animal growling) "What's that, Colonna?" "I'm pulling the buffalo out by his tail." "That's impossible!" "I don't ask questions, I just have fun!"

That last line could have been his catchphrase, for Colonna, like Bert "The Mad Russian" Gordon or Jack "Baron Munchausen" Pearl, was often used briefly to shake up the mundane proceedings with a few moments of lively nonsense. His actual catchphrase on Hope's show was a breezy opening cry of "Greetings, Gate!" Another well-used phrase was his grinning bark of "Whatsa matter? You crazy or something?" Still another Colonnaism, written for him by Jack Douglas, was "Who's Yehoodi?" which poked fun at the name of violinist Yehudi Menuhin. Colonna and most listeners were unaware that Menuhin's father had chosen the name (which translates as "The Jew") to proudly combat anti-Semitism.

A trademark manic bit of Colonna's was to shout "Hello" in a sketch, then "Good-bye," then grin, stare, and add, "Short day, wasn't it?" There was more than a touch of Groucho Marx to Colonna's brand of challengingly abrupt non sequiturs. From 1937 to 1940 Colonna recorded a series of novelty tunes including "Hector the Garbage Collector," "You're My Everything," "Where Is My Wandering Boy Soprano Tonight?" and "The Yogi Who Lost His Will Power."

Colonna appeared on the syndicated 1956 *Super Circus* show for children and guested on many television variety shows. He was never the same after a stroke in 1966. He was still noticeably weak when he made a guest appearance with Bob Hope on TV in 1976. When Jerry died a decade later, Hope recalled, "He was a dear friend, a great entertainer whom I traveled all over the world with for twenty-five years. He provided millions of laughs for millions of people. He delighted the entire world with his unique style of comedy—a great loss to the entertainment industry. I'll miss him."

SELECTED FILM APPEARANCES:
52nd Street (1937), *College Swing* (1938), *Naughty But Nice* (1939), *Comin' Round the Mountain* (1940), *Road to Singapore* (1940), *Ice Capades* (1941), *Star Spangled Rhythm* (1942), *Priorities on Parade* (1942), *Atlantic City* (1944), *It's in the Bag* (1945), *Road to Rio* (1947), *Kentucky Jubilee* (1951), *Meet Me in Las Vegas* (1956), *Road to Hong Kong* (1961).

TELEVISION SERIES:
The Jerry Colonna Show (1951)

COLLECTIBLES:
Music for Screaming (Decca), *Jerry Colonna Entertains at Your Party* (Bravo), *Let's All Sing With Jerry* (Liberty). His two books were *Who Threw That Coconut?* and *The Loves of Tullio* (a novel)

HANS CONREID
April 15, 1917–January 5, 1982

*T*all and theatrically imperious, Hans Conreid had film roles that were often confined to glaring, nostril-flaring eccentrics. He was well able to infuse his characters with a humorous but gloomy impatience and exasperation.

Born in Baltimore and raised in New York, Conreid graduated from the High School of Commerce in 1935. Having developed a flair for dialects, during his radio days he could imitate a variety of Germans, Frenchmen, Spaniards, Italians, and Greeks. He starred in dramas and in radio sitcoms including *My Friend Irma* (playing Professor Kropotkin) and *The Great Gildersleeve*. In 1937 he was in the cast for *Streamlined Shakespeare* with John Barrymore. Perhaps taking a cue from the self-

HANS CONREID, the veritable parody of a Shakespearean ham.

parodying Barrymore, Conreid developed a talent for imitating overdramatic Shakespearean actors and other grandiose types: "I am a big ham. Give me one laugh on stage and I am like a tiger who has tasted blood. I require a firm, restraining hand."

Sardonic or sarcastic rejoinders were always a part of lanky, angular Conreid's film character. In *Siren of Bagdad*, a tale of ancient times, he asks an Arab, "I beg your pardon. I realize they haven't been invented yet, but do you have a match?" In *The Gay Falcon* he has a very small role as a police sketch artist, but steals a scene with a comical look of disdainful disgust. His skill at ethnic voices still helped him land parts. For Orson Welles's *Journey Into Fear* he recalled, "I spoke in a Dutch accent and addressed the audience in French, English, and spoke to my assistant in German and Turkish, which they wrote on a blackboard." He said he was in dozens of films in which he played "pimply or weak Nazis." In 1953 he starred as a foppish, bizarre piano teacher who keeps little children prisoner at his massive piano in *The 5,000 Fingers of Dr. T*, scripted by Dr. Seuss.

Conreid's distinctive voice continued to serve him well in the fifties. He worked on *The Bullwinkle Show*, his best-known character being dastardly Snidely Whiplash in the "Dudley Do-Right" cartoons. He was the voice of Captain Hook in Walt Disney's cartoon version of *Peter Pan*. And on one of his few novelty albums, *Monster Rally*, he sang "The Purple People Eater" and "What Do You Hear From the Red Planet Mars?"

A popular raconteur on Jack Paar's *Tonight* show, Conreid later hosted *Fractured Flickers*, in which silent movies were rewritten with new dialogue. His acerbic presence included introductions and closings, such as: "Now this is Hans Conreid, bidding you good night from the entertainment capital of the world, of gimcrack joys and tinsel tragedies, where nothing is what it seems. That never-never land of make-believe—Washington, D.C."

Ethnic eccentrics continued to be Conreid's specialty. He played a Bulgarian sculptor in *Can-Can* on Broadway and landed his juiciest television role as the erratic Uncle Tonoose on *Make Room for Daddy*. Crusty, old, and obstinate, he was a lively attraction/distraction for Danny Thomas and reprised the role on *Make Room for Grandaddy*. Now firmly identified as a lovable old eccentric, Conreid played Tony Randall's father on *The Tony Randall Show* and made similar grandfatherly appearances on other sitcoms. His last role was in a cable version of *Barefoot in the Park*.

SELECTED BROADWAY APPEARANCES:
Can-Can (1953), *Tall Story* (1959)

SELECTED FILM APPEARANCES:
Dramatic School (1938), *It's a Wonderful World* (1939), *Maisie Was a Lady* (1941), *The Gay Falcon* (1941), *Blondie's Blessed Event* (1942), *Once Upon a Honeymoon* (1942), *Crazy House* (1943), *The Senator Was Indiscreet* (1947), *My Friend Irma* (1949), *On the Town* (1949), *Three for Bedroom C* (1952), *Siren of Bagdad* (1953), *The Twonky* (1953), *The Affairs of Dobie Gillis* (1953), *The 5,000 Fingers of Dr. T* (1953), *Bus Stop* (1956), *The Big Beat* (1958), *My Six Loves* (1963), *The Patsy* (1964), *The Brothers O'Toole* (1973), *The Shaggy DA* (1977), *The Cat From Outer Space* (1978), *Oh God Book II* (1980)

TELEVISION SERIES:
Pantomime Quiz (1950–52, 1955–57, 1962–63), *What's It For?* (1957–58), *The Danny Thomas Show* (1958–64), *Take a Good Look* (1959–61), *The Bullwinkle Show* (1961–62), *Hoppity Hooper* (1962), *Fractured Flickers* (1963), *Made in America* (1964), *Make Room for Grandaddy* (1970–71), *The Tony Randall Show* (1977–78), *American Dream* (1981)

COLLECTIBLES:
Dr. Seuss, Happy Birthday (Caedmon), *Little Toot Stories* (Caedmon), *Monster Rally* (RCA), *Peter and the Wolf* (Strand)

SCATMAN CROTHERS
Benjamin Sherman Crothers,
May 23, 1910–November 26, 1986

With a smile that could've blinded even Louis Armstrong, Scatman Crothers had a long career in music, stand-up, films, and television. Ironically, despite his many comedy credits, he may well be best remembered for his supporting roles in straight films: his warmth, courage, good nature, and sober sensitivity was a vital part of *One Flew Over the Cuckoo's Nest* and *The Shining*.

Born in Terre Haute, Indiana, Crothers grew up in a widely mixed neighborhood of Turks, Jews, Syrians, and Greeks. In a somewhat relaxed racial environment he dated white women without violent consequences. He admitted in *Scatman,* his autobiography, that his intentions of becoming a pastor were sidetracked by his amorous adventures. He had been preaching to children at his local church but told the pastor that he could no longer do it with a clear conscience: "I told him it was because I had committed fornication...I couldn't be no hypocrite and get up in front of those kids and preach...that's not right. A minister is supposed to set the example for members of his church. I couldn't be a hypocrite. But I definitely had the calling, and I would have been a good preacher if I hadn't let the Devil in."

Scatman entered show business at fourteen and got his nickname in the early thirties from the program director at a Dayton, Ohio, radio station fond of colorful nicknames for his stars. As Crothers recalled, "I

SCATMAN CROTHERS—he started out singing scat, then got laughs with his smiling style.

told him to call me Scatman because I do a lot of scat singing." Crothers sang novelty songs, told jokes, and formed his own group. He married a white woman in 1937 and the union lasted nearly fifty years. He recalled of his interracial marriage, "I did it before it was fashionable," but said it didn't create many problems because he didn't "make no big flauntin' issue of it. I was never the type to show her off. That was my private life." Ironically the couple had some of their most trying times when they lived in black neighborhoods and Mrs. Crothers was the target of derision.

Through the forties, Scatman's act consisted of jazz, comic songs, and classic black burlesque bits. He briefly played drums with the eccentric bop-comic Slim Gaillard (a 1946 musical short survives: *Dunkin' Bagels*). Crothers got his big radio break from Phil Harris, and together they recorded the 1948 novelty hit "Chattanooga Shoe Shine Boy." Soon he was billed in nightclubs as "The Great Scatman, Broadcast and Recording Star Comedian." He appeared on radio's sitcom *Beulah,* starring Hattie McDaniel, and joined Stan Freberg to supply the voices for "Wildman" and "Go Van Gogh" on the 1949 television puppet show *Time for Benny*. He had his own local Los Angeles TV show, *Dixie Showboat*, the first time a black starred in his own series. His cool comic versions of bebop and jazz musicians made him a regular on *The Colgate Comedy Hour* in the early fifties and led to his film career.

In *Meet Me at the Fair* he sang several songs, including "I Got the Shiniest Mouth in Town" (written by Stan Freberg) and his own "I Was There." He also wrote and sang two songs in *East of Sumatra* and played the pianist Smiley in *Walking My Baby Back Home*. In the fifties and sixties he tended to have roles that called for his good-natured smile, jazz singing, or both. He made several films with Jerry Lewis, including *The Patsy* in the role of a shoeshine man.

Crothers worked often on television, able to get more supporting roles by wearing a toupee and changing his familiar bald-headed look. He had a regular role on *Chico and the Man* as Louis the Garbageman, a fellow occasionally given to song: "I'm the man who empties your can—so stick out your can, 'cause here comes the garbage man!" A more controversial song, "Walk On, Nigger, Walk On," was sung by Scatman in the film *Coonskin*, one of several "blaxsploitation" movies Crothers made in the seventies.

Crothers did cartoon voices for *The Harlem Globetrotters* and other Saturday morning shows, played "Scat Cat" in Disney's *The Aristocats*, and parodied *Casablanca* pianist Dooley Wilson in *The Cheap Detective*. He actually played the Wilson role in the short-lived series *Casablanca*. One of his most satisfying roles was as an elderly jazzman on *One of the Boys*, the 1982 series starring Mickey Rooney.

Crothers became ill with cancer in 1986. Ronald Reagan sent him a get-well greeting in the hospital. When the cancer was in remission, Crothers went back to work, appearing on the TV series *Morningstar/Eveningstar* until he was hospitalized for the final time, his wife at his bedside.

Sometimes Crothers was attacked for "Uncle Tom" roles, but he said of the critics, "I don't pay them any mind. Feel sorry for them, though. Especially now. It's heaven for the young black man today. The door is open. All he's got to do is walk through it. He should use the energy he's burning up on being angry." He added, "Just because I play the part of a gangster doesn't mean I am one. Acting is just that—acting. And these youngsters should stop paying attention to what other folks are doing and spend that time working on developing their own wants."

SELECTED FILM APPEARANCES:
Yes Sir, Mr. Bones (1951), *Meet Me at the Fair* (1952), *Walking My Baby Back Home* (1953), *East of Sumatra* (1953), *Johnny Dark* (1954), *The Patsy* (1964), *The Family Jewels* (1965), *Three on a Couch* (1966), *Hello, Dolly!* (1969), *The Aristocats* (voice) (1970), *Lady Sings the Blues* (1972), *Linda Lovelace for President* (1974), *Coonskin* (1975), *One Flew Over the Cuckoo's Nest* (1975), *The Shootist* (1976), *Silver Streak* (1977), *The Cheap Detective* (1978), *Scavenger Hunt* (1979), *The Shining* (1980), *Zapped* (1982), *Twilight Zone, The Movie* (1983), *The Journey of Natty Gann* (1985)

TELEVISION SERIES:
Chico and the Man (1974–78), *One of the Boys* (1982), *Casablanca* (1983), *Morningstar/Eveningstar* (1986)

COLLECTIBLES:
Scatman issued many 78's, recorded a straight album *Rock 'n' Roll with Scatman* (High Fidelity, two cuts turning up on the Tops album *Music for a Mad Ball*) and a comedy album, *Comedy Sweepstakes* (Dooto). *Scatman* was published posthumously by William Morrow (Haskins and Crothers).

CASS DALEY
Catherine Dailey, July 17, 1915–March 22, 1975

A variation on the Martha Raye type of effervescent-but-plain manhunter, Cass Daley had teeth as prominent as Raye's but had usually less prominent comedy-relief roles.

When she was in her teens, kids made fun of her beanpole body, jutting butt, and buck teeth. She got some measure of revenge by winning amateur contests with her jokes and singing. The teenager worked in a factory, but her clowning—which included an imitation of the foreman—got her fired. At seventeen she became a hatcheck girl in a New Jersey nightclub, getting a chance to occasionally perform on stage. One of her favorite early numbers was "Please Don't Talk About Me When I'm Gone" while strumming the ukulele.

Daley sang at dance and "walkathon" marathons (a craze captured

CASS DALEY, at her daffy, manhunting best, makes a move on reluctant Walter Abel in *Star Spangled Rhythm*.

in the film *They Shoot Horses Don't They*). She married an agent who suggested she concentrate on comedy, and began adding more novelty songs to her act, perfecting it through nine years in vaudeville. Cass got her big break replacing Judy Canova in *The Ziegfeld Follies of 1936*.

Though she had grown up in Pennsylvania and later New Jersey, she ended up typed for rural rube roles. Her plain face and Olive Oyl body was always good for a laugh, and she didn't mind much. "I was never sensitive about my rear or my teeth," she once said. "They made money for me...have you ever noticed that all comediennes have buck teeth or a big mouth? Look at them: Martha Raye, Judy Canova, Carol Burnett, Kaye Ballard, right down the line..."

Daley began making film appearances in the forties, starting with *The Fleet's In*. She was especially effective in Olsen and Johnson's *Crazy House*, and in her own personal favorite, *Riding High*, teamed with eccentric dancer Gil Lamb. In that one she sang "Till the All Clear Comes" and "Willie the Wolf." At the same time she was also getting radio work. On *The Frank Morgan Show* in 1944 she evolved her catchphrase, "I said it and I'm glad!" She spent two years on *The Fitch Bandwagon* and had her own *Cass Daley Show* in 1950.

After beginning a family in 1949, Cass was more interested in her home life than her career. In 1967 she made a comeback in the film *The Spirit Is Willing* but was disappointed to find few offers of work after she made the TV talk show and variety circuit. In the seventies she toured in *The Music Man, The Apple of His Eye* with Buddy Ebsen, and 1972's nostalgic *The Big Show of 1936*. Her comeback ended with a shatter of glass. Alone in her apartment, the fifty-nine-year-old comedienne apparently fell and landed on her glass coffee table. A shard of glass jammed into her throat and she bled to death before her husband came home and discovered her.

SELECTED FILM APPEARANCES:
The Fleet's In (1942), *Riding High* (1943), *Crazy House* (1943), *Duffy's Tavern* (1945), *Out of This World* (1945), *Ladies Man* (1947), *Variety Girl* (1947), *Here Comes the Groom* (1951), *Red Garters* (1954), *The Spirit Is Willing* (1967), *The Phynx* (1970), *Norwood* (1971)

RICHARD DEACON
May 14, 1922–August 8, 1984

RICHARD DEACON, minus spectacles in pre-Dick Van Dyke days, makes a proposition to Doro Merande in *The Remarkable Mr. Pennypacker.*

Balding, deadpan, forever staring in tight-lipped exasperation over life's pettiest problems, Richard Deacon was the perfect choice to play any role calling for a ploddingly efficient flat-voiced drone.

Deacon was born in Philadelphia and raised in Binghamton, New York. After a childhood bout with polio briefly sidelined his schooling, he went on to become a medical student at Ithaca College. He entered the Army Medical Corps just as World War II was ending. Balding at twenty-two and already playing older men, he usually found himself in thankless film roles—but parts that the hungry actor still gave thanks for. He played it straight as a dour, scheming villain in one of his first decent-sized roles, *Abbott and Costello Meet the Mummy.* For years he had minor roles that barely gave him a chance to be funny. Pouchy eyed and solemn, he had a minute-long role in *The Birds* as a neighbor who watches Tippi Hedren deliver some birds to Rod Taylor's apartment.

Television helped Deacon find his comic style. It was on a Jack Benny show that he developed "the stare," his baleful, put-upon look of frustration. It was a reaction to Benny's narcissism. On one episode Jack announced, "My eyes are bluer than the feet of a Sicilian grape stomper." As an onlooker, Deacon glared in mute contempt. Benny broke up, crying "Now *that's* funny!" It was especially funny coming from a tall, rather solidly built man who towered over so many of his antagonists—but was reduced by his own civility (and timidity) to silent protest.

Gradually Deacon added variations: looks of pouty distaste, sulky disgust, and long-suffering disdain. Deacon readily admitted that he learned valuable lessons watching character comedians of the past: "The people I idolized were…Arthur Treacher…Franklin Pangborn… that kind of actor."

The tall, grim-looking bald man in the black glasses played Ward Cleaver's boss on *Leave It to Beaver* and wearily irate Mr. Baldwin, the IRS man, dealing with cackling Phyllis Diller on *The Pruitts of Southampton.* His ultimate TV role was Mel Cooley, the somewhat epicine brother-in-law of the boss on *The Dick Van Dyke Show.* The character was originally called Calvin Cooley, but somebody thought elderly Calvin Coolidge voters might object. All Mel wanted to do was perform his job adequately and by-the-rules. That he got the position not by merit, but by marrying the boss's sister, caused the comic battles between him and his nemesis Buddy Sorrell (played by Morey Amsterdam).

In script after script Morey heaped insults on Deacon's bald head: "You have all the charm of a sticky doorknob...your hair didn't fall out, it fell in and clogged your brain!" The laughs came not necessarily from Amsterdam but from the stolid, bleary-eyed looks of his long-suffering and slow-burning target. Deacon's simmering expression indicated that he could answer back, but was held in check by his own foolish sense of propriety and dignity.

Eventually, Deacon the actor began to get annoyed with his character's passivity: "I got a little paranoid about Morey always throwing a line at me. I guess I was beginning to take it personally, although I knew that he didn't mean it." He discussed the situation with producer Carl Reiner. When Reiner asked him how he felt deep down about the insults, Deacon muttered "Yech!"

This became Mel Cooley's catchphrase, and the laughs were even louder. Instead of ignoring the insults, he was fighting back. But the stoic masochist was permitting himself only one witless word of protest.

When allowed, Deacon's comic palette included mordant sarcasm. Again, it was always in reaction to antagonism. As the straight man on Morey Amsterdam's *Funny You Should Ask* album he got one of the biggest laughs just be a disdainful reaction. After a corny Amsterdam quickie, he muttered "That's charming." It even broke up Amsterdam.

With the exposure from *The Dick Van Dyke Show*, Deacon began to costar in light film comedies, always petulant, perplexed, and petty. The audience always liked him, feeling superior and sympathetic to the deadpan drone. One of the bachelor's last major sitcom parts was on *The Mothers-in-Law*, taking over from Roger C. Carmel as Kaye Ballard's husband. At sixty Deacon found a new profession: cooking show host. He starred in syndicated cooking show and authored one of the first microwave cookbooks.

SELECTED FILM APPEARANCES:
Abbott and Costello Meet the Mummy (1955), *Francis in the Haunted House* (1956), *The Solid Gold Cadillac* (1956), *Spring Reunion* (1957), *A Nice Little Bank That Should Be Robbed* (1958), *The Remarkable Mr. Pennypacker* (1958), *Lover Come Back* (1961), *That Touch of Mink* (1962), *The Patsy* (1964), *John Goldfarb, Please Come Home* (1965), *That Darn Cat* (1965), *Don't Worry, We'll Think of a Title* (1966), *The Gnome Mobile* (1967), *Enter Laughing* (1967), *Piranha* (1978), *The Happy Hooker Goes Hollywood* (1980), *Still the Beaver* (1983)

TELEVISION SERIES:
The Charlie Farrell Show (1956), *Date With the Angels* (1957–58), *Leave It to Beaver* (1956–63), *The Dick Van Dyke Show* (1961–66), *The Pruitts of Southampton* (1967), *The Mothers-in-Law* (1968–69)

COLLECTIBLES:
The cookbook *Richard Deacon's Micro Magic*. He appears as straight man to Morey Amsterdam in sketches on the latter's album, *Funny You Should Ask* (Marsh Records)

KENNY DELMAR
1910–July 14, 1984

KENNY DELMAR in his best-remembered guise of Sen. Beaure-guard Claghorn, making his point as gangsters Matt Willis (seat-ed left), Douglass Dumbrille (standing), and Ralph Sanford pre-pare to lay on hands in *It's a Joke, Son!*

As radio's longwind-ed, foghorn-loud Senator Beauregard Claghorn, Kenny Delmar was so overpower-ingly funny that few were offended by his stereotypi-cal Southern bluster: "Ah say, when I'm in New York I'll never go to the *Yankee* Stadium! I refuse to watch the Dodgers unless Dixie Walker's playing!"

The man behind the Southern senator was actu-ally born in Boston and raised in New York. He was always interested in show business and learned how to entertain a crowd by watch-ing his mother and aunt on stage. They were "The Del-mar Sisters" of vaudeville. At eight he briefly joined the act. When he was eighteen, some toughs broke his jaw while he strolled along Broad-way near 72nd Street.

It was feared that Delmar would be unable to continue his career, but he did, eventually becoming a versatile radio actor. He had three different roles in Orson Welles's 1939 Halloween panic broadcast *War of the Worlds*. Delmar worked mostly as an announcer (on *The March of Time* and *Your Hit Parade*) and was serving that function on *The Fred Allen Show* when "Senator Claghorn" was born in 1946. He claimed his interpretation of Allen's Southern senator was based on a loud rancher he met while hitchhiking in Texas.

As the most vocal member of "Allen's Alley," Claghorn would warn stentoriously, "I have the floor, don't try no filibuster!" and then floor Allen with corny jokes and terrible puns: "I was glad to see Sena-tor Aiken back. Achin' back! THAT'S A JOKE, SON!" "I *know it's a joke!*" Allen would grumble, but the oblivious Senator was still in high gear, shouting "I keep tossin' 'em and you just sidestep 'em! You're a regular sad sack." Than, pointing to the bags under Fred's eyes: "Sacks, that is!"

A nation of would-be comedians used Claghorn's catchphrase, shouting "That's a joke, son!" in defense of a bad one. Joke, that is. Ending a sentence with "that is" was another of the Senator's habits adopted by his fans. Senator Claghorn was fun in his cameo "Allen's Alley" appearances but couldn't sustain as a solo star. Kenny was cast

SELECTED BROADWAY APPEARANCE:
Texas, Li'l Darlin' (1949–50)

SELECTED RADIO APPEARANCE:
The Fred Allen Show

SELECTED FILM APPEARANCES:
It's a Joke, Son! (1947), *Strangers in the City* (1962)

TELEVISION SERIES:
School House (1949), *Good King Leonardo* (1960–61)

in the lead in one movie about the senator, *That's a Joke, Son!* but the pleasant little comedy didn't lead to more.

Still, the windy and wild braggart Delmar created was too good to disappear entirely. It was appropriated for a Warner Brothers Merrie Melodies cartoon series. Mel Blanc did the voice for the Claghorn-esque rooster "Foghorn Leghorn." Later Delmar himself began doing cartoon voices, notably portraying the dogged dog detective, "The Hunter," on the *King Leonardo* show. Through the sixties Delmar often spiced up bland radio commercials with a few jokes delivered in the forever bold and boisterous character of Senator Claghorn.

VERNON DENT
February 16, 1895–November 5, 1963

T he portly Vernon Dent is best remembered as the exasperated foil in dozens of Three Stooges shorts. Custard pie comedy was nothing new to Dent. He played various comic roles in dozens of silent era comedies.

Born in San Jose, Dent was originally a singer, but when silent film comic Hank Mann caught his act, Mann realized the hefty performer would have good presence in front of the cameras. Dent supported Mann in a series of films in 1919 and moved on to stooge for Billy Bevan, Larry Semon, and Mabel Normand, for a short time starring in his own comedy series in 1921, under the "Folly Comedies" banner. Dent was a regular in Harry Langdon's early short films, a bulky contrast to his baby-like friend. More than the traditional menacing heavy, Dent played a wide variety of characters in silent films, from oily con men to bumbling boyfriends, from eye-rolling brutes to big sissies.

During the sound era, Dent was reteamed with Harry Langdon in 1932 and 1933, then joined Columbia where he made feature films (he played Dutch Schultz in *The Shadow*) but worked more regularly in Three Stooges shorts. He permanently adopted his trademark thin gray mustache, and with his impressively stocky build, made a career out of standing in the way of the Stooges and paying the slapstick price for being so stubborn. Usually he played an over-worked businessman with no time to waste on slapstick nonsense. And so, to the glee of fans, he would suffer the insufferable clowning of the Stooges, his exasperation escalated from mild-mannered, almost whining complaints to sputtering outrage.

VERNON DENT in his usual role as target of the Three Stooges.

In the Stooges shorts, Dent occasionally got a chance to play broad slapstick (he was the demented brain surgeon Dr. D. Lerious in *From Nurse to Worse*). He sometimes played the benevolent boss. In *Dutiful But Dumb*, he was the editor of *Whack* magazine (slogan: "If It's a Good Picture, It's Out of Whack"). He actually sent the boys out on assignment and put up with their bumbling before they finally (miraculously) got the scoop. Usually he was just a hapless symbol of authority who was full of bluster—and ultimately full of pie. He took one in the face in *An Ache in Every Stake* and had more than his share in dozens of others. Much admired for his support work, Dent was praised by Stooge film producer-director Jules White: "Vernon was like the mounting for the ten-carat diamond."

Dent appeared in shorts with many other comedians including Charley Chase (*Teacher's Pest*) and Andy Clyde (*Share the Wealth*). He was in two W. C. Fields efforts—as the Secretary of Agriculture in *Million Dollar Legs* and billed somewhat crudely as "Fat Man in Train" for *You're Telling Me*.

For extra money and a lot of fun, Dent and his wife ran a concession stand in Westlake Park, selling ice cream and soda. His wife claimed it was here that Dent, sampling too much of the merchandise, developed diabetes. Some Stooge historians believed that Dent, like another Stooge support player Bud Jamison, was a Christian Scientist who had refused medical treatment, but this is simply not true.

Dent's eyesight began to fail him in the fifties, and by the time of

SELECTED FILM APPEARANCES:
(features) *Million Dollar Legs* (1932), *You're Telling Me* (1934); (shorts) *Marriage Humor* (1933), *Share the Wealth* (1936), *Calling All Doctors* (1937), *A Doggone Mixup* (1938), *Teacher's Pest* (1939), *Cold Turkey* (1940), *The Heckler* (1940), *From Nurse to Worse* (1940), *Dutiful But Dumb* (1941), *Crash Goes the Hash* (1944), *Defective Detectives* (1944), *Three Little Pirates* (1946), *Malice in the Palace* (1949), *Listen, Judge* (1952), *Knutzy Knights* (1954)

Stooge Shemp Howard's death, he had to be led to the casket to pay his last respects, placing his hand over Shemp's face. Dent accepted and adapted to his blindness and lived in comfortable retirement until he suffered a fatal heart attack in 1963.

ANDY DEVINE, garrulous, good-natured, gravel-voiced, and giggly.

ANDY DEVINE
October 7, 1905–February 18, 1977

When Andy Devine spoke, the words sounded like they had been coughed from a gravel gizzard up a washboard throat and out through tin teeth. It was such a distinctive, unnatural-sounding voice, people figured it had to have come by some bizarre childhood accident.

Andy obligingly told the story about the time he played with a curtain rod and pretended it was a trumpet. As he tooted into it, he fell down and it jammed it into the roof of his mouth. Sometimes Andy offered an alternate version: he was walking in the woods when he fell and a branch from a tree lodged in his throat, scrambling his vocal cords.

A 1941 press release for Devine when he was guesting on the radio show *Al Pearce and His Gang* reported "he got his gravel voice bench sitting" and cheering at college football games. In 1957 UPI reporter Jack Gaver noted a marked lack of "gravel" in Andy's voice during an interview. Andy admitted, "It comes out only when I have to project in acting." Considering his own statement, and the ability of impressionists (notably Will Jordan) to imitate him, there's no question that Andy's unique voice was something he could control.

Andy's first love was not acting, but football. Born in Flagstaff and a graduate of Arizona State College, the six-foot-two two-hundred pound Devine played pro ball before coming to California in 1925. His brawn helped him get extra work in films. He played a football player in his first major role, *The Spirit of Notre Dame* in 1931. Soon Andy Devine was getting regular roles and was often teamed with Richard Arlen or Leo Carrillo. Though no other name has been attributed to him for film roles, a few sources list his real name as "Jeremiah Schwartz." This has not been confirmed. References to his early years and family life, even in newspaper articles going back thirty years, routinely named his parents as Tom and Amy Ward Devine.

Through the thirties he often turned up as a cheerful sidekick in Westerns. He brought his colorful voice to *The Jack Benny Show* for Jack's Western "Buck Benny" sketches. Devine's greeting "Hiya, Buck!" became a popular catchphrase. A film based on the sketches, *Buck Benny Rides Again*, was rushed into production.

Along with Eddie "Rochester" Anderson, Devine and his gravel voice were used effectively to disrupt Benny's delivery and became almost a running gag itself. For some Benny shows he only made a cameo appearance, just enough to get the biggest laugh. In one episode, a parody of Dr. Jekyll and Mr. Hyde, Jack swallows a drug and in one dreadfully funny moment his voice sounds just like...Andy Devine's. In addition to the Benny radio show, Devine appeared often on *Lum and Abner*.

Thanks to radio's demand for distinctive comic voices, Devine's film career accelerated quickly. He was in demand for talkies that required some jarring talk and soon he was regularly offering comic support in two styles. His girth and jovial demeanor typed him as a jolly, chubby sidekick, a cheerful bumbler prone to a giggle and a laugh that sounded like a pocket full of spare change. Capable of twisting his face into furrow-browed sour looks of disapproval, Devine also took advantage of his bulk by playing gentle giants prone to grouse rather than fight.

Either way, Devine found work and by 1950 he claimed to have appeared in three hundred films, dramas as well as comedies and Westerns. At his current weight, that was one film per pound. In the early fifties he achieved new fame among young viewers for his work on two kid-oriented TV shows. As Jingles, sidekick to Guy Madison on *Wild Bill Hickok*, he was usually jolly, but his catchphrase was a whining wail of "Hey, Wild Bill! Wait for me!" As the host of *Andy's Gang*, Devine was again the friendly giant. The only time he'd begin his comic whine and his pouty complaints was when he was bedeviled by "Froggy the Gremlin," a wisecracking rubber frog puppet. Froggy would regularly trick Andy into painful slapstick, but Andy never held a grudge. He'd merely laugh and say, "You little rascal!" Froggy's response: "You great big square!"

Through the sixties the durable comic actor continued to play whining sidekicks and agitated elders in light films and stage productions. He was the voice of Friar Tuck in Disney's animated *Robin Hood*. He often

SELECTED FILM APPEARANCES:
We Americans (1928), *The Criminal Code* (1930), *Spirit of Notre Dame* (1931), *Three Wise Girls* (1932), *Destry Rides Again* (1932), *The Cohens and Kellys in Trouble* (1933), *Let's Talk It Over* (1934), *Hold 'Em Yale* (1935), *Chinatown Squad* (1935), *Romeo and Juliet* (1936), *You're a Sweetheart* (1937), *A Star Is Born* (1937), *Stagecoach* (1939), *Buck Benny Rides Again* (1940), *Flame of New Orleans* (1941), *Crazy House* (1943), *Ali Baba and the Forty Thieves* (1944), *The Ghost Catchers* (1944), *Follow the Boys* (1944), *The Gay Ranchero* (1948), *The Traveling Saleswoman* (1950), *The Red Badge of Courage* (1951), *Island in the Sky* (1953), *Around the World in 80 Days* (1956), *Adventures of Huckleberry Finn* (1960), *It's a Mad, Mad, Mad, Mad World* (1964), *Zebra in the Kitchen* (1965), *The Ballad of Josie* (1968), *The Over-the-Hill Gang* (1969), *Robin Hood* (voice) (1973), *Won Ton Ton, the Dog Who Saved Hollywood* (1976)

TELEVISION SERIES:
The Adventures of Wild Bill Hickock (1951–58), *Andy's Gang* (1954–55), *Flipper* (1964–65)

enjoyed summer theater work and played Captain Andy in many productions of *Show Boat*, including the 1957 Broadway revival. He acted in several Disney movies and had a final TV series role as Hap Gorman on *Flipper*. As he got older, Andy became more active in politics (he was honorary mayor of Van Nuys) and social causes, joining the board of directors of the Boy Scouts of Orange County and joining the committee to elect Ronald Reagan governor of California.

BILLY DeWOLFE
William Andrews Jones,
February 18, 1907–March 5, 1974

BILLY DeWOLFE, fastidious, precise, tight-lipped—and sometimes disguised as flower-hatted Mrs. Mergatroyd.

Tight-lipped, seemingly to the point of excruciating pain, Billy DeWolfe was a favorite for roles that called for a tense, pseudo-sophisticated and overly-articulate fussbudget. During the sixties he was especially active on television, playing the stuffy Vernon Bradley on *The Pruitts of Southampton*, petulant acting coach Jules Benedict on *That Girl*, bossy Roland B. Hutton, Jr. on *Good Morning, World*, and icily glaring Oliver Nelson on *The Queen and I.*

DeWolfe began his career as an acrobat and dancer, borrowing the last name of a theater manager in Quincy, Massachusetts, next door to his hometown of Wollaston.

He recalled, "Acrobats have the hardest job in the theater and get paid the least. Our dressing room was always on the top floor. If you danced you got a little more money and climbed less stairs." Part of the trio of "DeWolfe, Metcalf and Ford," Billy toured London for five years, appearing at the Palladium in 1933. He later developed a solo act in cabaret comedy, known for his pantomimes of how a woman takes a bath or puts on a girdle, and monologues as a woman carrying on an affair with the spotlight man and as "Mrs. Mergatroyd," a fussy old lady. He was convincing—despite his trademark neat and razor-thin mustache. "Women love to laugh, especially at themselves," DeWolfe said. "My Mrs. Murgatroyd was so effective that everybody who remembers it thinks I was dressed up like a woman." Actually, all he wore for his impersonation was a silly hat.

After navy service he began to appear in film musicals. *Blue Skies* and *Call Me Madam* were among his better efforts in the forties and fifties. He demonstrated quite a bit of versatility in *Blue Skies*, playing Bing Crosby's sidekick. In one scene he frightens a drunk by transforming himself (via a jacket worn backwards, sucked in cheeks, and a clumsy gait) into a Frankenstein monster. Later he suavely ends a conversation with a pretty girl by doing a backflip. And it's only after such masculine stunts that he gets a chance to do a turn as Mrs. Murgatroyd for Crosby's nightclub patrons. Two other key films for DeWolfe fans were a pair costarring Joan Caulfield, *Dear Ruth* and *Dear Wife*.

Broadway revues were also a prominent part of DeWolfe's career, especially in the fifties. He costarred with Hermoine Gingold as a pair of nattering old frumps in sketches for *John Murray Anderson's Almanac* and he was in drag again opposite Bea Lillie in a new production of *Ziegfeld Follies*. For a supermarket sketch he noted, "I did not shave my mustache. Of course, some people say they've seen mustached ladies in supermarkets!"

In his non-drag roles DeWolfe performed the function of a Franklin Pangborn or Arthur Treacher, dealing the star performer dart-like stares of disapproval, feigning superiority and, in moments of severe distress, actually hissing a few words of sarcastic protest. He got a lot of mileage out of prissily precise diction ("tissue" being pronounced "tiss-oo"). In talk show appearances with Johnny Carson, the highlight was Carson's straight line and Billy's well-timed, huffy reply:

"Busy are you, Billy?"

"Busy! Busy! Busy!"

SELECTED BROADWAY APPEARANCES:
John Murray Anderson's Almanac (1953), *Ziegfeld Follies* (1957), *How to Succeed in Business Without Really Trying* (1966)

SELECTED FILM APPEARANCES:
Dixie (1943), *Duffy's Tavern* (1945), *Miss Susie Slagle's* (1946), *Blue Skies* (1946), *Variety Girl* (1947), *The Perils of Pauline* (1947), *Isn't It Romantic?* (1948), *Tea for Two* (1949), *Lullaby of Broadway* (1951), *Call Me Madam* (1953), *Billie* (1965), *The World's Greatest Athlete* (1973)

TELEVISION SERIES:
That Girl (1966–67), *The Pruitts of Southhampton* (1967), *Good Morning, World* (1967–68), *The Queen and I* (1969), *The Doris Day Show* (1969–71)

COLLECTIBLES:
DeWolfe and Hermoine Gingold's sketches together are available on *Laugh of the Party* (Coral) and *Fun Time* (Coral)

DUDLEY DICKERSON clowns with the Three Stooges on the set of *Gem of a Jam.*

DUDLEY DICKERSON
November 27,1906–
September 23, 1968

Dudley Dickerson was only slightly overweight but he had round features and full, pinchable cheeks. The black comedian had plenty of porter, waiter and bellhop roles but thanks to his almost Muppet-like face, was instantly likable and fun to watch.

Although he was in many shorts with Andy Clyde, Vera Vague, and Charley Chase, even teaming with Hugh Herbert (as his valet) for a few titles, the Oklahoma-born actor is best remembered for his work in various Three Stooges shorts. It took a lot of talent to steal a scene or two from Moe, Larry, and Curly. In *Gem of a Jam* Dudley plays a night watchman who is aghast at coming across a weird looking dummy in his warehouse of theatrical props. It's Curly, who fell into a convenient trough of cement and dried into semi-stiffness. Rather than being scared, Dudley looks at it and says, "You sho' is ugly!" Curly tries to move and awkwardly follow the watchman to the nearest exit, and in a finely executed sequence Dudley keeps turning around to monitor the ugly, wayward thing that he can't get out of his sight.

Dickerson actually had a solo sequence in *A-Plumbing We Will Go.* He's the cook in a mansion that is under repair by the Stooges. When they inadvertently hook the plumbing into the electrical wiring, water fills up the lightbulbs until they burst. Dudley isn't about to be deterred. He turns up in full rain gear, ready to take on a storm. "This house has sure gone crazy!" Dudley mutters. He turns the dials on the stove and each burner becomes a water fountain, but he keeps struggling to work, doing several skillful slips and pratfalls on the wet kitchen floor.

Like Mantan Moreland and Willie Best, Dickerson couldn't avoid the elements of stereotype comedy that a writer or director would insist was "sure fire" entertainment. He did pop his eyes now and then, but at least if he had to show comic fear there was almost always a good reason. After all, in Stooges shorts there were plenty of gangsters, ghosts, and escaped lions running around—and the boys were not usually far behind him.

FIFI D'ORSAY

Yvonne Lussier,
April 16, 1904–December 2,1983

FIFI D'ORSAY, saucy pseudo-French comedienne, in a fashion pose.

Remembered as the lighthearted showgirl who duped the world into thinking she was really French, Fifi D'Orsay was at least born in the French-speaking city of Montreal.

She arrived in New York at twenty, dazzling Broadway producers with her sexy flashing eyes and cute way with a tune. How many showgirls could sing "Yes, We Have No Bananas" in French? She covered her lack of credits by announcing she had just arrived from the Follies Bergere.

She unabashedly made show-biz connections the old-fashioned way: by becoming a big star's girlfriend. She attached herself to the aging and usually drinking Ed Gallagher of Gallagher and Shean. "I became Mr. Gallagher's little sweetheart" she told writer Anthony Slide. "He was thirty-seven years older than me, but it was good for me because he knew all the little tricks of the business and I was a beginner. I wanted to learn everything about show business and he taught me—believe me…I was like a wife, but I wasn't his wife…I helped him because he was helping me, although it was no fun."

Billed as "Mademoiselle Fifi" in *The Greenwich Village Follies* of 1924, D'Orsay performed a comic sketch with Herman Berrens who tried to teach the mademoiselle how to play the piano. Many comic sketches played off her naïveté and coy French accent. In films she had success as a comic vamp. She delighted and intimidated Will Rogers in two early films, *They Had to See Paris* and *Young as You Feel*.

Over the years D'Orsay turned up in various films, brightening up a scene or two with her saucy eccentricity. In her fifties she was often cast in films as a comic "woman of the world," wry, still naughty, but usually bewildering thanks to her ostentatious manner and thick foreign accent. Fifi never disappointed her stage fans. She regularly toured with a nightclub act, singing songs and offering a few jokes. In her sixties she told ringsiders, "I'm old enough for Medicare—but not too old for men to care!"

MARGARET DUMONT, grande dame nonpareil, prepares to once again be "Groucho-ized"—wooed and insulted at the same time.

MARGARET DUMONT
October 20, 1889–
March 6, 1965

The immortal dowager, dignified Margaret Dumont deliberately stood in the way of the manic Marx Brothers, W. C. Fields and Abbott and Costello. Projecting a haughty invincibility, she refused to acknowledge their insulting slapstick. So she was subjected to it again and again. She never gave in. Neither did they. In fact, she was still in a comic war of insults with Groucho Marx in the sixties, guest-starring with him on TV's *The Hollywood Palace*.

The key to Dumont's eternal appeal was that however much her dignity was upset, she was never really hurt. Her grandiose obtuseness remained. In fact, the more ridiculously self-important she was, the funnier. She played a serious home owner in *Little Giant*, and was the recipient of a house full of dirt thanks to vacuum cleaning salesman Lou Costello. She was a bizarre love match for W. C. Fields in *Never Give a Sucker an Even Break*. But opposite the Marx Brothers, playing society matrons named Mrs. Teasdale, Mrs. Rittenhouse, Mrs. Upjohn, and Mrs. Claypool, she was much funnier. The loftier she played it, the more she was susceptible to down-to-earth insults.

She was a symbol of the establishment, both in attitude and in physique. Groucho Marx in *Duck Soup*: "You better beat it, I hear they're going to tear you down and put up an office building where you're standing…"

Dumont first met the Marx Brothers when she costarred in their second Broadway show, *The Cocoanuts*. Trained in opera, originally billed as Daisy Dumont, the Brooklyn-born singer-actress left show business to actually become a society matron, the wife of wealthy John Moller, Jr. After his death she returned to the stage in *The Rise of Rosie O'Reilly* opposite George M. Cohan. She played a social climber in *The Four Flushers* before going into *The Cocoanuts*. Groucho had several love-hate scenes with her in this one as well as *Duck Soup*:

Groucho: "Why don't you marry me?"

Dumont: "Why, marry you?"

Groucho: "You take me and I'll take a vacation. I'll need a vacation if we're going to get married. Married! I can see you right now in the kitchen, bending over a hot stove. But I can't see the stove…"

Dumont: "Rufus, what are you thinking of?"

Groucho: "…I suppose you'll think me a sentimental old fluff, but would you mind giving me a lock of your hair?"

Dumont: "A lock of my hair? Why I had no idea—"

Groucho: "I'm letting you off easy. I was going to ask for the whole wig."

In film after film, the naive but invariably rich widow Margaret Dumont was pursued, with mixed emotions, by Groucho. Now and then Dumont played opposite other comedians, suffering Groucho-esque insults even without Groucho. In *Kentucky Kernals*, she runs afoul of both Robert Woolsey and his partner Bert Wheeler:

SELECTED BROADWAY APPEARANCES:
The Summer Widowers (1910), *Go Easy Mabel* (1922), *The Rise of Rosie O'Reilly* (1923), *The Four Flushers* (1924), *The Cocoanuts* (1925), *Animal Crackers* (1928), *Shoot the Works* (1931), *Tell Her the Truth* (1932)

SELECTED FILM APPEARANCES:
The Cocoanuts (1929), *Animal Crackers* (1930), *The Girl Habit* (1931), *Duck Soup* (1933), *Kentucky Kernals* (1935), *A Night at the Opera* (1935), *Anything Goes* (1936), *Youth on Parole* (1937), *Wise Girl* (1937), *A Day at the Races* (1937), *At the Circus* (1939), *The Big Store* (1941), *Never Give a Sucker an Even Break* (1941), *The Dancing Masters* (1943), *Up in Arms* (1944), *The Bathing Beauty* (1944), *The Horn Blows at Midnight* (1945), *Little Giant* (1946), *Stop, You're Killing Me* (1952), *Auntie Mame* (1958), *Zotz* (1962), *What a Way to Go!* (1964).

TELEVISION SERIES:
My Friend Irma (1952–53)

"You look perfectly charming this morning."

"Oh, do you really think so?"

"No, but I had to say something…"

"I was never so insulted in my life!"

"Well, that's your fault. You don't get around enough."

Fans have seen Dumont opposite many others (Jack Benny in *The Horn Blows at Midnight*, Laurel and Hardy in *Dancing Masters*, and Red Skelton in *Bathing Beauty*) but through the thirties and forties Dumont was best as comic support for Groucho.

She knew the art of being a good straight woman. She explained it in a 1942 newspaper interview: "Script writers build up to a laugh, but they don't allow any pause for it. That's where I come in. I ad lib. It doesn't matter what I say. Just to kill a few seconds so you can enjoy the gag. I have to sense when the big laughs will come, and fill in, or the audience will drown out the next gag with its own laughter. I'm not a stooge. I'm a straight lady. The best straight woman in Hollywood. There's an art to playing straight. You must build up your man, but never top him, never steal the laughs from him."

"A wonderful dame," Groucho recalled of her, "I never had a foil like her. She took everything so seriously...I used to explain all the jokes to her. She was a serious woman. She was almost as big a star as we were. Everybody was crazy about Dumont. She was practically the fifth Marx Brother." She was treated like one of the family: "Once we took off all her clothes on a train we were all traveling on. You could hear her screaming all the way from the drawing room where she was, to where the engineer was blowing the train's whistle. She screamed and screamed but she loved it just the same. We took all her dignity away, both on and off the stage."

Dumont recalled that in the course of her stage and screen career with Groucho, "he pushed me out of windows, pulled chairs out from under me, broiled steaks in the fireplace, put frogs on the table and made life miserable in general—on the stage and off. I don't regret a minute of it."

Dumont continued to play the dowager on television (notably Mrs. Rhinelander on *My Friend Irma*) but the aging actress worked less often in the fifties. She once explained, "Try to find a play in which the supercilious society woman with the grand and haughty manner appears. She is no longer popular and I can't say I'm sorry, though I must admit she has been a gold mine to me." Fans were delighted when Dumont rejoined Groucho for an appearance on *The Hollywood Palace*. She died only a few weeks later.

CLIFF EDWARDS
June 14, 1895–July 17, 1971

There were two sides to Cliff Edwards's career. In the forties he took many little lighthearted roles, usually playing a bug-eyed comic character. In the twenties and thirties he was primarily a singer-musician affectionately called "Ukelele Ike."

"Ukelele Ike" had several hits, offering breezy versions of "Toot Toot Tootsie" and the snappy "Jada." The film *Hollywood Revue* caught him at the tail end of his crooning fame and the beginning of his comedy career. He sang "Nobody But You" seriously, then offered some novelty scat singing in a silly high-pitched voice. The little fellow with the bulging eyes was the comic butt of some jokes, huffing in mock jealousy over the film's other star singers, men who not only sang nicely but were good-looking as well. Just as music videos in the eighties and nineties helped dictate what fans heard on the radio, in the early thirties film appearances could catapult a star forward (Bing Crosby) or disappoint fans—as seemed to be the case with Cliff Edwards.

When the hits became fewer for the compact, aging crooner, he turned to suggestive comic songs like "I'm Gonna Give It to Mary With Love." It's about Mary Green, a lady about to get a surprise from Cliff: "Now I know that she has had it before. Mary's a gal that all the fellas adore. I'll let her take it right in her hand, 'cause I know she'll stroke it so grand. Like Jack and Jill we'll both get a thrill when I give it to Mary with love (my little kitten), when I give it to Mary with love." Each suggestive stanza ends with a surprise—the gift being a kitten, a necklace, or some other harmless item.

CLIFF EDWARDS (right) in his pre-Jiminy Cricket days, spiffily dressed for a night on the town with Eric Linden, Polly Walters, and Arline Judge in *Young Bride*.

In films, Edwards was usually typecast as a little wise guy who wasn't so wise, a fall guy whose brashness quickly turned to gulping, nervous timidity when challenged. Pop-eyed and ineffectual, he made a good sidekick for Western heroes of the day including Charles Starrett and Tim Holt.

Edwards was literally bug-eyed in his most famous movie role: Jiminy Cricket, sidekick to *Pinocchio*. The animated film classic not only preserves Edwards' unique comic voice (he was perfect as the wise yet easily concerned and flustered cricket), it contains the best example of his wistful charm as a singer: his solo song, "When You Wish Upon a Star."

SELECTED BROADWAY APPEARANCES:
The Mimic World of 1921 (1921), *Lady Be Good* (1924), *Lambs Gambol* (1925), *Sunny* (1925), *George White's Scandals of 1935* (1935)

SELECTED FILM APPEARANCES:
Hollywood Revue (1929), *Dough Boys* (1930), *Parlor, Bedroom and Bath* (1931), *George White's Scandals* (1934), *Gone With the Wind* (1939), *Flowing Gold* (1940), *Pinocchio* (voice) (1940), *The Monster and the Girl* (1941), *Overland to Deadwood* (1942), *Sagebrush Law* (1943), *Fun and Fancy Free* (voice) (1947), *The Man From Button Willow* (voice) (1965)

TELEVISION SERIES:
The Cliff Edwards Show (1949)

COLLECTIBLES:
Ukelele Ike Sings Again (Disneyland), *Pinocchio* (Disneyland), and collection of risque songs, *I'm a Bear in a Lady's Boudoir* (Yazoo)

LEON ERROL, one of the screen's longest-staggering drunk acts.

LEON ERROL
July 3, 1881–October 12, 1951

One of the funniest "drunks" in all show business, Leon Errol appeared in countless feature films as a realistically befuddled boozer: his legs rubbery, his brain pickled. He brought a special comic twist to his drunk roles. Rather than careening around in a happy daze, the balding, bespectacled comic often wore a frowning expression of discomfort and confusion, haplessly trying to struggle out of the mess he'd drunk himself into.

The frowns and grimaces of misery also came in handy for his "straight" series of nearly one hundred short film comedies (1938–51), in many of them as a henpecked husband (opposite Dorothy Granger). Most of them were mild appetizers supporting the feature picture. An earlier series (1934–37) was more experimental, including lively visual comedy and crisp vaudeville dialogue. The early *Should Wives Work?* received an Academy Award nomination. These shorts reflected Errol's early "pre-drunk act" comic inclinations.

The Australian-born comedian came to the U.S. by way of San Francisco. His first major comedy sketch, which was featured prominently in 1906's *The Baltimore Beauties* burlesque show, featured Tom Kennedy as a ventriloquist and Errol as his live dummy. Later Errol and his wife formed their own eccentric dance team and got a break appearing in *The Ziegfeld Follies of 1911* and the next four editions of the show. As he aged, the drunk character took over, but the wavering gait and the occasional falls could not have been timed to such perfection without his many years of dance training.

Unlike most comic drunks, Errol was not restricted to the narrow stereotype of a walk-on (or "stagger on"). Since he could play a wide range of older curmudgeons and eccentrics, he often supported the top comedians of his day in films that allowed him to drink moderately and act only mildly stewed. He costarred in *Never Give a Sucker an Even Break* with fellow ex-Ziegfeld star, W. C. Fields. He played Knobby Walsh, Joe Palooka's manager, in a series of movies for Monogram. He had the twin roles of Uncle Matt and Lord Basil Epping in the *Mexican Spitfire* comedy series with Lupe Velez. In Abbott and Costello's *The Noose Hangs High* it was he, not Abbott, who performed "the mudder's fodder" horse routine with Costello.

When he played these roles, drinking enough to be unreliable but not enough to be incoherent, he was often given more lines, and more of a chance to get a laugh from a joke rather than a stumble. In *Higher and Higher* (Frank Sinatra's starring debut) he plays a beleaguered father. Asked "Did you have more than one daughter?" he pauses for a moment to carefully consider the question. Then he blithely mutters, "Well, that of course I wouldn't know. My wife took care of those matters..."

SELECTED BROADWAY APPEARANCES:
Ziegfeld Follies (1911–15), *The Century Girl* (1916), *Hitchy-Koo* (1917–18), *Sally* (1920), *Louie the 14th* (1925), *Yours Truly* (1927), *Fioretta* (1929).

SELECTED FILM APPEARANCES:
Only Saps Work (1930), *Finn and Hattie* (1931), *Alice in Wonderland* (1933), *We're Not Dressing* (1934), *The Captain Hates the Sea* (1934), *Girl From Mexico* (1939), *Mexican Spitfire* (1939), *Mexican Spitfire Out West* (1940), *Never Give a Sucker an Even Break* (1941), *Where Did You Get That Girl?* (1941), *Mexican Spitfire's Baby* (1941), *Mexican Spitfire's Blessed Event* (1943), *Higher and Higher* (1943), *Invisible Man's Revenge* (1944), *Babes on Swing Street* (1944), *What a Blonde* (1945), *Joe Palooka* (1946), *Joe Palooka in the Knockout* (1947), *The Noose Hangs High* (1948), *Joe Palooka in the Big Fight* (1949), *Joe Palooka in the Counterpunch* (1949), *Footlight Varieties* (1951)

STUART ERWIN
February 14, 1902–December 21, 1967

STUART ERWIN, every hero's hapless pal.

Stuart Erwin was usually cast as a well-intentioned soul who made a bumbling mess of things. He was born in Squaw Valley, California, and his first acting assignments were on stage in Los Angeles shows including *The Open Gates* and *Women Go on Forever*. He attended the University of California at Berkeley, but in films, he rarely played a character with a college education.

Slapstick silent films were still the rage when Stu Erwin broke in, and he appeared in one of the last classics, *A Pair of Tights*. He and Edgar Kennedy played roles originally intended for Laurel and Hardy. In trying to defend their flapper girlfriends, the duo end up in a very Laurel and Hardy-ish ice cream fight.

For the sound era, mild-mannered Erwin still needed to be goaded into action. A low-key fellow with a round face, rounded features, and a relatively bland voice, it took an awful lot of comic degradation to get him riled enough to stand up for himself. Early in his film career he played the nice but punchy Joe Palooka in *Palooka* and was nominated for an Academy Award as Judy Garland's hayseed brother in *Pigskin Parade*.

Typical of his unassuming chump style was his costarring role in *International House*, playing an average guy with a below-average level of excitement. In one scene another man asks him about his marriage: "Didn't I hear something about you being sick the day before your wedding?" "Uh, it—it happened twice. That's why I didn't get married. Carol, uh, Miss Fortescue felt—well, you can imagine how she felt." "Discouraged." "Yes. So I resigned and went to America to the finest specialists." "Did they get you cleaned out all right?" "Every nickel!"

After spending the thirties and forties playing grumbling boyfriends and fumbling pals of the hero, Erwin emerged in the fifties as a father who didn't know best on the sitcom *The Stu Erwin Show*. It featured his real-life wife, June Collyer. As with many sitcoms of the era, comedy was mixed with moments of sage advice and warmhearted pathos. After the show ended, Erwin was cast in many straight acting parts, his worried demeanor well suited for such guest roles as a mousy embezzler on *Perry Mason*. He appeared in *Shadow Over Elveron*, a made-for-TV drama, just before his death.

SELECTED BROADWAY APPEARANCES:
Mr. Sycamore (1942), *Great to Be Alive!* (1950)

SELECTED FILM APPEARANCES:
Mother Knows Best (1928), *Happy Days* (1929), *The Exalted Flapper* (1929), *Paramount on Parade* (1930), *Maybe It's Love* (1930), *Only Saps Work* (1930), *Working Girls* (1931), *The Misleading Lady* (1932), *The Big Broadcast* (1932), *International House* (1933), *Going Hollywood* (1933), *Palooka* (1934), *Bachelor Bait* (1934), *The Band Plays On* (1934), *Women Are Trouble* (1936), *Pigskin Parade* (1936), *Dance, Charlie, Dance* (1937), *Small Town Boy* (1937), *Mr. Boggs Steps Out* (1937), *Hollywood Cavalcade* (1939), *Our Town* (1940), *Sandy Gets Her Man* (1940), *The Bride Came C.O.D.* (1941), *Cracked Nuts* (1941), *Blondie for Victory* (1942), *He Hired the Boss* (1943), *Heaven Only Knows* (1947), *Father is a Bachelor* (1950), *Son of Flubber* (1963), *The Misadventures of Merlin Jones* (1964), *Shadow Over Elveron* (1968)

TELEVISION SERIES:
The Stu Erwin Show aka *Trouble With Father* (1950–55), *The Greatest Show on Earth* (1963–64)

TOM EWELL
Yewell Tompkins, April 29, 1909

I n his best remembered films, Tom Ewell was the middle-aged comic fall guy taking a tumble over a statuesque blond. While viewers ogled Marilyn Monroe (*The Seven Year Itch*) and Jayne Mansfield (*The Girl Can't Help It*), they laughed at costar Ewell who reacted just the way most mere and mortal men would: with glassy-eyed gazes, fall guy wistfulness, and hopes so feverish he was sweating.

Ewell, a political science major at the University of Wisconsin, decided on an acting career after finding success with a local theater group and made his professional debut in 1928. One of his classmates also went into acting: Don Ameche. When Ewell came to Broadway, it was the street itself, not the theaters. He pounded the pavement but found little work, washing dishes for a living.

He got a few roles, but far more when he married his first wife Judith, daughter of Broadway producer George Abbott. Following his work in the play *John Loves Mary*, Ewell went out to Hollywood and made an unforgettable debut in *Adam's Rib*. He followed it with roles in two "Willie and Joe" World War II comedies (*Up Front* and *Back at the Front*). As a glum dogfaced soldier caught up in battle, he was the embodiment of the character in Bill Mauldin's gritty charcoal-sketch cartoons. Lou Costello saw his work, and since Ewell too was under contract at Universal, asked him to take a supporting role as a suicidal Yukon prospector in Abbott and Costello's *Lost in Alaska*. It was another role that called for Ewell's talents to make comedy out of misery.

TOM EWELL, every gal's hapless pal—even when lusting after Monroe and Mansfield on screen.

Ewell returned to Broadway for *The Seven Year Itch*, and when the film version arrived, Marilyn Monroe's costar got some recognition and respect as a somewhat unlikely leading man. Critics praised his ability to portray the foibles of an average man with a middle-age crisis. An actor without Ewell's depth might have been content with stereotypical comic lust and fluster. Ewell's reactions to Monroe, alternately lecherous, dazed, and worldweary, made the underlying desperation, desire, and need seem both human and humorous.

Ewell was called on to duplicate his success with a similar film, *The Girl Can't Help It*, opposite Jayne Mansfield, as well as *The Lieutenant Wore Skirts*, opposite Sheree North. These everyman comedies led to an average television sitcom in which he played a slightly rumpled real estate man dealing with a wife, mother-in-law, and house full of teen daughters. The show didn't last long, but did give Ewell the opportunity to brush up on his array of comic tricks, ranging from a wide-eyed look of disbelief to a sheepish grin of chagrin.

Ewell's next major exposure came in support of Robert Blake on the TV series *Baretta*. Through the eighties Ewell was often cast in melodramas playing fall guys, eccentrics, and men with sorrowful problems. Some of the actors who were now playing the hapless comic roles that once were Ewell's clearly showed his influence. Probably the best example is McLean Stevenson. He played parts that decades earlier might well have been typed for Tom Ewell: a slightly seedy, vaguely lusty, caring if care-worn middle-age man.

HERBIE FAYE
1899—June 28, 1980

HERBIE FAYE played weary and glum sidekicks, but always seemed to perk up playing second banana to Phil Silvers. He was with him in *Top Banana, Sergeant Bilko*, and this, the short-lived *New Phil Silvers Show*.

*H*is head bald, his mouth set in a grim downturn, his voice a New York-accented grumble, Herbie Faye invariably turned up as peptic cabdrivers, grousing building supers, put-upon salesmen, irascible bookies, and in his best continuing role, an aging and dour career soldier on Phil Silvers's TV series *You'll Never Get Rich*.

Never exactly Chaplin, Faye at least had the distinction of teaming with Chaplin's ex-wife Mildred Harris for a vaudeville act. Newcomer Phil Silvers wrote them a new routine—which called for a third actor—and so the duo became a trio. Harris was the draw, not her two stooges. Her vague fame in connection with Chaplin made her a curiosity item that intrigued audiences. Unfortunately she wasn't much of a comedienne and the trio rarely won repeat bookings.

According to Phil Silvers, Mildred Harris's cocaine problem was even more of a problem than her lack of comedy skills. Once she tried to liven up the show with a bit of suggestive stripteasing. After that night, the trio's bookings were quickly cancelled.

Silvers concocted a new act featuring Herbie and Herbie's chubby wife, Bobbie Caputo. In one scene, Silvers convinces Herbie that the best way to meet a girl is to drop his wallet, wait for a girl to pick it up, and then engage her in conversation. Bobbie walks by and Phil shouts "Let go of your wallet!" Herbie: "I can't." Phil: "Why not?" Herbie: "I got a Jewish cramp."

With gags like that, the act didn't last. Herbie and Bobbie remained on the vaudeville circuit as a duo, then Faye followed Silvers to Broadway, getting a second banana role in Phil's *Top Banana*. Faye later provided Silvers with key comic support on *You'll Never Get Rich* (better known in reruns as *Sergeant Bilko*) playing Private Fender, probably the oldest dogface in the army.

Faye was a familiar face in sitcoms into the seventies, his lemony look of long-suffering irritation good for a smile in a number of brief cameos. He was in several episodes of *The Odd Couple* getting chuckles as the building super who always had a gruff explanation for any problem. Unhappy with a wall cracked and marred after his "repair"? Don't ask him to do it over again. His solution: hang a few pictures!

Faye always brought a welcome lift to films when he made brief appearances. In the midst of some dreary doings in *Thoroughly Modern Millie*, for example, there was Herbie as a sighing, disgusted cab driver resigned to accepting a check for thirty-five cents from the newly arrived and naive country girl Millie. His last regular role was as Mr. Goldman, one of the Barnard Hughes's patients on the series *Doc*.

SELECTED BROADWAY APPEARANCES:
Wine, Women and Song (1942), *Top Banana* (1951)

SELECTED FILM APPEARANCES:
Top Banana (1954), *Come Blow Your Horn* (1963), *The Fortune Cookie* (1966), *Thoroughly Modern Millie* (1967), *The Night They Raided Minsky's* (1968)

TELEVISION SERIES:
Seven at Eleven (1951), *The Phil Silvers Show* (1955–59), *The New Phil Silvers Show* (1963–64), *Love Thy Neighbor* (1973), *Doc* (1975–76)

FRITZ FELD
Fritz Feilchenfeld, October 5, 1900

Forever playing maitre d's, odd foreign dignitaries, and peculiar artists, Fritz Feld contrasted his crisply efficient and haughty European demeanor with a sudden burst of eccentricity—slapping his palm up against his opened mouth to create a sudden loud POP. It was a comic salute, the oral version of clicking one's heels.

Early in his career, Feld played very different characters on stage: "I knew I was not a leading man. In Germany I played devils, hunch-

FRITZ FELD, haughty, efficient, eccentric—here with Billy Gilbert (left) and Judy Canova in *Sleepytime Gal*.

backs, witches and second gravediggers." He made his screen debut in *The Golem* and was a heavy in many silent films. He came to America in the Max Reinhardt Broadway production *The Miracle*, playing "The Piper."

Feld's characters were always intense, always passionate, always driven. When he applied the technique to comedies, he suddenly had a very successful career ahead of him. He admitted, "I play it very seriously. I feel that's what makes it funny. Rather than doing it burlesque, you see...I get very nervous and excited but basically I play it as if I'm serious."

His tendency toward abrupt and disconcerting reactions made him a favorite when a scene needed a quick, comic lift. He worked best when his sharp personality was matched in counterpoint against a star who was soft and vulnerable, traits shared by people as diverse as Carole Lombard and Lou Costello.

In *True Confessions*, Lombard is employed in the same house as butler Feld. She isn't sure about the boss, a lecherous type. "Where does his secretary usually do most of her work?" she asks. Feld's answer? A barking "Hah!"

In *Mexican Hayride* Feld played Lou Costello's elocution teacher. After trying to get Lou to breathe properly, he cries, "I would like to see you *inhale*!"

Feld's first big film role had him as an indignant desk clerk in *I Met Him in Paris*. After playing a hotel manager in *Idiot's Delight* he moved on to instantly burlesque the supposed intellectual superiority of doctors, psychiatrists, or any kind of instructor. In *Bringing Up Baby*, he's the strange Dr. Lehmann, who insists, "All people who behave strangely are not insane!" But he says it with an intense stare and a nervous tic. And in *The Affairs of Annabel*, he's a strutting eccentric director who is so full of odd mannerisms and strange ideas, someone shouts, "Take him to the psychopathic ward for observation!"

There was always something endearing about Fritz Feld's deluded characters, especially the maitre d's whose sense of self-importance Fritz regularly loved to shatter with exaggerated pomp and one loud mouth pop.

Feld created his trademark "pop" routine in Eddie Cantor's film *If You Knew Susie*. He recalled, "I was playing a head waiter. Mr. Cantor asked me to bring champagne. I had done a "click" sound in the older days but this time, I did the pop. They all laughed and wanted me to do it again." In the film, it's a brief sequence:

Cantor: "More champagne!"

Feld: "Champagne. (POP!) Coming up."

But everyone wanted him to do it again and again, and for over forty years, it seemed almost every film appearance required at least one solid pop.

Nearly four decades after his first mouth-popping roles, he played a fastidious hotel manager in Gene Wilder's film *The World's Greatest Lover*. For this brief bit, Fritz blew a kiss to his fans and to actress Carol Kane. Of course, when his hand came away from his mouth, there was a resounding POP. Anything else would have been a disappointment.

One of the most beloved character comedians, Fritz spent many years as a board member of the American Federation of Television and Radio Artists (AFTRA), tallied up over one thousand appearances in films, radio and TV, and was happily married since 1940 to actress Virginia Christine (probably best known as "Mrs. Olsen" in a series of coffee commercials on TV in the sixties). He continued to make television appearances in the eighties (on *Amazing Stories, Magnum, P.I.,* and others) and was honored when a theater in Crestwood Hills Park, Brentwood was renamed the Fritz Feld Community Theatre.

SELECTED FILM APPEARANCES:
The Golem (1917), *I Met Him in Paris* (1937), *Hollywood Hotel* (1937), *Tovarich* (1937), *Bringing Up Baby* (1938), *Artists and Models Abroad* (1938), *Gold Diggers in Paris* (1938), *I'll Give a Million* (1938), *Idiot's Delight* (1939), *At the Circus* (1939), *Mexican Spitfire's Baby* (1941), *Shut My Big Mouth* (1942), *Henry Aldrich Swings It* (1943), *Phantom of the Opera* (1943), *Knickerbocker Holiday* (1944), *The Secret Life of Walter Mitty* (1947), *The Noose Hangs High* (1948), *Mexican Hayride* (1948), *You Gotta Stay Happy* (1948), *O. Henry's Full House* (1952), *Jail Busters* (1955), *The Errand Boy* (1962), *Who's Minding the Store?* (1963), *The Patsy* (1964), *Wicked Dreams of Paula Schultz* (1968), *The Comic* (1969), *Hello, Dolly!* (1969), *Herbie Rides Again* (1974), *The Sunshine Boys* (1975), *Won Ton Ton, the Dog Who Saved Hollywood* (1976), *Silent Movie* (1976), *Freaky Friday* (1976), *The World's Greatest Lover* (1977), *All the Marbles* (1981), *History of the World—Part I* (1981), *A Fine Mess* (1986), *Barfly* (1987)

NORMAN FELL
March 24, 1924

With large, sad eyes and a gasping, dispeptic expression, Norman Fell made a career out of playing unhappy employees or disapproving employers. It didn't matter whether he was the boss or the bossed: he was miserable.

Born in Philadelphia, Fell first performed in school productions at Central High. He recalled, "I enjoyed acting and marveled that one could get paid for doing it." He spent World War II in the Pacific, flying cargo planes, noting, "I was getting shot at for eight thousand pounds of toilet paper." He graduated from Temple University in 1950 where he majored in drama. After study with Stella Adler, he appeared in

NORMAN FELL (in dark suit), comic fall guy and sometimes no-nonsense dramatic actor, surrounded by *The Boys* buddies (from left) Lionel Stander, Allen Garfield, Norm Crosby, and Jackie Gayle.

dozens of fifties TV dramas. Along with Jack Klugman, another Philadelphian noted for hangdog expressions, Fell at first tended to play dramatic roles on stage and television that called for a downtrodden loser.

In 1958 he began making films, appearing in *Ocean's Eleven* and *The Rat Race*. His baleful look was utilized when he joined dozens of other comic character players in *It's a Mad, Mad, Mad, Mad World*, playing a cab driver. His serious side was seen as Steve McQueen's no-nonsense superior in *Bullitt*. A few years later, Fell blended the right touch of comic suspicion and menace to unnerve Dustin Hoffman in *The Graduate*. (Fell played the proprietor of Hoffman's off-campus rooming house.) It was his big break, one that he thought had come nearly ten years earlier when he was singled out for his work in *The Rat Race*. "All I got out of it was a scrapbook of good notices. However, after *The Graduate* my phone started ringing."

Eventually Fell was cast in an endearing supporting role: landlord Stanley Roper on *Three's Company*. The running gag was his grim curiosity about the sex lives of his three tenants (Suzanne Somers, Joyce DeWitt, and John Ritter). His own sex life with "wife" Audra Lindley left much to be desired—especially desire.

The depressed landlord has no interest in his sharp-tongued wife, a fact she is always quick to complain about. "This house means a lot to me," he tells her. "How come you never say that about me!" she asks. Deadpan, he grumbles, "You're not in a rising market." She counters: "Neither are you!"

Fell would find many more sitcom roles calling for an actor who could get quick laughs with a long-suffering personality. He briefly starred in a spin-off series, *The Ropers*, and in 1989 costarred with Norm Crosby in a cable series called *The Boys*. The busy performer admitted, "Survival is the key word for me…I've always been more comfortable inching my way along."

Most of Fell's best roles have allowed for a certain amount of vulnerability. Even if he plays an unsympathetic part, viewers have to feel a little sorry for such a loser. Of his most famous role, Mr. Roper, Fell says "I think audiences like him because they can say 'Here's a guy who's lower than we are.'" Fell was always a fall-guy fans could fall for.

SELECTED FILM APPEARANCES:
Pork Chop Hill (1959), *The Rat Race* (1960), *Ocean's Eleven* (1961), *It's a Mad, Mad, Mad, Mad World* (1963), *Quick Before It Melts* (1964), *Fitzwilly* (1967), *The Graduate* (1967), *Bullitt* (1968), *If It's Tuesday This Must Be Belgium* (1969), *Rabbit Test* (1970), *Catch-22* (1970), *The End* (1978), *Paternity* (1981), *Transylvania 6-5000* (1985), *For the Boys* (1991)

TELEVISION SERIES:
Joe and Mabel (1956), *87th Precinct* (1961–62), *Dan August* (1970–71), *Needles and Pins* (1973), *Three's Company* (1977–79), *The Ropers* (1979–80), *Teachers Only* (1982–83), *The Boys* (1989)

PARKER FENNELLY
October 22, 1891–January 22, 1988

Fred Allen based his favorite radio character, Titus Moody, on his own New England upbringing. Maine-born Parker Fennelly was perfect as the crusty but doleful, wistful old gent who admitted he was "Moody b' name, Moody b' nature." His taciturn quintessential Down East nature suggested it was a sin to say one word more than necessary.

His high voice had a hoot owl's hoarseness, each sentence was pushed tightly through his teeth, squeezed so hard the "s" words were squashed into a lisp. This would be most evident in his later television commercials for Pepperidge Farm in the sixties. The slogan as delivered by Fennelly: "Pepp'idge Fahm Remembarsh."

Fennelly was not just an established character actor on stage before joining Fred Allen in "Allen's Alley." He also wrote three

PARKER FENNELLY, definitive drawling Down-Easterner, too preoccupied to notice Doro Merande's predicament in *The Russians Are Coming! The Russians Are Coming!*

Broadway plays—*Fulton of Oak Falls* in 1937, and two early forties efforts, *Two Story House* and *Cuckoos on the Hearth*. Earlier, he toured the legendary Chattaqua circuit doing Shakespeare. After his success with the Titus Moody character, Fennelly was typecast in similar rural roles for films, replacing Arthur Hunnicutt (who replaced Percy Kilbride) in the waning *Ma and Pa Kettle* series.

Today his fame endures as Titus Moody. His catchphrase to Fred Allen was a hail but weary "Howdy, Bub!" The homely hometown world of Titus Moody could be pretty silly:

Allen: "Say, Mr. Moody, you sound a little hoarse."

Fennelly: "I know. I got a cold in the head."

Allen: "Well how could you get a cold in the head?"

Fennelly: "Got a run in mah stocking cap. Before I cut the cat's tail off I was catchin' cold all the time…when the winter's freezin' cold, a short-tailed cat don't keep the door open so long comin' into the house."

Typical of Titus's world is this vignette, delivered with deadpan detachment:

"Last hobby I had was givin' moose calls. One mornin' at daybreak I went up to the top of a hill. I put on an old fur coat and a fur cap. I got down on all fours. I let out a moose call…a big she-moose come over the hill, runnin'. She nuzzled up to me and started lickin' my fur cap… I got up and explained as best I could. A big tear come in her eye. She turned and walked away…somewhere in them hills tonight…there's a moose with a broken heart. So long, Bub!"

After his Pepperidge Farm commercials, TV viewers got a last look at Fennelly when he played Mr. Purdy on Andy Griffiths's *Headmaster* series of the early seventies.

SELECTED BROADWAY APPEARANCES:
Mister Pitt (1924), *Small Timers* (1925), *Florida Girl* (1925), *Faust* (1927), *Babbling Brookes* (1927), *Country Chairman* (1936), *Our Town* (1944), *Happily Ever After* (1945), *Live Life Again* (1945), *Loco* (1946), *Southwest Corner* (1955), *Carousel* (1956)

SELECTED FILM APPEARANCES:
Lost Boundaries (1949), *The Whistle at Eaton Falls* (1951), *Ma and Pa Kettle on Old MacDonald's Farm* (1957), *It Happened to Jane* (1959), *The Russians Are Coming! The Russians Are Coming!* (1964), *Angel in My Pocket* (1969)

TELEVISION SERIES:
Headmaster (1970–71)

STEPIN FETCHIT
Lincoln Theodore Monroe Perry,
May 30, 1896–November 19, 1985

STEPIN FETCHIT, whose slow moves regularly got fast chuckles.

S tepin Fetchit looked funny with his shiny bald dome, questioning eyes, parted mouth, and hanging lower lip. He acted funny with his stammering, shuffling, and slowly-timed walk that took skill to execute. But the result of his creation was a stereotype used by others (Willie Best, most notably) and abused by even more, until he became a source of pain as much as pride to black America. He was the first black to make a million dollars in films, but he did it with a "dumb" comic style that poked fun not just at himself but at an entire race.

Born in Jamaica (he was named after several U.S. presidents), he was in minstrel shows and later performed with a partner. The duo called themselves "Step and Fetchit," supposedly after a Baltimore racehorse. After going solo he landed one of his first important roles, playing Gummy in *Hearts of Dixie*, a 1929 film with an all-black cast. The character had "gum legs," and Fetchit made the most of his rubbery walk.

Subsequently, Fetchit's character veered further and further toward cartoonish parody. He was a favorite in films depicting Southern lifestyles with nostalgia and he played a variety of menials on and off the plantation. Fetchit was the comic support for Will Rogers four times: *The Country Chairman, Judge Priest, David Harum,* and *Steamboat Round the Bend*. His slow ways comically irked Rogers, but it was clear that the two were really friends. Some of their byplay is just plain silly. In *Judge Priest*, Will Rogers wants to know, "Why aren't you wearing shoes?" Stepin Fetchit has the answer: "I'll save 'em in case my feet wear out."

Fetchit recalled in 1971, "I was the first Negro militant. When people saw me and Will Rogers together like brothers, that said something to them." But by 1971, whatever Fetchit was saying to fellow blacks was not being heard. He had become the personification of the Uncle Tom stereotype. His very name a reminder of black humiliation, he had trouble finding work, especially in the turbulent late sixties and early seventies. He insisted that he had gotten equal pay to his white costars and that he had made an important contribution to film comedy. He claimed that it was he who blazed the trail for modern black comedians. "All the things that Bill Cosby and Sidney Poitier have done wouldn't be possible if I hadn't broken that law. I set up thrones for them to come and sit on."

Through the years, Stepin Fetchit made millions and spent millions. He was a millionaire in 1937 and bankrupt in 1947 and back in the money by 1957, then unable to find work in 1967. He even tried stand-up and released an album on the Vee-Jay label. He was cheered for his work in John Ford's *Steamboat Round the Bend* in 1935 and Ford's *The Sun Shines Bright* in 1953, then jeered a generation later. In the late seventies, Stepin Fetchit was cast in a few movies; some people recognizing him for the grand comedian he was, but others still wary of what he represented.

SELECTED BROADWAY APPEARANCES:
Three After Three (1939), *Walk With Music* (1940)

SELECTED FILM APPEARANCES:
In Old Kentucky (1927), *Show Boat* (1929), *The Ghost Talks* (1929), *The Big Fight* (1930), *The Prodigal* (1931), *Stand Up and Cheer* (1933), *Charlie Chan in Egypt* (1935), *Dimples* (1936), *On the Avenue* (1937), *Elephants Never Forget* (1939), *Zenobia* (1939), *Miracle in Harlem* (1948), *The Sun Shines Bright* (1953), *Amazing Grace* (1974), *Won Ton Ton, the Dog Who Saved Hollywood* (1976)

JAMES FINLAYSON, Scottish vaudevillian who came to America only to find Laurel and Hardy the bane of his life.

JAMES FINLAYSON
August 27, 1877–
October 9, 1953

Beloved for his comic support of Laurel and Hardy, bald little James Finlayson was a "reaction" comedian. In his role as an observer scrutinizing every wrong move and every illogical word the boys made, Finlayson cued the laughs and kept them going as he furiously squinted or exhaled a huffy breath of indignation. When things really got out of hand, Finlayson performed his famous "double take and fade away," shaking his head, arching one eyebrow, and then shrinking back in disbelief and hapless chagrin.

Born in Scotland, a graduate of Falkirk College, Finlayson journeyed to America in 1912 and appeared in vaudeville before joining the ranks of the prospering silent film comedians. Bald even then, sporting a little mustache (on screen only), the little fellow with the piercing dark eyes and large ears made dozens of films before he arrived at Hal Roach Studios and met Stan Laurel. He supported Laurel in solo films (*Smithy* is probably the best) and occasionally starred in a short (notably *Yes, Yes, Nanette*, with costar Oliver Hardy). He became a member of the Laurel and Hardy stock company with one of the duo's first efforts, *Love 'Em and Weep* in 1927.

Usually playing an authority symbol who gets caught up and brought down, the scrappy Scot sometimes got a chance to perpetrate his own laughable violence. His most memorable silent short was *Big Business* (1929) in which he played a home owner who doesn't want to be bothered by door-to-door Christmas tree salesmen Stan and Ollie–especially in July! The reciprocal violence escalates as the feisty, fiery Finlayson does a manic job of destroying their car while they do damage to his windows and door.

Another highlight was the 1929 short *Men o' War*. This time in his familiar guise of the bothered, bewildered observer, a soda jerk who greets every new outrage with a new squint of disbelief, disgust, and high dudgeon. In the sound era, Finlayson's clipped delivery added to his comic character but in *Pardon Us*, it was his visual reactions to Laurel and Hardy's blithely silly verbal humor that made the comedy routines even more memorable. As a teacher:

Finlayson: "Now then, what is a blizzard?"

Stan: "A blizzard is the inside of a buzzard."

Finlayson: (after a furious double take) "Three goes into nine how many times?"

Stan: "Three times."

Finlayson: "Correct."

Stan: "And two left over!"

Finlayson: (scowling at Ollie) "What are YOU laughing at?"

Ollie: "There's only one left over!"

Finlayson: (another doubly furious take)

From the twenties through the forties, as long as Laurel and Hardy were a hot comedy team, James Finlayson was with them, literally at full steam.

SELECTED FILM APPEARANCES:
Married Life (1920), *Smithy* (1924), *Yes, Yes, Nanette* (1925), *Welcome Home* (1925), *Do Detectives Think* (1927), *The Second Hundred Years* (1927), *Ladies Night in a Turkish Bath* (1928), *Lady Be Good* (1928), *Men o' War* (1929), *Hoosegow* (1929), *Chickens Come Home* (1930), *Big Business* (1930), *The Dawn Patrol* (1931), *Pardon Us* (1931), *Our Wife* (1931), *Pack Up Your Troubles* (1932), *Fra Diavolo* (1933), *Bonnie Scotland* (1935), *The Bohemian Girl* (1936), *Way Out West* (1937), *The Toast of New York* (1937), *Blockheads* (1938), *The Flying Deuces* (1939), *A Chump at Oxford* (1940), *Saps at Sea* (1940), *To Be or Not to Be* (1942), *The Perils of Pauline* (1947), *Grand Canyon Trail* (1948), *Royal Wedding* (1951)

JOE FLYNN
November 8, 1924–July 19, 1974

A short, slightly squashed man with glasses that always seemed to tilt slightly askew in times of trouble, Joe Flynn specialized in irritated bosses and businessmen. A sneering little martinet who demanded respect, he was forever fuming because everyone around him knew him for what he was: a pipsqueak who happened to be in a position of power. Audiences loved to see him squall out orders—and squirm when they weren't carried out.

Educated at Notre Dame and the University of Southern California, at first Flynn endured many minor film roles (including a doctor's ineffectual assistant trying to control Lon Chaney Jr., the electrically revived *Indestructible Man*). His talents as a comic character man emerged in full when he was cast as Capt. Wallace B. Binghamton on *McHale's Navy*. The glowering, diminutive actor was a perfect comic contrast to beefy, chuckling Ernest Borgnine, who always got the best of Flynn. His catchphrases included a slow-burning bark "What? What? What?" as chaos began to envelope him, and ultimately a charred, miserable snarl of "I could just scream!"

JOE FLYNN, pretty much always the pompous pipsqueak.

Flynn was cast in similar roles in a variety of light, family-oriented Disney movies in the sixties and seventies. Behind the scenes, he was a vice president of the Screen Actors Guild, known for taking strong and definite stances on the issues—unlike his most famous character, Captain Binghamton.

Flynn died in his swimming pool in the summer of 1974. Police theorized that he took a dip in the late afternoon or at night, and had a heart attack. He was married and had two sons. Dennis Weaver, SAG

SELECTED FILM APPEARANCES:
This Happy Feeling (1958), *Cry for Happy* (1961), *Lover Come Back* (1962), *McHale's Navy* (1964), *McHale's Navy Joins the Air Force* (1965), *Divorce, American Style* (1967), *Did You Hear the One About the Traveling Saleslady?* (1968), *The Love Bug* (1969), *The Computer Wore Tennis Shoes* (1970), *The Barefoot Executive* (1971), *Million Dollar Duck* (1971), *The Strongest Man in the World* (1975)

TELEVISION SERIES:
The George Gobel Show (1958–59), *The Adventures of Ozzie and Harriet* (1960–62), *The Bob Newhart Show* (1961–62), *The Joey Bishop Show* (1961–62), *McHale's Navy* (1962–66), *The Tim Conway Show* (1970)

president at the time of Flynn's death, commented to *Variety*, "Joe was one of our most independent officers. Following his conscience, he always spoke openly on all guild matters. Always questioning, always searching, he set an example for others to follow. Wit and humor were Joe's stock in trade, and thank goodness he was never without them..."

FRANK FONTAINE
April 19, 1920–August 4, 1978

Forever linked with Jackie Gleason for his role as "Crazy Guggenheim" on Gleason's variety show, Frank Fontaine's comic routines had a strong vaudevillian flavor. He recalled, "When I was a boy, my father was in vaudeville and my mother went with him. Sometimes my brother and I went with them and I went to fifty-three schools. But sometimes we didn't and we were boarded out. I don't want my kids ever missing going to the ball game, or being without their dad..."

It was that sentiment that inspired Fontaine—father of eleven children–to try and become as rich and successful in show business as he could. He was variously a singer, actor, comic and impressionist in the forties. He sang with Vaughn Monroe's band and appeared in a number of films. On stage he got lots of laughs with a sketch called "The Sweepstakes Ticket Winner," about a goofy goon who gurgles and cackles with glee as he describes winning the prize. He starts from the very

FRANK FONTAINE, amiable in film support, later famous for baffling Jackie Gleason as "Crazy Guggenheim."

beginning ("I was jus' sittin' around, I wasn't doin' nothin' see...") and then, after reciting the winning number with plenty of histrionics (gasping "OH! OH! OH! on the zeroes), he goes into gooey giggles and goose-like cackles.

The laughs were entirely in the jolly idiot character Frank created ("John L. C. Savony") and his bizarre laugh. With a too large hat jammed down over his ears, and an ill-fitting jacket somewhat askew, and slightly punch-drunk, he performed the routine on *The Ed Sullivan Show* in 1948, and on two record albums. CBS tabbed him to star in his own radio sitcom, *The Frank Fontaine Show*, all about his problems raising all those kids. He appeared on *The Paul Winchell Show* in 1957, and in 1962 played "Crazy Guggenheim" to Jackie Gleason's sketch character, Joe the Bartender. Looking alarmingly simpleminded, "Craze" would greet his buddy Joe the Bartender, with a "stiff palm-out hand wave, accompanied by popping eyes and that demented grin." How original the mannerisms were is hard to tell. That description by author Stanley Green was about Dave Chasen in a 1924 *Earl Carroll Vanities* show with Joe Cook. Green called Chasen's gestures "much-copied."

For his audience in the sixties, Fontaine's "Crazy Guggenheim" was definitely an original. He would visit Joe the Bartender just to tell him terrible jokes: "Two little mice went in swimming. And one of the mice started to drown. The other mouse dragged him out and tried to save him. How did he do it? He gave him mouse-to-mouse restitution!"

After becoming aggravated with "Craze's" silly gestures and lovably stupid antics, Joe would become forgiving and misty—and ask Craze to sing a tune for him. This was the cue for Fontaine to warble a serious number in his deep, syrupy baritone.

After Gleason's show left the air, Fontaine continued performing, putting an act together that was part straight stand-up, part visit with "Crazy Guggenheim," and part songs. The act was successful, but not enough to meet all Fontaine's financial needs. The IRS took his house in settlement of back taxes in 1971. He had to take to the road, appearing in resurrected vaudeville touring shows like the *Roy Radin Revue*. The road ended in Spokane, Washington. Fontaine was attending the convention of the National Order of Eagles, having helped raised money for them. Shortly after the ceremony in which he was thanked for helping their cause, he suffered a heart attack.

SELECTED FILM APPEARANCES:
Nancy Goes to Rio (1950), *Stella* (1950), *Call Me Mister* (1951), *The Model and the Marriage Broker* (1952)

TELEVISION SERIES:
The Swift Show (1949), *Scott Music Hall* (1952–53), *The Jackie Gleason Show* (1962–66)

COLLECTIBLES:
Fontaine's comedy albums include *Idiot's Delight* (guest star) and the promotional release "Five Exciting New Radio Shows" (CBS). He also recorded many "straight" singing albums including *Songs I Sing on the Jackie Gleason Show* (ABC Paramount). "The Sweepstakes Winner" routine is on Capitol compilation albums *Comedy Hits* and *They're Still Laughing*

PAUL FORD
Paul Ford Weaver, November 2, 1901–April 12, 1976

Paul Ford didn't enter show business until he was nearly forty. Still known as Paul Weaver back then, he had a wife, five kids, and a varied résumé of dead-end jobs including magazine salesman. He had barely lasted a year at Dartmouth and now had to find some kind of lasting employment.

After producing a puppet show at the 1939 World's Fair, he began to explore the world of show business a bit deeper. He found good luck in radio, frequently performing on soap operas. When he flunked an audition, Paul Weaver returned later, signing "Paul Ford" to the call sheet. He got the part—and kept the name.

The middle-aged actor became a "new face" on Broadway. His was a comic one, with small, tired basset hound eyes, prominent jowls and a tentative, worried frown to his mouth. He had a distinctive voice prone to muttering whines and grim asides. He made a perfect comic authority figure with just the right amount of self-doubt hiding behind the tight-lipped, stony facade. After several productions he was singled out for his supporting role as Colonel Purdy in *Teahouse of the August Moon*.

Brooks Atkinson in the *New York Times* praised his performance as "immensely funny and immensely winning." Ford played

PAUL FORD, alone in a leaky boat and sporting a typically sunken "nothing ever goes right" expression.

a bank president on the short-lived sitcom *Norby* in 1954, and then appeared in the film version of *Teahouse of the August Moon*. He brought his military bearing to television as semi-stoical, long-suffering Colonel Hall on Phil Silvers's Sergeant Bilko series, *You'll Never Get Rich*. While Bilko hustled his schemes, wary Colonel Hall tried to keep his composure, his stern visage clearly ready to crumble in frustration every time he was tricked.

Ford returned to the stage, joining the ensemble Broadway cast of *The Thurber Carnival*. He finally got a chance to actually star in a show when he played hapless Harry Lambert in *Never Too Late*, a past-middle-age gent who discovers that he's going to become a father. He says with stoic detachment, "There's all kinds of happiness. This is the happiness that everybody isn't too happy about." Ford repeated his starring role in the film version.

Having starred on Broadway, the veteran actor was now deemed by network executives suitable for

SELECTED BROADWAY APPEARANCES:
Decision (1944), *Lower North* (1944), *Kiss Them for Me* (1945), *As We Forgive Our Debtors* (1947), *Command Decision* (1947), *Brass Ring* (1952), *Teahouse of the August Moon* (1953), *Good as Gold* (1957), *Whoop-Up* (1958), *The Thurber Carnival* (1960), *Never Too Late* (1962), *Three Bags Full* (1966), *What Did We Do Wrong?* (1967), *Three Men on a Horse* (1969)

SELECTED FILM APPEARANCES:
Perfect Strangers (1950), *Teahouse of the August Moon* (1956), *The Matchmaker* (1958), *Who's Got the Action?* (1962), *The Music Man* (1962), *Never Too Late* (1965), *The Russians Are Coming! The Russians Are Coming!* (1966), *The Spy With a Cold Nose* (1967), *The Comedians* (1967)

TELEVISION SERIES:
Norby (1954), *You'll Never Get Rich* (a.k.a *Sergeant Bilko*, a.k.a. *The Phil Silvers Show*) (1955–59), *The Baileys of Balboa* (1964–65)

a starring role on TV. He played gruff but lovable Sam Bailey, owner of a charter boat on *The Baileys of Balboa*. His first mate was Sterling Holloway and another member of the cast was young Judy Carne. The series didn't last but the chance for him to be the center of attention after so many years as an ensemble player, was a fine tribute and he continued to find plentiful assignments on stage and in films through the sixties.

WILLIAM FRAWLEY
February 26, 1887–March 3, 1966

WILLIAM FRAWLEY, a cantankerous but lovable grump for forty years in films and television.

William Frawley made a career out of playing comically tough and gruff types, though by the time he got to television, he'd mellowed slightly into grumpy and dumpy. He played himself; his costars recalled that Frawley was essentially the same sour, hard-drinking, but somewhat sentimental guy he played in comedy.

He started out as a singer, joining the church choir at home in Burlington, Iowa. Defying his mother, who had her suspicions about show people, young Bill was soon touring vaudeville with a piano player named Franz Rath. Their act was called "A Man, a Piano, and a Nut." In 1914 Frawley decided that it was more fun to tour with Edna Broedt. They married, and as "Frawley and Louise" made their way along the tough vaudeville circuit for over a decade.

After their divorce, song-and-dance-man Frawley appeared in some Broadway shows and eventually landed a film contract. As a wise guy with a jaundiced eye and a salty mouth, he could play either a shady character or a detective in support roles. He was a tough nightclub boss menacing Abbott and Costello in *One Night in the Tropics* and ten years later, on the side of the law, he was the detective unable to believe his eyes in *Abbott and Costello Meet the Invisible Man*.

True to his curmudgeonly nature, Frawley dismissed his film career in one line: "I played in ninety-six pictures, maybe one or two good ones." Fans who have pondered on the thought, point to *Miracle on 34th Street* as one. He played the Tammany Hall toughie who tells a judge to watch his step before ruling "there ain't no Santy Claus."

The no-nonsense comic used the same tactics to get his big break in television. The moment he found out about Lucille Ball's prospective sitcom in late 1950, he called her personally and pitched himself, trading in on their past work together. Lucy was surprised. She barely remembered him from *Ziegfeld Follies*, the 1946 film they were both in. But the more she thought about it, the more she realized how perfect Frawley would be as cantankerous Fred Hobart Mertz, her downstairs neighbor. Once Frawley promised to curb his well-known drinking habit, he was signed.

Frawley never promised to curb his tongue and he regularly insulted his TV "wife," Vivian Vance. The crusty actor was quickly bored with the weekly routine, which he likened to "eating stew every night—stale and not a bit funny." Whether always intentional or not, Frawley got a lot of laughs. It was his half-hearted enthusiasm in some scenes, the awkward way he sometimes stood while waiting for something to do, and his laconic slow takes and wisecracks. His dour presence offered a comic contrast to Lucy's frantic slapstick.

Following *I Love Lucy*, Frawley was cast as the acerbic comic support to three wholesome boys and genial Fred MacMurray in *My Three Sons*. The aging actor required prostate surgery a few years after the show's premiere and health problems prevented his return to the series. Fans missed him, but his view of his sitcom work was even less charitable than that of his film career. He had little to say about *My Three Sons*, and of *I Love Lucy* he grunted, "I just took the money and ran."

SELECTED BROADWAY APPEARANCES:
Merry Merry (1925), *Bye Bye Bonnie* (1927), *She's My Baby* (1928), *Here's Howe!* (1928), *Carry On* (1929), *Sons o' Guns* (1929), *She Lived Next to the Firehouse* (1931), *Tell Her the Truth* (1932), *Twentieth Century* (1932), *The Ghost Writer* (1933)

SELECTED FILM APPEARANCES:
Surrender (1931), *Moonlight and Pretzels* (1933), *Shoot the Works* (1934), *The Lemon Drop Kid* (1934), *Hold 'Em Yale* (1935), *Alibi Ike* (1935), *Three Cheers for Love* (1936), *Double or Nothing* (1937), *Something to Sing About* (1937), *Professor Beware* (1938), *St. Louis Blues* (1939), *Huckleberry Finn* (1939), *Golden Gloves* (1940), *One Night in the Tropics* (1940), *Blondie in Society* (1940), *Cracked Nuts* (1941), *Footsteps in the Dark* (1941), *It Happened in Flatbush* (1942), *Whistling in Brooklyn* (1943), *Going My Way* (1944), *Lady on a Train* (1945), *Ziegfeld Follies* (1946), *Miracle on 34th Street* (1947), *Monsieur Verdoux* (1947), *The Babe Ruth Story* (1948), *The Lone Wolf and His Lady* (1949), *Kill the Umpire* (1950), *The Lemon Drop Kid* (1951), *Rhubarb* (1951), *Abbott and Costello Meet the Invisible Man* (1951), *Safe at Home* (1962)

TELEVISION SERIES:
I Love Lucy (1951–57), *The Lucy-Desi Comedy Hour* (1957–60), *My Three Sons* (1960–64)

COLLECTIBLES:
William Frawley Sings the Old Ones (Dot)

VINCENT GARDENIA
Vincent Scognamiglio, January 7, 1922–December 9, 1992

Known for comic excitability, usually with a little ethnic top-spin, Vincent Gardenia won a Best Supporting Actor Tony Award for *The Prisoner of Second Avenue* in 1971 and was a respected stage actor before a national TV audience got to know him as ample, middle-age Frank Lorenzo, the sensitive and passionate husband of Edith Bunker's friend Irene on *All in the Family*. A

VINCENT GARDENIA, the beloved "King of Brooklyn," excitable in comedy and dangerous in drama.

good cook, jowly Frank could lose himself in an intense reverie over a vichyssoise. When the boorish Archie Bunker complains that the soup is cold, Frank first registers dismay—then rhapsodizes his response: "If you heat up vichyssoise—it *weeps*!"

The role marked Gardenia's second comic encounter with Jean Stapleton (Edith Bunker). Shortly before, he played her fussy husband in the film *Cold Turkey*.

Born in Naples, young Vincent came to Brooklyn with his father, an actor and singer. The family name changed after an admirer told his father, "You sing like a gardenia." Vincent was three when he played a shoeshine boy in one of his father's productions. He recalled, "We'd play the old Yiddish theaters on Second Avenue when they were empty…we'd tour Italian neighborhoods in Staten Island, the Bronx and Queens, as well as our own Brooklyn."

After World War II service, Gardenia made his Broadway debut as a blind man in *The Visit* in 1958. After that he began moving back and forth between the stage and films, making his movie debut in *Mad Dog Coll* in 1961 playing mobster Dutch Schultz. He was nominated for a Best Supporting Actor Academy Award for *Bang the Drum Slowly* in 1974. Gardenia was often cast as a tough, if comically down-to-earth type, but often added a touch of humor and human nature. It was his idea to give his detective character in *Death Wish* a heavy cold. He reasoned that his character was "beleaguered…I felt the bad cold emphasized that."

As he aged into slight portliness, his dangerous edge seemed to soften as well, his tough guys now merely stubborn or petulant, undone by their inner sentimentality. Gardenia made the most of turning a scowl into a sappy, good-natured smile of compliance. The warmhearted usually bespectacled actor never strayed from his Brooklyn beginnings: he lived there in a house with his sister and her family until he died. He smiles, saying, "When I go out, everybody knows me. Most of the people I run into I've known since we were kids. You don't have ties like this in L.A." Cooking continued to be his main hobby. He preferred to remain in New York for stage work.

He made indelible impressions in a variety of Broadway shows over the years, from Neil Simon's *God's Favorite* in 1974 to Larry Gelbart's *Sly Fox*. In the nineties, he spent several years in the Off-Broadway show *Breaking Legs*, as the agitated restaurant owner fighting with an unmarried daughter and a room full of his mob-connected business associates. He died while on tour with the show. In films, Gardenia was the sour, dangerous flower shop owner, Gravis Mushnick, in *Little Shop of Horrors* and received another Best Supporting Actor Oscar nomination for his richly ethnic role in the Italian family comedy *Moonstruck* as Cher's straying father.

"After *Moonstruck*, the number of scripts sent to me quadrupled," he admitted. But he turned down sitcoms for New York stage work. "I don't want to do them [sitcoms]," he said, "why put this burden on me at my age…I mean, the house is already paid for."

In 1990, Gardenia, having lived most of his life in Brooklyn, was given a singular honor, being named King of Brooklyn.

SELECTED BROADWAY APPEARANCES:
The Visit (1958), *The Prisoner of Second Avenue* (1972), *God's Favorite* (1974), *Sly Fox* (1977), *Ballroom* (1978), *Glengarry Glen Ross* (1984), *Breaking Legs* (1990)

SELECTED FILM APPEARANCES:
Mad Dog Coll (1961), *A View From the Bridge* (1962), *Where's Poppa?* (1970), *Cold Turkey* (1970), *Little Murders* (1971), *Bang the Drum Slowly* (1974), *The Front Page* (1974), *The Manchu Eagle Murder Caper Mystery* (1975), *Greased Lightning* (1977), *Heaven Can Wait* (1978), *Home Movies* (1979), *Movers and Shakers* (1985), *Little Shop of Horrors* (1986), *Moonstruck* (1988), *Age-Old Friends* (1989)

TELEVISION SERIES:
All in the Family (1973–74), *Breaking Away* (1981)

ANITA GARVIN
February 11, 1907

A durable comic actress in silent and sound shorts, Anita Garvin costarred in dozens of efforts, playing everything from a hostile wife (in Leon Errol's *Truth Aches*) to a snooty glamour puss (*Show Business* with ZaSu Pitts and Thelma Todd). She began her career as a Mack Sennett bathing beauty, moved on to Christie studios, and ultimately became a regular with Hal Roach. Typical of her style was *A Pair of Tights* with Stu Erwin and Edgar Kennedy. She plays a happy-go-lucky flapper who urges her boyfriend into slapstick mayhem, even if she ends up getting in on the action as well.

ANITA GARVIN, once again losing her dignity to Laurel and Hardy, this time in *From Soup to Nuts*.

Laurel and Hardy fans especially remember her comic moment in *From Soup to Nuts*, as a society woman trying desperately to eat a cherry on her plate, chasing it around and around with her spoon while her tiara falls over her eyes. In *The Battle of the Century*, she had a memorable vignette as the rather proper young lady who accidentally slips on a thrown pie. As she falls her skirt billows open, allowing a significant amount of the gooey dessert to make a rear entry—a fact acknowledged by one priceless shake of the leg as she walks away. Audiences laughed harder at her reaction than any other's in the film: thanks to her own perception of the brief role. She made her character so airy and above it all that when she gets involved in the mayhem, the audience feels it's her just dessert.

After her marriage in the thirties Garvin spent most of her time at home with her husband and children. She played Mrs. Stan Laurel in *Be Big* but, despite his efforts to change her mind, she turned down subsequent work roles and Mae Busch began getting Garvin-type roles whenever Stanley needed a screen wife. In January of 1991, the home-bound Garvin was given a new wheelchair by her ever loyal fans. She said at the ceremony, "I haven't made a picture in over forty years—and I get fan mail from all over the world! It's absolutely amazing."

ALICE GHOSTLEY, whose career bloomed playing wallflowers and odd clinging vines.

ALICE GHOSTLEY
August 16, 1926

S he was an unforgettable face in *New Faces of 1952*, the campy singer of "The Boston Beguine," her musical remembrance of a romantic evening: "It was a magical night with romance everywhere. There was something in the air. There always is, in Boston. We went to the Casbah, that's an Irish bar there. The underground hideout of the D.A.R. there…. We danced in a trance and I dreamed of romance. Till the strings of my heart seemed to be knotted. And even the palms seemed to be potted. The Boston Beguine was casting its spell and I was drunk with love—and cheap muscatel."

For decades, the pensive, woeful Ghostley played similar damaged ducklings and soured soubrettes. While some who were influenced by her moved from character roles to stardom (Carol Burnett), Ghostley would remain an integral, memorable ensemble player. She was one of the anguished stepsisters (Kaye Ballard the other) in the Julie Andrews production of *Cinderella* on TV, and appeared in S. J. Perelman's *The Beauty Part* and *The Thurber Carnival* on Broadway.

Born in Missouri and educated at the University of Oklahoma, Ghostley came to Manhattan in 1950. For many years she was best known for her New York stage and cabaret work, earning a Tony Award in 1965 for *The Sign in Sidney Brustein's Window*. Early on she was typecast as a comic spinster, even though she was married. Her marriage to actor Felice Orlandi lasted over forty years.

In films and on television, Ghostley regularly played silly sad sacks and neurotic, wanly grimacing flakey females that sometimes seemed like *New Faces* buddy Paul Lynde in drag. "I don't see myself that way," she said, "but everybody else does. Maybe it's because I don't look like anybody else." She was a series regular on *Bewitched* as Esmerelda and on *Designing Women* as Bernice.

SELECTED BROADWAY APPEARANCES:
New Faces of 1952 (1952), *Sandhog* (1954), *All in One* (1955), *Shangri-La* (1956), *The Thurber Carnival* (1960), *The Beauty Part* (1962), *The Sign in Sidney Brustein's Window* (1964), *Annie* (1978)

SELECTED FILM APPEARANCES:
New Faces (1954), *To Kill a Mockingbird* (1962), *My Six Loves* (1963), *Rabbit Test* (1978), *Grease* (1978), *Not for Publication* (1984)

TELEVISION SERIES:
Captain Nice (1967), *Jonathan Winters* (1967–69), *Bewitched* (1969–72), *Designing Women* (1988–)

She continued to enjoy stage work, playing Miss Hannigan on Broadway in *Annie,* and in 1988 and 1989 joining the national touring company of *Nunsense,* playing Sister Mary Regina of the Order of the Little Sisters of Hoboken.

BILLY GILBERT
William Gilbert Baron, September 12, 1894–September 23, 1971

Casting agents knew him as Billy "The Sneezer" Gilbert, a big, blustery fellow who could liven up a scene with a sneeze. But not just an ordinary sneeze. Gilbert had a vast repertoire of them. He could almost bring down the house with one of his full-force blasts, the kind that had the star comics rolling their eyes or diving for cover.

But it was even funnier when the three-hundred-pounder began his itchy-nosed, weepy-eyed gasps, and as everyone ran for cover, he issued a weak and fluttery, little old lady's sneeze. The camera stayed on Gilbert as he blushed and smiled with embarrassment.

BILLY GILBERT, the big man with the big sneeze, getting the help of Shemp Howard, a frequent screen pal, in sorting out Helen Gilbert's problem in *Three of a Kind*.

Gilbert's most famous supporting role was in Disney's *Snow White and the Seven Dwarfs*. He was the undisputed choice for the part of "Sneezy."

But sneezing wasn't all that Gilbert could do. Almost as large as both Oliver Hardy and Stan Laurel put together, Billy was a formidable foe in many of the duo's best comedies. He could play anything from a blustery, bulge-eyed big-game hunter to an imposingly haughty doctor or professor with a stereotypical German accent, a thick black mustache, and a monocle. The comedy was always in how the boys could destroy Billy's dignity and leave him howling and gesticulating outrageously. The thing about Billy Gilbert was that he would never go gentle into that good fade-out. He was always dangerous right to the end.

One of Gilbert's most memorable roles capped the long battle Laurel and Hardy had getting a piano up those incredible stairs in *The Music Box*. Once the boys finally get the piano into Gilbert's house, he enters to register furious anger. "I HATE PIANOS!" he bellows, taking an ax to the offending instrument and nearly bludgeoning the boys as well. His anger finally subsiding into bathetic remorse, he signs for the destroyed piano, only to get squirted in the face with ink. Now he takes up his shotgun and Stan and Ollie leave the scene in a hurry.

The reliable comedy veteran had been in show business almost all his life. If not actually born in a trunk, Gilbert was at least born in a dressing room. It belonged to his parents, a pair of traveling singers who tried to liven up the vaudeville trail with opera and light classics. Gilbert spent many years in vaudeville before arriving in Hollywood and becoming a human pillar of comic support.

Aside from Laurel and Hardy, Gilbert visited his grandiose arrogance and eccentric dignity on the Three Stooges and the team of Thelma Todd and ZaSu Pitts. He was briefly part of two comedy teams himself. He and Ben Blue were paired as "The Taxi Boys" and later he made a few feature films with fellow stooges Shemp Howard and Maxie Rosenbloom.

At the start of World War II, Gilbert joined Charles Chaplin in making *The Great Dictator*. During the war, Gilbert and his wife traveled the country and the world as members of the USO, entertaining soldiers. Back home, on December 9, 1942, Billy's foster son committed suicide. The thirteen-year-old boy left a note near the rifle: "Grandmother wouldn't believe me."

After the war, Gilbert chose stage work more often than films, appearing in a revival of *The Chocolate Solider* in the mid-forties and later replacing Walter Slezak in the hit Broadway show *Fanny*. Gilbert suffered a stroke in 1963 but returned to show business within a year. The tried and true comedy of burlesque and vaudeville was alive and well in Las Vegas revues so Gilbert journeyed there for several shows, and in 1970 he guested on a Johnny Carson special called *Sun City Scandals*, a last bow celebrating fifty years in comedy.

SELECTED BROADWAY APPEARANCES:
The Chocolate Soldier (1947), *The Buttrio Square* (1952), *Fanny* (1956)

SELECTED FILM APPEARANCES:
Noisy Neighbors (1929), *The Music Box* (1932), *Million Dollar Legs* (1932), *Flying Down to Rio* (1933), *One Hundred Men and a Girl* (1937), *Snow White and the Seven Dwarfs* (voice) (1937), *Blockheads* (1938), *Happy Landing* (1938), *Destry Rides Again* (1939), *The Great Dictator* (1940), *His Girl Friday* (1940), *Arabian Nights* (1942), *Crazy House* (1945), *Anchors Aweigh* (1945), *The Kissing Bandit* (1949), *Five Weeks in a Balloon* (1962)

GEORGE GIVOT
1903–June 7, 1984

A vaudevillian who often performed comic monologues as "The Greek Ambassador," tall, dark-haired George Givot differed from most ethnic comedians of the thirties and forties. While most tended to be wild of eye, or hair, Givot was rather charming. An ancestor of sorts to Bronson Pinchot, who created the winning character of immigrant Balki on TV's *Perfect Strangers*, Givot found humor in his peculiar accent and the amusing way he misunderstood people and baffled them with what

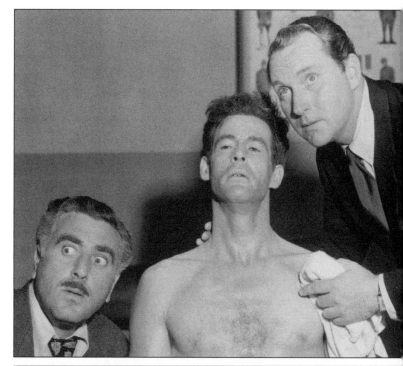

GEORGE GIVOT, wide-eyed English-mangler, in a scene from *Behind the Rising Sun* with Robert Ryan (center) and Don Douglas (right).

SELECTED BROADWAY APPEARANCES:
The Constant Sinner (1931), *Americana* (1932), *Pardon My English* (1933), *Mexican Hayride* (1944), *Wonderful Town* (1958), *Do Re Mi* (1961)

SELECTED FILM APPEARANCES:
The Chief (1933), *Hollywood Party* (1934), *When's Your Birthday?* (1937), *Wake Up and Live* (1937), *Marie Walewska* (1938), *Hollywood Cavalcade* (1939), *DuBarry Was a Lady* (1943), *Step Lively* (1944), *Riff Raff* (1946), *Three Sailors and a Girl* (1953), *The Lady and the Tramp* (voice) (1955)

TELEVISION SERIES:
Stop Me If You've Heard This One (1949), *Versatile Varieties* (1949)

he thought were perfect, logical-sounding sentences.

Triviasts also know him for being a member of a fake "Three Stooges" group. Givot, Bobby Calahan, and Curly Howard appeared together in the 1934 MGM short *Roast Beef and Movies*. This wasn't a real teaming, however. Curly and his true team members Moe and Larry were all under contract to MGM and occasionally all three were called on for miscellaneous supporting assignments between official Three Stooges shorts and feature roles.

Born in Russia but raised in Omaha where he was adopted after his parents died, Givot attended the University of Chicago intent on a law career. Somehow, he got sidetracked. Known for a fine Maurice Chevalier impression, Givot was a regular on radio and developed a talent for a variety of accents. He went on to appear in small roles in dozens of feature films, and was the voice of Tony the restaurant owner in Disney's *Lady and the Tramp*. His career extended to the early days of television when he was a panelist on *Stop Me If You've Heard This One*, and then hosted his own *Versatile Varieties* show.

Typical of Givot's style was his role as a tailor in Ed Wynn's early starring effort, *The Chief*. In a scene that was really more like a five minute vaudeville turn, Givot tries to sell Wynn a suit that would look "magnifeesum," and be fit for "the President for the United Snepps." The used suit had been previously owned by "an ambasstador" who had taken his own life by committing "sewerpipes."

Wynn has a hard time following him, but evidently so did all of Givot's customers: "Beezness is rotten. As matter of fact, day by each and more by better I'm getting less by day and more by night!"

JAMES GLEASON
May 23, 1886–April 12, 1959

There were plenty of roles for James Gleason, a man whose lessons in life seemed written on his face. There was a feisty glint in his eye that could signal both amusement and wariness. His tongue seemed firmly in his cheek as he appraised the latest comic problem confronting him, sagely choosing a reaction somewhere between quiet determination and doleful exasperation.

The warm, indulgent side of his comic persona was best seen in *The Yellow Cab Man*, as he played the patient old cabbie who tolerated

Red Skelton's painful slap-stick mistakes. The crankier, slow-burning side could be observed in *The Penguin Pool Murder Case* and *The Plot Thickens,* two of the thirties movies in which he played the chagrined lawman Oscar Piper. With many a head shake and sigh, he had to follow amateur sleuth Hildegard Withers (Edna May Oliver) through her crime solving escapades.

JAMES GLEASON, glib, sarcastic, often caustic, and here over-dressed as he interrupts monocled (?) Lawrence Grant's bath in *Clear All Wires.*

Born in New York, Gleason developed an inter-est in show business from his parents, who had their own stock company. His wife, Lucile, also came from a show business family, and when they married in 1906, they joined her father in a touring vaudeville act. They ended up in Oregon for sev-eral years, performing in a variety of plays. Gleason began writing some himself. Then they moved to Broadway.

Gleason wrote and starred in several Broadway productions includ-ing *Is Zat So?* (1925) and *The Shannons of Broadway* (1927). He also wrote *Rain or Shine* (1928) and *Puffy* (1928). When he came to Holly-wood, he cowrote several films including a version of his Broadway show *Fall Guy* (1930), *Beyond Victory* (1931), *The Bowery* (1933), and *Change of Heart* (1934). But soon he would become better known for his long-suffering and hotly simmering character roles.

Though he often played thankless roles, the wiry, streetwise little guy with the grayish white hair and thin mustache did get some appreci-ation for all his supporting roles. He received an Academy Award nomi-nation for *Here Comes Mr. Jordan* and even had his own short-lived film

SELECTED BROADWAY APPEARANCES:
Charm School (1920), *Like a King* (1921), *The Deep Tangled Wildwood* (1923), *The Lady Killer* (1924), *Is Zat So?* (1925), *Lambs Gambol* (1925), *The Shannons of Broad-way* (1928)

SELECTED FILM APPEARANCES:
Polly of the Follies (1922), *The Flying Fool* (1929), *The Swellhead* (1930), *Puttin' On the Ritz* (1930), *Blondie of the Follies* (1932), *The Penguin Pool Murder* (1932), *The Plot Thickens* (1936), *Forty Naughty Girls* (1937), *The Higgins Family* (1938), *On Your Toes* (1939), *Here Comes Mr. Jordan* (1941), *Arsenic and Old Lace* (1944), *Once Upon a Time* (1944), *The Bishop's Wife* (1947), *The Life of Riley* (1949), *The Yellow Cab Man* (1950), *We're Not Married* (1952), *The Last Hurrah* (1958)

BERT GORDON, Eddie Cantor's favorite "Russian" preparing to lay on a definitive "How do you do!!!"

comedy series at budget-minded Republic Studios. It was called *The Higgins Family.*

In the forties, things were rough for Gleason's own family. On Christmas Day, 1945, his son, a sergeant in the Signal Corps, fell to his death from a hotel window. Lucile Gleason died of a heart attack in 1947, but James (always "Jimmy" to his fans) continued on, appearing in some of his most memorable roles: *The Life of Riley, The Yellow Cab Man, We're Not Married,* and a year before his death, *The Last Hurrah.*

BERT GORDON
*Barney Gorodetsky, 1898–
November 30, 1974.*

His catchphrase was a heavily-accented enthusiastic greeting of "How do you do!" Only Bert Gordon, nicknamed "The Mad Russian," would be so simultaneously friendly but aggressive.

Born not in Russia but in New York City, Gordon was literally a stagestruck kid. At twelve, he was part of vaudeville's "The Stage Struck Kids." Two years later, he joined another kid act, "The Newsboy Sextette," which included Walter Winchell and Bert Wheeler. Then he was one of "The Nine Crazy Kids" that featured Bert Lahr and Jack Pearl. After that, he decreased the numbers. He teamed with his brother Harry for a while, then went out as a single.

It was on radio's *Eddie Cantor Show* that he achieved his fame, appearing for over a decade as the "Mad Russian," neatly countering the blandly high-pitched star: "How do you do!" "Russian, what are you doing here?" "I am a travel agent. In fact, traveling is mine hobo." "You don't mean hobo, you mean hobby." "You travel on your salary, I'll travel on mine!"

The Mad Russian's charm incorporated many aspects of Jewish comedy. Gruffness would suddenly give way to a shrug of surprise or conciliation. An act of foolishness would get, instead of a scolding, his knowing, grandfatherly catchphrase, "Silly boy!" Ultimately, his "madness" was more wide-eyed confusion and eccentricity.

Cantor always addressed Gordon simply as "Russian," which had to have been annoying to any Russians listening. After all, Mrs. Nussbaum, Amos and Andy, and Fibber McGee never were identified solely by a one-word racial greeting. Then again, the Mad Russian wasn't much on language: "Russian, I bet you don't even know the alphabet!" "I don't know what? I'll show you! A, B, C!" "Go on." "There's more?"

One of the biggest laughs in the stellar *Thank Your Lucky Stars* was Gordon's brief cameo. As a patient under a sheet, all he did was rise from the bed, his eyes bulging, his ears sticking out, his black mop of fluffy hair billowing in all directions. "How do you DO!" he cried, like an insane Jack-in-the-Box.

The method to Gordon's "madness" worked well for sharp walk-ons and brief guest roles. He could get worked up in one minute, then shrug in resignation the next. The third minute? That belonged to somebody else. Gordon was well-remembered for his film bits and his many radio appearances on a wide variety of shows. Through the Cold War of the fifties and the menace of Khrushchev, there was still one "Mad Russian" who could raise a smile. One of Gordon's last TV appearances was in a mid-sixties episode of *The Dick Van Dyke Show* in an episode saluting old-time radio comedy.

SELECTED FILM APPEARANCES:
New Faces of 1937 (1937), *Outside of Paradise* (1938), *Sing for Your Supper* (1941), *She Gets Her Man* (1945)

COLLECTIBLES:
Bert Gordon is "The Mad Russian" opposite Joe Penner on the compilation album *Jest Like Old Times* (Radiola) and battles Eddie Cantor on *Son of Jest Like Old Times* (Radiola). He also plays "Colonel Pickling" in the Jewish parody album *My Fairfax Lady* (Jubilee Records) opposite Joel Gray.

GALE GORDON
Charles T. Aldrich, Jr., February 2, 1906

One of the favorite targets of sitcom stars, young (Dennis the Menace) and young at heart (Lucille Ball), Gale Gordon played stuffy bankers, rule-obsessed school principals, and humorously glowering, slow-burning curmudgeons.

His father, Charles T. Aldrich, was a vaudevillian who once played the Palace on Broadway in 1928. His mother, Gloria Gordon, was a performer as well. Her long career included the role of Mrs. O'Reilly on *My Friend Irma* and cameos as one of the elderly members of the Jack Benny fan club on Jack's TV show.

After some work on Broadway, notably in *The Daughters of Atreus* in 1936, Gordon became a regular on radio, playing "Flash Gordon" and later the district attorney in *Big Town*. In comedy, Gordon developed an officious and unctuous character, as exemplified by Mayor La Trivia on *Fibber McGee and Molly*, Rumson Bullard on *The Great Gildersleeve*, and Rudolph Atterbury on Lucille Ball's series *My Favorite Husband*. Gordon came by his measured speech pattern as a child. After surgery on his cleft palate he needed to take lessons in enunciation.

Gordon's first TV sitcom was *Our Miss Brooks*, playing the school principal, Osgood Conklin. He was doing Conklin at the same time Lucille Ball wanted him for the part of Fred Mertz on *I Love Lucy*. Gor-

GALE GORDON, invariably glowering in disgust as Lucille Ball's favorite television foil.

don had to turn Lucy down. After replacing the late Joseph Kearns as George Wilson's brother, John, on *Dennis the Menace,* Gordon earned his most lasting fame by spending a decade groaning, wringing his hands, and casting his eyes to the heavens as Lucille Ball's long-suffering boss, banker Theodore J. Mooney, on *The Lucy Show.*

Gordon cast a cocked, disapproving eye at various comedy stars in his film appearances but was soon typed as Mr. Mooney as the years with Lucy rolled by. On *The Lucy Show* and then on *Here's Lucy,* now playing her brother-in-law, Harrison Carter, he was forever doomed to participate in Lucy's well-intentioned but hairbrained schemes. It got worse over the years. Early in *The Lucy Show,* Mr. Mooney was president of Connecticut's Danfield First National Bank and Lucy just a customer. The format changed and, at San Francisco Westland Bank, she was now his secretary!

It was all sweet suffering. Either Gordon's "banker character" was true to life, or he grew into it—Gordon became the head of the Chamber of Commerce in his adopted town of Borrego Springs, California, and was even elected mayor. When Lucy decided to try another sitcom, *Life With Lucy* in 1986, she coaxed Gordon out of retirement to costar. He explained to writer Richard Lamparski that he had no great aspirations as an actor, especially that late in his career. "I have no regrets...but I also have no illusions about my capabilities. A Hamlet I never was. From time to time someone needs a character actor who can yell. That's my specialty, yelling—at stars, mostly." There was one woman he didn't yell at: his wife, Virginia Curley. In one of his last stage appearances, he and she costarred in a stock production of *On Golden Pond.*

SELECTED FILM APPEARANCES:
Here We Go Again (1942), *A Woman of Distinction* (1950), *Rally Round the Flag, Boys* (1958), *Don't Give Up the Ship* (1959), *Visit to a Small Planet* (1960), *All Hands on Deck* (1961), *Sergeant Deadhead* (1965), *Speedway* (1968)

TELEVISION SERIES:
Our Miss Brooks (1952–56), *The Brothers* (1956–57), *Sally* (1958), *Pete and Gladys* (1960–62), *Dennis the Menace* (1962–63), *The Lucy Show* (1963–68), *Here's Lucy* (1968–74), *Life With Lucy* (1986)

CHARLOTTE GREENWOOD

*Frances Charlotte Greenwood,
June 25, 1893–
January 18, 1978*

CHARLOTTE GREENWOOD, the long-legged eccentric dancer and comic sidekick, impersonates Carmen Miranda as Edward Everett Horton does some fishing in *Springtime in the Rockies*.

As the self-proclaimed "only woman in the world who can kick a giraffe in the face," the tall and leggy Charlotte Greenwood was a major star on stage. From 1909 to 1912 she was paired with little Eunice Burnham in a musical comedy act. Next, she sang and eccentricly danced with Sidney Grant. At five-foot-ten she could fling a high kick over the head of her five-foot-two partner.

After playing Letitia (Letty) Proudfoot in the 1914 Broadway hit *Pretty Mrs. Smith,* she appeared in five stage sequels between 1915 and 1935. Letty's personality was evident in this little ditty: "I may not be so pretty, and I don't dress like a queen./I may not be so witty, I am over sweet sixteen./My fame is not my fortune. It looks like the morning after./But I still maintain that I retain–bing bing! My girlish laughter!"

Charlotte was charming with her bright round eyes, wispy blond hair, and puckish little smile. She was not the ingenue, not with her long body, long face, and long nose, but even in her later support roles in film comedies she was far from the stereotyped homely man-chaser.

In the twenties Greenwood played the Palace on Broadway in vaudeville sketches like "Movieland" and "Her Morning Bath." The latter was about a woman taking a bath and getting ready for a job interview—only to run into problems with the meter reader, the iceman, and ultimately a burglar.

The plain-looking, high-kicking comedienne toured the world, landing in Hollywood where her eccentric style served as comic contrast to many shorter and less ebullient comedians. From a series of short subjects for Educational Pictures in the mid-thirties she went on to cast a disapproving eye at Eddie Cantor in drag in *Palmy Days* and tried to arouse Buster Keaton in *Parlor, Bedroom and Bath.* Featured in only the last third of that film, she provided many of its highlights with her hilarious comic choreography, stomping about in a hotel room, hoisting her legs over the sofa, and trying desperately to teach love-shy Buster the art of seduction.

Charlotte played Betty Grable's pal in *Springtime in the Rockies,* a film that featured one of Greenwood's inimitable dance routines. Greenwood's talent continued to amaze other comics. Groucho Marx was in attendance at a White House gathering where Charlotte entertained with her comic high kicks. Turning to Eleanor Roosevelt, Groucho said, "That's what you could do if you just put your mind to it."

Capable of verbal comedy as well as dance acrobatics, Greenwood appeared on radio in the forties with *Life With Charlotte* and *The Charlotte Greenwood Show.* She toured for two years in *I Remember Mama* and played Aunt Eller in the film version of *Oklahoma!* Nearly forty years after she first amused Broadway audiences, Greenwood was back, costarring in *Out of This World.* She nearly walked out of it, though, declaring that times had changed and Cole Porter's lyrics were awfully risqué. She retired to work for the Christian Science Church.

ALAN HALE, JR., hefty and happy, spending time with good little buddy Bob Denver and lovely Tina Louise in *Gilligan's Island.*

ALAN HALE, JR.
March 8, 1918–
January 2, 1990

For much of his movie career, Alan Hale Jr. played the same parts as his father—gentle giants. Alan was often the sidekick to an adventure hero, just as Alan Hale Sr. was. Hale Sr. played Little John in *Robin Hood* (1922), *The Adventures of Robin Hood* (1938), and *Rogues of Sherwood Forest* (1950). After his father's death in 1950, and looking quite a bit like him, Hale Jr. began appearing regularly in action films. He didn't play comic parts at first, but was just another brawny extra, as in *It Happens Every Spring,* as a college baseball player trying to hit a few doctored balls off Ray Milland.

He had the lead on the early spy TV show *Biff Baker,* then played the smiling railroader *Casey Jones.* He recalled, "I thought Casey Jones was a nice character and the program was entertaining, but we didn't seem to click. We were betwixt and between [making] Casey for adults or for kids. Apparently it showed."

Six years later, Hale tried out for the role of Jonas Grumby, "The Skipper" on *Gilligan's Island.* The part was originally planned for an actor named Carroll O'Connor. Hale was hearty, perfect for the Oliver Hardy-ish role. While the stare into the camera was pure Ollie, most of Hale's other mannerisms were pure jolly—especially his catchphrase, a robust "Hi little buddy!" to mousy little Gilligan. Hale's cartoonish versions of the slow-burn, the exasperated grimace, and the melt from happy smile to wan disbelief all delighted young viewers. They appreciated his softened, cheerful version of an authority figure. As on *Casey Jones,* most wondered whether the show was intended for adults or kids. Adult critics hated it, but it's since enjoyed two decades of reruns as a daytime kid's show.

Hale followed *Gilligan's Island* with *The Good Guys* (again with Bob "Gilligan" Denver), but, like several members of the *Gilligan's Island* cast, found himself forever typed for his role on the show. For a guest appearance on a *Batman* episode, starring Vincent Price, Hale had a cameo as the proprietor of "Gilligan's Restaurant."

Hale ended up at a California restaurant called "The Lobster Barrel," now serving as a "good will greeter." His latter day acting roles were mostly in *Gilligan's Island* specials and reunions. Married with two daughters and a son, he voiced no complaints about his acting career: "I've had a wonderful time in the business. It's shown me the world and introduced me to great people." When he died, costar Tina Louise recalled, "He had that great warmth, great smile—he was the original Santa Claus."

SELECTED FILM APPEARANCES:
All-American Coed (1942), *To the Shores of Tripoli* (1942), *Thank Your Lucky Stars* (1943), *Monsieur Beaucaire* (1946), *One Sunday Afternoon* (1948), *It Happens Every Spring* (1949), *Kill the Umpire* (1950), *The Gunfighter* (1950), *The Big Trees* (1952), *The Rogue Cop* (1954), *The Indian Fighter* (1955), *The Lady Takes a Flyer* (1957), *North Avenue Irregulars* (1978), *The Fifth Musketeer* (1979), *Hambone and Hillie* (1983)

TELEVISION SERIES:
Biff Baker, USA (1952–53), *Casey Jones* (1958), *Gilligan's Island* (1964–67), *The Good Guys* (1969)

CHARLES HALL always expected the worst from Laurel and Hardy, and got it. He's peevish over the boys' mischief in *Leave 'Em Laughing.*

CHARLES HALL
August 19, 1899–
April 13, 1959

Like his friend Stan Laurel, Charles Hall was born in England and schooled in comedy in Fred Karno's vaudeville troupe. In America, Hall became one of Laurel and Hardy's most enduring antagonists, appearing in forty-seven films with the duo. He worked with some other film comedians as well— Buster Keaton, Wheeler and Woolsey, even Abbott and Costello. Rarely did he get to display the comic venom he showed Laurel and Hardy. In W. C. Fields's *Million Dollar Legs* he had a very minor role as one of the Olympic athletes from Klopstokia.

Hall often played a mean-tempered little guy, which for comic purposes meant he was matched against huge Oliver Hardy. He usually had good reason to be ticked off. In *Tit for Tat*, he thinks Ollie has dallied with his wife. After all, he's just seen Ollie come out of his wife's bedroom window laughing and saying, "I've never been in a position like *that* before!" Of course it was all a sitcom mistake— and little Charlie is ready to bully the bigger but softer and rounder Ollie.

The little bulldog won't mount an all-out attack, he just wants to take a bite out of his giant foe, a nippy little show of bravado. Charlie slashes Ollie's hat. Ollie in turn throws potato salad at Charlie. Charlie snaps an electrical appliance onto Ollie's nose and zaps it. Ultimately Charlie is subjected to a raw egg shampoo, tought a final lesson in a game of one-upmanship he should never have started.

Unlike the more cartoonish foes of Laurel and Hardy (James Finlayson, Billy Gilbert, and perennial cop Edgar Kennedy), Hall looked like an average guy and was cast in scenes that showed how even an average guy (delivery boy in *Twice Two*, desk clerk in *Snaps at Sea*) could become exasperated with Stan and Ollie. In *Come Clean* he's at the ice cream counter seething at having to announce the flavors available— and hearing requests for everything else: "We're *out* of orange, *goose*-berry, and chocolate!"

It was Hall who, in *Battle of the Century*, set off the most memorable pie fight in movie history. After taking a tumble thanks to Ollie, Hall smashes him in the face with a pie, leading to another, and another. That was Hall's role in so many Laurel and Hardy films: strike or be struck.

Hall worked in movie comedies for over twenty years and even turned up on television occasionally: briefly in an episode of *The Abbott and Costello Show* (called "The Fall Guy") and as a contestant on Groucho Marx's *You Bet Your Life*.

SELECTED FILM APPEARANCES:
(shorts) *Battle of the Century* (1927), *Leave 'Em Laughing* (1928), *Two Tars* (1928), *Wrong Again* (1929), *Double Whoopie* (1929), *Angora Love* (1929), *Below Zero* (1930), *Laughing Gravy* (1930), *Come Clean* (1931), *Any Old Port* (1932), *The Music Box* (1932), *Twice Two* (1933), *Tit for Tat* (1934),*The Live Ghost* (1935), *Thicker Than Water* (1935), *Our Relations* (1936); (features) *Sons of the Desert* (1933), *Cock-eyed Cavaliers* (1934), *Kentucky Kernals* (1934), *Pick a Star* (1937), *Saps at Sea* (1940), *One Night in the Tropics* (1940)

COLLECTIBLES:
British writer Ray Andrew's self-published book, *On the Trail of Charles Hall,* collects interviews from those who remembered Hall during his vaudeville and movie days. The book was often sold at *Sons of the Desert* conventions.

THURSTON HALL
May 10, 1882–February 20, 1958

A heavy-set character man who usually played humorously pompous senators, doggedly dignified businessmen, and gruff fathers, Thurston Hall blustered his way through small roles in dozens of films. As soon as he appeared, he easily set the tone for a scene: the hero was never in serious trouble because Hall's throat-clearing, jowly consternation, and windy posturing clearly showed that behind the authority figure was a muddled slow-thinker who could be persuaded to do most anything.

Early in his career, Hall was a leading man and a dapper figure with the ladies. Married in 1914, he was divorced in 1926 after his wife claimed he had deserted her three years earlier. The sordid tale of the Broadway actor's flings made the local newspapers. His wife told reporters, "Shortly after he left, I went to the Taft Hotel in New Haven and found him living there with another woman. When I discovered this he said to me, 'I have a kink in my brain. I wish I knew what is making me do this to you. You have been the best

THURSTON HALL, out of his banker pinstripes and into cowboy garb for a change of pace.

wife in the world.'"

In the twenties, Hall earned up to $20,000 a year on Broadway. When he played Senator Cassius Clayborn in the 1926 hit *Still Water,* critic Alexander Woollcott raved, "He succeeds in capturing the very aroma of an American politician." Hall won praise as Jake Smith in the Don Marquis comedy *Everything's Jake* and moved out to Hollywood for ripe cameo roles that seemed to hark back to Senator Cassius Clayborn. He played a good-natured, befuddled senator in *Sherlock Holmes Goes to Washington.* He's only mildly surprised to be in the midst of a murder case. When the murderer is revealed right in front of his eyes, he offers one of his hearty, impersonal congratulations: "You're a smart fella, Holmes." Then it's back to business.The ultimate businessman, Hall amused a new generation when he moved on to television in the early fifties. His best role was as the crusty soul of dignity and propriety, bank president Humphrey Schuyler, forever dismayed at the lighthearted antics of his vice-president, Cosmo Topper, in the *Topper* series.

MARGARET HAMILTON
December 9, 1902–May 16, 1985

Margaret Hamilton said that in her career in comic support, she generally played "a cantankerous cook or acidulous aunt with a corset of steel and a heart of gold." She played a variety of spinsters, some puritanical and snippy, others merely gruff. Her defining role as the witch in *The Wizard of Oz* was really just another spinster part, one that gave her a chance to utter some very amusing lines. How many truly evil witches would chortle, as they're melting to death, "What a world, what a world!"

A kindergarten teacher from Cleveland, Hamilton began her stage career at the Cleveland Playhouse. Shortly after, she put together a one-woman show, dubbed "A program of Charm and Comedy. Heartrending and Humorous Songs of 1840, 1890, 1929." She performed parodies of 1840-styled art singers ("The Bird of Spring" by O. W. Withington), sang campy 1890s tunes ("Don't Swat Your Mother, It's Mean" and "She's More to Be Pitied Than Censured") and sent up 1929's radio fare with songs ("Moanin' Low") and satire ("featuring Winnie and Freddie, the Ever Ready Underwear Twins.") Years later

Hamilton recalled that "the whole thing was put together with spit and prayer, and I did it at various lunches and clubs and ladies luncheons and they all thought it was lovely."

She appeared as Betty the Housekeeper for three years on the radio serial *Doctor's Wife* and spent another three as Aunt Effie on *The Couple Next Door*. She had a successful stage role as a grape-eating eccentric in *Another Language* on Broadway, and moved on to films. With her slim face, long nose, and pursed lips, she was the embodiment of prissiness and sourness, playing parts in a variety of classic comedies from *Nothing Sacred* to *Mad Wednesday* (as Harold Lloyd's unwed sister), facing off against comedy teams Fields and West (*My Little Chickadee*) and Abbott and Costello (*Comin' Round the Mountain*).

She played so many housekeeper and maid roles that of her predictable role in the film *Twin Beds* she told a reporter, "I just never get my man. Everybody makes everybody else but I still make beds!" She added, "The only time the movie moguls allowed me a bit of romance was in *Stablemates* when I made eyes at Wallace Beery. But my obvious ogling was obviously unsuccessful!"

Over the years, "Spinster" Hamilton (in real life she was married until 1938 and had a son, now a successful financial adviser in the Far East) continued to play maids and cooks, and in the sixties turned up as a parody of a proper "Republican old lady" on episodes of *That Was*

MARGARET HAMILTON, screen spinster nonpareil and filmdom's most famous witch.

SELECTED BROADWAY APPEARANCES:
Another Language (1932), *Dark Tower* (1933), *The Farmer Takes a Wife* (1934), *Outrageous Fortune* (1943), *The Men We Marry* (1948), *Fancy Meeting You Again* (1952), *Annie Get Your Gun* (1958), *Goldilocks* (1958), *Save Me a Place at Forest Lawn* (1963), *Show Boat* (1966), *Oklahoma!* (1969), *Our Town* (1969), *The Devil's Disciple* (1970)

SELECTED FILM APPEARANCES:
Chatterbox (1936), *Laughing at Trouble* (1937), *You Only Live Once* (1937), *Nothing Sacred* (1937), *A Slight Case of Murder* (1938), *The Adventures of Tom Sawyer* (1938), *Mother Carey's Chickens* (1938), *The Wizard of Oz* (1939), *Angels Wash Their Faces* (1939), *My Little Chickadee* (1940), *The Villain Still Pursued Her* (1940), *The Invisible Woman* (1940), *George White's Scandals* (1945), *Janie Gets Married* (1946), *Faithful in My Fashion* (1946), *Mad Wednesday* (1947), *Texas, Brooklyn and Heaven* (1948), *The Red Pony* (1949), *People Will Talk* (1951), *Comin' Round the Mountain* (1951), *Thirteen Ghosts* (1960), *Rosie!* (1968), *Angel in My Pocket* (1969), *The Anderson Tapes* (1971), *Brewster McCloud* (1971), *Journey Back to Oz* (voice) (1974)

TELEVISION SERIES:
Ethel and Albert (1953–56)

the Week That Was. She was in the touring companies of many popular shows (notably *A Little Night Music* in the seventies) and had a second career in TV commercials, playing "Cora," the spunky spinster with a penchant for telling every friend and neighbor about Maxwell House coffee. She lived on Gramercy Park in New York and was fond of local stage work until a broken hip curtailed her career in 1981. She had been rehearsing a new play at the time, *Kudzu.*

Of her fame in *The Wizard of Oz,* she said, "I don't resent it at all, but there are other things I'd rather be remembered for. And I do wish parents wouldn't allow any child under five to see it. It gives them nightmares. I didn't allow my own son to see it until he was nine." She was always tolerant of fans who pointed her out as "the witch," and fans who simply pointed her out as somebody they thought they knew: "People remember my face, even if they don't remember my name. They have to remember my face. Who could forget it?"

RICHARD HAYDN, who brought screen prissiness to a high art.

RICHARD HAYDN
March 10, 1905–April 25, 1985

A British character actor noted for his comically severe looks and the foolish pomp of his affectations, Richard Haydn was generally cast as butlers, prissy neighbors, or snooty eccentrics. He got a lot of mileage from his stares, sulks, and the exquisite ripeness of his flutey nasal voice. In *And Then There Were None* he plays the butler, the soul of decorum even as his dinner guests are being murdered one by one. Noting the depleted ranks, he asks mournfully, but with a trace of pique, "How many of you will be for dinner tonight?"

When the guests become suspicious of him, wondering if the butler actually did it, his reactions—wounded sullenness, offended distress, and a few whining words of doubtful dignity—gave the film its needed comic relief.

Haydn worked in a secretarial job with London's Gaiety Theatre before venturing on stage in 1926 as a chorus boy in *Betty in Mayfair.* He later appeared in *This Year of Grace* by Noel Coward, and starred in a two-man drag act playing an opera diva. Finding limited success, he left show business for some very odd jobs, including the supervision of a banana plantation in Jamaica. After a hurricane wrecked the place, Haydn joined local theatrical companies and made his way back to England where he developed a new solo act as "Mr. Carp," a fish imitator. The silly fellow, all seriousness in his demand for quiet attention, would plant his feet firmly heel to heel (to steady himself), take a deep breath, and suddenly transform his intense features into a ridiculous mouth-gaping fish face.

He arrived on Broadway in 1939 for a Coward revue *Set to Music,* and followed it with *Two for the Show.* In both productions he offered monologues and absurd comic poems as Mr. Carp. Haydn soon mounted his film career which extended into the sixties. He was a favorite in small comic parts but did win critics over with his serious role in *The Green Years.* He also directed a few films: *Miss Tatlock's Millions, Dear Wife,* and *Mr. Music.* Haydn lent his voice to the caterpillar in *Alice in Wonderland* and went on to schoolmaster and headmaster parts in *Her Twelve Men, Toy Tiger,* and *Clarence the Cross-Eyed Lion.* His last part was a cameo as a messenger in *Young Frankenstein.*

In the sixties Haydn sometimes appeared on TV. He played an arrogant writer with a complex against machines on *The Twilight Zone.* On an episode of *The Dick Van Dyke Show* he reprised his "Mr. Carp" routine. He also performed a recitation about his confrontation with a bully, telling of staring the ruffian down with a well-aimed cry of "Who cares for you?" Naturally, this stopped the bully. Briefly: "And then he hit me!"

SELECTED BROADWAY APPEARANCES:
Set to Music (1939), *Two for the Show* (1940)

SELECTED FILM APPEARANCES:
Charley's Aunt (1941), *Ball of Fire* (1941), *Forever and a Day* (1943), *And Then There Were None* (1945), *Cluny Brown* (1946), *The Green Years* (1946), *Singapore* (1947), *Forever Amber* (1947), *The Late George Apley* (1947), *Sitting Pretty* (1948), *Alice in Wonderland* (voice) (1951), *The Merry Widow* (1952), *Her Twelve Men* (1954), *Jupiter's Darling* (1955), *Toy Tiger* (1956), *Please Don't Eat the Daisies* (1960), *Five Weeks in a Balloon* (1962), *The Sound of Music* (1965), *Clarence the Cross-Eyed Lion* (1965), *The Adventures of Bullwhip Griffin* (1967), *Young Frankenstein* (1974)

COLLECTIBLE:
The Journal of Edwin Carp, a book by Haydn

GEORGE "GABBY" HAYES
George Frances Hayes, May 7, 1885–February 9, 1969

A New Yorker who became the prototype for dozens of grizzled old Western sidekicks, George Hayes worked in vaudeville as a singer and dancer and had a varied career in character parts before he clicked as comedy relief. He won chuckles in a series of John Wayne Westerns for Monogram. He was called "Windy" when he joined William Boyd's *Hopalong Cassidy* series and turned into "Gabby" when he joined Roy Rogers at Republic.

He was a tough old cuss. "My name is Cactus, mister," he said in *In Old Santa Fe,* "and don't you forget that I'm prickly!"

Hayes made over one hundred Westerns, including *Trail Street,* one of several with Randolph Scott. "You talk about winds and cyclones," he enthuses in it. "One time the wind blew so hard it blew the chicken feathers right off the chickens onto the ducks and the duck

GEORGE "GABBY" HAYES, ornery Western sidekick of sidekicks.

feathers onto the chickens! Funniest thing you ever saw, to hear them ducks crowin' and the chickens quackin'!" He always lived up to his "Gabby" nickname.

Hayes won over new fans with a kiddie TV show in 1950, telling tales about the Old West and introducing guests like his pal Roy Rogers. The older he got, the funnier he became, with his squinty eyes, random teeth, scruffy gray beard, and catchphrase "You're darn tootin'!"

In real life Hayes took pains to distance himself from his screen character. Said costar Kirby (*Sky King*) Grant: "He was very serious minded...an extremely dapper dresser, beautiful clothes. His beard was beautifully trimmed and he kept his teeth in when he wasn't making a picture."

He could still be an ornery cuss. Late in his career, when asked to reflect on all those golden Westerns he made, Hayes snapped, "I hate 'em. Simply can't stand 'em. They always are the same, you have so few plots—the stagecoach holdup, the rustler, the mortgage gag, the mine setting, and the retired gunslinger. Why, I made all those movies and hardly knew I was acting in them."

SELECTED FILM APPEARANCES:
Smiling Irish Eyes (1929), *Riders of the Desert* (1932), *Texas Buddies* (1932), *The Fighting Champ* (1932), *Sagebrush Trail* (1933), *The Gallant Fool* (1933), *The Man From Utah* (1934), *In Old Santa Fe* (1934), *Tumbling Tumbleweeds* (1935), *The Hoosier Schoolmaster* (1935), *Bar 20 Rides Again* (1935), *The Plainsman* (1936), *Mr. Deeds Goes to Town* (1936), *Hopalong Cassidy Returns* (1936), *Bar 20 Justice* (1938), *The Arizona Kid* (1939), *Young Bill Hickok* (1940), *The Melody Ranch* (1940), *Calling Wild Bill Elliott* (1943), *Marshal of Reno* (1944), *Don't Fence Me In* (1945), *Song of Arizona* (1946), *Badman's Territory* (1946), *My Pal Trigger* (1946), *Wyoming* (1947), *Return of the Badmen* (1948), *Albuquerque* (1948), *El Paso* (1949), *Cariboo Trail* (1950)

TELEVISION SERIES:
The Gabby Hayes Show (1950–54)

HUGH HERBERT
August 10, 1887–March 12, 1952

HUGH HERBERT, silly giggler who made "woo woo" good for a laugh.

Hugh Herbert's mannerisms are famous—but usually not associated with Hugh Herbert. His fluttery finger movements became a Huntz Hall trademark. His own excited little cry of "woo woo!" was surpassed by Curly Howard's. And his grandfatherly charm and perplexed raised eyebrows seemed mild compared to the cartoonish Ed Wynn.

Herbert, who hailed from Binghamton, New York, did not become a major comedian because he looked fairly normal and didn't exaggerate his mannerisms. But precisely because he was only a mild eccentric, he was always at work in comic support roles, lending a little mild mayhem to movie musicals and other star's comedies.

Herbert could play all kinds of parts: a censor (*Footlight Parade*), the Secretary of the Treasury (*Million Dollar Legs*), or a preoccupied poet (*The Perfect Specimen*). He appeared in a few Wheeler and Woolsey films, playing a detective in *Hook, Line and Sinker* and a sea captain in *Diplomaniacs*.

Though he always managed to throw his "woo woo" giggle into his roles, his characters were believably silly. In *Gold Diggers of 1935* he was an authority on snuff who noted, "I work till my brain gets fogged." Of his hobby, he insisted: "Snuff is not to be sneezed at!" As the good-natured poet in *The Perfect Specimen* he announced, "My wife has great taste. She left me! Woo woo!"

His "woo woo" got a workout in *Gold Diggers in Paris,* where, as a Frenchman, he cries, "These American people are so peculiar! Woo woo!" By the time the film ends, Rudy Vallee and even a talking dog are "woo wooing" too.

Quite often directors used his laugh as punctuation for a scene. He'd poke his head in a doorway, eye what was going on, tilt his eyes upward and "woo woo!" He played a silly gumshoe in Olsen and Johnson's *Hellzapoppin* who regularly popped up just to take a closer look at the proceedings. Through camera trickery the detective could change his disguises instantly just by ducking behind a tree. "Don't ask me how I do it, folks!" Hugh grinned.

Occasionally Herbert was tested with meatier roles. He was "Snout" in the 1935 *Midsummer Night's Dream,* and played five different drag roles in *La Conga Nights*—as a mother and four sisters! He even had his own series of shorts for Columbia in the forties. His costars were a blond leading lady (Christine McIntyre) and an eye-popping black sidekick (Dudley Dickerson), both regulars in Columbia's *Three Stooges* shorts.

Hugh was witty in private life. He was puffing a cigar at the Friar's Club when insult comic Jack E. Leonard got a whiff of it. As the smoke billowed, Jack griped, "Don't you ever inhale?" Said Herbert: "Not with *you* in the room."

Often used as an eccentric extra attraction, not a star, Hugh Herbert would never make it into *Who's Who,* but he certainly knew how to "woo woo!"

STERLING HOLLOWAY
January 4, 1905–November 23, 1992

S terling Holloway's voice had all the power of a moth trying to flutter off a sticky marshmallow. But it was that high husky voice, prone to occasional flute-like squeaks, that made him famous. He used it in many Walt Disney cartoons, portraying Kaa the snake in *The Jungle Book,* Roquefort the mouse in *The Aristocats,* and lovable *Winnie the Pooh.*

In live-action films, the drawling comedian from Cedartown, Georgia, usually played bumpkins—wide-eyed, wild-haired stringbeans. When he didn't, he played eccentric parts: the frog in the all-star 1933 version of *Alice in Wonderland* and a plum tree in *The Blue Bird* in 1940. For *International House* he played a dancing sailor, doing a few eccentric steps as he serenades an Oriental sweetheart. Meanwhile the chorus sings: "She was a Japanese tea cup—and he was just a mug."

As a delivery boy in *Gold Diggers of 1933* all Holloway had to do was stand in the doorway and let the camera focus on his silly face— the pursed lips, the big ears, unruly shock of fluffy hair, and simple-minded gaze. That got a laugh. Then he had a line of dialogue. A chorus girl hands him a five dollar tip and says, "Buy yourself a yacht." The rube twitters, "Oh! But I get SO seasick!" Though he occasionally played a substantial role, Holloway's goofy looks and silly voice made him a quick "human joke" for walk-ons. He recalled, "I delivered so many telegrams and jerked so many sodas I got tired of it."

In *Look Who's Laughing,* he plays Rusty, a jerky soda jerk, waiting on Charlie McCarthy, who is guzzling sodas as if they were beers, trying to drown an aching heart. Charlie's been jilted and Holloway sympathizes: "Ain't women awful? What fools we morons be!"

Holloway got very tired of playing the fool. It wasn't what he'd envisioned after he had first gotten some good notices on Broadway in the 1925 *Garrick Gaieties* revue. The 1926 edition featured an early tune by a promising duo named Rodgers and Hart, and it was Holloway who sang it: "Mountain Greenery." While he was beloved for his little comic turns in films and his funny faces and funny voice, he wanted an opportunity to play a good dramatic role, or at least win some serious critical attention.

STERLING HOLLOWAY, wistful rube with the flutey voice, never got the girl on screen and was lucky even to be next to her (here she's Lynne Roberts in *Saddle Pals*).

SELECTED BROADWAY APPEARANCES:
Evil Doers of Good (1923), *The Failures* (1923), *Roseanne* (1923), *Fata Morgana* (1924), *Garrick Gaieties* (1925), *Get Me in the Movies* (1928), *The Shoestring Revue* (1928), *Garrick Gaieties* (1930), *A Midsummer Night's Dream* (1934), *The Grass Harp* (1952)

SELECTED FILM APPEARANCES:
(shorts) *Not the Marrying Kind* (1933), *Heartburn* (1934), *Sterling's Rival Romeo* (1934), *Double Crossed* (1935), *Bring 'Em Back a Lie* (1935), *Mr. Wright Goes Wrong* (1946), *Man or Mouse* (1948) (features) *Casey at the Bat* (1927), *Blonde Venus* (1932), *American Madness* (1932), *Elmer the Great* (1933), *International House* (1933), *Alice in Wonderland* (1933), *Gold Diggers of 1933* (1933), *Dancing Lady* (1933), *The Merry Widow* (1934), *The Gift of Gab* (1934), *Life Begins at Forty* (1935), *Palm Springs* (1936), *The Woman I Love* (1937), *Behind the Mike* (1937), *Professor Beware* (1938), *Look Who's Laughing* (1941), *Dumbo* (voice) (1941), *Bambi* (voice) 1942), *The Lady Is Willing* (1942), *The Three Caballeros* (voice) (1944), *Sioux City Sue* (1946), *Alice in Wonderland* (voice) (1951), *It's a Mad, Mad, Mad, Mad World* (1963), *Winnie the Pooh* (voice) (1966), *Winnie the Pooh and the Honey Tree* (voice) (1964), *The Jungle Book* (voice) (1967), *Live a Little, Love a Little* (1968), *The Aristocats* (voice) (1970), *Won Ton Ton, the Dog Who Saved Hollywood* (1976), *Super Seal* (1976), *Thunder on the Highway* (1977)

TELEVISION SERIES:
The Life of Riley (1953–58), *Willy* (1955), *The Baileys of Balboa* (1964–65)

COLLECTIBLES:
Holloway's charming records include: *Peter and the Wolf* (Disneyland), *Just So Stories* (Disneyland), *The Three Little Pigs* (Disneyland), *Winnie the Pooh* (Disneyland) and *More Mother Goose* (Disneyland)

Now and then Holloway had a chance. Between 1933 and 1935 he starred in a dozen shorts for Universal and in another group for Columbia between 1946 and 1948.

His real breakthrough came with his voice work for Disney, where there was often a touch of pathos to the cartoon characters he did and the critical response to the movies was always enthusiastic. He would forever earn the admiration of the children who grew up watching these memorable Disney cartoons. They also remembered him fondly from the early days of television. Holloway played Waldo Binny on *The Life of Riley* in the early to mid fifties, and was lovably befuddled in several absent-minded professor roles on *Superman* ("Uncle Oscar" in two episodes, "Professor Twiddle" in another). He was also a regular in the 1955 version of *Willy*, a short-lived comedy series. In the sixties he briefly appeared with Paul Ford in *The Baileys of Balboa*.

Through the later years of his career, the lifelong bachelor was more often heard and not seen—re-maining one of the best known and most revered comic voice men at Disney Studios.

EDWARD EVERETT HORTON (right), watches with his typical fey expression as Robert Paige confronts Robert Benchley sneaking into his house in *Her Primitive Man*.

EDWARD EVERETT HORTON
March 18, 1886–
September 29, 1970

A tall and spindly master of fussy mannerisms, including a clucking tongue and a disapproving gaze, Edward Everett Horton appeared in hundreds of films, often as a butler or male secretary. Always worried by any impropriety, Horton was forever raising an eyebrow and uttering impotent little phrases of old maidish consternation like "My word! Well, really!" (to Deanna Durbin in *Lady on a Train*) or "Oh Dear Dear!" (to Fred Astaire in *Top Hat*).

Always driven by a need to do whatever is correct, he won't even act unless he can find the correct word first. In *The Perfect Specimen* he observes that Joan Blondell has crashed her car through a fence. After an "Oh my word!" and a "Dear, Dear!" or two, he babbles his concern: "You're in a pickle! A predicament! A…" "A spot?" "No, no, from the Latin! A dilemma!"

It was a cheeful dilemma for Horton to play these characters. "I have my own little kingdom," he once said. "I do the scavenger parts no one else wants, and I get well paid for it." He probably winked when he said that. A sly grin and a throaty little "heh heh" giggle were also a part of his screen character—to show that the conservative fuss-budget often vicariously enjoyed some of the incorrect, or downright naughty behavior he witnessed.

Born in Brooklyn, Horton made his stage debut in a drag role while a student at Columbia University. He took parts in Gilbert and Sullivan operettas with the Dempsey Light Opera Comedy on Staten Island and from there joined other stock companies. He began producing plays and starred when the parts suited him, alternating roles with his friend Franklin Pangborn.

The thin, six-foot-two actor loved the stage and worked in summer theater productions all through his career. He played his favorite character, Henry Dewlip in *Springtime for Henry,* more than three thousand times in different productions over the years. He began his career in silent films, one of his best, the starring role as the English butler in the 1923 version of *Ruggles of Red Gap.*

SELECTED BROADWAY APPEARANCES:
Among the Married (1929), *Springtime for Henry* (1940), *Carousel* (1965)

SELECTED FILM APPEARANCES:
Too Much Business (1922), *Ruggles of Red Gap* (1923), *The Hottentot* (1929), *Wide Open* (1930), *Kiss Me Again* (1931), *Six Cylinder Love* (1931), *The Front Page* (1931), *Trouble in Paradise* (1932), *Alice in Wonderland* (voice) (1933), *Design for Living* (1933), *Kiss and Make Up* (1934), *The Gay Divorcée* (1934), *Going Highbrow* (1935), *Top Hat* (1935), *His Night Out* (1935), *The Perfect Specimen* (1937), *Lost Horizon* (1937), *Oh Doctor* (1937), *College Swing* (1938), *Holiday* (1938), *Little Tough Guys in Society* (1938), *Ziegfeld Girl* (1941), *Bachelor Daddy* (1941), *Here Comes Mr. Jordan* (1941), *I Married an Angel* (1942), *The Gang's All Here* (1943), *Thank Your Lucky Stars* (1943), *Arsenic and Old Lace* (1944), *Her Primitive Man* (1944), *Earl Carroll's Sketchbook* (1946), *The Ghost Goes Wild* (1947), *The Story of Mankind* (1957), *Pocketful of Miracles* (1961), *It's a Mad, Mad, Mad, Mad World* (1963), *Sex and the Single Girl* (1964), *The Perils of Pauline* (1967), *Cold Turkey* (1970)

TELEVISION SERIES:
Holiday Hotel (1950), *The Bullwinkle Show* (1961–62), *The Cara Williams Show* (1964–65), *F Troop* (1965–67)

In films, Horton was consistent: the fretful fellow with semi-effeminate mannerisms. In *Top Hat* he has a girl, but this worries him: "I met her at the bird house at the zoo...I took her to the cinema, then we had dinner, then I took her to another cinema, and then I fear I forgot myself and let her kiss me!" Ginger Rogers recalled: "Horton was exactly the same as he appeared on the screen. He loved comedy and behaved in a comical manner all the time. Consequently, we couldn't take our eyes off him, for fear of missing the topper to whatever he was doing."

He was the Mad Hatter in *Alice in Wonderland,* fretted over his wife having not one but two lovers in *Design for Living* and played the nervous and grousing comic relief in *Lost Horizon.* Through the forties and fifties he maintained his unique position as the only nattering nuisance that viewers actually enjoyed seeing, his mild fluster more endearing than annoying.

Four decades after he made his silent film debut, Horton's unique voice made him a TV favorite, as narrator of "Fractured Fairy Tales" on *The Bullwinkle Show*. He added his trademark knowing laugh to each story's punny punchline.

Horton was active even into his eighties when his chin was pin-striped with wrinkles and he looked like he was about to fall over. He played the frail head of a tobacco company in *Cold Turkey* and had a memorable continuing role as an ancient Indian chief on TV's *F Troop*. He filmed an episode of *The Governor and J. J.* which ran two weeks after his death.

For years Horton lived placidly with his mother in the San Fernando Valley, collecting a half-million dollars worth of antiques. He maintained the property after her death and sometimes noticed a few fans making a pilgrimage to his house. The address was easy to find—his was the only home on "Edward Everett Horton Lane." He and his brother George had invested wisely in real estate, which included a huge tract of property Horton puckishly called "Belleigh Acres."

ARTHUR HOUSMAN, whose sozzled sophisticate brightened up hundreds of scenes.

ARTHUR HOUSMAN
October 10, 1889–April 8, 1942

"I was born in New York and educated there," Arthur Housman recalled. "When my mother wanted me to go to college, I went out and got a position so I'd have a good excuse to get out of more education."

Housman went into vaudeville, then worked in silent films for the Edison company. He achieved modest success in the *Waddy and Arty* film series of 1914. He was very busy on stage early in his career but did appear in several features in the silent era, including *Manhandled* and *The Bat*. Before long, one aspect of his comic persona, his ability to play a drunk, predominated.

Not being much for rubber-legged theatrics, Housman was usually called on to play a refined, sozzled sophisticate (complete with mandatory top hat and mustache), or the garden-variety barfly (with a pleasant if grizzled, leathery face, the mustache a little thicker) downing the drinks and inviting company.

Housman wandered into a lot of comedy stars, usually in bar scenes, and usually bent on having them join him for a few. He worked with Harold Lloyd (*Movie Crazy* and *Feet First*), Mae West (*She Done Him Wrong*), W. C. Fields (*Mrs. Wiggs of the Cabbage Patch*), and Laurel and Hardy (*Our Relations*, as well as several shorts including *The Fixer Uppers, Scram,* and *The Live Ghost*). In *Scram* it was Housman, in full tuxedo, who staggers home and can't get into his mansion and requests the assistance of Stan and Ollie. Never-

SELECTED FILM APPEARANCES:
Under the Red Robe (1923), *Manhandled* (1924), *The Bat* (1926), *Fools for Luck* (1928), *The Singing Fool* (1928), *Feet First* (1930), *Movie Crazy* (1932), *She Done Him Wrong* (1933), *Mrs. Wiggs of the Cabbage Patch* (1934), *Our Relations* (1936), *After the Thin Man* (1936), *A Family Affair* (1937), *Step Lively Jeeves* (1937), *Blondie Takes a Vacation* (1939), *Go West* (1940), *Public Enemies* (1941)

mind that, until he's inside, he's too soused to realize it isn't his house.

Asked to name his favorite comedy role, Housman sounded a bit like one of his inebriated characters: "Don't ask me to name the characters, for I can't remember them. But I like 'boob' parts pretty well. I've had a lot of them to play and I like them. I like any comedy part, though." Like any guy with a few drinks in him, Housman was mellow about what he wanted out of life: "My great ambition? Oh, to have a few million dollars and a chicken farm."

SHEMP HOWARD
Samuel Horwitz, March 17, 1895–November 23, 1955

Only one of the Three Stooges managed to enjoy a separate solo career: Shemp Howard, brother of Curly and Moe. The "original" third stooge in vaudeville and when the boys made their first films for Fox, Shemp left them in 1933, aggravated over being pushed around, onstage and off, by the trio's straight man at the time, Ted Healy. Curly joined, Healy eventually left, and the trio of Moe, Larry and Curly began their series of popular shorts for Columbia Pictures. Whither Shemp?

At first a promising star comedian, Shemp made thirty shorts for Vitaphone between 1933 and 1937. He moved to Columbia where his two brothers were Stooging, and made eighteen more solo short films through 1946. Between 1934 and 1937, he was also in a series of low budget *Joe Palooka* shorts playing Joe's manager, Knobby Walsh, a seemingly tough and confident wise guy who always seemed to unravel with confusion and complaints.

All through those years Shemp had supporting roles in feature films, most of them trading on his character of the outwardly gruff and baleful smart aleck who turned out to be all bluff.

He was very useful in mysteries and dramas, livening up a scene in a Charlie Chan film, *Murder Over New York*. While hunting for a Hindu suspect, Charlie's son Jimmy sits in front of a police lineup of Hindus and remarks, "They're beginning to look alike to me." One of the Hindus is Shemp! Hauled out of the lineup he insists he's a real fakir, not a faker, declaring "Through me, souls are cleansed." The cops wash his face and reveal him to be a white con artist named Shorty McCoy, the Canarsie Kid. It's a highlight of comic relief, solely due to Shemp's

SHEMP HOWARD, stooging with Lou Costello, Bud Abbott, and a distracted Hillary Brooke.

character change from wise guy to hapless stooge.

Shemp had the same personality in real life. He admitted to an interviewer that he was a homely guy ("I'm a beast!") but his rough exterior—squinty eyes, potato nose, lumpy face, big ears and greasy hair—hid a core of pure marshmallow. Shemp's fears and superstitions were legend. Moe recalled that his brother was a bedwetting child prone to whining. The adult Shemp was afraid of cars and took trains as much as possible. He always carried rubbers in his pocket in case of rain and a walking stick to fend off dogs. He was even a stooge in business, opening a nightclub in 1939 that *Variety* called "a losing struggle" and "a waste of acreage."

As comic support in films, Shemp was also a loser, his film time whittled down by jealous comics accusing him of upstaging them. It wasn't Shemp's fault. He really didn't do much, but being ineffectual was part of his act! He was a fall guy whether he took a pratfall or not. He did virtually nothing in Abbott and Costello's *Buck Privates,* other than grumble at Lou Costello, "What are you, a wise guy or a salesman? I've been around." But just by trying to keep up with Lou, and failing, he upstaged the rotund star. (He stooged for Abbott and Costello in five films.) In W. C. Fields's *The Bank Dick,* Shemp played the bartender at the Black Pussy Cat Cafe, yet all he did was walk down the street whistling, and in one scene make up a Mickey Finn for a customer, giving

SELECTED BROADWAY APPEARANCES:
A Night in Spain (1927), *A Night in Venice* (1929)

SELECTED FILM APPEARANCES:
(solo shorts) *In the Dough* (1933), *Close Relations* (1933), *Here Comes Flossie* (1933), *Pugs and Kisses* (1934), *Henry the Ache* (1934), *Corn on the Cop* (1934), *Knife of the Party* (1934), *A Peach of a Pair* (1934), *While the Cat's Away* (1936), *The Choke's on You* (1936), *Boobs in the Woods* (1940), *Pick a Peck of Plumbers* (1944). (Stooge shorts) *Hold That Lion* (1947), *Brideless Groom* (1947), *Sing a Song of Six Pants* (1947), *Heavenly Days* (1948), *Who Done It* (1949), *Don't Throw That Knife* (1951), *The Pest Man Wins* (1951), *Gents in a Jam* (1952), *Rip, Sew and Stitch* (1953), *Creeps* (1956). (Feature films) *Headin' East* (1938), *The Bank Dick* (1940), *Buck Privates* (1941), *In the Navy* (1941), *San Antonio Rose* (1941), *Hold That Ghost* (1941), *Hellzapoppin* (1941), *The Invisible Woman* (1941), *Pittsburgh* (1942), *Private Buckaroo* (1942), *Crazy House* (1943), *Three of a Kind* (1944), *Crazy Knights* (1944), *Trouble Chasers* (1945), *Blondie Knows Best* (1946), *Africa Screams* (1949)

COLLECTIBLES:
Several "All Shemp" videos were released by Columbia House while various entrepreneurs have issued cassettes of the few public domain Stooge shorts Shemp made and some of the obscure shorts he made for Van Beuren as well as Vitagraph. Channel 13 Video, for example, offers *Shemp Steps In,* featuring four shorts: *Why Pay Rent, The Choke's on You, His First Flame,* and *A Peach of a Pair.*

Fields a squinty nod once the potion was ready. And, in Olsen and Johnson's *Hellzapoppin,* he was funny because he was *trying* to be. Acting very much like a second banana, he'd rush into a scene with a quick gag: "Wanna buy a stove? It's hot!" Some fans insist that while Shemp was a funny guy, he was even funnier unintentionally. He was a scream when he was trying hard (as in Stooge shorts where he made lame jokes, idiotic faces, and uttered squawky "ib ib ib ib" noises whenever he was distressed or choking).

Shemp (he got the name from his mother and her Lithuanian accented version of Sam) rejoined the Three Stooges when his brother Curly suffered a stroke in 1946. Shemp hadn't lost his touch. After all, a few years earlier, he, Billy Gilbert and Maxie Rosenbloom had formed a variant on the Three Stooges, starring in *Three of a Kind, Crazy Knights,* and *Trouble Chasers.*

Shemp remained a member of the Three Stooges until his sudden death from a heart attack in 1955. Gone and for many years forgotten when Stooges shorts featuring "the original Curly" became a hit on television, he was rediscovered by fans who began to appreciate the peculiar charm of hapless second banana Shemp. In the late eighties Columbia Home Video began to issue a series of "All Shemp" tapes to go with the popular "All Curly" volumes.

MARTY INGELS
Martin Ingerman, March 9, 1936

MARTY INGELS, second banana turned agent, here with wife Shirley Jones.

A cheerful brand of wide-eyed nebbish, Marty Ingels varied from other "jerk" comics of the day, mellowing the goofiness with good nature. With his crooked smile, eager-to-please disposition, and mild fumbling, he could play believable support characters in films and on television.

The Brooklyn-born actor worked in summer stock in Pennsylvania, created a stand-up routine, and appeared in the Broadway show *Kelly.* Considered possibly another Red Skelton or Danny Kaye, he came to Hollywood and was briefly the protégé of Jerry Lewis. He claims Lewis's film *The King of Comedy* was based on the real-life way small-time comic Marty doggedly tried to win the attention of the famous comedian. Jerry signed him up at $1,000 a week but cut him from his film *Ladies Man,* destroying Ingels, who had taken out ads on the trade papers promoting his appearance. He made his film debut in an oddity called *Armored Command,* a sixties World War II movie starring Howard Keel.

Ingels as a performer will probably remain best known for his short-lived TV sitcom *I'm Dickens—He's Fenster.* With John Astin as Harry Dickens, Marty played Arch Fenster, the dizzy carpenter with the high, husky voice and blameless grin who always seemed to get into trouble. As a problem-prone, sweet-natured loser, Ingels guested regularly in sitcoms including *The Dick Van Dyke Show,* and had his own solo act in nightclubs. Unfortunately Ingels suffered from a variety of phobias, insecurities and anxieties. "Anxiety is an awful disease," he says, "because you have no idea why you are so fearful. It just takes you apart piece by piece and renders you totally unable to deal with simple things." After struggling with his career, he unraveled during a mid sixties *Tonight Show* appearance. Following a comic set and a stint on the couch with Johnny Carson, Ingels was quietly watching Carson interview drummer Buddy Rich when he suffered a panic attack that had him twitching. The audience laughed even as Ingels fought his way to his feet and lurched toward the curtains, collapsing backstage.

He remained in his apartment for nine months, hardly moving from his bed, sometimes lying flat against the floor. He was a bundle of symptoms: "They take all forms, defy logic, and grip you without any apparent warning. I was afraid of height, of looking up or looking down. Afraid of crowds. Afraid of open spaces…I was afraid of being away from my home…I am still afraid of flying."

Ingels would never become a top banana, but he remained a very capable supporting comic. He was Norman Crump on Phyllis Diller's sitcom *The Pruitts of Southampton,* costarred in a West Coast production of *The Pajama Game* and made several more film appearances. He married actress Shirley Jones, who was with him as he learned to separate his pushy-klutz screen persona from real life, and cope and overcome his fears. (Once he picked her up in a motor home for a date so that he wouldn't have to technically "leave the house.")

After 1976 he found a more lucrative show business career. He became a successful talent agent. "Ingels Inc." produced 14,000 commercials in eleven years. His agency found celebrities willing to promote products. As he said, "I'm in the perfect business now. I get Mr. A and Mr. B, I fight the whole world and get them together, I sit back and watch them do their business. I get a little piece of the action and it's a wonderful business and I'm very good at what I do."

In 1990 he and his wife Shirley cowrote a dual autobiography, *An Unlikely Love Story,* that included a section of advice on coping with life and creating an enduring marriage. He counseled

SELECTED FILM APPEARANCES:
Armored Command (1961), *The Horizontal Lieutenant* (1962), *Wild and Wonderful* (1964), *The Busy Body* (1967), *For Singles Only* (1968), *How to Succeed With Sex* (1970)

TELEVISION SERIES:
I'm Dickens—He's Fenster (1962–63), *The Pruitts of Southampton* (1967)

COLLECTIBLES:
Shirley and Marty: An Unlikely Love Story, an autobiography.

readers to "repress nothing," realize the virtue of "vulnerability," learn "self esteem," and to lift "all the weight off your shoulders" by "truth…the purest communication there is." High on Ingels's top ten list was "Humor. Easier said than done, but do it, find it, feel it, look for partners with it. Life's absurd as it is. Try laughing at it. Just make the *sound* first. It's contagious and medicinal and addictive."

LOU JACOBI
Louis Jacobovitch, December 28, 1913

LOU JACOBI, the twinkly-eyed comedian who makes Woody Allen and millions of others laugh.

A heavy-set Jewish character comedian with a little mustache and twinkling eyes, Lou Jacobi could play anything from a harried husband in *Don't Drink the Water* to a comically absurd transvestite (with a mustache) in *Everything You Ever Wanted to Know About Sex*. As the dumpy bartender in *Irma La Douce* he had a unique philosophy of life. To be honest in a dishonest world "is like plucking a chicken against the wind— you'll only wind up with a mouth full of feathers."

The Toronto-born actor appeared on stage as early as *The Rabbi and the Priest* in 1924. His father, who was in the Yiddish theater, discouraged his son from entering the profession, so for many years Jacobi made his living as a violinist. At thirty-nine he ventured to England and it was there that his acting career began. His first triumph was a serious role on Broadway as Mr. Van Daan in *The Diary of Anne Frank* but after that he generally found important supporting roles in comedy. Woody Allen became a booster. Jacobi recalled, "He saw me in *Come Blow Your Horn*. He said, 'I'm going to write a play for you," and he wrote *Don't Drink the Water.* Later Woody wrote him the highlight role in *Everything You Always Wanted to Know About Sex*. A big Jacobi fan when Lou played in *Don't Drink the Water* on Broadway, Woody Allen recalled, "Lou got every laugh and twenty more from his body language. He's a funny human."

In the sixties Jacobi headed an ensemble cast in several comedy albums, including *When You're in Love the Whole World Is Jewish* and *You Don't Have to Be Jewish*. The latter offered classic old jokes told anew: "I'm in women's wear," Jacobi says in a thick Jewish accent. "You may have heard of us. Finkelstein and O'Brien…I'm O'Brien!"

Over the summer in 1976 Jacobi starred in his own television series *Ivan the Terrible* as a head waiter in a Moscow hotel. He continued to play key comedy roles on stage, TV, and films, often getting laughs on sight. A running gag in *Amazon Women on the Moon* was poor Lou as a typically elderly Jewish hubby, wandering around in his underwear, totally lost, calling out to his wife. He started the nineties as busily as ever with his memorable role in *Avalon*. Always ebullient, in 1991 he said he never worried much about the roles he lost or the slow periods in his career: "We are in the rejection business. If we're in a flop it's normal. If we're in a hit—it's wonderful! I love my work. How many people do you know love their work and get paid for it?"

SELECTED BROADWAY APPEARANCES:
The Diary of Anne Frank (1955), *The Tenth Man* (1959), *Come Blow Your Horn* (1961), *Fade Out, Fade In* (1964), *Don't Drink the Water* (1966), *Norman Is That You?* (1970), *The Sunshine Boys* (1974), *The Cheaters* (1978)

SELECTED FILM APPEARANCES:
Irma la Douce (1963), *The Last of the Secret Agents* (1966), *Cotton Comes to Harlem* (1970), *Little Murders* (1971), *Everything You Ever Wanted to Know About Sex But Were Afraid to Ask* (1972), *Roseland* (1977), *The Lucky Star* (1980), *Arthur* (1981), *Chu Chu and the Philly Flash* (1981), *My Favorite Year* (1982), *Amazon Women on the Moon* (1987), *Avalon* (1990)

TELEVISION SERIES:
The Dean Martin Show (1971–73), *Ivan the Terrible* (1976), *Melba* (1986)

COLLECTIBLES:
You Don't Have to Be Jewish (Kapp), *When You're in Love the Whole World Is Jewish* (Kapp), *Al Tijuana And the Jewish Brass* (Capitol), *The Yiddish Are Coming* (Verve), *Bunnicula* (Caedmon)

BUD JAMISON
William Edward Jaimison, February 15, 1894–September 30, 1944

Remembered as a perennial nemesis of the Three Stooges, whether he played (an impressively versatile) array of stereotypical fussy butlers, Irish cops, burly cowboys, or British aristocrats, Jamison had a career stretching back to such early Chaplin films as *A Night Out, The Champion* and *The Tramp* (all in 1915). The California-born ex-vaudevillian was a bit player then, rarely getting billing under his slightly altered last name. In *The Tramp,* for example, he's one of three hobo thugs out to steal money from Charlie (and run away with Edna Purviance).

Jamison remained a semi-visible member of the Chaplin stock company through *The Floorwalker* in 1916 and *A Dog's Life* in 1918. After working in a few Harry Langdon films (*The Chaser* and *Heart Trouble*) he began the sound era stooging in dozens of Andy Clyde's early shorts including *Bulls and Bears, No, No Lady,* and *Heavens! My Husband.* He turned up in Thelma Todd and ZaSu Pitt's *Strictly Unreliable* in 1932 and played Charley Frobisher, a kibbitzing golf friend in W. C. Fields's *The Dentist* the same year.

In 1934 he began working regularly with the Three Stooges and deserves some distinction for being the very first man to poke Curly and Larry in the eye in a Columbia short (*Woman Haters*). Though he also costarred in Charley Chase shorts between 1937 and 1939, he seemed to find his comic element with the Stooges, especially when he was reduced to inhaling deeply, glaring, and uttering a hushed, frustrated rebuke. As the butler in *Crash Goes the Hash* (1944) he scoffs at the trio, "Such levity! You remind me of the Three Stooges." Their answer: "Hey! That's an insult!"

Jamison was a Christian Scientist and had refused treatment when he became ill in September of 1944. According to his death certificate, the fifty-year-old actor died of mesenteric thrombosis. The autopsy also revealed carcinoma in his right kidney and calculi (stones) in his bladder and left kidney.

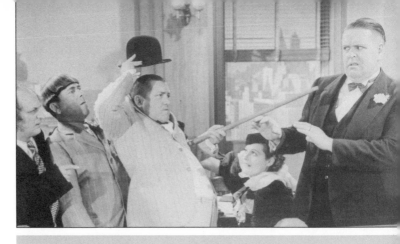

BUD JAMISON, whether playing con men or effete butlers, invariably ended up under the scrutiny of the Three Stooges.

SELECTED FILM APPEARANCES:
(shorts) *His New Job* (1915), *A Night Out* (1915), *The Champion* (1915), *The Bank* (1915), *Lonesome Luke* (1917), *A Dog's Life* (1918), *Darwin Was Right* (1929), *The Dentist* (1932), *In a Pig's Eye* (1934), *Woman Haters* (1934), *Men in Black* (1934), *Uncivil Warriors* (1935), *Hoi Polloi* (1935), *Disorder in the Court* (1936), *Dizzy Doctors* (1937), *Wee Wee Monsieur* (1938), *Tassels in the Air* (1938), *Violent Is the Word for Curly* (1938), *Three Sappy People* (1939), *Dizzy Detectives* (1943), *Crash Goes the Hash* (1944). (Features) *The Chaser* (1928), *Heart Trouble* (1928), *Ticket to Paradise* (1936), *Blondie* (1938), *Topper Takes a Trip* (1939), *Li'l Abner* (1940), *Holiday Inn* (1942), *Lost in a Harem* (1944), *Nob Hill* (1945)

ALLEN JENKINS
Alfred McGonegal, April 9, 1900–July 20, 1974

How did Allen Jenkins describe his sad, comic face? "An oyster," he said in the film *Maisie Gets Her Man*, "the resemblance is very strong today."

Although he was able to play a variety of put-upon, hard-luck mugs, Jenkins's nasal New York voice and hangdog expressions typed him as a comically wary and weary sidekick to everyone from George Sanders (The Falcon) to Warren William (Perry Mason). He played cab drivers and hapless henchmen in dozens of films. One of his rare roles as a policeman was in voice only: as Officer Dibble on the cartoon series *Top Cat*. Around that time he summed up his long career in films: "I was in one hundred seventy-eight movies in which I was a stumblebum hood, but lovable. Always lovable. I was the stupid, engaging one."

ALLEN JENKINS, who was usually the mousy guy driving the cab for the stars at Warners and Universal.

Staten Island-born Jenkins started his career dancing in the Broadway show *Pitter Patter* with another hoofer, James Cagney, and went on to become one of Cagney's movie business friends known in Hollywood at that time as the "Irish Mafia." In 1932 he played a comic tough guy on stage in *Blessed Event* and came to Hollywood to repeat the part. Always self-deprecating, Jenkins recalled "I was in the right place most of the time. Just leaving when a notice for auditions arrived. In the right restaurant when the director was casting. Things like that. The country is full of good actors, great actors. They never got a break or the right role."

In his prime in the thirties, Jenkins was making up to twenty-five hundred dollars a week. He had a shot at comedy team stardom when he and Hugh Herbert got together for *Sh! The Octopus!* but the film didn't impress the critics. Jenkins remained a busy supporting player, one of those guys moviegoers always loved to see even if they couldn't attach a name to his glumly pouting visage. "You know me," he says in *The Gay Falcon,* "never remember a name, always forget a face." By the fifties, having spent lavishly on having a good time, he took any role he could get, even playing in an Ann Corio burlesque revue. For a time he was a car salesman.

The New Yorker loved one thing about California: sailing and deep sea diving. The "oyster faced" actor had a passion for photographing abalone: "One thing the abalone have taught me—they pay no more attention to an ocean liner than they do a rowboat. They probably know that eventually both will join them in Davey Jones's locker!"

Married, with two children, Jenkins enjoyed his fame, up to a point. Seeing his own films at

SELECTED BROADWAY APPEARANCES:
Pitter Patter (1920), *Rain* (1923), *Glory Hallelujah* (1926), *Potash and Perlmutter, Detectives* (1926), *The Front Page* (1928), *The Last Mile* (1930), *Five-Star Final* (1930), *Wonder Boy* (1932), *Blessed Event* (1932), *Something For the Boys* (1943), *My L.A.* (1951)

SELECTED FILM APPEARANCES:
The Girl Habit (1931), *Rackety Rax* (1932), *42nd Street* (1933), *Blondie Johnson* (1933), *I've Got Your Number* (1934), *Jimmy the Gent* (1934), *The Case of the Howling Dog* (1934), *While the Patient Slept* (1935), *The Case of the Curious Bride* (1935), *The Case of the Lucky Legs* (1935), *Ready, Willing and Able* (1937), *Sh! The Octopus!* (1937), *Dead End* (1937), *Gold Diggers in Paris* (1938), *Torchy Plays With Dynamite* (1939), *Destry Rides Again* (1938), *Brother Orchid* (1940), *The Gay Falcon* (1941), *Maisie Gets Her Man* (1942), *The Falcon Takes Over* (1942), *Stage Door Canteen* (1943), *Lady on a Train* (1945), *The Senator Was Indiscreet* (1947), *Behave Yourself* (1951), *The Wac From Walla Walla* (1952), *Pillow Talk* (1959), *Doctor, You've Got to Be Kidding* (1967), *The Front Page* (1974)

TELEVISION SERIES:
The Duke (1954), *Hey Jeannie* (1956–57), *Top Cat* (voice) (1961–62)

night didn't excite him. "It bugs me. I come home at night and want to relax and turn on the TV and there is that chiseled Jenkins pan, with that Brooklyn Irish accent saying "Seen them get away in a black car, boss—headin' for Canarsie."

GORDON JONES
April 5, 1911–June 20, 1963

Gordon Jones's most famous role as a comedy foil consisted of two words: "Ohhh! Costello!" As Mike the Cop on TV's *Abbott and Costello Show* that was about all he ever said. Then he'd shake his head in frustration and chase after Lou, stumbling over his own feet. Being a fall guy to a fall guy was quite an ignominious job.

Jones's early days were full of glory. At UCLA he was "Bull" Jones, football

GORDON JONES, football star turned leading man in B movies (here with Betty Furness in *They Wanted to Marry*) turned big lug and stooge to Abbott and Costello.

star. He held the school record in the shot put, tossing the iron pill forty-eight feet, nine inches. After college he turned pro and played with the L.A. Bulldogs before becoming a radio announcer. In 1935 the handsome, Iowa-born athlete tried the movie business. In *Night Waitress* he was actually a leading man opposite Margot Grahame.

Jones went to Broadway in 1940 for *Quiet Please!* This was a turning point for him: "I'd never been on the stage before, and the first time I got a laugh from a live audience I thought I was a terrific comic." The same year, Jones played "The Wreck" in the play *My Sister Eileen* with Rosalind Russell. As the name implies, he was there for his threatening physique—which, since all he wore was underpants, was constantly on display.

In 1941 he told an interviewer for the *Brooklyn Eagle,* "I've been playing down that athletic business for the last eight years, ever since I got out of school." He found that people had an adverse reaction: "They think a guy that's played football is a crackpot...a complete dimwit." Unfortunately, dimwit roles predominated after he returned from World War II.

First Lieutenant Jones met Abbott and Costello when he played Jake Frame, one of the cowboy villains in *The Wistful Widow of Wagon Gap.* He would play a variety of big lugs in films, always the butt of the joke. A few years later, and he was Mike the Cop, a cross between Nat

133

SELECTED BROADWAY APPEARANCES:
Quiet Please! (1940), *My Sister Eileen* (1940)

SELECTED FILM APPEARANCES:
Up in the Air (1941), *Blonde From Singapore* (1941), *The Feminine Touch* (1941), *They All Kissed the Bride* (1942), *My Sister Eileen* (1942), *The Secret Life of Walter Mitty* (1947), *The Wistful Widow of Wagon Gap* (1947), *A Foreign Affair* (1948), *Mr. Soft Touch* (1949), *Tokyo Joe* (1949), *Corky of Gasoline Alley* (1950), *Sound Off!* (1952), *Gobs and Gals* (1952), *The Monster That Challenged the World* (1957), *Battle of the Coral Sea* (1959), *Everything's Ducky* (1961), *Son of Flubber* (1963)

TELEVISION SERIES:
The Abbott and Costello Show (1951–53), *The Ray Milland Show* (a.k.a. *Meet Mr. McNulty*) (1953–54)

Pendleton and Jack Carson: big, tough, but slow-burning and always wearing a pained expression. His comic support was sometimes just a snort, but when it came to registering exasperation, he was one of the best. The classic big guy vs. little guy confrontations always ended badly for the big guy. But viewers somehow loved the way he lost.

CAROL KANE
June 18, 1952

A quirky variation on the Goldie Hawn school of the saucer-eyed blond innocent, Carol Kane has been embraced by fans who find her vulnerable, comical, and cute. Speaking for the other side is critic John Simon: "You have to have a stomach for ugliness to endure Carol Kane—to say nothing of the zombielike expressions she mistakes for acting."

Kane had her best successes playing immigrants. First came *Hester Street.* Then she was an Emmy winner for her role in *Taxi* in 1983, as Simka Gravas, the woman who married the even more bizarre Latka (Andy Kaufman). She played Gene Wilder's quirky immigrant wife in *The World's Greatest Lover.* While she clearly was chosen to lend support to a flamboyant or star comedian in many films, she always seemed to have a few moments to contrast them with her offbeat charm. This subtle eccentricity made her a popular talk show guest, playing off David Letterman with coy smiles, giggles, and the baby-talk that made her seem like a cross between a dizzy Gracie Allen and a nervous Diane Keaton.

CAROL KANE, whose unique voice and cadence bespoke an endearing quirkiness in comedy as well as drama.

Always a bit different, Carol Kane became a vegetarian at fourteen, and at sixteen toured the country in *The Prime of Miss Jean Brodie.* A few years later she was costarring in *Carnal Knowledge* with Jack Nicholson, who gave the young actress some good advice ("Watch Bette Davis and Peter Lorre" to learn film technique). By twenty-two, she was an Academy Award nominee for *Hester Street.* Cleveland-born Kane fascinated a variety of directors from Sidney Lumet (*Dog Day Afternoon*) to Woody Allen (*Annie Hall*).

Through the eighties and into the nineties, Kane has often injected more of a sharp edge into her screen characters—like a candy-covered apple that might just have a razor blade in it. She played a little innocent who isn't as defenseless as she seems in *Pandemonium.* In this parody of *Carrie* the wide-eyed girl has the power of telekinesis. She admits calmly, "It all started when I went on the pill." After several people are murdered, someone says "If we knew about the killings, I wouldn't have come." "I would have!" she chirps. Why she'll even have lunch at the House of Bad Pies, where Tuesday's special—is served on Thursday.

In *Scrooged* she played the deceptively birdlike and sweet Ghost of Christmas Present, but got most of her laughs from comic acts of hard-kicking aggression. In *The Lemon Sisters* she was an inept singer prone to accidentally smacking people in the face or using her microphone cord as a bolo rope, sending the microphone into the audience.

Of that film, the *New York Times* tactfully noted, "You can make up your own lemon jokes." Kane moved back to television, costarring in *American Dreamer* with Robert Urich, and other shows.

SELECTED FILM APPEARANCES:
Is This Trip Really Necessary? (1970), *Desperate Characters* (1971), *Carnal Knowledge* (1971), *The Last Detail* (1973), *Dog Day Afternoon* (1975), *Hester Street* (1975), *Harry and Walter Go to New York* (1976), *Annie Hall* (1977), *The World's Greatest Lover* (1977), *The Muppet Movie* (1979), *Norman Loves Rose* (1982), *Over the Brooklyn Bridge* (1984), *Racing With the Moon* (1984), *Jumping Jack Flash* (1986), *Ishtar* (1987), *Scrooged* (1988), *License to Drive* (1988), *Flashback* (1990), *The Lemon Sisters* (1990), *My Blue Heaven* (1990), *When a Stranger Calls Back* (1993)

TELEVISION SERIES:
Taxi (1981–83), *All Is Forgiven* (1986), *American Dreamer* (1990), *Brooklyn Bridge* (1992)

MARVIN KAPLAN
January 24, 1927

Marvin Kaplan usually played a mild mannered, fumbling, nebbishy sort of character in films and on TV. Usually wearing nerdish glasses and looking rather glum. He was perfect as a hapless but sympathetic fall guy, his dull Brooklyn accent coming out in a soft whine. While a pouting delivery and wallflower personality are hardly lovable traits, Kaplan's outlook, suggesting that fate was working against him, seemed to strike a chord with viewers.

Kaplan hadn't planned on a show business career: "I come from the Williamsburg section of Brooklyn. I graduated from Eastern District High School in Brooklyn, but then I went out to California where I became interested in theater at U.S.C." He wrote his thesis on the techniques of turning stage plays into radio plays and was set for a career as a writer when he was spotted by Constance Collier in a production of

MARVIN KAPLAN, who personified nerds before the term was coined, screws up his courage to face down gangster Sheldon Leonard in *Behave Yourself.*

The Doctor in Spite of Himself. On her recommendation to Katharine Hepburn, Kaplan got a part in *Adam's Rib* in 1949.

Several other film roles followed, but it was TV's *Meet Millie* that got him noticed—in the role of schlumpy Alfred Prinzmetal. Sometimes, instead of comic reluctance and resignation, Kaplan would try and fight back against the forces that were bringing him down. In *It's a Mad, Mad, Mad, Mad World* he was the pudgy co-owner of a gas station that's being wrecked by a berserk Jonathan Winters. Without veering into a stereotype of effeminancy, Kaplan makes the most of helpless shouts and cries as he tries to screw up his courage and subdue the madman but ends up running for cover. It's one of the highlights of the film.

Occasionally Kaplan appeared in dramas, notably an episode of *Mod Squad* where he played a Jewish merchant tormented by anti-Semitic juvenile delinquents. Television work was always plentiful for him in the sixties and seventies, though he still had aspirations of writing scripts and casting himself in a serious remake of the Peter Lorre film *M.* Kaplan was always anxious for a good stage role, too, and played the Cowardly Lion in a production of *The Wizard of Oz.* In Los Angeles, he appeared in the 1969 revival of *Uncle Vanya.*

Fans also remember him as the voice of the conciliatory "Choo Choo" on the animated series *Top Cat* and as Henry the telephone lineman on the long-running sitcom *Alice.* Of the cute sidekick cat role, Kaplan remarked back in 1961, "Choo Choo is partly an extension of me, or rather, with his warmth, honesty and a certain humility, he represents the best of what I should be." Ever honest, the bachelor had to admit that waiting for him at home was not a pet cat but a dog.

SELECTED FILM APPEARANCES:
Adam's Rib (1949), *I Can Get It for You Wholesale* (1951), *Angels in the Outfield* (1951), *Behave Yourself* (1951), *Wake Me When It's Over* (1960), *It's a Mad, Mad, Mad, Mad World* (1963), *A New Kind of Love* (1963), *The Great Race* (1965)

TELEVISION SERIES:
Meet Millie (1952–56), *Top Cat* (voice) (1961–62), *Chicago Teddy Bears* (1971), *Alice* (1977–85)

STUBBY KAYE
Martin Wilson, November 11, 1918

Stubby of physique, but possessing a comical swagger, Stubby Kaye was best known for portraying Nicely Nicely Johnson in both the stage and screen versions of *Guys and Dolls,* singing the showstopping number, "Sit Down, You're Rocking the Boat."

Another key role for the cheerful, balding actor was Marryin' Sam in the musical *Li'l Abner.* He sang the show's best tune, "Jubilation T. Cornpone," about a dubious Confederate war hero: "When we almost had 'em but the issue still was in doubt./Who suggested the retreat that turned it into a rout?/Why it was Jubilation T. Cornpone,/old tattered and torn pone, he kept us hidin' out!" The singer lent a certain bizarre touch to the comic Western *Cat Ballou,* as he and Nat King Cole deadpanned the title tune and appeared regularly as troubadours in the film, adding musical punctuation to the action.

Kaye's career as a comedian began shortly after he graduated from De Witt Clinton High School in the Bronx. He was the straight man for Robert Alda when the two teamed in 1938. He got bigger, physically, billed as "the Extra Padded Attraction" for his two-hundred-seventy-pound, five-foot-seven physique. As for stardom, he wasn't getting bigger, having to swap a solo act for ensemble work in burlesque: "You've heard of the top banana in burlesque? I wasn't even the bottom plum. I was about the thirty-seventh stooge—caught the stripper's clothes when they were thrown off stage." Gradually he became noticed for more than his trademark girth: a robust effervescence.

Following his Broadway successes, the roly-poly comic became a favorite with kids, hosting the sixties TV game show *Shenanigans.* In 1976 he filmed a pilot called "Side by Side" about a retired cop. Kaye came back to Broadway for the burlesque musical *Grind,* which lured him away from his British wife and home in England. A few years later,

STUBBY KAYE, roly-poly Nicely Nicely Johnson on stage and screen (flanked here by Johnny Silver and Frank Sinatra) who gave a welcome kick to many films over four decades.

SELECTED BROADWAY APPEARANCES:
Guys and Dolls (1950), *Li'l Abner* (1956), *Everybody Loves Opal* (1961), *Good News* (1974), *The Ritz* (1975), *Grind* (1985)

SELECTED FILM APPEARANCES:
Guys and Dolls (1955), *Li'l Abner* (1959), *Forty Pounds of Trouble* (1963), *Sex and the Single Girl* (1964), *Cat Ballou* (1965), *The Way West* (1967), *Sweet Charity* (1968), *The Cockeyed Cowboys of Calico County* (1970), *The Dirtiest Girl I Ever Met* (1973), *Six Pack Annie* (1975), *Who Framed Roger Rabbit* (1988)

TELEVISION SERIES:
Shenanigans (1964–65)

he returned to Hollywood, livening up the film *Who Framed Roger Rabbit* with his role as gangster Marvin Acme. It was just the last in a series of supporting roles calling for Kaye's special talents in portraying loud but likable, tough but round and tender wise guys.

LARRY KEATING, Gracie Allen and George Burns's snide TV neighbor who played comic support in many films before and after.

LARRY KEATING
April 13, 1896–August 26, 1963

Crusty curmudgeon Larry Keating was always on hand for a mordant glare, raised eyebrow, and snide remark. He rarely seemed to play people with wit or flair; his was the garden-variety cynicism of a weary suburban neighbor, the aging husband dragged along to a boring cocktail party, or the boss whose slow burn was mostly indigestion.

Keating didn't find his niche in films until the fifties, and it was really only late in the decade when sitcom-styled movies like *Who Was That Lady?* became popular that Keating had a chance to work effectively. Keating was busy on TV during that period, having replaced Fred Clark as Harry Morton, George Burns's grouchy neighbor on *The George Burns and Gracie Allen Show.* The stereotype took. A few years later he became Roger Addison, next door neighbor to Alan Young on *Mr. Ed,* and was as acerbic as ever. In one episode he and his wife have an argument over an expensive present she'd like him to get for her. "I'll have that string of pearls!" she cries. His dry comeback: "You'll have to dive for them."

Keating died of leukemia during the show's run. Sadly, he was not only at a peak of activity with the TV series, he was also in demand for films. His last, *The Incredible Mr. Limpet,* was released posthumously in 1964.

SELECTED FILM APPEARANCES:
Song of the Sarong (1945), *Mr. 880* (1950), *The Mating Season* (1951), *Francis Goes to the Races* (1952), *Monkey Business* (1952), *She's Back on Broadway* (1953), *Daddy Long Legs* (1955), *The Best Things in Life Are Free* (1956), *The Buster Keaton Story* (1957), *Who Was That Lady?* (1960), *Boys' Night Out* (1962), *The Incredible Mr. Limpet* (1964)

TELEVISION SERIES:
The Hank McCune Show (1950), *The George Burns and Gracie Allen Show* (1954–58), *The George Burns Show* (1958–59), *Mr. Ed* (1961–63)

PATSY KELLY
Sarah Veronica Kelly,
January 21, 1910–September 24, 1981

One of the most appealing "wisecracking dames" to come out of Brooklyn, Patsy Kelly began her show business career as a dancer, her classmate a pretty young hopeful named Ruby Keeler.

Patsy's big break came in 1926 when she accompanied her brother to an audition. Comic Frank Fay chose *her* as his new stooge instead. The routine they developed was far from Burns and Allen, more like Milton Berle vs. a female ringsider, and after weathering a barrage of joking put-downs, Kelly had enough. Thanks to old friend Ruby Keeler, now a Broadway star, Patsy found new jobs, eventually playing with Al Jolson in *The Wonder Bar* and Clifton Webb in *Flying Colors,* where producer Hal Roach spotted her.

Patsy was the good-natured but brassy counterpoint to blond, classy Thelma Todd in a series of memorable comic shorts in the early thirties as replacement for Todd's first partner, ZaSu Pitts. The far more streetwise Patsy was perfect for the new style of tough comedy that became a force at the time thanks to such Brooklyn and New York-bred teams as the Three Stooges and the Marx Brothers, both featuring glowering cynics (Moe Howard and Groucho Marx).

PATSY KELLY, the good dame who was always ready with a wisecrack or a caustic quip.

Sweet Thelma and simmering Patsy made nearly two dozen shorts together through 1935 as the top female comedy team in Hollywood. Their best shorts include *Beauty and the Bus* in 1933, *Bum Voyage, Babes in the Goods,* and *Maid in Hollywood* in 1934, and *Sing, Sister Sing, Twin Triplets,* and *Top Flat* in 1935. Kelly's caustic quips were always an important part of the action. In *Babes in the Goods,* she's a brash saleswoman as a picky, annoying customer holds up a garment and asks, "Will the colors run?" Patsy: "Not till they see you in it."

The chemistry between the two actresses might have led to feature films but in 1935 Thelma Todd died mysteriously. A later biography (*Hot Toddy*) theorized murder at the hands of ex-lover gangster Lucky Luciano. Kelly struggled to find a new partner. Among her choices was Polish-born comedienne Lyda Roberti. They made a 1937 film together, *Nobody's Baby,* but Roberti died in 1938. (She reportedly dieted herself into a heart attack at age twenty-nine.) Kelly even teamed with Thelma Todd's old partner, ZaSu Pitts, but there wasn't much interest in their 1941 effort, *Broadway Limited.*

Able to add some sting to roles calling for a sassy chorine, salty salesgirl, or stewing best friend of the pretty star, Patsy found herself in demand for brief feature film roles. In *Pick a Star* Kelly is prickly indeed. Her star-struck girlfriend sighs over a suave actor (Mischa Auer). "It must be wonderful to be pointed out." Kelly cracks, "Dillinger didn't think so." Later, meeting Auer herself, she's unimpressed. "Mind if I smoke?" he asks. "I don't care if you burn," she tells him.

Sometimes it wasn't so much what Patsy said, but the knowing way she said it. She was Jean Harlow's sidekick in *The Girl From Missouri*. An old man is trying to grab a good time with Patsy. Her response: "Look at this. Death takes a holiday." Later, when Harlow's behavior seems suspicious, Patsy is quick with a put-down: "Say, did somebody ask you to sniff a little white powder?"

In the fifties Kelly, who never married, was a combination gal Friday and costar for Tallulah Bankhead. She toured in *High Time* (1953) and *Dear Charles* (1955), and came out of the lean decade with *Please Don't Eat the Daisies* in 1960. In a revival of *No, No Nanette* with Ruby Keeler, Patsy Kelly staged another comeback, winning a Tony Award. She followed this with the Debbie Reynolds revival of *Irene*. Fans were happy to see the perennial favorite in a new costarring role, playing Brigid Murphy in a TV series called *The Cop and the Kid* with Charles Durning. She continued to take on television and film assignments, turning up on an episode of *Love Boat* just a year before she died.

PERT KELTON
October 14, 1907–October 30, 1968

She looked sort of pert, especially when she was a child star in vaudeville beginning at age three, but as an adult, Pert Kelton found that her snub nose and bitter smile typed her as a wisecracking woman of the world. In the thirties she was the typical New York chorus girl (though she was born in Great Falls, Montana), young and tender-looking outside but tough as an old boot inside. As she got older, she got tougher, and was cast as the original no-nonsense Alice Kramden, in Jackie Gleason's "Honeymooners" sketches on *Cavalcade of Stars*.

Hard luck seemed to be with Pert Kelton at either end of her film career. She seemed on the verge of a breakthrough when she costarred with Patsy Kelly, replacing the late Thelma Todd, in a short called *Pan Handlers*. But the team of Kelly and Kelton ended right there. For the next short, she was replaced by Lyda Roberti.

Fans of Pert Kelton have had to scout the late night TV listings to find some of the obscure films that gave her a few moments to do her stuff. She had some satiric singing moments as a tin-eared chorus girl in *Hooray for Love* in 1935. She was Constance Bennett's sidekick in *Bed of Roses*, a tough paloma just paroled from prison, hitching a ride by propositioning a trucker right outside the gates. She got the ride, plus an extra two bucks which she proudly tucked into her stocking.

PERT KELTON, brash girlfriend to stars (here it's Frances Langford in *The Hit Parade*) long before becoming TV's first Alice Kramden.

Earning a couple of dollars in show business wasn't always easy, but Kelton continued to find roles in films and on Broadway, ultimately landing what seemed to be another big chance: Jackie Gleason's comic foil in "Honeymooners" sketches, Alice Kramden. She was her usual tough self, but the times were tougher. McCarthy-era gossip had painted her red: a Communist sympathizer. She was replaced by Audrey Meadows.

With the end of the witch-hunts, the aging Kelton was allowed to work again, and true to form, she was often cast in roles that required a strong presence. To the end, and against any comedian, she remained unbowed and uncompromising.

SELECTED BROADWAY APPEARANCES:
Sunny (1925), *Five O'Clock Girl* (1927), *Du Barry* (1932), *Bed of Roses* (1933), *All in Fun* (1940), *Any Day Now* (1941), *Guest in the House* (1942), *Lady Behave* (1957), *The Music Man* (1957), *Greenwillow* (1960), *Come Blow Your Horn* (1961), *I Was Dancing* (1964), *Spofford* (1967)

SELECTED FILM APPEARANCES:
The Bowery (1933), *Annie Oakley* (1935), *Kelly the Second* (1936), *Cain and Mabel* (1936), *The Hit Parade* (1937), *Rhythm of the Saddle* (1938), *You Can't Take It With You* (1938), *Whispering Enemies* (1939), *The Music Man* (1962), *Love and Kisses* (1965), *The Comic* (1969)

TELEVISION SERIES:
Cavalcade of Stars (1951)

EDGAR KENNEDY, the slow-burn specialist, in an optimistic moment from one of his domestic comedy shorts.

EDGAR KENNEDY
April 26, 1890–November 9, 1948

There's something Laurel and Hardy, W. C. Fields, Olsen and Johnson, Harold Lloyd, Wheeler and Woolsey, and the Marx Brothers all have in common.

All annoyed Edgar Kennedy. As a bartender to Harold Lloyd and a judge presiding over a case involving W. C. Fields, Kennedy would slide an anguished hand across his eyes and bald dome and wonder how long he was expected to endure their declarations. Faced with slapstick from most of his other antagonists, he'd try to keep his calm while his mouth shut in a steely line and he glowered with mounting fury. The term "slow burn" was popularized in describing the master at it: Edgar Kennedy.

You could tell just by looking at him that you could fry an egg on his steaming forehead, but several comedians pushed the slow burning Kennedy even further. Stan Laurel did it because he didn't know any better. In *A Perfect Day* he seems to constantly slam a car door on frustrated Edgar's gouty foot.

Harpo and Chico Marx just wanted to see what would happen when Edgar finally *did* explode. They teased lemonade vendor Edgar in *Duck Soup,* stealing his hat and then setting fire to it. Of course, even when he finally did get it all off his chest, screaming, shouting, and even attempting some slapstick retaliation, he never won. Yes, he did knock over Harpo and Chico's peanut vending stand, but then Harpo took a foot bath in Kennedy's lemonade, leaving aggravated Edgar to shudder in chagrin. And that wasn't enough; while Edgar is at home bathing, who suddenly rises from the bathwater? Harpo! And all Edgar can do is stare in disbelief.

A former vaudevillian and Keystone Cop (Mack Sennett spotted him initially when he was a boxer on the West Coast), Kennedy became a regular at Hal Roach's studio where he played annoyed cops and sour relatives in a variety of Laurel and Hardy and Our Gang comedies. He turned up in many other comedies in the thirties and was rewarded with his own series of comedy shorts. Called *The Average Man,* it had a long run (1931–48) with Edgar handling domestic situation comedy with a burdensome wife (Florence Lake) and mother-in-law (Dot Farley). The mild antics were fine for their time, but Edgar worked best in supporting roles opposite more formidable foes. He was a flustered detective unable to solve a case without Edna May Oliver's sleuthing in *The Penguin Pool Murder,* played a judge in Olsen and Johnson's *Crazy House,* and was the warden trying to deal with Wheeler and Woolsey in *Hold 'Em Jail.*

Kennedy sometimes did get to do more than burn or fluster. In *Unfaithfully Yours* he played a lowbrow detective with a love of highbrow music. This irritated conductor Rex Harrison, who had to endure Kennedy's enthusiasm: "Nobody handles Handel like you handle Handel!"

SELECTED FILM APPEARANCES:
Tillie's Punctured Romance (1914), *The Knockout* (1914), *The Great Vacuum Robbery* (1915), *Skirts* (1923), *Going Crooked* (1926), *A Pair of Tights* (1928), *They Had to See Paris* (1929), *The Penguin Pool Murder* (1932), *Duck Soup* (1933), *Tillie and Gus* (1933), *Twentieth Century* (1934), *Murder on the Blackboard* (1934), *Kid Millions* (1934), *Woman Wanted* (1935), *The Bride Comes Home* (1935), *Mad Holiday* (1936), *A Star Is Born* (1937), *Super Sleuth* (1937), *It's a Wonderful World* (1939), *Charlie McCarthy, Detective* (1939), *Laugh It Off* (1939), *Li'l Abner* (1940), *Sandy Gets Her Man* (1940), *Blondie in Society* (1941), *Snuffy Smith, Yard Bird* (1942), *The Falcon Strikes Back* (1943), *Air Raid Wardens* (1943), *Crazy House* (1943), *It Happened Tomorrow* (1944), *Anchors Aweigh* (1945), *Mad Wednesday* (1947), *Variety Time* (1948), *Dig That Gold* (1948), *My Dream Is Yours* (1949)

COLLECTIBLES:
Edgar Kennedy Slow Burn Festival video

Kennedy was a favorite through the thirties and forties, one of the irreplaceable masters of comic support. It wasn't easy to make anger and frustration funny. The audience had to be able to root for the comic bully without feeling too sorry for the beleagured, rather likable Edgar. Very few actors ever mastered a "slow burn." Not even Edgar's brother, Tom Kennedy, who was a veteran comic support player. But with his hefty build and befuddled pig's face, he generally had little more than buffoon roles (such as running after the stowaway Marx Brothers as a ship's officer in *Monkey Business*).

Married, with two children, Kennedy continued to work despite the debilitations caused by throat cancer. He died two days before a testimonial dinner planned in his honor. His brother Tom died in October of 1965.

GUY KIBBEE
March 6, 1882–May 24, 1956

Guy Kibbee looked like a jollier, more benign William Frawley. His comedy roles included stuffy old men and rich, silly sugar daddies. In *42nd Street,* he is financing a musical, smitten by the star Dorothy Brock (Bebe Daniels). "I'd like to do something for you, if you'd do something for me," he leers. The lady braces for the worst. What does the old goat want of her? With a goofy, toothy smile, the old guy makes his request: "Call me Abner!"

Another typical part was Nathaniel Peabody in *Gold Diggers of 1933.* The fuddy-duddy plays Dick Powell's trustee, determined to keep him away from gold diggers and actresses. But the foxy old fellow can't help himself as he breaks into a dreamy, dopey smile over the memory of one such floozie: "She called me Fuffy! Don't know why she did…"

GUY KIBBEE (left), who specialized in sly old codgers, repasting with ZaSu Pitts and Hugh Herbert during a comic interlude in *Dames*.

He sighs happily, "Showgirls are excellent in their way. Attractive creatures. Even fascinating…"

The balding, white-haired Kibbee had some good lines in *The Joy of Living* with Irene Dunne. "I've been drinking over forty years," he declares, "and I haven't acquired the habit yet."

After working on a Mississippi showboat as a teenager and making the rounds of vaudeville, El Paso-born Kibbee finally arrived on Broadway in *Torch Song* in 1930. The following year he made his film debut in *Man of the World*. He briefly starred in his own *Scattergood Baines* comedy film series in the early forties but was more in demand as a reliable ensemble player, his distracted daydreamers, spry old codgers and sly, straying conservatives always adding color to the proceedings.

In 1946 he returned to Broadway to star in *A Joy Forever*. Health problems curtailed his career. Married, with two sons and a daughter, he contracted Parkinsons Disease in 1951 and later required constant medical care. The *New York Times* reported that in his last year, "despite his illness…he was still the Guy Kibbee of infectious laughter and the almost inexhaustible supply of jokes. He was held in warm affection." When his nursing home screened a copy of a *Scattergood Baines* film six months before his death, he summed it up in two words: "kinda funny."

SELECTED BROADWAY APPEARANCES:
Torch Song (1930), *Marseilles* (1930), *A Joy Forever* (1946)

SELECTED FILM APPEARANCES:
Man of the World (1931), *Laughing Sinners* (1931), *Blonde Crazy* (1931), *Fireman Save My Child* (1932), *They Just Had to Get Married* (1932), *42nd Street* (1933), *Gold Diggers of 1933* (1933), *The Wonder Bar* (1934), *Babbitt* (1934), *Merry Wives of Reno* (1934), *Big-Hearted Herbert* (1934), *While the Patient Slept* (1935), *Don't Bet on Blondes* (1935), *I Married a Doctor* (1936), *Don't Tell the Wife* (1937), *The Joy of Living* (1938), *It's a Wonderful World* (1939), *Mr. Smith Goes to Washington* (1939), *Scattergood Baines* (1941), *Scattergood Rides High* (1942), *Scattergood Survives a Murder* (1942), *Whistling in Dixie* (1942), *The Horn Blows at Midnight* (1945), *Gentleman Joe Palooka* (1946), *Fort Apache* (1948), *Three Godfathers* (1948)

PERCY KILBRIDE
July 16, 1888–December 11, 1964

reluctant yokel, lanky Percy Kilbride was a popular Broadway costar through the thirties. His one complaint at the time: "I always want to have a serious part. They never give me any."

He played the spry and droll caretaker in *George Washington Slept Here* and, when Jack Benny scouted the show as a film possibility, Kilbride was discovered: Benny recalled, "Mr. Kimber was played by an actor with an absolutely deadpan face, nasal voice, and rasping delivery. I went out of my mind when I saw him…I thought Kilbride stole the show…one of the wildest performances I had ever seen and I laughed every time he opened his mouth. I laughed even before I heard his lines."

PERCY KILBRIDE breaks his traditional deadpan demeanor to cut capers with Marjorie Main in *Ma and Pa Kettle at Waikiki.*

Told by Jack Warner that Kilbride might steal the film from him, Benny said, "You're goddam right he will…without Kilbride, you've got nothing!" During filming, Benny laughed so hard he often blew a dozen takes in a row: "They threatened to throw me out of the picture if I didn't stop laughing at Kilbride. I stopped by not sleeping the night before we did scenes with him and I came on the set so exhausted that I simply didn't have the strength to laugh at him….He was a strange little man…what he played in movies was the person he was in life. He lived all alone. He had no friends. He wanted just so much salary for his work. He wouldn't take more and he wouldn't take less. He was a self-reliant, independent New Englander."

Typical of Kilbride's dry rustic humor was his deadpan line in *The Egg and I*: "I don't hold with too much water…rusts the bones."

Lifelong bachelor Kilbride lived in a boarding house at 1966 N. Beachwood Drive in Hollywood. Among the other guests with a furnished room there was James Finlayson. Percy kept temporary quarters because, as he wrote to a friend in 1944, "visions of New York keep rising before me…I'm a 'city feller' and New York is always a temptation."

As it turned out, Hollywood kept him busy. After playing Pa Kettle in *The Egg and I,* he starred with Marjorie Main in the successful low-budget *Ma and Pa Kettle* series. The success certainly didn't go to his head. He said, "There's no kick in doing him over and over again…the fun of being an actor is to meet the challenge of creating new characters."

Though it was his most famous part, Kilbride quit the role, replaced by Arthur Hunnicutt and later Parker Fennelly. His own favorite role was as a blackmailer in Broadway's *Little Brown Jug*. On September 21, 1964, he and a friend were hit by a car in Hollywood. His friend was killed. Kilbride underwent brain surgery on November 11 and died a month later.

SELECTED BROADWAY APPEARANCES:
The Buzzard (1928), *Adam's Apple* (1929), *Getting Even* (1929), *The Up and Up* (1930), *Louder, Please!* (1931), *The Great Magoo* (1932), *Whatever Possessed Her* (1934), *Name Your Poison* (1936), *Day in the Sun* (1937), *Sunup to Sundown* (1938), *Censored* (1938), *The Flying Ginzburgs* (1938), *When We Are Married* (1939), *George Washington Slept Here* (1940), *Two Story House* (1941), *Cuckoos on the Hearth* (1941), *Little Brown Jug* (1946)

SELECTED FILM APPEARANCES:
George Washington Slept Here (1942), *Crazy House* (1943), *Knickerbocker Holiday* (1944), *State Fair* (1945), *The Egg and I* (1947), *You Gotta Stay Happy* (1948), *Feudin', Fussin' and a-Fightin'* (1948), *Ma and Pa Kettle* (1949), *Ma and Pa Kettle Go to Town* (1950), *Ma and Pa Kettle Back on the Farm* (1951), *Ma and Pa Kettle at the Fair* (1952), *Ma and Pa Kettle on Vacation* (1953), *Ma and Pa Kettle Hit the Road* (1953), *Ma and Pa Kettle at Home* (1955), *Ma and Pa Kettle at Waikiki* (1955)

LEONID KINSKY (standing), doing his traditional "crazy Russian" (as Bogart called him), ponders his next move with fellow "spies" Florence Marly and Leon Belasco in *Gobs and Gals*.

LEONID KINSKY
April 18, 1903

Bogart called him a "crazy Russian" in *Casablanca,* and that was pretty much the type of role Leonid Kinsky played. The tall, angular Russian with the long putty-tipped nose seemed to veer between roles that required an eccentric and others that only needed a stooge who could appropriately register dumb frustration and hapless dismay. Most fans recall the eccentric side in *Casablanca,* though his role as the coy bartender was slim. As for the stooge, he played an assistant to the villain Trentino in the Marx Brothers' *Duck Soup.* How useful was he? "You have muddled everything!" Trentino shouts in frustration.

Born in St. Petersburg, where he began his theatrical career as a mime, Kinsky came to the United States in 1921, working in a Chicago restaurant-theater. After the stock market crash he tried a new profession and eventually joined the road tour of Al Jolson's *Wonder Bar*. His first major break was a role in Ernst Lubitsch's *Trouble in Paradise*.

SELECTED FILM APPEARANCES:
Trouble in Paradise (1932), *Duck Soup* (1934), *We Live Again* (1934), *Rhythm on the Range* (1936), *Make a Wish* (1937), *Flirting With Fate* (1938), *Professor Beware* (1938), *On Your Toes* (1939), *He Stayed for Breakfast* (1940), *Weekend in Havana* (1941), *That Night in Rio* (1941), *So Ends Our Night* (1941), *The Talk of the Town* (1942), *Casablanca* (1942), *Can't Help Singing* (1944), *Monsieur Beaucaire* (1946), *Gobs and Gals* (1952)

TELEVISION SERIES:
The People's Choice (1956–58)

In the sixties and seventies Kinsky concentrated more on writing and producing than acting. He retained his ties to Russia as an adviser, helping to determine which Hollywood films would be worth importing. He told writer Richard Lamparski that the Russians had a unique view of Leonid's ethnic acting: "When I play Russians in movies, they made me so exaggerated no real Russian believed me."

FUZZY KNIGHT
John Forrest Knight,
May 9, 1901–February 23, 1976

A vaudevillian ever since he graduated from the University of West Virginia, John Knight was a comedian, drummer, songwriter, and bandleader, appearing in *Earl Carroll's Vanities* (1927) and *Here's How* (1928) well before turning up in films.

Fans of Westerns got to know Knight well as the sidekick to a number of screen stars. He worked with Johnny Mack Brown (1929–43), Tex Ritter (1942–43), Rod Cameron (1944), Kirby Grant (1945–46), Jimmy Edison (1950), and Whip Wilson (1951–52). Grant told Western film author David Rothel, "Fuzzy was a genuinely funny person. Some of the sidekicks were not really funny… but a lot of what Fuzzy did for comedy was improvised on the set. The lines, the bare bones were there, but Fuzzy fleshed them out with his own brand of humor and

FUZZY KNIGHT (right), beloved Western sidekick, joins Jennifer Holt and Hank Worden in *Tenting Tonight on the Old Campground*.

gimmicks, double takes, and things of that sort."

He was billed as "Fuzzy" due to his raspy, fuzzy logic voice. He may have had some fuzzy stubble but did not wear a beard. His distinctive vocals netted him a hit single: "Twilight on the Trail" from the movie *Trail of the Lonesome Pine.*

His best remembered roles in other films were in support of Mae West and W. C. Fields. As hapless stooge Cousin Zeb to W. C. Fields in *My Little Chickadee,* he asks the card player, "Is this a game of chance?" Fields replies, "Not the way I play it, no." In Mae West's *She Done Him Wrong,* he's a wisecracking piano player. A singer tells him, "Ever since I sang that song, it's been haunting me." His answer: "It should. You murdered it."

ELSA LANCHESTER, London music hall performer turned longtime movie eccentric, proved to be more than the bride of Frankenstein.

ELSA LANCHESTER
Elizabeth Sullivan,
October 28, 1902–December 26, 1986

Yes, Elsa Lanchester was *Bride of Frankenstein,* immortal for her bird-like stare, angry swan hissing, and electric Brillo hairstyle. But she was more:

She was a nude model. She sang risque comic songs. She was a bohemian friend to H. G. Wells and Aldous Huxley. She earned extra money as a correspondent in divorce cases. She married one of the great actors of her time—who happened to be homosexual. And she was a hit through the fifties and sixties for her revival of bouncy, bawdy British Music Hall songs, eventually coming to Broadway in a one-woman show.

And from the forties in films to the seventies on television, she was a delightful comic support player. Her dignity was often challenged but, happily enough, she was usually strong-willed enough to win out, pressing into service her twin weapons of stubborn righteousness and implacable eccentricity. In her Academy Award-nominated supporting part opposite husband Charles Laughton in *Witness for the Prosecution,* she plays the nurse who is constantly foiled in trying to keep him from bad habits (smoking) and cultivating good habits (taking his medicine).

In a typical late television role, on Bill Cosby's early seventies sitcom, she played a dotty old lady trying to save trees in a hopeless but heroic act of conservation in the face of highway construction. She never gives up, pushing her now dumpy body along to the next tree, her chipper British accent intact and her round, expressive eyes still shining with indomitable spirit.

Elsa was spirited early on. Encouraged by her radical socialist parents, she enrolled in an all-boys school. After studying with Isadora Duncan in Paris, the seventeen-year-old began singing risque tunes in skimpy costumes. One of her titillating tidbits: "I may be fast, I may be loose, I may be easy to seduce. I may not be particular—to keep the perpendicular!"

She married Charles Laughton in 1929 and costarred on stage and in films together. (On the British stage, she was Peter Pan to Laughton's Hook.) They were compatible more as friends than lovers. Laughton told her, "I've got a face like an elephant's behind." When she discovered his homosexual affairs and told him it didn't matter, Laughton was moved to tears. "I wish Charles had not cared so much about the other kind of beauty, the beauty he sought in others," she wrote after his death, sad to find that "he needed secret and degrading episodes."

Elsa spent a decade (1941–51) performing with Los Angeles' Turnabout Theater Company, often singing comic songs. She brought them to Broadway in the early sixties. But it was in films that most fans knew her. She worked with Danny Kaye in *The Inspector General,* as the wife of the mayor (Gene Lockhart),

SELECTED BROADWAY APPEARANCES:
Payment Deferred (1931), *The Tempest* (1934), *They Walk Alone* (1941), *No Strings* (1942), *The Party* (1958), *A Zany Evening With Elsa Lanchester* (1960), *Elsa Lanchester Herself* (1961)

SELECTED FILM APPEARANCES:
The Constant Nymph (1927), *Day Dreams* (1930), *The Stronger Sex* (1931), *The Officer's Mess* (1931), *The Private Life of Henry VIII* (1933), *The Private Life of Don Juan* (1934), *David Copperfield* (1935), *Bride of Frankenstein* (1935), *The Ghost Goes West* (1936), *Rembrandt* (1936), *The Beachcomber* (1938), *Ladies in Retirement* (1941), *Tales of Manhattan* (1942), *Thumbs Up* (1943), *Lassie Come Home* (1943), *The Spiral Staircase* (1946), *The Razor's Edge* (1946), *The Bishop's Wife* (1947), *The Big Clock* (1948), *The Inspector General* (1949), *Dreamboat* (1952), *Androcles and the Lion* (1952), *Three-Ring Circus* (1954), *Witness for the Prosecution* (1957), *Bell, Book and Candle* (1958), *Mary Poppins* (1964), *That Darn Cat* (1965), *Easy Come, Easy Go* (1967), *Blackbeard's Ghost* (1968), *Me, Natalie* (1969), *Willard* (1971), *Arnold* (1973), *Terror in the Wax Museum* (1973), *Murder by Death* (1976)

TELEVISION SERIES:
The John Forsythe Show (1965–66), *Nanny and the Professor* (1971)

COLLECTIBLES:
Cockney London (Verve), *Elsa Herself* (Verve), *Songs for a Smoke-Filled Room* (Hi-Fi, reissued as *Bawdy Cockney Songs,* Tradition), *Songs for a Shuttered Parlor* (Hi-Fi, reissued as *More Bawdy Cockney Songs,* Tradition; the two Tradition albums released on one CD as *Elsa Lanchester, The Bride of Frankenstein Sings*); two autobiographies, *Charles Laughton and I* and *Elsa Lanchester Herself*

played a bearded lady in the Martin and Lewis comedy *Three-Ring Circus,* and was the frumpy, feisty parody of Miss Marple in Neil Simon's *Murder by Death.*

In 1983 she published her autobiography, *Elsa Lanchester Herself,* acknowledging the one supporting role that brought her the most fame and annoyance. Of *The Bride of Frankenstein,* she admitted, "I'm flattered that I'm recognizable in a part I played in the 1930s.... Apart from the discomfort of the monster makeup and all the hissing and screaming I had to do, I enjoyed working on the film." Her main complaint was being unable to enjoy her customary breaks for tea. As the bandage-wrapped bride, "I drank as little liquid as possible. It was too much of an ordeal to go to the bathroom...accompanied by my dresser!"

HARVEY LEMBECK (right), in his traditional role as the streetwise Brooklynite, connives with Robert Strauss in the film version of *Stalag 17*, both repeating their stage roles.

HARVEY LEMBECK
April 15, 1923–January 5, 1982

He knew comedy so well he could teach it. In fact, many young comics remember Harvey Lembeck more fondly as their mentor, than as the rough but good natured kid from Brooklyn he played in so many fifties and sixties comedies.

Originally part of a dance act, "The Dancing Carrolls," Lembeck journeyed far from New York to study at the University of Alabama. He enlisted in the army during World War II, transferred to the marines, and ended up spending several years in the navy on a submarine. It gave him a lot of training for what would become his stereotypical role in the fifties: one of the lowly dogfaces in service comedies.

After graduating from New York University in 1947, he arrived on Broadway as "Insignia" in *Mister Roberts* and followed it with another war comedy, *Stalag 17.* He turned up in the film version of *Stalag 17* as well as *You're in the Army Now* and *Willie and Joe Back at the Front.* He always seemed to be cast as the placating little guy with a Brooklyn-accented voice of reason. Due to his runty size, the streetwise wise guy had to be humorously cautious when it came to danger; prone to trying to think his way out of trouble and keep his pals out of danger as well.

In both the stage and film version of *Stalag 17,* he was Shapiro, the guy in charge of keeping the slaphappy and powerful "Animal" (Robert Strauss) in check. He usually did it with a placating if homely remark, like: "How dumb can you get, Animal?" He and Strauss were teamed again a decade later for another service comedy, *The Last Time I Saw Archie.*

On television, Lembeck had a similar role, serving as one of the voices of reason, semiliterate though it may have been, trying to reign in the scheming Phil Silvers as Sergeant Bilko. The part of Corporal Rocco Barbella (the real name of boxer Rocky Graziano, used as a tribute) nearly went to Buddy Hackett. When Hackett turned it down, Lembeck made the part his, nasal-voiced Rocco becoming the helpful little sidekick trying to keep up with Bilko's fast strides into trouble.

With Broadway work and a TV show shot in New York, Lembeck had no reason to move from his home in Queens, where he had a wife and two kids, Michael and Helaine. Among Lembeck's costarring highlights in the fifties were the comedy sketches he did with Nancy Walker in *Phoenix '55,* the part of Ali Hakim in *Oklahoma!* (the 1958 revival) and the chance to sing "Brush Up Your Shakespeare" alongside Jack Klugman in the TV version of *Kiss Me Kate* starring Alfred Drake.

In the sixties, Lembeck played Erich Von Zipper in a series of *Beach Party* movies. He made for a comic leather-jacketed villain—a cocky little guy with a ridiculously misplaced air of self-confidence and toughness. While fans found Lembeck lovable in parts that placed him in the same league with humorous upstarts like Leo Gorcey and Arnold Stang, film and TV producers didn't seem to see him as anything else. On stage he was able to expand his range, playing Sancho Panza in a touring company of *Man of La Mancha.* He performed the role at the White House for Lyndon Johnson.

For fifteen years Lembeck ran a comedy workshop, coaching young stars including Robin Williams and John Ritter. In 1981 he made a few appearances on *Mork and Mindy,* and also appeared on a Lily Tomlin special, but he mainly devoted his attention to his teaching, and to producing television specials featuring new talent. He was shooting an episode of *C.H.I.Ps* at the time of his death. His son, Michael, went on to become an actor and director on television.

SELECTED BROADWAY APPEARANCES:
Mister Roberts (1948), *Stalag 17* (1951), *Wedding Breakfast* (1954), *Phoenix '55* (1955), *South Pacific* (1957), *Oklahoma!* (1958)

SELECTED FILM APPEARANCES:
You're in the Navy Now (1951), *Willie and Joe Back at the Front* (1953), *Stalag 17* (1954), *Between Heaven and Hell* (1956), *Sail a Crooked Ship* (1962), *A View From the Bridge* (1962), *Beach Party* (1963), *Bikini Beach* (1964), *Pajama Party* (1964), *Muscle Beach Party* (1964), *The Unsinkable Molly Brown* (1964), *Beach Blanket Bingo* (1965), *Ghost in the Invisible Bikini* (1966), *The Spirit Is Willing* (1967)

TELEVISION SERIES:
Sgt. Bilko (a.k.a. *The Phil Silvers Show*) (1955–59), *The Hathaways* (1961–62), *Ensign O'Toole* (1963–64)

SHELDON LEONARD, veteran comic tough guy (and latter-day TV producer), mugs with Leo Gorcey.

SHELDON LEONARD
Sheldon Bershad,
February 22, 1907

"For more than twenty years I made a good thing of coming on like an ape...muttering 'all right Louie, drop da gun'" According to comic bad guy Sheldon Leonard, his role called for "a sort of Runyonesque character, who wasn't mean and vicious, but a slightly pixilated hoodlum who'd do nothing more violent than steal bridges and sell hot ferryboats."

Sheldon sometimes played a real bad guy, but more often he burlesqued his own image in films menacing Abbott and Costello, Brown and Carney, the Bowery Boys, Martin and Lewis, and others. He eventually turned up as a Damon Runyon character in *Guys and Dolls*. On radio, Leonard played the racetrack tout ready to give Jack Benny a tip on anything from horses to trains. He turns up at the train depot, muttering: "Take the Super Chief—it's got a good rail position...the Super Chief will beat El Capitan into Chicago by six lengths...take my word for it, the Super Chief is a sleeper."

One of Leonard's first jobs was at the New York Stock Exchange. It was an auspicious morning: "The crash had started. I was in at nine in the morning and by two in the afternoon I was out of a job."

Though Leonard spent a lifetime talking out the side of his mouth in a low, menacingly enunciated Brooklyn accent, he was far from his thug image. After attending Stuyvesant High in New York, he came to Syracuse University on an athletic scholarship. Aside from starring on the football, water polo, and swim teams, he was president of the dramatics society. He spent the thirties working on Broadway and reading scripts for producers George S. Kaufman and George Abbott. He recalled, "I developed an objectivity about scripts which an actor doesn't have; he only notices his own part."

After his years as a comic Hollywood heavy, Leonard put is knowledge of scripts and his on-the-job training in production to work. In 1953 he became a partner with Danny Thomas on a series of successful TV shows and went on to produce hit sitcoms including *Make Room for Daddy, The Bill Dana Show, The Dick Van Dyke Show,* and *The Andy Griffith Show.* He also produced *I Spy,* taking a chance on a stand-up comic with no acting experience, Bill Cosby.

He said there was no formula to his TV sitcom success: "It would be nice if there was a way to intellectualize comedy, reduce it to rules and formulas. It would make us feel so much more secure…comedy does not survive analysis. If you tell your wife a joke and all you get in response is a puzzled look and 'What's funny about that?' don't try to explain. Let it go. Change the subject."

SELECTED BROADWAY APPEARANCES:
Hotel Alimony (1934), *The Night Remembers* (1934), *Having Wonderful Time* (1937), *Kiss the Boys Goodbye* (1938)

SELECTED FILM APPEARANCES:
Another Thin Man (1939), *Lucky Jordan* (1942), *Hit the Ice* (1943), *To Have and Have Not* (1944), *Zombies on Broadway* (1945), *It's a Wonderful Life* (1946), *The Gangster* (1947), *Sinbad the Sailor* (1947), *If You Knew Susie* (1948), *Jinx Money* (1948), *Take One False Step* (1949), *Behave Yourself* (1951), *Abbott and Costello Meet the Invisible Man* (1951), *Stop, You're Killing Me!* (1952), *Money From Home* (1953), *Guys and Dolls* (1955), *Pocketful of Miracles* (1961)

TELEVISION SERIES:
The Duke (1954), *Big Eddie* (1975)

Leonard remained on the production side of the business, winning good critical notices for the sitcom *My World and Welcome to It.* The four-time Emmy Award-winner occasionally took an acting role, starring in the short-lived series, *Big Eddie.* He played Cliff Huxtable's hospital boss in a poignant episode of *The Cosby Show.* In 1990 Leonard appeared on an episode of *Murder She Wrote* in a familiar Brooklyn mug guise, playing Bulldog Kowalski, an old detective still snooping around after a twenty-five-year-old homicide, hoping to finally crack "da moida."

SAM LEVENE
Samuel Levine, August 28, 1905–December 20, 1980

An energetic, Runyonesque New York actor, Sam Levene seemed to specialize in heart-of-gold hoods and querulous police detectives. Either way, the heroes who encountered him weren't sure if he was really as tough—or as smart—as he seemed. That he was subject to the same moments of doubt marked him as a perfect comic foil and durable ensemble player.

Levene was about to go to work in the garment center of New York when he took a chance on acting school. He made his stage debut in 1927 in *Wall Street* but his big break came seven years later when he played the comic tough guy Patsy in *Three Men on a Horse* in 1935. The way he said them, threats seemed more ridiculous than murderous: "If ya ever show your face around here again you'll carry it out between two buns like hamboiger!"

Levene appeared in the movie version the next year and many more films that called for an actor who, with a semi-knowing squint and an elaborate show of tongue-in-cheek shrewdness, turns tough mug remarks into light comedy. In *Shadow of the Thin Man,* he's the hard-boiled inspector trying to solve a case. Examining a gun: *"So,* it hasn't been *fired?* It must be using a new perfume—black powder!"

SAM LEVENE, New Yorker through and through, whether playing hard-boiled comic hoods or no-nonsense detectives, as here in *Crossfire* with Robert Ryan (left) and Steve Brodie.

Levene's love of the stage remained throughout the years. He regularly returned to Broadway. After his first film roles, he was back to play Gordon Miller, the con man theatrical producer, in *Room Service*. In the forties he once again returned from Hollywood to reestablish his stage credentials, earning praise for his role as Sidney Black in *Light Up the Sky,* once more playing an explosive, high-pressure producer. A few years later he created the role of Nathan Detroit in *Guys and Dolls. Variety* called it "among the classic comedy portrayals in U.S. musical legit." He went on to play opposite Jack Albertson on Broadway in *The Sunshine Boys,* and made less and less films in the seventies.

To film fans accustomed to a dark-haired feisty player in classic Hollywood productions, he was almost unrecognizable in his brief role as an aging friend of Lee Strasberg in *And Justice for All.* It was a surprise to read the credits and discover that the funny scene-stealer commiserating with Strasberg on the pleasures and pitfalls of eating a Thanksgiving turkey was none other than Sam Levene.

The colorful star never retired. He was back on Broadway in the 1980 production *Horowitz and Mrs. Washington,* but died later that year, a few days before Christmas.

SELECTED BROADWAY APPEARANCES:
Headquarters (1929), *Three Times an Hour* (1931), *Wonder Boy* (1931), *Dinner at Eight* (1932), *Yellow Jack* (1934), *Three Men on a Horse* (1935), *Room Service* (1937), *Margin for Error* (1939), *A Sound of Hunting* (1945), *Light Up the Sky* (1948), *Guys and Dolls* (1950), *The Matchmaker* (1954), *The Hot Corner* (1956), *Make a Million* (1958), *Heartbreak House* (1959), *The Good Soup* (1960), *Let It Ride* (1961), *The Devil's Advocate* (1961), *The Last Analysis* (1964), *Nathan Weinstein, Mystic, Connecticut* (1966), *Three Men on a Horse* (revival) (1969), *Paris Is Out!* (1970), *The Royal Family* (1975), *Horowitz and Mrs. Washington* (1980)

SELECTED FILM APPEARANCES:
Three Men on a Horse (1936), *Mad Miss Manton* (1938), *Golden Boy* (1939), *Crossfire* (1947), *The Babe Ruth Story* (1948), *Sweet Smell of Success* (1957), *Act One* (1963), *Such Good Friends* (1971), *And Justice For All* (1979)

RICHARD LIBERTINI
May 21, 1943

Originally a "Stewed Prune," later a barking dog, a cracked wizard, and a South American dictator with a Señor Wences obsession, Richard Libertini specializes in offbeat roles. Sometimes he's only on screen for a minute or two (as in *Bonfire of the Vanities*) but when a flagging movie needs a quick, quirky shot of comedy, quirky Libertini is the one to choose.

Libertini established a name for himself early as an inventive improv comedian. While still attending Boston's Emerson College he joined the Greenwich Village revue *Stewed Prunes.* Later he hooked up with the Second City improvisation group and performed with it in Chicago, New York, and London. He was also in the cast of Broadway *The Mad Show,* singing a parody of Dylanesque protest singers. With partner McIntyre Dixon, he created a bizarrely memorable routine with the two as animal impressionists. At first the audience had no idea why Libertini was suddenly woofing and barking. Realizing that

RICHARD LIBERTINI, among the quirkiest of the current comic supports, is the whimsical fakir in *All of Me.*

he was now playing a dog master of ceremonies, they watched him bark his introduction of Dixon, another dog, who could imitate sheep, a cat, and even a human being saying "Down, boy!"

Libertini guest starred on a variety of sitcoms including *The Mary Tyler Moore Show, Newhart* and *Barney Miller,* and was the Godfather for a few seasons on *Soap.* He also enjoyed playing the trumpet, both professionally (for over a decade) and as a hobby. He began making films in the late sixties, often stealing several key scenes, even opposite comedy superstars.

One of his best roles in the seventies was as General Garcia, the overwhelmingly eccentric dictator in *The In-Laws* who loves doing Señor Wences impressions, rhapsodizes over paintings on black velvet, and hates it when anyone notices the "Z" for Zorro scar on his cheek. In *All of Me* with Steve Martin and Lily Tomlin, Libertini once again proved a delightful scene-stealer as the tall, dark, jibbering swami who can't quite control his spiritual magic. He had one of the few bright moments in *Bonfire of the Vanities* playing a Bronx schoolteacher having troubles with his kids. As he puts it, "they're either cooperative or life threatening."

As an expert at dialect comedy, Libertini wrings laughs from most any phrase. In *Best Friends*, he gets the film's first laughs when he conducts a marriage ceremony. As a Mexican justice of the peace, he calls out for the couple to repeat "I Dee An Doe!" Finally they realize he means, "I thee endow."

In 1988 Libertini starred as a comedy writer in the short-lived sitcom *Family Man*. Two years later the balding, bearded actor costarred in *The Fanelli Boys* as Father Angelo. In 1991 his unique brand of eccentricity led to his being cast as a flaky cop opposite Robert Guillaume in *Pacific Station*. Libertini's character was into new-age teas, "sharing" emotions, and pursuing a healthy mind and body. He often imparted his offbeat concepts to Guillaume. In the pilot episode, he tried to get his stodgy partner to stop arguing with his wife and see her point of view: "When I was married, we had a rule—never go to bed angry." "So why did you get divorced?" "Going without sleep for six months was too much for her."

GEORGE LINDSEY
December 17, 1929

A cheerful proponent of country comedy, George "Goober" Lindsey has specialized in film and television roles that firmly stereotyped him as a goofy hayseed. Sometimes he grinned as if he didn't have a thought in his head. Sometimes he put on a doleful expression that sadly suggested he was trying to find a thought in his head. Either way, Lindsay made it look easy.

Actually, Lindsey put in many years of work as he trained to become an actor and comedian. Born in Jasper, Alabama, he attended Florence State College on an athletic scholarship, ending up a member of the Alabama Sports Hall of Fame. After three years in the air force, where he performed in hundreds of talent contests and service shows, he became an English teacher at Hazel Green High School. Then he made the big career move. Coming to New York to get his masters degree in education at Hunter College, he began to study acting at the American Theatre Wing School.

He brought hip, country-tinged comedy to The Duplex and other New York clubs. Patrons were intrigued by his ideas for songs, like "The Let's Give Up Our Inhibitions So We the Neanderthal Can Invent the

Round Wheel and Improve Our Way of Life Blues." Lindsey appeared on Jack Paar's show in the spring of 1961 and then went to Hollywood for *The Alfred Hitchcock Hour, The Twilight Zone,* and other TV shows that cast him as "killers, dopers, bodyguards, and all kinds of men of the black hat."

Lindsey's comedy break came with *The Andy Griffith Show.* He had the role of Gomer Pyle—until Jim Nabors was tested—but later turned up as Gomer's cousin "Goober." He played the same rube role in the spin-off *Mayberry R.F.D.,* and later joined the cast of *Hee Haw.* While George "Goober" Lindsey remained firmly rooted in country comedy, urban critics continued to blast his genre of humor. Lindsey insisted there was a difference "between a hillbilly show and a rural show. But funny is funny."

Lindsey appeared in a number of films as well as TV shows including *Gunsmoke, Banaceck,* and *M*A*S*H* (the latter a memorable episode in which he played a hell-raising good ol' boy whose comical obnoxiousness is more distracting than the war). He lent his voice to several Disney cartoon characters and carved out a stand-up act for Las Vegas and the banquet circuit. He'd begin with a few words about his roots: "I'm from Jasper, Alabama. It's a small town—we got two things we're very proud of. Night and day! It's not too hard to tell we was poor—when you saw the toilet paper dryin' in the clothesline…"

He raised $450,000 to build the George Lindsey Aquatic Center at the Alabama State Hospital for the Mentally Retarded and raised over a million dollars for the Special Olympics. He continued to take supporting roles in films and extended his sense of humor to his personal life. Visitors to Lindsey's Tarzana, California, home always noticed the stuffed animal trophies decorating his walls—each one fitted with crossed eyes.

GEORGE LINDSEY, Gomer Pyle's hayseed cousin, Goober, proved adept at being a second banana country style.

MARION LORNE
Marion Lorne MacDougall,
August 12, 1888–May 9, 1968

An actress who got funnier as she grew older, Marion Lorne was beloved for her protrayals of eccentric and downright dotty ladies. She had small roles in many films and was memorable on television as the forgetful Aunt Clara on *Bewitched*.

Lorne appeared often in Broadway productions of the late twenties and early thirties before leaving for her native London where she lived with her husband, theater manager Walter Hackett. They came back to America in 1942. After his death she concentrated on her career, replacing Josephine Hull during the Broadway run of *Harvey* and acting in many more theatrical productions.

In films, she was the addled mother Robert Walker wanted knocked off in Hitchcock's *Strangers on a Train*. Hitchcock recalled, "She was more than an actress in England; she was an institution.

MARION LORNE, never forlorn but always forgetful, seems to be onto a new maxim: seeing is not always believing.

She played English teacher Mrs. Gurney on *Mr. Peepers* in the early fifites, and, according to costar Tony Randall, was pretty much the same offstage as on, slightly fogbound. She may have had good reason to act befuddled. During the run of *Mr. Peepers* she said, "I'm a nervous type as you might have realized.... It takes me a long time to learn a part, and here every week I have to learn a new one and sometimes they're still rewriting it up to the last minute."

Over the years Lorne perfected her particular brand of perplexed old lady, utilizing a flustered stammer and an incongruous stare as if it was *the other* person who was at fault for not understanding her.

She played herself in sketches on *The Garry Moore Show*, and went on to her greatest fame on *Bewitched*. The role of the kindly but confused Aunt Clara seemed to revitalize interest in her. She had a small part in *The Graduate* and seemed ready to balance more film roles with her work on *Bewitched*. Lorne was living alone at 130 East 39th Street in Manhattan when she suffered a fatal heart attack. Not long after that, her name was read at the year's Emmy Awards—for Outstanding Performance by a Supporting Actress in a Comedy Series, for *Bewitched*, edging out costar Agnes Moorehead.

On the set of *Bewitched* her fellow actors saw the craft behind her seemingly effortless fumbling. At a rehearsal one day, she missed a line and producer Bill Asher told her it was funny and not worth changing. Marion insisted on doing it over, saying, "I have to know exactly how to say it before I screw it up."

SELECTED BROADWAY APPEARANCES:
Pansy's Arabian Night (1924), *Sorry You've Been Troubled* (1929), *Hyde Park Corner* (1934), *London After Dark* (1937), *Harvey* (1948), *Dance Me a Song* (1950)

SELECTED FILM APPEARANCES:
Strangers on a Train (1951), *The Girl Rush* (1955), *The Graduate* (1968)

TELEVISION SERIES:
Mr. Peepers (1952–55), *The Garry Moore Show* (1958–61), *Bewitched* (1964–68)

DONALD MacBRIDE (left), scowler without peer, helps try to scare information out of not-too-cooperative Oliver Blake with the help of policeman Tom Kennedy (Edgar's brother) and Johnnie Berkes in *Blonde Alibi.*

DONALD MacBRIDE
June 23, 1893–June 21, 1957

A master of comic menace, prone to upturned eyebrows and grimacing snarls, wrathful Donald MacBride played tough guys and slow-burning villains opposite many comics including Abbott and Costello, the Marx Brothers, and TV's *My Friend Irma.*

Before playing hotel managers, detectives and irritated store owners, Brooklyn-born MacBride worked as a singer, appearing in *George White Scandals of 1923* in songs and sketches. His big break was in *Room Service* on Broadway. When the Marx Brothers signed to do the film version, they insisted on one particular costar. "Our choice among Broadway coworkers in the picture," Groucho Marx announced, "is

SELECTED BROADWAY APPEARANCES:
George White's Scandals of 1923 (1923), *Glory for All* (1937), *Room Service* (1937)

SELECTED FILM APPEARANCES:
Room Service (1939), *Here Comes Mr. Jordan* (1941), *Topper Returns* (1941), *Love Crazy* (1941), *The Invisible Woman* (1941), *They Got Me Covered* (1942), *The Thin Man Goes Home* (1944), *Abbott and Costello in Hollywood* (1945), *Good News* (1947), *The Egg and I* (1947), *The Seven Year Itch* (1955)

TELEVISION SERIES:
My Friend Irma (1952–54)

MacBride...his is a performance that out-wickeds anything that Bill Brady ever gave us in *Way Down East*. And he does his stuff without the aid of a snowstorm."

MacBride didn't mind being the comic villain: "Can I help it if autograph seekers avoid me? I never turned down anybody for anything.... All comedians are at heart devils. What about the practical joker? Somebody has to get hurt to get the laughs, right? Look back through the pages of melodrama and what do you find? You find the majority of the 'curse you, gal' creatures grinning at their crimes.... I've got to boil and I love it. I'm the nicest man around the house you ever saw. My wife is mighty pleased.... for I never have to lose my temper anymore at home. I save it all for my part."

Though censors forced him to change "hells" and "damns" to a scream of "Jumping Butterballs!" MacBride had a field day as the man trying to evict the Marx clan in *Room Service*. When the film came out, the New York *Daily Mirror* insisted that MacBride got "a shade more laughs than the stars." His clenched teeth, bulldog jaw, disdainful glare, and mordant sneer made him a welcome foe for many subsequent comedians. He could vary his brand of poison from chilling calm to a sarcastic parody of good nature to the ultimate ulcerous growl and bellow. The reliable man of movie menace found himself in demand during the early days of television. He played Irma's boss, Milton J. Clyde, on *My Friend Irma* and was still working a year before his death, appearing in an episode of "Director's Playhouse" in July of 1956.

GAVIN MacLEOD
Allan See, February 28, 1931

A pleasant performer specializing in easy-going nice guys and mild-mannered patsies as well as, in earlier days when he had hair, no-good movie hit men and gunsels, Gavin MacLeod had his best successes late in his career as Murray Slaughter, the mildly sarcastic TV newswriter on *The Mary Tyler Moore Show* and the cheerful Captain Merrill Stubing of *The Love Boat*. For many years earlier he had to endure thankless roles from the inept and petty foil to Peter Sellers (*The Party*) to the wistful nonentity Happy Haines, one of the more pliable members of *McHale's Navy*.

Born in Mt. Kisco, schooled at Ithaca College, MacLeod studied drama after air force service and took the last name of his drama coach. Though he would eventually make a good living with likable characters who displayed gentle, ironic touches of humor, he had a miserable struggle to reach success. Early in his career he was worried about every role he got: "My identity came from the size of the parts I was playing." With a wife and two kids, he had to make a tough decision; keep on struggling or take a small but steady-paying job on *McHale's Navy.*

GAVIN MacLEOD, character actor (usually gunsels) to comic support as TV's Murray Slaughter to the big time as captain of *The Love Boat.*

"My agent said don't take it. My wife said don't take it..." He took it anyway. The money kept him just barely ahead of the creditors. The fulfillment was nil. "I would have, like, two lines a week: 'What are we gonna do now, Skip?'" In films he hardly had better luck. In *The Party* he played a tense and pushy producer having no luck taking Claudine Longet to bed or even keeping his toupee on his head. "Meshugah!" he yells at Peter Sellers. "I'm not your sugar!" Sellers insists. With such limited film and TV success, MacLeod saw a bleak future: "I started drinking, I got into diet pills, and so I tried twice to do myself in. I'll tell you what turned me around. Jesus Christ turned me around."

MacLeod's next sitcom role proved to be his big break, the wry Murray, forever supporting Mary Tyler Moore and needling Ted Knight. *The Love Boat* helped him coast along for more years of comfortable living and fame. MacLeod never forgot where the inspiration came from and shared his convictions in a 1985 broadcast with Jim and Tammy Bakker of the P.T.L. Ministry. "This is overpowering for me," he said, weeping. MacLeod remained anchored in his *Love Boat* fame, appearing in commercials for a luxury liner of that name and in 1990 starring in a made-for-TV reunion movie which didn't thrill *New York Post* television critic David Bianculli, who pronounced it "a real sinker...the most reprehensible excursion at sea since the Exxon Valdez."

MacLeod's faith remained vital to his own happiness: "I have peace. I have happiness. And if something doesn't go the way I think—I say that doesn't make any difference—*he* knows what he's doing."

SELECTED BROADWAY APPEARANCES:
The Captain and the Kings (1962)

SELECTED FILM APPEARANCES:
I Want to Live! (1958), *Compulsion* (1959), *Operation Petticoat* (1959), *McHale's Navy* (1964), *McHale's Navy Joins the Air Force* (1965), *The Sand Pebbles* (1966), *The Party* (1968), *Kelly's Heroes* (1970), *Murder Can Hurt You* (1980), *The Love Boat Valentine Cruise* (1990)

TELEVISION SERIES:
McHale's Navy (1962–64), *The Mary Tyler Moore Show* (1970–77), *Love Boat* (1977–86)

MARJORIE MAIN, garrulous hillbilly on the screen but a lady when filming stopped.

MARJORIE MAIN
Mary Tomlinson,
February 24, 1890–April 10, 1975

*I*n *Murder He Says,* a tough hillbilly woman presides over a brood of yahoo murderers who like to poison people. One person timidly wonders who will be next. "Well waddya wanna do," comically tough Marjorie Main growls, "live forever?"

In the forties and fifties, the harsh, scratchy-voiced actress was the bumptious queen of rural film comedy starring in the *Ma and Pa Kettle* series. She also played bold, big-boned battle-axes in comedies opposite everyone from Fred MacMurray to Lou Costello. According to Costello's daughter, Paddy, Main was unintentionally funny during the making of *Wistful Widow of Wagon Gap.* Paddy recalled that Main amazed her father. "She broke him up. He said that before they could do a scene, Marjorie would have to go sit in a corner somewhere and talk to her dead husband and get his permission to do the scene! And after the deceased husband gave his permission, she would go out and do the scene! Well, this just blew Dad away."

Most fans were surprised that the assorted flint-eyed, funny harridans (who were even more hideous when they tried to coquette and act cute) bore no relation to the real-life Main, who led a life of quiet and refined dignity.

The daughter of a reverend, she was born in Acton, Indiana, and studied drama at Franklin College and later Hamilton School of Dramatic Expression (in Lexington, Kentucky). She taught acting at Bourbon College in Paris, Kentucky, then performed with a touring Shakespeare company and other drama troupes. W. C. Fields brought her to New York for his show *The Family Ford.* She subsequently starred in a variety of Broadway plays, retiring after marrying psychologist/clergyman Dr. Stanley Krebs. She resumed her career following his death.

She won excellent reviews for her role as Joseph Downey's weary mother in the gangster drama *Dead End* and appeared opposite Humphrey Bogart in the film version. She made a logical partner for burly Wallace Beery in several early films, but after her ill-tempered comic roles in *Murder He Says* and *The Egg and I,* she was partnered with Percy Kilbride for the *Ma and Pa Kettle* series that brought her fame— and permanent typecasting as a garrulous hayseed. After nine profitable Kettle potboilers and the classy *Friendly Persuasion,* she retired from the screen in 1957.

162

CHUCK McCANN
September 2, 1936

CHUCK McCANN, goofy comic and mimic known for his Oliver Hardy impersonation and his jaunty "Hi, guy!"

An amiable performer whose light, good nature is a contrast to his hefty build, Chuck McCann began his career as a stand-up comic and mimic, and through the years made cameo sketch appearances and commercials as everyone from Stan Laurel and Oliver Hardy to John F. Kennedy and Ed McMahon. His most famous original character was the title role in *The Projectionist,* a cult comedy classic.

Born in Queens Village, young McCann demonstrated a tendency toward slapstick when he jumped out of his bedroom window carrying a bedsheet: he was trying to understand how parachutes operated. McCann's father, Val, worked as a musical arranger at the Roxy Theater and taught accordion; his grandfather, Jack, rode a unicycle with Buffalo Bill's Wild West Show. After attending Andrew Jackson High School, Chuck began his show business career in small clubs and on variety shows hosted by Garry Moore and Steve Allen. Later he had a local children's show, *Let's Have Fun,* in New York (1959–65), on which he had kids laughing with his impressions of comic strip characters (Dondi, Little Orphan Annie, etc.)

SELECTED FILM APPEARANCES:
The Heart Is a Lonely Hunter (1968), *The Projectionist* (1971), *Silent Movie* (1976), *They Went That-a-Way and That-a-Way* (1978), *C.H.O.M.P.S.* (1979), *Rosebud Beach Hotel* (1985), *Hamburger...The Motion Picture* (1986), *Thrashin'* (1986), *Cameron's Closet* (1989)

TELEVISION SERIES:
Let's Have Fun (a.k.a. The Chuck McCann Show) (1959–65), *The Garry Moore Show* (1966–67), *Turn On* (1969), *Happy Days* [not the Ron Howard sitcom] (1970), *Far-Out Space Nuts* (1975), *Van Dyke and Company* (1976), *All That Glitters* (1977), *A New Kind of Family* (1979–80), *Semi-Tough* (1980)

COLLECTIBLES:
Sing Along With Jack (Colpix), *Everything You Always Wanted to Know About the Godfather But Don't Ask* (Columbia), *Miss Casino Comedy Show* (video cassette)

and great comedians (Laurel and Hardy). Meanwhile for their parents he recorded *Sing Along With Jack,* an album that tried to outdo Allan Sherman's *My Son the Folksinger* and Vaughn Meader's *The First Family* by combining concepts: John F. Kennedy (McCann) singing folk songs.

McCann continued to costar on comedy albums (he was Marlon Brando in a *Godfather* parody album of 1972) and began a promising film career in a serious role playing Alan Arkin's deaf mute friend in *The Heart Is a Lonely Hunter.* He had the lead in the cult classic comedy-fantasy, *The Projectionist,* but was used mainly in support after that, a reliable performer in roles calling for an earnest, good-natured big guy with the common touch. Ironically in the sixties one of his best comic characters was used in a TV commercial for a deodorant. He and a sleepy, depressed fellow (played by Bill Fiore) shared a mutual medicine cabinet in adjoining apartments in a modern high-rise. McCann's catchphrase was a goofy, cheery "Hi, Guy!" whenever the two men opened the cabinet.

Over the years, McCann continued to vary his roles between comedy for kids and for adults. In 1975 he was cocreator, cowriter, and star of *The Far-Out Space Nuts* Saturday morning comedy series. Two years later he played Bert, the house-husband to Lois Nettleton, on *All That Glitters.*

The divorced father of three was known in the eighties primarily for his flawless impressions of Oliver Hardy and W. C. Fields on TV commercials, including a series for a windshield wiper company. The six-foot-three, two hundred-fifty-pounder also developed an accurate Ed McMahon parody which he used often, including a 1989 Rodney Dangerfield cable special satirizing *The Tonight Show.*

HATTIE McDANIEL
June 10, 1895–October 26, 1952

Though often stereotyped as a comic maid, Hattie McDaniel made the most of her roles. In *Hattie,* his 1989 biography of her, Carlton Jackson wrote that in most films, "she was slow and bumbling like Stepin Fetchit" but also "cantankerous...in the America of the mid-thirties both North and South, it was something different, to say the least, to see a black person act this aggres-

HATTIE McDANIEL, whose cantankerous comic maids invariably took the star down a peg or two, deals Ann Sheridan in *George Washington Slept Here.*

sively toward whites."

Born in Wichita, Hattie won a gold medal in Denver for her teenage recital of "Convict Joe" for the Women's Christian Temperance Union. She grew up singing with her brother Otis in vaudeville and appearing with J. M. Johnson's Mighty Modern Minstrels. She came to California in 1931 and appeared on the *Optimistic Donuts* show on KNX radio in Los Angeles. Her later radio appearances included programs starring Amos and Andy and Eddie Cantor. The amply-built Hattie sang in films (she performed "Ice Cold Katie" with Willie Best in Cantor's *Thank Your Lucky Stars*) but became best known as a domestic. One rueful look from her to her employer was enough to set an audience chuckling, as in *Alice Adams.* Sometimes the laughs came from malaprops. In *Since You Went Away* she insisted that when her job as a maid ended each day she was on her own: "When I finishes my work, I wants my solitude and I wants my privitation."

Occasionally she got her hands on an important role. Her work in *Gone With the Wind* was fairly straight but included a lot of fussing and fretting humor. "You can't show your bosom 'fore three o'clock!" she warns Vivien Leigh as Scarlett O'Hara. For her performance as Mammy she became the first black performer to win an Academy Award. At the podium, having received an ovation from the greatest stars in Hollywood, she said, "It makes me feel very humble, and I shall always hold

SELECTED FILM APPEARANCES:
I'm No Angel (1933), *Judge Priest* (1934), *Babbitt* (1934), *Imitation of Life* (1934), *Traveling Saleslady* (1935), *Alice Adams* (1935), *Libeled Lady* (1936), *Show Boat* (1936), *The Bride Walks Out* (1936), *Don't Tell the Wife* (1937), *The Wildcatter* (1937), *Everybody's Baby* (1939), *Zenobia* (1939), *Gone With the Wind (1939)*, *The Male Animal* (1942), *George Washington Slept Here* (1942), *Johnny Come Lately* (1943), *Thank Your Lucky Stars* (1943), *Three Is a Family* (1944), *Margie* (1956), *Song of the South* (1946), *Mr. Blandings Builds His Dream House* (1948), *Family Honeymoon* (1948)

TELEVISION SERIES:
Beulah (1951) [as the second of three actresses to play the role]

COLLECTIBLES:
Hattie (by Carlton Jackson)

it as a beacon for anything that I may be able to do in the future." She began weeping with emotion, adding, "I sincerely hope that I shall always be a credit to my race, and to the motion picture industry." She went on to appear in over eighty films.

On radio and later on television she took over the role o0f the comic maid "Beulah." She didn't use a stereotyped dialect for the part. Her version of the domestic was one that seemed to know a lot more than her boss did. When asked about playing maids so often in films, Hattie had an answer. "Hell," she said, "I'd rather play a maid than be one."

JOHN McGIVER, whose snob appeal brought smiles to moviegoers, terrifies mousy Agnes Gooch (Jane Connell) in *Mame.*

JOHN McGIVER
November 5, 1913–September 9, 1975

A balding, perfectly moon-faced actor with a petulant, precise speech pattern, John McGiver was ideally cast as a wryly witty if overbearing boss, or an exasperated underling. He was very popular in sitcom-styled films and TV shows in the sixties and early seventies.

McGiver was born in New York City and graduated from Fordham University, earning a master's degree at Columbia. He taught at Christopher Columbus High School in the Bronx (Anne Bancroft, then Anna Maria Italiano, was a student). McGiver wrote the Broadway play *All Gaul Is Divided* in 1947 but recalled, "I became very contented teaching English, and writing radio and television scripts over the weekends. I was satisfied with my life, and satisfied that I was earning a living in the best, most sensible way for me." In 1955 he happened to sub for a friend in an Off-Broadway show, was seen by an agent, and subsequently cast in a *Studio One* TV episode. More work followed until, at forty-two, he became a full-time actor.

After several key roles on Broadway, he moved out to California for films, instantly typed for his slow-burning glare and tight-lipped looks of chagrin.

On television McGiver guested on *The Twilight Zone* and became a regular on *The Patty Duke Show.* Married, with ten children, McGiver ultimately got his own sitcom, *Many Happy Returns,* about life in a department store. It didn't last long, but McGiver remained a busy performer, appearing in several more programs. In films he is probably best remembered as the staid and religious man who turns out to be an

SELECTED BROADWAY APPEARANCES:
All Gaul Is Divided (1947), *Cloud 7* (1958), *Drink to Me Only* (1958), *God and Kate Murphy* (1959), *A Thurber Carnival* (1960), *A Cook for Mr. General* (1961), *Happiness Is Just a Little Thing Called a Rolls Royce* (1968), *Our Town* (1968), *The Front Page* (1968)

SELECTED FILM APPEARANCES:
I Married a Woman (1958), *Breakfast at Tiffany's* (1961), *Mr. Hobbs Takes a Vacation* (1962), *Who's Minding the Store?* (1963), *Man's Favorite Sport?* (1964), *Marriage on the Rocks* (1965), *The Spirit Is Willing* (1967), *Fitzwilly* (1967), *Midnight Cowboy* (1969), *The Great Man's Whiskers* (1971), *The Apple Dumpling Gang* (1975)

TELEVISION SERIES:
The Patty Duke Show (1963–64), *Many Happy Returns* (1964–65), *Mr. Terrific* (1967), *The Jimmy Stewart Show* (1971–72)

obsessed fanatic in a moment of black comedy in *Midnight Cowboy.* Of his acting style, McGiver modestly said, "I'm no Method actor, not one of those young fellows who screw up their faces and wonder what's meant by this and what's behind that. Arthur Treacher once said, 'I say lines, I take my money, and I get along home.' That's me."

FRANK McHUGH
May 23, 1898–September 11, 1981

The ultimate sidekick at Warner Brothers, Frank McHugh was comic relief in dramas and a bewildered straight man to others in comedies. He played wise-cracking reporters, punchy boxers and good-natured drunks, all in support of the leads. He seemed to be permanently attached to James Cagney, having played his buddy Spud in *The Crowd Roars,* his chum Droopy in *Here Comes the Navy,* and his pal Danny in *The Roaring Twenties,* and in many others.

On his own, McHugh played Quince in *A Midsummer Night's Dream* (also with Cagney) and Windy in *Mighty Joe Young.* He was William Powell's sidekick in *I Love You Again,* bringing

FRANK McHUGH as the almost always good-natured best friend to all the Warner leading men of the thirties and forties.

in the laughs more from his Runyonesque enthusiasm and breathless bafflement than any particular comedy line. He rarely seemed to get a quotable gag or perform a memorable bit of physical comedy but he got chuckles from his reactions; like the people watching in the audience, he seemed powerless to prevent comic or dramatic disaster. All he

167

SELECTED BROADWAY APPEARANCES:
The Fall Guy (1925), *Fog* (1927), *Excess Baggage* (1927), *Tenth Avenue* (1927), *Show Girl* (1929), *A Funny Thing Happened on the Way to the Forum* (1963), *Finian's Rainbow* (1967)

SELECTED FILM APPEARANCES:
The Dawn Patrol (1930), *The Widow From Chicago* (1930), *Traveling Husbands* (1931), *The Front Page* (1931), *The Crowd Roars* (1932), *The Blessed Event* (1932), *42nd Street* (1933), *Elmer the Great* (1933), *Footlight Parade* (1933), *Here Comes the Navy* (1934), *Let's Be Ritzy* (1934), *Midsummer Night's Dream* (1935), *Gold Diggers of 1935* (1935), *Three Men on a Horse* (1936), *Mr. Dodd Takes the Air* (1937), *The Roaring Twenties* (1938), *The Fighting 69th* (1938), *City for Conquest* (1940), *Going My Way* (1944), *Bowery to Broadway* (1944), *State Fair* (1945), *The Velvet Touch* (1948), *Mighty Joe Young* (1949), *It Happens Every Spring* (1953), *There's No Business Like Show Business* (1954), *The Last Hurrah* (1958), *Say One for Me* (1959), *Easy Come Easy Go* (1967)

TELEVISION SERIES:
The Bing Crosby Show (1964–65)

could do was look on in surprise, or shake his head and mutter with deadpan earnestness, "Gee, that's tough."

McHugh occasionally had a starring chance, like *He Couldn't Say No,* about a mild mannered fellow who buys a nude statue of his dream girl—and ultimately meets her—but he didn't have enough charismatic comedy inventions to last through a whole feature.

Born in Homestead, Pennsylvania, Frank left his parents' McHugh Stock Company for vaudeville in his late teens. In the twenties he was active on the stage both on Broadway (*The Fall Guy*) and in London (*Is Zat So*). He was married in 1928 and through the thirties and forties made his name in Hollywood movies. He took occasional stage roles in his later years, coming back to Broadway for *A Funny Thing Happened on the Way to the Forum* in 1963. He made his sitcom debut in 1964 as the handyman Willie Walters on *The Bing Crosby Show.*

He and James Cagney remained pals all their lives, both returning to New England after their Hollywood years. At the time of his death McHugh was living in retirement in Cos Cob, Connecticut, with his wife and two children.

HOWARD McNEAR
January 27, 1905–January 3, 1969

I n the eighties a minor cult formed around character comedian Howard McNear, the man who played flustered, fussy barber, Floyd Lawson on *The Andy Griffith Show.* Floyd was a fairly lame personality, a windy natterer prone toward useless gossip, but there was something about his mild, wistful fluttering and hesitant, cautionary tones that seemed to amuse fans. Floyd sometimes got excited, but always seemed to try and hold it in, his "Ooooh, Andy..." coming with inhaled breathiness.

Born in Los Angeles, McNear attended the Oatman School of the Theater, and appeared in plays as a leading man. Even as the aging Floyd, complete with glasses, McNear wore a dapper pencil mustache that gave a hint of what he was like as a suave youth. A durable radio performer, McNear appeared on *Gunsmoke* (1952–61) playing Doc Adams opposite William Conrad's Matt Dillon.

On television, McNear had appeared often as Mr. Hamish on *The George Gobel Show* and guested frequently on *The Jack Benny Show*. When he worked on Andy Griffith's show, the star recalled that McNear was like his character, "nervous" but a "kind, kind man." McNear had a stroke in 1963. His recovery was helped considerably when he was invited to return. He did, after two years, but couldn't walk well. He stayed behind his barber's chair and the camera angles had to avoid his weakened left side (one arm was now fairly useless). Still, Floyd the Barber was back.

HOWARD McNEAR, always making a gentle nuisance of himself, enjoys Brian Donlevy's confrontation with Jerry Lewis in *The Errand Boy*.

Married with two sons and a daughter, McNear would have his greatest fame after his death, and in the late eighties when companies advertising in rock magazines began selling "Floyd" T-shirts with pictures of the famous barber on them. Fans watching reruns waited for those rare moments of Floyd the Barber's sappy reveries. Like the time he recalled… "I always did want to be a barber. Even when I was a little kid. I used to practice on cats…we had the baldest cats in the county."

SELECTED FILM APPEARANCES:
The Long, Long Trailer (1954), *Bundle of Joy* (1956), *Bell, Book and Candle* (1958), *Anatomy of a Murder* (1959), *The Errand Boy* (1961), *Irma La Douce* (1963), *Kiss Me, Stupid* (1964), *The Fortune Cookie* (1966)

TELEVISION SERIES:
The Brothers (1956–57), *The Andy Griffith Show* (1960–68)

KAY MEDFORD
Margaret Kathleen O'Regan, September 14, 1914–April 10, 1980

Kay Medford told the New York *Daily News* in 1964, "I started playing sexpots, nymphos, prostitutes, gun molls with wet lips and cigarettes dangling, then madams, and now mothers." Typical of her early performances was her role opposite Vincent Price in the Broadway comedy *The Playhouse*. Critic Walter

KAY MEDFORD, showing her deadpan Jewish mother style even though she was Irish.

Kerr wrote that "Miss Medford has a rueful lower lip, disillusioned eyes…you feel that everything is against Miss Medford…you love her for her unquenchable spirit."

The older the bleary-eyed, caustic, long-suffering actress got, the funnier she became. On Broadway she played Dick Van Dyke's mother in *Bye Bye Birdie* and Barbra Streisand's in *Funny Girl.* "I'm playing another Jewish mommala," she said at the time. "I'm not even Jewish, I'm Irish."

Born and raised in New York, she was an orphan at fifteen. She later found work as an artist and lived in Greenwich Village with a roommate. Through writer Whitney Bolton, she met director Mervyn LeRoy. "Maybe you can do some art posters for him," said Bolton. But when LeRoy came up to visit, he came away convinced that Medford, the daughter of stage actress Mary Reagan, was worth a screen test.

Medford made several films and was even more effective on stage. She did impressions of Johnny Ray, Tallulah Bankhead, and Bette Davis in *Talent '52.* The self-proclaimed "nasal New Yorker" spoofed Tennessee Williams plays and Doris Day films in the 1955 *Almost Crazy* revue, and was a critics favorite for years in subsequent shows and film appearances.

Medford scored one of her best stage successes in *Don't Drink the Water,* replacing Vivian Vance. Woody Allen pronounced her performance "hysterically funny."

SELECTED BROADWAY APPEARANCES:
Paint Your Wagon (1951), *The Little Clay Cart* (1953), *Talent '52* (1952), *The Playhouse* (1954), *Almost Crazy* (1955), *Wake Up Darling* (1956), *A Hole in the Head* (1957), *Bye Bye Birdie* (1960), *The Heroine* (1963), *Pal Joey* (1963), *Funny Girl* (1964), *Don't Drink the Water* (1966)

SELECTED FILM APPEARANCES:
The War Against Mrs. Hadley (1942), *Swing Shift Maisie* (1943), *A Face in the Crowd* (1957), *Butterfield 8* (1960), *The Rat Race* (1960), *Ensign Pulver* (1964), *The Busy Body* (1967), *Funny Girl* (1968)

TELEVISION SERIES:
To Rome With Love (1969–70), *The Dean Martin Show* (1970–73)

She was active on TV in the sixties and seventies, mostly in sitcoms. She had completed an episode of *Barney Miller* and was making the film *Honky Tonk Freeway* in 1981 when she became too ill to work. Geraldine Page took her place, but for those who recalled her vitality—especially on the stage in the sixties, Kay Medford was one of the irreplaceable.

170

VICTOR MOORE
April 24, 1876–July 23, 1962

balding, pudgy, very funny little man, Victor Moore sometimes played a scowling, impatient businessman but more often appeared as a befuddled, easily intimidated patsy.

Born in Hammonton, New Jersey, he and his wife Emma Littlefield had some success with a vaudeville sketch called "Change Your Act." They first performed it in 1903, and toured with it for years. It was based, in part, on the abuse of Moore. Meek and timid, he calls out to the lighting crew "Mister, hey mister! Spotlight, you know, spotlight, like we rehearsed!" He gets more and more woeful each time the (fake) stage manager shouts at him to come up with something fresh.

In the late twenties Moore came to Broadway with a string of hits that culminated with his role as ineffectual Vice President Alexander Throttlebottom of *Of Thee I Sing*. The Pulitzer Prize–winning play costarred William Gaxton as President Wintergreen. Moore was soon typecast as the insecure, worried nobody thrust into a position of power. The vice president is so unimportant, he isn't even recognized by a

VICTOR MOORE, wonderfully befuddled as always, only thinks he's been dealt a winning hand.

White House tour guide, who asks, "What kind of fellow is he?" Moore answers, "He's all right. He's a nice fellow when you get to know him, but nobody wants to know him." "What's the matter with him?" "There's nothing the matter with him. He's just vice president." "What does he do all the time?" "He sits around in the parks, and feeds the pigeons…the other day he was going to join the library, but he had to give two references so he couldn't get in."

Dumpy little Moore and tall straight-man Gaxton teamed on Broadway in a subsequent sequel, *Let 'Em Eat Cake*, as well as *Anything Goes, Leave It to Me, Louisiana Purchase, Hollywood Pinafore,* and *Nellie Bly.*

While Moore had dabbled in film as early as 1915 (as the star of the very brief *Chimmie Falden* series and *The Clown*, a sentimental feature), it was in the sound era that Moore's woeful demeanor and groaning voice brought memorable laughs.

In *Gold Diggers of 1937* he's moaning Broadway producer J. J. Hobart, always walking around like a tired, overstuffed duck, whining "Gimme one of my pills, I'm havin' a dizzy spell." Even the sight of half-nude chorus girls doesn't inspire him. As they parade by him in bathing suits he murmurs, "They'll catch their death of cold." In *Zieg-*

SELECTED BROADWAY APPEARANCES:
45 Minutes From Broadway (1906), *The Talk of the Town* (1907), *The Happiest Night of His Life* (1911), *See You Later* (1919), *Easy Come Easy Go* (1925), *Oh, Kay!* (1926), *Funny Face* (1927), *Hold Everything* (1928), *Of Thee I Sing* (1931), *Let 'Em Eat Cake* (1933), *Anything Goes* (1934), *Leave It to Me!* (1938), *Louisiana Purchase* (1940), *Hollywood Pinafore* (1945), *Nellie Bly* (1946), *On Borrowed Time* (1953), *Carousel* (1957)

SELECTED FILM APPEARANCES:
Chimmie Falden (1915), *The Clown* (1917), *The Man Who Found Himself* (1925), *Heads Up* (1930), *Gift of Gab* (1934), *Gold Diggers of 1937* (1936), *We're on the Jury* (1937), *Meet the Missus* (1937), *Life of the Party* (1937), *Radio City Revels* (1938), *Louisiana Purchase* (1941), *Star-Spangled Rhythm* (1942), *Riding High* (1943), *It's in the Bag* (1945), *Duffy's Tavern* (1945), *Ziegfeld Follies* (1946), *A Kiss in the Dark* (1949), *We're Not Married* (1952), *The Seven Year Itch* (1955)

field Follies he utilized his vaudeville experience in a sketch as the nervous little man whose zealous lawyer keeps angering the judge. All he wants to do is "Pay the Two Dollars" but nobody's listening. At least he got wiser as he got older. In *We're Not Married* he's the perplexed justice of the peace who's unfortunately not licensed to perform weddings, much to the subsequent dismay of several couples he'd earlier united. In his last film, *The Seven Year Itch* with Marilyn Monroe, he played a plumber who walks in on her bubble bath.

"You're an old darling that everybody's taking advantage of," he was told in *Gold Diggers of 1937,* but thanks to his cuddly, dumpy looks and inoffensive ways, everybody seem to love the hapless, helpless, gentle Mr. Moore.

POLLY MORAN (right) prepares for inevitable screen mayhem with thirties screen partner Marie Dressler in *Reducing*.

POLLY MORAN
Pauline Therese Moran,
June 28, 1883–January 25, 1952

She was a silent film clown who favored raucous comedy, and Polly Moran's low style was perfectly suited to her times. She was very popular in Mack Sennett comedies circa 1915, and made a comeback teamed with Marie Dressler in the early thirties.

Born in Chicago, she quit school to join a touring company and starred in light opera and musical comedy. While playing vaudeville on the Orpheum circuit and in Europe she developed her own "nut" solo act as an eccentric singer and comedienne. There was nothing subtle about her man-chasing demeanor. And there was nothing subtle about the result, which usually was a blow to her dignity and a pratfall to the floor. The buxom comic would do anything for a laugh. She once blackened her eyes with makeup, insisting she hurt herself jumping rope without a bra.

Martha Raye and many others would take on Moran-styled roles, but in her day Polly got big laughs as everything from messy housewives to garrulous "Sheriff Nell," comic terror of the old West. After slow years in the late twenties she made a comeback with *The Callahans and the Murphys* costarring Marie Dressler. The two played battling, hard-drinking Irish women—drawing protests from various Irish groups, which especially resented the classic scene in which two ladies splashed beer down each other's shirts. Polly and Marie continued to make knockabout comedies in the late twenties and early thirties with Moran—the antagonistic troublemaker—usually the one to take the flop in the mud or the pie in the face.

After Dressler's death, Moran's comic parts became smaller and smaller. Polly drifted back to two-reelers in 1936. On July 15 that year, she had her second husband, Martin Malone, arrested. Newspapers headlined the story. He had tried to kill her, screaming in a drunken tirade that someone had called him "Mr. Polly Moran." She said that he fired a gun at her but it jammed. She wanted a divorce. A month later, she changed her story: "He never threatened me with a gun. I thought it would be a good lesson to the boy if I told officers to take him away and lock him up. I thought it would teach him not to be playing with guns." The truth evidently lay somewhere in between. He was fined $100 by a judge and set free.

SELECTED FILM APPEARANCES:
Ambrose's Little Hatchet (1915), *Madcap Ambrose* (1916), *She Loved Him Plenty* (1918), *Skirts* (1921), *The Callahans and the Murphys* (1927), *Bringing Up Father* (1928), *Hollywood Revue* (1929), *Caught Short* (1929), *Reducing* (1930), *Politics* (1931), *Prosperity* (1932), *The Passionate Plumber* (1932), *Alice in Wonderland* (1933), *Two Wise Maids* (1937), *Tom Brown's Schooldays* (1940), *Adam's Rib* (1949), *The Yellow Cab Man* (1950)

Polly had invested well from her silent film years. She had a nine-room mansion with two servants and a chauffeur. Still, she longed to make more films. Republic Studios hoped to duplicate the Dressler-Moran successes by teaming Polly with grouchy British comedienne Alison Skipworth, but there was not much interest in their two films, *Two Wise Maids* and *Ladies in Distress*. Polly remained in semi-retirement until 1949 when she began a belated, short-lived comeback with a role in *Adam's Rib*.

MANTAN MORELAND
September 3, 1901–September 28, 1973

A chunky black comedian, wide-eyed Mantan Moreland was known for his raspy voice, comic scowling, and good-natured reticence. He often played the hired help—a chauffeur or servant—but got a lot of mileage out of earthy indignance and comical grousing. He had enough charm to make his moments of hesi-

MANTAN MORELAND in his traditional role as chauffeur for boss Charlie Chan and number-one son (Sidney Toler and Benson Fong).

tence, self-preservation and doubt funny rather than annoying. That he could get laughs as much from low-key reactions as patented high jinks is evident from his simple catchphrase, a wistfully amused "Mm, mm, ain't that somethin'."

Unfortunately, the Moreland repertoire also included some stereotypical comical cowardice, ranging from high-pitched screams to eye-rolling expressions of fear. In his most famous role, Birmingham Brown, the cautious chauffeur to Charlie Chan, he had many comic highlights that still survive, but there seemed to be one too many frenzied cries of "Mistah Chan!" and jokes that were racially offensive. Roland Winters as Chan: "Go on in...you'll be harder to see in the dark." Mantan: "Don't worry, I'm gonna blend in with the darkness!"

Born in Louisiana, and always claiming that his first name was not some kind of bad racist pun but a common name down South, Moreland was in show business most of his life. He said he began as a barefoot dancer in minstrel shows as early as 1912 and worked with the Hagenbeck Wallace circus when he was fourteen. He made his way through vaudeville, toured Europe in *Blackbirds of 1928,* and returned to the States in various shows and reviews. He eventually teamed with Flournoy Miller and learned Miller's "anticipation" or "interruption" style in comedy routines. Moreland would subsequently perform it at the Apollo Theater, in films (especially the later low-budget, short-on-script Chan films at Monogram), and in nightclubs. Here, with his partner from the fifties and sixties, Livinggood Pratt, the humor is in the split-second anticipation of what the other is going to say:

"Mantan, what's your brother doin'..." "He's gonna get married... he's gonna marry the daughter of–" "She's a nice girl. Listen, let me tell you something.... One time I—" "That was her sister!..." "Now that's funny, just the other day I was talkin' to her father and the first thing I—" "That was your fault. What you should've done—" "I did!" "See that, Livinggood? That's why I like to talk to you. 'Cause you and I seems to agree with each other!"

Moreland made his film debut in 1939 in Joe Louis's *Spirit of Youth.* He had bit parts in 300 movies, and despite his often criticized stereotype Charlie Chan antics, went on to star in many films for black-oriented companies like Million Dollar Productions and Dixie National, which rarely played outside black theaters.

Moreland worked regularly on radio's *Duffy's Tavern* in 1951 and 1952 and starred in twelve episodes of the TV show *Michael Shayne, Detective* in 1958. Probably his best role in the latter part of his career was the 1957 all-black stage production of *Waiting for Godot.* He took Bert Lahr's part in that one. Despite the prestige of that role, he remained best known for his old supporting comedy roles and Chan films and was haunted by some of the moments of glaring bad taste. In 1959 he admitted, "Millions of people may have thought that my acting was comical but I know now that it wasn't always so funny to my own people."

SELECTED BROADWAY APPEARANCES:
Blackbirds (1928), *Lew Leslie's Blackbirds of 1930* (1930), *Singin' the Blues* (1931), *Blackberries of 1932* (1932), *Yeah-Man* (1932), *Shuffle Along of 1933* (1933), *Waiting for Godot* (1957)

SELECTED FILM APPEARANCES:
Spirit of Youth (1937), *Next Time I Marry* (1938), *Gang Smashers* (1938), *Harlem on the Prairie* (1938), *Two-Gun Man from Harlem* (1938), *Star Dust* (1940), *Viva Cisco Kid* (1940), *While Thousands Cheer* (1940), *Mr. Washington Goes to Town* (1940), *Cracked Nuts* (1941), *Up in the Air* (1941), *King of the Zombies* (1941), *A-Haunting We Will Go* (1942), *The Strange Case of Dr. X* (1942), *Mexican Spitfire Sees a Ghost* (1942), *The Palm Beach Story* (1942), *Hit the Ice* (1943), *Cabin in the Sky* (1943), *You're a Lucky Fellow Mr. Smith* (1943), *The Chinese Cat* (1944), *Bowery to Broadway* (1944), *Charlie Chan in the Secret Service* (1944), *See Here, Private Hargrove* (1944), *The Shanghai Cobra* (1945), *Mantan Messes Up* (1946), *Mantan Runs for Mayor* (1946), *Shadows Over Chinatown* (1946), *Tall, Tan and Terrific* (1946), *The Chinese Ring* (1947), *Docks of New Orleans* (1948), *Best Man Wins* (1948), *The Feathered Serpent* (1948), *Sky Dragon* (1949), *Enter Laughing* (1967), *Watermelon Man* (1970), *The Biscuit Eater* (1972), *The Young Nurses* (1973)

COLLECTIBLES:
That Ain't My Finger (Laff), *Elsie's Sportin' House* (Laff), *Tribute to the Man* (Laff)

After suffering a stroke in 1963, Moreland moved from New York to California with his wife, Hazel, and daughter, Marcella. He returned to work, making risque party albums, joining Livinggood in USO shows in the Orient, and guesting with Moms Mabley on a memorable episode of Bill Cosby's first TV sitcom. While many black performers who had allowed themselves to play stereotyped roles in the thirties and forties were spurned in later years, Moreland seemed to have slightly better luck finding work.

PAT MORITA
Noriyuki Morita, June 28, 1936

A stand-up comedian and sitcom costar through the sixties and seventies, diminutive Pat Morita played off his amused tolerance for bigotry and his ability to slyly joke back. In the early sixties he was sometimes billed as "The Hip Nip." In 1964 he opened at the Copa in New York replacing Sam Cooke, a gig he got because of complete ethnic confusion. The Copa's owner thought "Pat Morita" sounded Italian.

In films, Pat sometimes had embarrassing roles (he was in stereotypical Oriental garb and thick glasses as a comic henchman in

PAT MORITA, the hip, sly proprietor of the local teen hangout in *Happy Days*, was an ethnic stand-up comic turned Oscar-nominated dramatic actor.

Thoroughly Modern Millie) but on TV sitcoms, producers recognized his comic style and gave him roles that played off his deadpan cool. In a guest spot on *The Odd Couple* he was a Japanese restaurant owner trying to get investors. He claimed yuppies couldn't get enough of the cuisine: "They think it's hip to eat Nip." He was able to fend off Redd Foxx on *Sanford and Son,* even though his name on the series, "Ah Chew," was something to sneeze at. And on *M*A*S*H* he guested during the first season as Capt. Sam Pak, making gentle fun of Caucasian misconceptions. Hawkeye Pierce (Alan Alda) debates Major Burns with Pak listening in:

Pierce: "It wouldn't hurt us to speak their language." Burns: "I don't need any of your lip." Pierce: "Lip is Sam's cousin." Burns: "Oh, Pish posh!" Pak: "Pish Posh? That's my mother's family."

Another episode allowed Morita to comically diffuse stereotypical thinking. Colonel Blake (McLean Stevenson) is at his wit's end. "Sam, what's Korean for suicide?" Sam looks surprised: "That's Japanese. We don't do that schtick."

Morita played Arnold, proprietor of the drive-in restaurant where Richie and the Fonz hang out with their friends on *Happy Days,* and the same character on the short-lived *Blansky's Beauties.* He was also the star of the series, *Mr. T and Tina,* briefly, before returning to *Happy Days.*

After years of comic support the short, graying character actor reverted to his real Japanese name, Noriyuki Morita and scored his

SELECTED FILM APPEARANCES:
Thoroughly Modern Millie (1967), *The Shakiest Gun in the West* (1968), *Where Does It Hurt?* (1972), *Cancel My Reservation* (1972), *Every Little Crook and Nanny* (1972), *Evil Roy Slade* (1972), *A Very Missing Person* (1972), *Punch and Jody* (1974), *Human Feelings* (1978), *For the Love of It* (1980), *Jimmy the Kid* (1982), *The Karate Kid* (1984), *The Karate Kid II* (1986), *The Karate Kid III* (1989)

TELEVISION SERIES:
The Queen and I (1969), *Sanford and Son* (1974–75), *Happy Days* (1975–76), *Mr. T and Tina* (1976), *Blansky's Beauties* (1977), *Happy Days* (1982–83), *Ohara* (1987), *The Karate Kid* (voice) (1989–90)

COLLECTIBLES:
You Gotta Have Wa by Robert Whiting (Harper Audio)

greatest success as Mr. Miyagi in *The Karate Kid* (earning an Oscar nomination) and two sequels. Morita admitted he was far from an expert in the sport: "I'm not a black belt. I'm more a black and blue belt; a bruised belt. Boy, have I been belted...everybody believes I know what I'm doing...."

Despite his newfound fame as a serious actor, Morita was still called upon for stereotypical but lighthearted roles. In 1990 he appeared in ads as "The Colgate Wisdom Tooth," a variation on the "wise old Oriental philosopher" character. His wisdom was confined to words of mouth, like: "The freshness should not leave one's mouth as soon as one's toothbrush does."

BURT MUSTIN
February 8, 1884–January 28, 1977

BURT MUSTIN, twinkly-eyed old-timer who invariably induced smiles, "marries" Judith Lowry in TV's *Phyllis* as Cloris Leachman beams.

Bald, turtle-faced Burt Mustin played twinkle-eyed "old-timers in a variety of sitcoms over the years. Perhaps one reason why he seemed so spry and full of good nature and enthusiasm was that acting was something fresh and new to him. He didn't start his professional career until he was sixty-seven.

He had graduated from Pennsylvania Military College in 1903 with a degree in engineering and spent nearly forty years in Pittsburgh selling cars (the Oakland Sensible Six, the Franklin, and later Lincolns and Mercurys). He moved to Tucson for his health in 1942, selling hearing aids and acting in amateur productions as a hobby. After playing the janitor in *Detective Story* in Phoenix, he was asked to repeat the role in the movie version: "I had an agent and a contract before I ever hit Hollywood—a nice way to break in."

In films, Mustin was typed as a handyman or a hayseed. On TV he played Gus the Fireman on *Leave It to Beaver,* Jud Crowley on *The Andy Griffith Show,* and was occasionally the ancient bank vault guard on Jack Benny's show. With his wide-eyed sincerity and cheerful brand of old codger mannerisms, Burt could steal scenes with just a line or two. In *Cat Ballou,* he played a befuddled old Westerner confronting an outlaw: "Can you loan me a bullet, Kid? You remember me, old...old...." then he wandered away unable to recall his own name.

Mustin got his best part in years as Justin Quigley in episodes of *All in the Family,* a wry and spry senior citizen who runs away from a retirement home to get married. In real life, Burt was married in 1915 and the union lasted until his wife's death fifty-four years later. Asked for his secret to long life he said, "I watch my diet, I keep good, decent hours. I never drink, nor do I smoke. And I was married to the same woman for over fifty years—and never played around."

He was still working in his nineties, acting in some episodes of *Phyllis.* He married Mother Dexter (Judith Lowry) in one episode—which was the last for both of them. Aged veteran Lowry died November 29, 1976, shortly before the episode was aired. Mustin had said of the episode, "This is it. I've had it. But it's a classy way to go." It was. He died the following January 28.

SELECTED FILM APPEARANCES:
Detective Story (1951), *The Sellout* (1952), *Just Across the Street* (1952), *She Had to Say Yes* (1953), *Rally Round the Flag Boys* (1959), *Snow White and the Three Stooges* (1961), *The Thrill of It All* (1963), *Son of Flubber* (1963), *What a Way to Go!* (1964), *Cat Ballou* (1965), *The Reluctant Astronaut* (1967), *Speedway* (1968), *The Love Bug* (1969), *The Over-the-Hill Gang* (1969), *Now You See Him, Now You Don't* (1971), *Mame* (1974)

TELEVISION SERIES:
A Date With the Angels (1957–58), *Leave It to Beaver* (1957–59), *Ichabod and Me* (1961–62), *The Andy Griffith Show* (1961–66), *The Funny Side* (1971), *All in the Family* (1973–76), *Phyllis* (1976)

JACK NORTON, the dapper screen drunk, shares Max Baer and William Bendix's amazement in *Taxi, Mister!*

JACK NORTON
Mortimer J. Naughton, 1889–October 15, 1958

Jack Norton, the dapper man with the pencil mustache, was one of the great comic drunks in films and vaudeville. A good actor, he seemed to be having a great time downing his drinks, even though he confessed that what looked like whiskey in his glass " was either cold tea or Coke or burnt sugar—or a mixture of all three." He confessed that in movie scenes "gin was water and wine was ginger ale with a little bicarbonate of soda in it."

Married to Lucille Healy of the Healy Sisters, the Brooklyn-born vaudevillian bought a comic song called "Follow the Car Tracks, They'll Take You Home." He performed it as a drunk, had a hit routine, and remained drunk on stage ever since, staggering his way through vaudeville and the *Ziegfeld Follies* in 1923 and 1924 when he teamed with ex-boxer James J. Corbett.

Used for a quick laugh, Norton found steady employment as an unsteady drunk in dozens of films. Probably no actor has been in more movies for a shorter amount of time than Norton, who, in a typical bit in *Thank Your Lucky Stars,* barely staggers past Bette Davis before he's gone. It annoyed him that sometimes he didn't even get a film credit. As he said in 1945, "I've been soused in front of the cameras at least fifty times. Along comes Ray Milland in *The Lost Weekend.* He gets drunk once and everybody says he's going to get an Academy Award. It isn't fair. Then again, maybe it is. Milland stays tipsy for five days [in the film] and all I ever do is reel in and reel out in three to ten minutes."

Norton rarely had more than a few lines of dialogue. In *Blue Skies* he's a customer in Bing Crosby's nightclub: "I want a drink." "Don't you think you've had enough?" "If I think I had enough, would I ask for more?"

It's been widely reported that Jack was a teetotaler. A 1945 interview in the *New York Herald-Tribune* disproves that: "Let's put it this way, I'm acquainted with the taste of alcohol. I'd be lying if I said I didn't drink...but while most of my drunk roles are comedy characterizations, I see no humor in a man who is mentally sick, which is what an alcoholic is."

Norton played a variety of boozers, from the mildly tipsy type to the falling down drunk: "One day a director bawled me out for overplaying a scene. He told me that no drunk ever got so blotto and still stayed on his feet. What the director didn't know was that I had watched him at a party two nights before and was just copying the way he acted then. No, I didn't tell him."

SELECTED BROADWAY APPEARANCES:
The Ziegfeld Follies (1923, 1924), *Earl Carroll's Vanities* (1925), *The Florida Girl* (1925), *Five O'Clock Girl* (1927)

SELECTED FILM APPEARANCES:
Cockeyed Cavaliers (1934), *Don't Bet on Blondes* (1935), *A Day at the Races* (1937), *Thanks for the Memory* (1938), *It's a Wonderful World* (1939), *The Ghost Breakers* (1940), *The Bank Dick* (1940), *The Farmer's Daughter* (1940), *The Palm Beach Story* (1941), *Louisiana Purchase* (1941), *The Fleet's In* (1942), *It Ain't Hay* (1943), *Hail the Conquering Hero* (1944), *Ghost Catchers* (1944), *The Big Noise* (1944), *Hold That Blonde* (1945), *The Naughty Nineties* (1945), *Bringing Up Father* (1946), *Blue Skies* (1946), *The Kid From Brooklyn* (1946), *Mad Wednesday* (1947), *Variety Time* (1948)

DAVE O'BRIEN
David Poole Fronabarger,
May 31, 1912–November 8, 1969

Handsome in the manner of good natured lugs like B-film actor Dick Foran, Texas-born Dave O'Brien spent most of his early movie career playing bit parts and working as a stuntman. A part-time welder when he arrived in Hollywood in 1928, he starred in a 1938 drama *The Burning Question,* which was unintentionally hilarious. Rereleased decades later as *Reefer Madness* it became a cult classic. O'Brien had few starring roles in the thirties, mostly appearing as a chorus dancer (*42nd Street* and *Footlight Parade*) and a villain in obscure Westerns (*Whirlwind Horseman* and *Gun Packer*).

In the forties O'Brien starred in a series of *Pete Smith Specialty* shorts. Initially hired for his ability to take falls, he developed an amusing slow burn as he went from annoyance and frustration to ultimate destruction. In the shorts, he was constantly beset by pests— "Movie Pests," "Bus Pests," etc. Whether he was trying to watch a film, ride the bus, go shopping, or relax at home, there was always somebody to poke an elbow in his ribs, crumble his newspaper, trip him up, and drive him to distraction (and a thundering fall). The erstwhile stuntman was so good at falling that the last entry in the series, *Fall Guy,* was literally a collection of O'Brien's greatest hits. One stunt comedy, *Wrong Way Butch,* a comic look at industrial mishaps, won an award from a government safety group as a good "cautionary" film to screen for workers. O'Brien and Smith accepted their award from President Truman himself.

O'Brien (under the name of David Barclay) sometimes directed comedies in the Pete Smith series. Author Leonard Maltin noted that "as a director Dave was equally skillful. One beautiful visual gag from *I Love My Wife But...* comes to mind. Whenever a husband accompanies his wife on a shopping trip, hubby invariably catches the eye of an embarrassed female shopper in the vicinity. In this case, it's an older woman buying a girdle. By using the sundry mirrors that fill the salesroom (and O'Brien's ingenious camera angles) he makes it impossible for their eyes not to meet, in mutual embarrassment."

O'Brien starred in B-Westerns in the forties as well, sometimes earning a starring role. In semiretirement in the fifties O'Brien wrote comedy material (most often sight gags and pantomime bits) for Red Skelton's TV series, eventually earning an Emmy for his work.

DAVE O'BRIEN, sometimes B movie lead in the forties when not doing slow burns in "Pete Smith Specialty" shorts, enjoys a moment with Jinx Falkenburg in *Tahiti Nights.*

180

The eighty Pete Smith shorts (often featuring real-life wife Dorothy Short) turn up on television from time to time while *Reefer Madness* remains the comic high point in O'Brien's feature film career. Fans of action adventure films might remember O'Brien best in one film sandwiched between his unintentional

and intentional comedies. Not exactly the leading man type, he did get a chance at it when he played *Captain Midnight* in a 1942 serial.

VIRGINIA O'BRIEN
April 18, 1921

One of the strangest ways to perk up films in the forties was to insert a specialty number featuring the deadpan singing of Virginia O'Brien. Unforgettably odd, O'Brien looked as beautiful and beguiling as any pop singer of the day—except that she didn't smile. She sang fast-paced jazz-tinged ditties with an unnerving stare, not moving a muscle except for those in her frantic lips.

She claimed that her unusual style was the result of an unhappy stage experience. Literally frozen with fear, she sang a number on stage without moving. The result was uproarious laughter from the audience.

O'Brien impressed MGM's head, Louis B. Mayer, with her unusual style. Her studio connections via an uncle, director Lloyd Bacon, didn't hurt. While other comic performers with unusual gifts could do their set pieces anywhere, walking into a scene just to stutter, sneeze, or use a catchphrase, O'Brien was at a slight disadvantage. She needed to be showcased in a musical number. In over a dozen films her appearances were as comic relief to the straight songs in musicals.

Her most popular number is probably the swinging "Rockabye Baby" in the Marx Brothers' *The Big Store*. She also deadpanned her way through "Take It Easy" in the film *Two Girls and a Sailor* and "Saloma" in *DuBarry Was a Lady*.

VIRGINIA O'BRIEN, the poker-faced forties comedienne and singer, tries to lay a kiss on frequent costar Red Skelton in *Merton of the Movies*.

The poker-faced singer's husband during the forties was a lot more animated: Kirk Allyn, star of the movie serial *Superman*. After they were divorced in the fifties, O'Brien remarried and attempted comebacks several times as a straight singer in local California nightclubs.

UNA O'CONNOR eeks out some laughs, breaking the tension during *Bride of Frankenstein*.

UNA O'CONNOR
Agnes Teresa McGlade,
October 23, 1880–February 4, 1959

Outrageous screaming and bawling typed Una O'Connor as somewhat strident comic relief in the classic horror films directed by James Whale: *The Invisible Man* (her first American-made picture) and *Bride of Frankenstein*.

Born in Belfast, Ireland (some sources say 1893), O'Connor was two when her mother died and her father moved to Australia. The youngster stayed behind with an aunt and attended convent schools. She graduated with an M.A. from South Kensington School of Arts and planned to become a teacher. After attending the Abbey Theater School in Dublin, she found stage work instead, making her debut in 1911. She appeared on Broadway often in the twenties, and after appearing in the British stage version of Noel Coward's *Cavalcade* headed for Hollywood to make the film. (She had made some movies in Great Britain as early as 1929.)

She was nearly turned back. A doctor aboard ship discovered she had a "leaky heart valve" and a special board of inquiry at Ellis Island was convened before she could be let into the country. Though she'd appeared on Broadway on previous visits, now she needed her film studio to sign a paper indicating she would "never need public aid in this country." Finally she was free to go West and begin her film career. It lasted over twenty years, despite her heart problems.

With her head cocked in parrot-like poses, her large eyes a contrast to her pinched nose and tight mouth, O'Connor was typecast as an old pest and nuisance—which is why audiences were more amused then sympathetic to her shriek-fits. They also were happy to see someone clearly more frightened than they were when the Invisible Man or the Frankenstein monster arrived on the scene.

She was a barmaid in the former and a lady's maid in the latter, and played maid roles in *The Adventures of Robin Hood,* and in both the Broadway and film versions of *Witness for the Prosecution.* She was also Mrs. Gummidge in the Selznick production of *David Copperfield.* For an odd change of pace she attempted a French accent to play Jeanette MacDonald's maid in *Rose Marie.* She admitted that whether she scream-

SELECTED BROADWAY APPEARANCES:
The Fake (1924), *Autumn Fire* (1926), *The Ryan Girl* (1945), *The Linden Tree* (1948), *The Shop at Sly Corner* (1949), *The Enchanted* (1950), *Witness for the Prosecution* (1954)

SELECTED FILM APPEARANCES:
Cavalcade (1933), *The Invisible Man* (1933), *All Men Are Enemies* (1934), *Chained* (1934), *The Barretts of Wimpole Street* (1934), *David Copperfield* (1935), *Bride of Frankenstein* (1935), *Father Brown, Detective* (1935), *Little Lord Fauntleroy* (1936), *Call It a Day* (1937), *The Adventures of Robin Hood* (1938), *We Are Not Alone* (1939), *Lillian Russell* (1940), *Strawberry Blonde* (1941), *Three Girls About Town* (1941), *My Favorite Spy* (1942), *Holy Matrimony* (1943), *The Canterville Ghost* (1944), *The Bells of St. Mary's* (1945), *Cluny Brown* (1946), *Ivy* (1947), *The Corpse Came C.O.D.* (1947), *Adventures of Don Juan* (1948), *Witness for the Prosecution* (1957)

ed or merely clucked her tongue in annoyance, domestic roles were her lot: "I'm a slavey whether I like it or not." She said she was usually unrecognized by fans without "my usual frumpy clothes and makeup."

Unmarried, she lived at the Windsor Hotel on 58th Street in Manhattan until arteriosclerosis required her admission to the Mary Manning Walsh Home. She was well enough to leave and appear in *Witness for the Prosecution* in Hollywood, but it was to be her final film.

EDNA MAY OLIVER
Edna May Nutter, November 9, 1883–November 9, 1942

*E*dna May Oliver was comedy's definitive New England spinster. She came by her Bostonian primness honestly. Her mother, Ida Nutter, was a descendant of John Quincy Adams. Edna starred in light opera productions and played the piano in an all-woman orchestra before coming to Broadway in 1917's *Oh Boy!* She began making films in 1923, winning praise for her role as a tipsy Bible saleswoman in *Let's Get Married* (1925). In 1928 she married a stockbroker. They were divorced after five years.

Through the thirties and forties, Edna May Oliver played a variety of stiff-spined film spinsters, most of them with a sniffy nose and stuffy manner. If disapproving retorts and withering glares were not enough to get the message across, the lady did the sensible thing: she brawled. As the proper Miss Pross in *A Tale of Two Cities* she had audiences cheering when she finally lost her temper. Fans found her memorable as the nurse in *Romeo and Juliet,* Aunt March in *Little Women,* the Red Queen in *Alice in Wonderland,* and Aunt Betsey Trotwood in *David Copperfield.*

What separated her from other spinster types was her shrewd wit,

EDNA MAY OLIVER, haughty and sniffy-nosed, strikes a typically fretful pose.

doleful tolerance of inferiors, and self-depreciating humor. Her most popular film character was Hildegarde Withers, schoolteacher turned detective in three comedy-mystery films: *The Penguin Pool Murder, Murder on the Blackboard,* and *Murder on a Honeymoon.* She always had a sassy comeback for her friend, exasperated detective Oscar Piper (James Gleason). In *The Penguin Pool Murder* she huffed at him: "I'm a schoolteacher, and I might have done wonders with you if I'd caught you early enough." And to a sexy secretary putting on lipstick: "When you've got your disguise on, I'd like to ask you a few questions. That is, if you can talk through all that makeup!" Oliver eventually left the series, replaced by Helen Broderick and later ZaSu Pitts. A TV movie version of Miss Withers (*A Very Missing Person*) starred Eve Arden.

In comedy, Edna's humor often came from her attempts to maintain her composure no matter what the chagrin. She played a wife in Wheeler and Woolsey's *Half Shot at Sunrise* who uses her regal if goose-like voice and haughty sarcasm to deal with her two-timing army officer husband. "You don't seem to realize the problems I have," he grumbles. She pauses, then enunciates: "I don't see how they could have a war without you. I know *I couldn't.*" Her husband sulks, "You'd have the last word with an echo."

Oliver's influence certainly extended to Carol Burnett, who often seemed to use a variation of Edna's horsey-faced huffiness in her own comic portrayals of well-read and well-bred older women. For her memorable role as pioneer widow Mrs. McKlennan, frontier neighbor to Claud-ette Colbert and Henry Fonda, Oliver received an Academy Award nomination for *Drums Along the Mohawk,* and was making films up to her untimely death, on her birthday, at age fifty-nine. She had no relatives or children. An actress, Virginia Hammond, was at her bedside during her last days. Once asked to create an epitaph for her tombstone, Edna May Oliver offered these words: "It might have been worse."

SELECTED BROADWAY APPEARANCES:
Oh Boy! (1917), *My Golden Girl* (1920), *Wait Till We're Married* (1921), *Wild Oats Lane* (1922), *Ice-Bound* (1923), *Cradle Snatchers* (1925), *Show Boat* (1928)

SELECTED FILM APPEARANCES:
Wife in Name Only (1923), *Manhattan* (1924), *The Lady Who Lied* (1925), *Lovers in Quarantine* (1925), *Let's Get Married* (1926), *Hook, Line and Sinker* (1930), *Fanny Foley Herself* (1931), *Laugh and Get Rich* (1932), *Cracked Nuts* (1931), *Hold 'Em Jail* (1932), *The Penguin Pool Murder* (1932), *The Great Jasper* (1933), *Meet the Baron* (1933), *Little Women* (1933), *Alice in Wonderland* (1933), *We're Rich Again* (1934), *Murder on the Blackboard* (1934), *Murder on a Honeymoon* (1935), *David Copperfield* (1935), *A Tale of Two Cities* (1935), *Romeo and Juliet* (1936), *Rosalie* (1937), *Little Miss Broadway* (1938), *Nurse Edith Cavell* (1939), *Drums Along the Mohawk* (1939), *Pride and Prejudice* (1940), *Lydia* (1941)

J. PAT O'MALLEY
March 15, 1904–February 27, 1985

J. PAT O'MALLEY, jolly Britisher who played lovable hobos and cheerful eccentrics, gives the old chin-up to James Franciscus in *Four Boys and a Gun*.

For two decades J. Pat O'Malley was the sitcom world's favorite Irish grandpa, garrulous old codger, and lovable hobo. He was also well known for his jolly, comic voices in Disney cartoons.

Born in Burnley, Lancashire (some sources say 1901), O'Malley was originally a tenor on songs like "By the River Sainte Marie," sung when he was a member of Jack Hylton's British dance band. O'Malley toured America with Hylton in the thirties. He also performed Lancashire dialect comedy including Stanley Holloway numbers like "Albert and the Lion." O'Malley even published a book of "Albert" poems as well as routines about "Erbert Pinwinkle the Lancashire Lad." He went on to costar on radio's *Alec Templeton Time* and to tour with the popular pianist.

On Broadway he was the befuddled British detective in Agatha Christie's *Ten Little Indians,* and in movies and on TV O'Malley worked extensively for Walt Disney, appearing on the "Spin and Marty" episodes of *The Mickey Mouse Club* and doing cartoon voices. It was O'Malley as the walrus and the carpenter and both Tweedle Dum and Tweedle Dee in *Alice in Wonderland.*

O'Malley appeared often in films, but even more often in television sitcoms, giving any episode instant warmth and humor when he went through his paces as a cheerful eccentric with years of happy memories and plenty of time to share them. In the sixties he played Rob Petrie's cheerful father on *The Dick Van Dyke Show* (though the

SELECTED BROADWAY APPEARANCES:
But Not Goodbye (1944), *Ten Little Indians* (1944), *Of Thee I Sing* (1952), *Seagulls Over Sorrento* (1952), *Home Is the Hero* (1954)

SELECTED FILM APPEARANCES:
Alice in Wonderland (voice) (1951), *Witness for the Prosecution* (1957), *101 Dalmatians* (voice) (1961), *Son of Flubber* (1963), *Mary Poppins* (1964), *The Jungle Book* (voice) (1967), *Star!* (1968), *Hello, Dolly!* (1969), *Cheyenne Social Club* (1970), *The Gumball Rally* (1976), *Cheaper to Keep Her* (1980)

TELEVISION SERIES:
My Favorite Martian (1963–64), *Wendy and Me* (1964–65), *The Dick Van Dyke Show* (1964–66), *The Rounders* (1966–67), *A Touch of Grace* (1973), *Maude* (1975–77)

COLLECTIBLES:
O'Malley wrote a book called *The Lancashire Lad*

EUGENE PALLETTE, frog-voiced, long-suffering heavy whose pompousness was always good for a laugh.

portly, bulbous O'Malley hardly resembled the slim, sharp-featured Van Dyke). In the seventies, he costarred with Shirley Booth in *A Touch of Grace* and had one of his last continuing roles as Bert Beasley, who married Mrs. Naugatuck (Hermoine Baddeley) on *Maude.*

EUGENE PALLETTE
July 8, 1889–September 3, 1954

A cross between a frog and a basketball in build and appearance, Eugene Pallette was a round, overstuffed character actor with a uniquely gruff voice. If a part called for an agitated, blustery businessman or a semibright detective, Pallette was there. In fact he was "there" before Hollywood knew what to do with him. It was a considerably slimmer Pallette who was used by D. W. Griffith in *Birth of a Nation* (as a soldier) and *Intolerance* (the role of Latour).

"I made a hundred pictures a year in my first four years here," Pallette recalled. "Believe it or not, I was Norma Talmadge's leading man [circa 1916]. Of course in those days I only weighed one hundred thirty-five pounds." He also appeared in Douglas Fairbanks's *Three Musketeers.*

Pallette's parents were actors. They were on tour in Kansas performing in East Lynne when Eugene was born. Pallette became an actor, but it wasn't always smooth going. A touring company stranded him in Portland, Oregon, when the manager ran off with the funds. He worked as a streetcar conductor for six months before finding film extra work in Los Angeles around 1910. His silent film career ended with World War I. After the war he made over $140,000 in a Texas oil investment. He thought he knew the business world pretty well, but when he lost all his money during subsequent transactions, he suffered a nervous breakdown.

After a year in the hospital, Pallette came back to films. During the sound era the five-foot-nine actor ballooned up to three hundred pounds and had a fifty-one-inch waist. He said, "At first it hurt my vanity when I got a sideways look at my figure. But then I found I could capitalize on it; I could get good character parts." He added, "If you're twice as big as the other fellow, you've got twice the chance to hog the scene."

Roly-poly Pallette stole quite a few scenes in *My Man Godfrey,* playing the exasperated, grim father who pays the bills for his extravagant wife and daughters. When the girls go out on a scavenger hunt looking for a "forgotten man," Pallette snaps, "if you want a forgotten man—you'll find me home in bed!" Later, reflecting on his family life he says, "All you need to start an asylum is an empty room and the right kind of people."

SELECTED FILM APPEARANCES:
The Birth of a Nation (1915), *Intolerance* (1916), *Ghost House* (1917), *Tarzan of the Apes* (1918), *The Three Musketeers* (1921), *The Canary Murder Case* (1929), *The Green Murder Case* (1929), *The Benson Murder Case* (1930), *Kibitzer* (1930), *Huckleberry Finn* (1931), *Half-Naked Truth* (1932), *Made on Broadway* (1933), *The Kennel Murder Case* (1933), *Friends of Mr. Sweeney* (1934), *Steamboat Round the Bend* (1935), *The Ghost Goes West* (1936), *My Man Godfrey* (1936), *Topper* (1937), *The Adventures of Robin Hood* (1938), *Mr. Smith Goes to Washington* (1939), *The Lady Eve* (1941), *The Bride Came C.O.D.* (1941), *Are Husbands Necessary?* (1942), *The Big Street* (1942), *Tales of Manhattan* (1942), *It Ain't Hay* (1943), *Heaven Can Wait* (1943), *Sensations of 1945* (1944), *Step Lively* (1944), *The Cheaters* (1945), *In Old Sacramento* (1946), *Suspense* (1946)

Writers seemed to relish embellishing Pallette's roles to accommodate his trademark griping. Playing an engineer who loves to gamble in *Shanghai Express* he grumbles, "What future is there in being a Chinaman? You're born, eat your way through a handful of rice, and you die. What a country."

All types of people could aggravate Pallette. He played Henry Fonda's father in *The Lady Eve,* McCann, the politician in *Mr. Smith Goes to Washington,* and Sergeant Heath in the *Philo Vance* film series. In *It Ain't Hay* he spent ninety minutes trying to get the better of Abbott and Costello, while in *The Big Street,* he was Damon Runyon's Nicely Nicely Johnson, a decade before the character turned up on Broadway in *Guys and Dolls.*

A mobile fat man, Pallette demonstrated some versatility fencing left-handed against Basil Rathbone in *The Mark of Zorro,* and right-handed against Erroll Flynn in *The Adventures of Robin Hood.* Though the character comedian earned $125,000 a year that didn't mean he could stop complaining. As he said, "If there is one thing I like to gripe about it's how tough it is to be funny."

FRANKLIN PANGBORN
January 23, 1893–July 20, 1958

The biggest fussbudget in films, Franklin Pangborn played a variety of stuffy clerks, floorwalkers, and bureaucrats, most of them as prissy as they were precise. Best known for his support roles opposite W. C. Fields, Pangborn took abuse as the alternately fawning and dubious film producer in *Never Give a Sucker an Even Break* and the inanely dutiful bank examiner in *The Bank Dick.*

In the latter, as J. Pinkerton Snoopington, the perfect picture of propriety in pince-nez glasses, bowler hat, and neatly trimmed mustache, Pangborn paid the price for his persnickety personality. As with most characters Pangborn played, he missed audience sympathy not only because of his pruney nature, but the hypocrisy of his rule-making. He's the sober man who, at Fields' sly urging, will sneak several drinks at the Black Pussy Cafe, as long as they sit in a corner where

FRANKLIN PANGBORN, moviedom's premiere fussbudget, is not amused as Betty Kean tries to get a rise out of him in *Moonlight Masquerade*.

nobody will see them. He considers himself far more intelligent than the average man, with the mentality to tackle complicated bank accounts, but actually has less common sense than most:

Doctor: "Take two of these pills in a glass of castor oil for two nights running, then you skip one night."

Snoopington: "I thought you said I wasn't to take any exercise."

Doctor: "You take me too literally."

In the course of the film, Snoopington is drugged into nausea and takes a fall from a hotel window, both highlights of hilarity. What made him so funny was the dronish devotion to duty that kept him coming back for more. As he says: "If duty called I would go into the tsetse fly country of Africa and brave sleeping sickness if there were books to be examined!"

Born in Newark, New Jersey, Pangborn found his first stage role in a local production of *The Power Behind the Throne* in 1911. When it came time to tour in stage productions, he ran into paternal disapproval: "My father was a member of a life insurance company and both he and mother frowned on my stage aspirations. To mention the stage to my mother was to bring a tragic look on her face and a sob in her voice." They wouldn't give him a suitcase for his trip. "One of the neighbors gave me one. I will never forget saying goodbye to mother. It was a tragedy. My heart was broken, as our boat steamed up the Hudson and on leaving the boat I found my trunk also broken. I carried shoes, socks, ties, shirts and suits up the street in my arms, crying softly to myself for mother."

Pangborn worked hard, eventually touring with many great stars, including Alla Nazimova (*The Marionettes*) and Pauline Frederick (*Joseph and His Brethren*). He served in the infantry during World War I and was gassed and wounded at the Battle of Argonne. After more stage work following the war, he made a movie short with Lupino Lane in 1927 and as a comedian saw his career take off following his work in *My Man Godfrey* in the mid-thirties. He was the antagonist for Jack Benny in *George Washington Slept Here*, Olsen and Johnson in *Crazy House*, and Harold Lloyd in *Mad Wednesday*.

Living quietly along with a protective clique of neighboring gay actors and Hollywood technicians, Pangborn made a hobby out of buying small cottages and resort homes, then sprucing them up and redecorating them for lucrative resale.

Among the many fans of the petulant Pangborn was Jack Paar, who tried to bring the veteran performer's style to television on *The Tonight Show* in the late fifties. "I thought it would be a riot to have someone like him be the announcer," Paar recalled of "that gay little guy...It was funny but only for shock. It didn't last more than two weeks because dear Franklin could not ad-lib in character. He was an actor who could only read lines. We had no script, so back he went to Hollywood. And then Hugh Downs took over...." Pangborn died not long afterward following surgery for recurrent intestinal problems.

Pangborn's self-described "aptitude for false dignity" had given him a long career as the prissy and pompous fellow all dressed up and ready for a slapstick fall. He once said, "No knockabout clown in patched pantaloons had to take the punishment regularly meted out to the comedian unlucky enough to have become identified with dress clothes."

> **SELECTED FILM APPEARANCES:**
> *Exit Smiling* (1926), *Getting Gertie's Garter* (1927), *The Sap* (1929), *Lady of the Pavements* (1929), *Cheer Up and Smile* (1930), *International House* (1933), *Design for Living* (1933), *Imitation of Life* (1934), *She Couldn't Take It* (1935), *Mr. Deeds Goes to Town* (1936), *My Man Godfrey* (1936), *Step Lively Jeeves* (1937), *Stage Door* (1937), *Topper Takes a Trip* (1939), *The Bank Dick* (1940), *Never Give a Sucker an Even Break* (1941), *Sullivan's Travels* (1941), *George Washington Slept Here* (1942), *The Palm Beach Story* (1942), *Crazy House* (1943), *Hail the Conquering Hero* (1944), *The Horn Blows at Midnight* (1945), *Mad Wednesday* (1947), *Down Memory Lane* (1949), *My Dream Is Yours* (1949), *The Story of Mankind* (1957), *Oh Men! Oh Women!* (1957)

LEE PATRICK
November 22, 1906–November 25, 1982

Flipping the channels on late night television, a viewer finds that anything is possible. On one station there's a sexy girl with a knowing smile, her wisecracks giving some life to a drab drama. On another station there's a dithery old lady who makes a fool of herself with her scolding and confusion. The strange thing is: they are both Lee Patrick, at different ends of her corner.

Inheriting the fluttery roles Billie Burke used to play, New York-born Lee Patrick amused television fans as Henrietta, the fretful wife on the TV version of *Topper*. She played similar parts through the fifties and sixties, including Nick Adams's pushy, matchmaker mother in *Pillow Talk*.

But early in her career, Lee Patrick was anything but a huffy old biddy. Probably her most enduring youthful screen role was Sam Spade's sly and sexy secretary, Effie Perine, in *The Maltese Falcon*. In many of these early films Lee was a wisecracking bad girl. After playing a stripper and a bubble dancer in two successive films, she

LEE PATRICK, a sly businesswoman here, casts a knowing glance at Leo Carrillo in *Larceny With Music*.

snapped, "Every day I'm getting better and better by going lower and lower."

Lee's comic flair was promoted by George S. Kaufman who cast her in the two Broadway shows that solidified her reputation. In *June Moon* (both the original and the revival five years later), she was the nasty but witty redhead Eileen. In *Stage Door,* she was the smart-talking blond, Judith. Of her *June Moon* role she recalled, "There is an old stage superstition that if the actors, during the rehearsal of a comedy, laugh at the lines the audience won't." Her part, "which was supposed to be full of belly laughs, hardly got a grin from the cast." Sure enough, the audience loved the show: "That superstition might still be the bunk, but I must admit a great fondness for it."

Sometimes there was unintentional comedy onstage. In another production she had to deliver a soliloquy in her nightgown. As she was performing the bedroom scene, a bat flew around the theater. After the monologue, she simply got into bed, and pulled up the covers. The curtain came down and, with a spotlight on it, the bat was captured.

In films, Lee missed out on many good parts. Her agent, Zeppo Marx, let several slip by, but she recalled vetoing even more. Not particularly driven toward stardom, she was happily married to writer Tom Wood. After her starlet phase, she appeared on radio (including a series called *The O'Neills*) and landed a few amusing mature roles, like the part of a snide actress in Jack Benny's *George Washington Slept Here.* Annoyed at playing summer stock in the boondocks, she complained about the theater that was once a barn: "Take the pigs out before they put the hams in."

After *Topper* and some sixties film comedies she retired, except for a cameo in *The Black Bird,* an affectionate parody/sequel to *The Maltese Falcon.* She didn't mind playing Sam Spade's Effie Perine again, and she didn't mind getting letters from fans who, watching rerun after rerun, still knew her best for her Henrietta Topper. In New York in 1982 with her husband to celebrate her birthday, she appeared on *Good Morning, America* to talk about *Topper* and her old films. She died a few weeks later.

SELECTED BROADWAY APPEARANCES:
The Green Beetle (1924), *The Backslapper* (1925), *Baby Mine* (1927), *Matrimonial Bed* (1927), *The Common Sin* (1928), *June Moon* (1929), *Rock Me, Julie* (1931), *Blessed Event* (1932), *June Moon* (revival, 1933), *Slightly Delirious* (1935), *Knock on Wood* (1935), *Curse You Jack Dalton* (1935), *Stage Door* (1936), *Michael Drops In* (1938)

SELECTED FILM APPEARANCES:
Strange Cargo (1929), *Border Cafe* (1937), *Crashing Hollywood* (1938), *Invisible Stripes* (1940), *Million Dollar Baby* (1941), *The Maltese Falcon* (1941), *George Washington Slept Here* (1942), *Jitterbugs* (1943), *Larceny With Music* (1943), *See My Lawyer* (1945), *Keep Your Powder Dry* (1945), *Mildred Pierce* (1945), *Mother Wore Tights* (1947), *Inner Sanctum* (1948), *The Fuller Brush Girl* (1950), *Vertigo* (1958), *Auntie Mame* (1958), *Pillow Talk* (1959), *Visit to a Small Planet* (1960), *Summer and Smoke* (1961), *Wives and Lovers* (1963), *The New Interns* (1963), *7 Faces of Dr. Lao* (1964), *The Black Bird* (1975)

TELEVISION SERIES:
Topper (1953–55), *Mr. Adams and Eve* (1956–57)

ALICE PEARCE
October 16, 1919–March 3, 1966

ALICE PEARCE, whose plain looks and deadpan quips brightened countless scenes, seems preoccupied with doing June Allyson's nails in *The Opposite Sex*.

Remembered for her role as Gladys Kravitz, the snoopy neighbor on *Bewitched,* rubber-faced Alice Pearce tended to play sour or eccentric characters in films and on stage. As Lucy Schmeeler, the plain-looking girl with a bad cold, she was comic relief in *On the Town*. Plain she was, with her angular nose and thin but jowly face.

Pearce could handle songs as well as comedy, which made her a valuable performer on the New York stage in the forties. Her lively stand-up cabaret act once played for over a year at the Blue Angel. Her stage success helped her land her own TV variety show in 1949. Back then fifteen minute shows were common and hers was broadcast on Friday nights at 9:45—until it was cancelled three months later.

She continued stage work in the fifties after duplicating her role in the film version of *On the Town*. In the sixties she lent her dowdy appearance and comically dyspeptic personality to sitcom films like *Kiss Me, Stupid* and *The Glass Bottom Boat*. Her parts weren't always long, mostly because they needed no setup. One glare from Pearce and viewers instantly knew that this was going to be one of the petty, sourball antagonists for the comic heroine.

Most slow-burn comics reach some sort of climax in their frustration, but Pearce was funny because the reaction she produced was simple: "just let her burn." The prime example of this was her frustrated Gladys Kravitz, forever trying to prove that her neighbor is a witch. But Samantha the witch (Elizabeth Montgomery) never squelched her. Samantha just outwitted Gladys and let her keep right on burning.

SELECTED BROADWAY APPEARANCES:
New Faces of 1943 (1942), *On the Town* (1944), *Look Ma, I'm Dancin'* (1948), *Small Wonder* (1948), *Gentlemen Prefer Blondes* (1949), *The Grass Harp* (1952), *Dear Charles* (1954), *Fallen Angels* (1956), *Copper and Brass* (1957), *The Ignorants Abroad* (1960), *Midgie Purvis* (1961), *Sail Away* (1961)

SELECTED FILM APPEARANCES:
On the Town (1949), *The Belle of New York* (1952), *How to Be Very Very Popular* (1955), *The Opposite Sex* (1956), *Tammy and the Doctor* (1963), *The Disorderly Orderly* (1964), *Kiss Me, Stupid* (1964), *Dear Brigitte* (1965), *The Glass Bottom Boat* (1966)

TELEVISION SERIES:
The Alice Pearce Show (1949), *Jamie* (1953–54), *One Minute Please* (1954–55), *Bewitched* (1964–66)

COLLECTIBLES:
During her cabaret days in the late fifties Pearce recorded *Monster Rally* (RCA) with Hans Conreid. She made the most of novelty songs like "I'm in Love With the Creature From the Black Lagoon" and the old Phil Harris hit, "The Thing."

Pearce, the funny-looking self-proclaimed "chinless wonder," had been hunting for a good sitcom role for a while. She had auditioned for Grandmama on *The Addams Family* but missed and got *Bewitched* instead. She enjoyed playing the only slightly less garish Mrs. Kravitz: "Playing strange, sweet oddballs is exactly my cup of tea."

Hardly a dull and dour crone off camera, Pearce and husband director Paul Davis spent much of their time at the art gallery they had opened in Hollywood. She won an Emmy for *Bewitched* in 1966, but it was a posthumous honor. She died of cancer a few months before the awards show.

JACK PEARL, "Baron Munchausen" of radio and early talkies, strikes an uncharacteristically romantic pose with Edna May Oliver in *Meet the Baron.*

JACK PEARL
October 29, 1895–December 25, 1982

One of his generation's most amusing German dialect comics, Jack Pearl was "Baron Munchausen," or simply "The Baron," teller of tall tales. His ridiculous lies would have even outraged the original Baron von Munchausen. When the whoppers got progressively more outlandish, his straight man would protest. And Jack would fire back his catchphrase: "Vas you dere, Sharlie?"

The catchphrase became popular for anyone needing a comeback for a doubter or disbelieving dope. In fact, some forty years after the Baron's fame, Marlon Brando (in the book *Conversations*) used it twice when an interviewer began making suppositions. The actor added, "That's the great phrase that sustains me from one problem to another."

Pearl grew up on the Lower East Side of New York City. The kid costarred in one of the many vaudeville versions of Gus Edwards's "School Days" sketch. Walter Winchell and George Jessel were also in the cast, which drew laughs from various ethnic characters in the classroom. Jack used a German accent even then. In 1930 Pearl became the Baron with Cliff Hall as his straight man.

For awhile, audiences couldn't get enough of his eccentric humor and ridiculously exaggerated German accent. "I went to correspondence school," he'd say, trilling the "r" and pronouncing "school" as "shkool." "They threw me out from there...I played hooky." "You played hooky from a correspondence school? How is that possible?" "I sent them an empty envelope!"

Pearl starred on Broadway, had his own radio show, and was groomed for film greatness in *Meet the Baron.* Jimmy Durante was his flustered sidekick in that one, with the Three Stooges in supporting roles. Unfortunately the film showed Pearl's character to be amusing but one-dimensional, better used in small doses and in support of other stars. He remained popular for a time on radio where various hosts, such as Rudy Vallee, enjoyed getting a brief, befuddling visit from the irascible, impossible Baron.

As the thirties wore on, Pearl's welcome wore out, his outrageous accent in questionable taste after the rise of Nazi Germany, his catchphrase done to death. Ironically, he'd been afraid to disappoint the crowd by not exclaiming "Vas you Dere, Sharlie?" at some point during every sketch.

Pearl was hoping to turn his luck around with a role in *Yokel Boy* on Broadway. Phil Silvers was a costar. Silvers claimed in his autobiography that preview audiences were "bored with Dutch dialect at $4 a seat" and that Pearl was ruining the show. During one performance, Silvers started marching around the stage. "Vat iss dat?" the distracted Pearl had to ask. "The parade passing you by," snapped Silvers. And Pearl was soon gone from *Yokel Boy.*

Silvers later regretted his cruelty, but the cruel truth was that Pearl had less and less opportunities for work in the fifties and sixties. For some old-fashioned laughs and nostalgia Jackie Gleason used him on his old variety show, but for the Baron, the TV horizon was barren. Thirties film and the golden age of radio turned out to have been Pearl's golden age as well.

SELECTED BROADWAY APPEARANCES:
The Dancing Girl (1923), *A Night in Paris* (1926), *Artists and Models* (1927), *Pleasure Bound* (1929), *International Revue* (1930), *Ziegfeld Follies* (1931), *Pardon My English* (1933), *One Flight Down* (1937), *All for All* (1943)

SELECTED FILM APPEARANCES:
Meet the Baron (1933), *Hollywood Party* (1934)

COLLECTIBLES:
They're Still Laughing (Capitol), *Golden Age of Comedy* (Evolution)

NAT PENDLETON
August 9, 1895–October 12, 1967

Not every big dope in films is really a big dope. Nat Pendleton was just acting when he played goofy gangsters, befuddled cops, and the dim sergeant to Abbott and Costello in *Buck Privates.*

A descendant of Revolutionary War hero Gen. Nathaniel Greene, Nathaniel Greene Pendleton graduated from Columbia University with a degree in engineering. He was also captain of the wrestling team and an Olympic medalist in 1920.

Intelligent and strong, Pendleton varied his early careers between brainy jobs and brawny ones. The

NAT PENDLETON, the brawny lug, in a respite between bouts as foil for such comedy teams as the Marx Brothers and Abbott and Costello.

brainy jobs included working as an auditor for Standard Oil, and owning an
import-export business that
made use of his ability to
speak French and Spanish.
Among the brawny jobs was
working for the Mexican
police in tracking down the
infamous Emiliano Zapata.
After forming his own True
Story Films in 1921 and producing one movie, Pendle-
ton got in front of the cameras. His imposing physique
helped him get parts calling
for a stereotyped big lug: an ambulance driver in a series of *Dr. Kildare*
films and Lieutenant Guild in a pair of *Thin Man* movies. Pendleton
rarely had a comic line, but made the most out of a frustrated expression or a hapless cry of "There's somethin' fishy goin' on here!" (one of
his lines in *It's a Wonderful World*). "Aw gee," he told Bogart in *Swing
Your Lady*, "talk United States, will ya."

After playing the grouchy comic foil in *Buck Privates* Pendleton was
rewarded with the starring role of *Top Sergeant Mulligan*, which the New
York *Daily News* called, "Monogram's ill-fated effort to get a facsimile of
Buck Privates," complete with a comedy team—Frank Faylen and
Charles Hall.

Pendleton continued to play dense cops (*It's a Wonderful World*),
Runyonesque crooks (*Baby Face Harrington*), and, sporting a silly curly
blond wig, a strongman nemesis to the Marx Brothers in *At the Circus*.
His thankless job always included "dem and dose" dialogue which was
a bit embarrassing. Nat recalled what happened when he took his
grandmother to see him in a film in 1946: "The way I murdered gram-
mar almost murdered Grandma!"

ZASU PITTS
January 3, 1898–June 7, 1963

Erich Von Stroheim took her seriously but everyone else laughed at
ZaSu Pitts, the flustery girl with the woefully moaning voice,
owlish eyes, and fluttering hands. She was invariably cast as a
spindly comic spinster or cautious sidekick to a livewire girlfriend.
Named after two aunts, Eliza and Susan, Kansas-born ZaSu grew up
in Santa Cruz. After being laughed at for attempting dramatic recita-
tions, she did comic monologues in high school like "Mrs. Smart
Learns How to Skate," and with some encouragement from her mother, tried show business after graduation.

A strange, thin girl whose odd appearance was more alluring than homely, ZaSu had potential in silent films. After much rejection, she found bit parts at Universal and eventually subbed for Gale Henry in some comedy shorts for the Joker comedy division in 1917. She was written into Mary Pickford's *The Little Princess,* and was given the lead by an admiring King Vidor in *Better Times* (the first of her many comic wallflower roles). She played more comic parts until being cast as a prostitute in *The Fast Set.* This impressed Erich Von Stroheim, who pronounced her "the screen's greatest tragedienne." With her baleful eyes, quivering intensity, and long hair down to her waist, she was unforgettable as Trina in *Greed.* She played a princess in another Von Stroheim film, *The Wedding March,* but soon was firmly typed as the comic maid or spinster. Ernst Lubitsch used her in *Monte Carlo* and *The Man I Killed.*

ZASU PITTS, the flustery girl with the sad eyes and the fluttery hands, wonderfully woeful from silents to TV.

Pitts starred in the silent version of *All Quiet on the Western Front,* but when her voice caused audience snickers, her scenes in the sound version were reshot with a replacement. Von Stroheim couldn't understand why his former leading lady was now being given comedy parts exclusively. "Some people do think she is funny looking," he admitted, "but I think art must weep when ZaSu plays a comedy role."

In talkies, ZaSu's doleful voice accentuated her comedic qualities, and after playing opposite Leon Errol (*Finn and Hattie*) and Will Rogers in *Mr. Skitch,* she was teamed with Thelma Todd for a series of comedy shorts. The forlorn, querulous actress was the hapless foil to smart and sexy Thelma. Impressionists loved to imitate the "oh me, oh my" wearily singsong cadence of the endlessly complaining ZaSu. Her voice was the inspiration for Popeye's girlfriend, Olive Oyl.

Some of the shorts, like *Sneak Easily* and *Asleep in the Feet,* featured Pitts more than Todd, indicating her promise as a solo. After a contract dispute with producer Hal Roach, Pitts quit the series in favor of more feature film work. She never became a big star on her own but remained one of the most popular character comediennes in films. She quipped, "I'm always the hired help." She amused audiences in maid roles in *Ruggles of Red Gap* and *No, No Nanette* and played Miss Hazy in *Mrs. Wiggs of the Cabbage Patch.* The *New York Times* applauded: "The patient and doleful Miss Hazy has become the fluttering ZaSu Pitts, and, for no more pious reason than to make you roar, she has been provided with a suitor in the outlandishly funny person of W. C. Fields." A few years later, Fields paid some kind of compliment to his slim, dizzily wayward costar. In *Never Give a Sucker an Even Break,* he admonishes young Gloria Jean, "You want to grow up and be dumb like ZaSu Pitts?"

Over the years, Pitts continued to play modest roles in every medium. She was a frequent guest on radio, including the *Lum and Abner* show, played a librarian in the Broadway play (written especially for her) *Ramshackle Inn,* and amused her fans by taking over Edna May Oliver's "Miss Withers" role in a pair of detective comedies opposite James Gleason.

Television audiences who were unaware of her supporting work with Thelma Todd, with Slim Summerville in several films, or with James Gleason, got a chance to appreciate her when she played Esmeralda Nugent opposite Gale Storm on the vintage sitcom, *Oh Susanna* (originally titled *The Gale Storm Show*). One of her last roles was as a phone operator in *It's a Mad, Mad, Mad, Mad World.*

Far from the spinster she played, Pitts had a daughter and son, and was living comfortably with her second husband, a realtor named John E. Woodall, at the time of her death.

MAE QUESTEL
Mae Kwestel, September 13, 1912

Betty Boop, Olive Oyl, Little Audrey, Winky Dink, and Casper the Friendly Ghost: Mae Questel did them all. No woman has had greater success with such varied comic voices in cartoons. But, as Mae pointed out to her fans, "I like being me and not just a voice." She enjoyed stepping out from behind the anonymous microphone and was typed for roles requiring an eccentric, tough, strident-voiced Jewish mother, proud and feisty. She was "Mrs. Portnoy" in book and record parodies of *Portnoy's Complaint* in the sixties, the aggravating "Aunt Bluebelle" in paper towel TV commercials in the seventies and ended the eighties playing Woody Allen's mother in *New York Stories*.

Born in the Bronx, a graduate of Morris High School, Mae's placid life at 1165 Anderson Avenue changed after winning a talent contest imitating the "Boop-Boop-a-Doop" girl, singer Helen Kane. She appeared often in vaudeville, and in 1930 Frank Loesser wrote a novelty tune for her, "I'm the Kind of Girl You Can Bet Is Chased." She appeared at the Palace as part of an unusual trio; her costars were a piano player named Fred Coots and baseball star Waite Hoyt. Her act included impressions of Fanny Brice, Maurice Chevalier, and Marlene Dietrich, but it was her Helen Kane mimicry that proved the most lucrative.

In 1931 she parlayed the Kane imitation into the voice for the Betty Boop cartoons. Two years later, parodying ZaSu Pitts, she gave voice to Popeye's sweetheart, Olive Oyl. She recorded "Sweet Betty, Don't Take My Boop-Boop-a-Doop Away" in 1933, along with "Animal Crackers in My Soup" (1935) and "At the Codfish Ball" (1936). In addition to hundreds of cartoons, Mae appeared on radio programs from *Perry Mason* to *The Henry Morgan Show* and, replacing Shirley Booth, *Duffy's Tavern*. She guested regularly on TV too, from *The Goldbergs* to *The Bob Newhart Show*. On Broadway she played Gertrude Berg's friend in *A Majority of One* and Nancy Dussault's cute, advice-giving mom in *Bajour*.

Never one for retiring, and hardly a retiring personality, the comedienne used her vocal talents in *Who Framed Roger Rabbit* and won notices for her work as Sadie Millstein in *New York Stories*. She first met Woody Allen when she recorded the song "Chameleon Days" for his film *Zelig*. The ageless Questel ("rhymes with compel," she said), mother of two sons, was always ready for a good role accentuating her humorously spirited personality. She said in 1990, "I feel like an old bag but I don't act like one!"

MAE QUESTEL, Betty Boop personified, with Jack Barry on the fifties TV kiddies show, *Winky Dink and You.*

SELECTED BROADWAY APPEARANCES:
Doctor Social (1948), *A Majority of One* (1959), *Enter Laughing* (1963), *Bajour* (1964)

SELECTED FILM APPEARANCES:
Wayward (1932), *A Majority of One* (1961), *It's Only Money* (1962), *Move* (1970), *Funny Girl* (1968), *Hot Resorts* (1984), *Who Framed Roger Rabbit* (voice) (1988), *New York Stories* (1988)

TELEVISION SERIES:
Stop Me If You've Heard This One (1949)

COLLECTIBLES:
Mrs. Portnoy's Retort (Musicor; a book version is also available), *Faustus and Everyman* (Caedmon), *Betty Boop Soundtracks* (Mark 56), a book version

EDDIE QUILLAN
March 31, 1907–July 19, 1990

He had an infectious smile, and a bright personality, and could double take with the best of them. Early in his career Eddie Quillan usually played the peppy thirties preppy, striding boldly into all kinds of sitcom trouble with flash and panache. *Big Money* in 1930 was one of his better efforts, along with *The Tip-Off*. In that one, he plays a bright-eyed radio mechanic. Nothing bothers this fellow. "Listen Ethel," he tells a coworker, "the wolf's at the door again.

EDDIE QUILLAN, enthusiastic second banana and double-take champ, discussing matters with Marjorie Rambeau in *Strictly Personal*.

SELECTED FILM APPEARANCES:
College Kiddo (1927), *Noisy Neighbors* (1929), *The Sophomore* (1929), *The Godless Girl* (1929), *Girl Crazy* (1932), *Strictly Personal* (1933), *Mutiny on the Bounty* (1935), *Big City* (1937), *The Grapes of Wrath* (1940), *Margie* (1940), *Flying Blind* (1941), *It Ain't Hay* (1943), *This Is the Life* (1944), *Song of the Sarong* (1945), *A Guy Could Change* (1946), *Sideshow* (1950), *Brigadoon* (1954), *Ladies' Man* (1961), *Who's Got the Action?* (1962), *Promises Promises* (1963), *Move Over Darling* (1963), *The Ghost and Mr. Chicken* (1966), *Angel in My Pocket* (1969), *How to Frame a Figg* (1971), *The Strongest Man in the World* (1975)

TELEVISION SERIES:
Valentine's Day (1964–65), *Julia* (1968–71), *Hell Town* (1985)

How's chances of gettin' five bucks on my salary till payday?" "Nothin' doin'." "Okay. If things get too tough—I'll eat the wolf!"

A former vaudevillian from Philadelphia, Eddie joined his brothers and a sister as "The Rising Generation." He was discovered by Mack Sennett when the troupe played Los Angeles' Orpheum Theater in 1925. Intending him to take the place of Harry Langdon, Sennett gave the bright-eyed young man scripts loaded with Langdon's brand of humor and even made Quillan duplicate Langdon's white-face makeup.

After working in many Sennett shorts starting in 1926 with *A Love Sundae*, Quillan began making features for Cecil B. De Mille. His big break with De Mille seemed like something out of a typical Quillan sitcom. The plucky kid had stopped to help a stranded motorist fix his car. The grateful man turned out to be a De Mille assistant who made sure Eddie got an audition.

Eddie's brother Joe Quillan was also making a move in the world of comedy, writing on radio for *Our Miss Brooks*, *The Eddie Cantor Show*, and *The Kate Smith Show*. Through the thirties and forties, Quillan usually played a smart bellhop or a grinning cab driver. He had bit roles in some classic pictures: a lovesick sailor in *Mutiny on the Bounty* and a radio mechanic in *The Grapes of Wrath*. His enthusiasm never waned. He was active in television sitcoms during the late sixties and early seventies, still playing lively characters like Grover Cleveland Fipple on *Valentine's Day* and Eddie Edson the amusing mailman on *Julia*.

CHARLOTTE RAE
Charlotte Lubotsky, April 22, 1926

Skilled at playing a variety of neurotics, for decades plump Charlotte Rae seemed typed as an overwrought housewife or a fidgety saleswoman. She was the histrionic Sylvia Schnauzer on *Car 54, Where Are You?* her homely angst leading to wide-eyed, emotional outbursts like this:

"Leo, please, before you take off your shoes and your feet swell up—

take me out! I'm going stir crazy...I find myself praying the building will catch on fire! At least we'll go out together...I wanna see what the outside world looks like...Take me anywhere, Leo! A movie, an ice cream parlor! Let's just stand on a street corner! Ha ha! Maybe we'll see an accident!"

Rae, who received her B.S. degree from Northwestern University won some early attention on Broadway playing excitable Mammy Yokum in *Li'l Abner*. She also developed a comedy act with music that made her welcome in clubs like the

CHARLOTTE RAE, who in the matter of comic support was almost always on the verge of collapse, giving a lesson here to the cast of *Hello Down There:* (from left) Ken Berry, Janet Leigh, Tony Randall, Jim Backus, a young Merv Griffin, and Roddy McDowall.

Village Vanguard. Then for films and television she carved out a niche playing nervously giggling saleswomen on the edge of their sanity, housewives faintly hiding their miseries behind crooked smiles, and Jewish mothers trying not to worry their kids by how much they worry.

She was Molly the Milkman on *Sesame Street*, a burbling Tupperware saleslady in an episode of *All in the Family*, received an Emmy nomination as Maureen Stapleton's friend in the 1975 TV movie *Queen of the Stardust Ballroom*, played Woody Allen's mother in *Bananas*, and parlayed the supporting TV role of Mrs. Garrett the housekeeper on *Diff'rent Strokes* into a starring one on *The Facts of Life*.

In 1990 Rae won a rave notice in the *New York Times* for an Off-Broadway revival of Samuel Beckett's *Happy Days*. The *Times* critic wrote, "...best known for her comic performances, Miss Rae aims for lightness and achieves it as called for...[she] is most adept at projecting the character's earthy humor." This was earthy humor, all right. Beckett's stage directions called for the star of this essentially "one-woman show" to perform buried up to her waist in earth.

SELECTED BROADWAY APPEARANCES:
Three Wishes for Jamie (1952), *The Threepenny Opera* (1954), *The Littlest Revue* (1956), *Li'l Abner* (1956), *The Beauty Part* (1962), *Henry IV* (1968), *Morning, Noon and Night* (1968), *Dr. Fish* (1970)

SELECTED FILM APPEARANCES:
Hello Down There (1969), *Bananas* (1971), *The Hot Rock* (1972), *Queen of the Stardust Ballroom* (1975), *Rabbit Test* (1978), *Hair* (1979), *The Triangle Factory Fire Scandal* (1979), *The Facts of Life Go to Paris* (1982)

TELEVISION SERIES:
Car 54, Where Are You? (1961–63), *Hot L Baltimore* (1975), *The Rich Little Show* (1976), *Diff'rent Strokes* (1978–79), *The Facts of Life* (1979–86)

RAGS RAGLAND, who played so dumb even goofy Red Skelton used him as a stooge.

RAGS RAGLAND
John Beauregard Ragland,
August 23, 1905–August 20, 1946

When an interviewer asked the aging Bud Abbott to name his favorite comedian, he answered: Rags Ragland. When asked to name some of the performers he recalled working with, Bud's answer was the same. Rags Ragland. Many other older comedians had fond remembrances of Rags Ragland, an actor who was not such a great laugh-getter (he mainly played big, happy oafs) but was a colorful character who enjoyed going out on the town drinking and carousing.

Phil Silvers loved to relate a typical Rags anecdote. A young comic named Bobby Morris was working in a burlesque sketch with Rags, enthusiastically mugging to the audience, stealing the scene. Rags told the kid, "Don't move on my lines or I'll nail you to the stage." Bobby kept at it—and Rags kept his word, literally nailing him to the stage and leaving him squirming through the subsequent comic scenes and stripper numbers.

Born in Kentucky, Ragland began as a boxer, then broke into show business as a burlesque second banana, spending eleven years working on the bill with most of the great stars of his day. He made it to Broadway for *Who's Who* and played a sailor in *Panama Hattie*. In films as an MGM contract player in the forties, he was so dumb, even dumb guys used him for a stooge. The good natured big lug played Red Skelton's sidekick Sylvester in *Whistling in Brooklyn*, and its two sequels, forever coming up with malaprops like "I had a pre-medicated idea!" Red sneers, "You can't even spell cat." Rags: "When I come to words like that I just ignore 'em." Rags stooged for Red in six films.

Ragland had signed a new contract with MGM in 1946 and had been rehearsing with Phil Silvers to team up for nightclub work when he collapsed and died of Bright's disease and uremic poisoning.

SELECTED BROADWAY APPEARANCES:
Who's Who (1938), *Panama Hattie* (1940)

SELECTED FILM APPEARANCES:
Ringside Maisie (1941), *Whistling in the Dark* (1941), *Sunday Punch* (1942), *Maisie Gets Her Man* (1942), *Panama Hattie* (1942), *Whistling in Dixie* (1942), *DuBarry Was a Lady* (1943), *Girl Crazy* (1943), *Whistling in Brooklyn* (1943), *The Canterville Ghost* (1944), *Her Highness and the Bellboy* (1945), *Anchors Aweigh* (1945), *Abbott and Costello in Hollywood* (1945), *Ziegfeld Follies* (1946), *The Hoodum Saint* (1946)

ERIK RHODES

Earnest Sharp,
February 10, 1906–
February 17, 1990

ERIK RHODES played fake lotharios and vain gigolos with the best of them, including a screenful of second bananas in *Top Hat*: Edward Everett Horton, Eric Blore, and Helen Broderick.

"Sometimes I faked my Italian so well that people thought I actually was Italian," recalled suave Erik Rhodes. "They were surprised to hear me speak regular English."

The man who played the preening Tonetti in *Top Hat* and the posturing Beddini in *The Gay Divorcée* (repeating his stage role) was born in El Reno, Oklahoma. After graduating from the University of Oklahoma, he came to New York on an acting scholarship but admitted that following a few small roles on stage, he was reduced to singing in a speakeasy: "My career really began in a speakeasy, although I sang in high school and in college. My voice seemed all right for the place and I remained in speakeasies for a couple of years and was about ready to give up and go back to Oklahoma when I landed a small part in the revue *Hey Nonny Nonny!*"

Someone felt he would go places a lot faster—if he changed his name. Earnest Sharp became Erik Rhodes, and Erik Rhodes landed the part of the amusingly vain gigolo who acts as correspondent ready to admit adultery in *Top Hat*. A concern is whether or not he'll not only admit to it for the divorce, but try to commit the act as well. He huffs, "With me, strictly business! My slogan: 'Your wife is safe with Tonetti! He prefers spaghetti!'"

In *The Gay Divorcée*, Rhodes had another standout role as an eccentric designer given to excitable declarations: "Never again will I allow women to wear my dresses!" After playing the foppish Beddini ("I am rich, I am pretty!") and the equally dramatic Tonetti ("I am delightful!"), Rhodes discovered, "If you were successful doing something once, they wanted you to keep doing it."

Once in a while Rhodes got away from the ethnic eccentrics, but usually he was still the foppish playboy. He was Max Corday in *Charlie Chan in Paris*, a jaunty boor in a top hat who says to the great detective, "Me velly happy know you. Maybe you like-y have-y little drink-y!" Chan answers in perfect English, "Very happy to make acquaintance of charming gentleman." Chan adds severely, "Me no like-y drinkee now. Perhaps lay-tah." Corday stiffens momentarily at his gaffe, then chuckles and airily goes off to get a drink, feeling he could certainly use it after such a faux pas.

Rhodes figured he could use a break from playing the guy who invariably loses Ginger Rogers to Fred Astaire and returned to the stage in the forties. He co-starred as the butler on *The Gloria Swanson Hour* during the early days of television. In addition to Broadway work, he appeared in stock in *The King and I, Blithe Spirit, Cactus Flower, 1776,* and *The Boy Friend*, often getting one of the lead roles instead of comic relief. He supplemented his income with TV commercials for everything from Benson & Hedges to Duncan Hines. His last TV appearance was as the Duke of Exeter on *The Adams Chronicles* on PBS in 1976.

The longtime bachelor had finally married in 1972, and after his wife's death in 1984 he returned to Oklahoma where he lived in comfortable retirement.

LYDA ROBERTI, Poland's contribution to American screen's comic vampdom.

LYDA ROBERTI
May 20, 1906–March 12, 1938

A comic vamp in several thirties comedies, Lyda Roberti was memorable as the femme fatale "Mata Machree," adding some satiric sexuality to the W. C. Fields comedy *Million Dollar Legs*. Few fans today realize she was parodying Greta Garbo in *Mata Hari*, her haughty, naughty demeanor burlesquing the techniques of a serious and simpering exotic sex goddess.

Born in Poland, the daughter of a popular circus clown, Roberti performed in a trapeze act with her sister Manya. The duo fled Warsaw during the Russian Revolution and worked in an American nightclub in Shanghai. Lyda ultimately came to America and after working as a glamorous stooge for a comic at Brooklyn's Paramount Theater, was discovered by Lou

Holtz for Broadway's *You Said It*. She introduced "I've Got a Cousin in Milwaukee" in that show, and literally became an overnight sensation.

Her sexy comic numbers and all-out vamping for laughs made her the standout in several shows. In *Pardon My English* she was still stooging. Jack Pearl nibbled her arm and told the audience, "It's pork—but I'll eat it." In the following year's *Roberta* she wowed the crowd singing the tune "I'll Be Hard to Handle."

In Hollywood she was often cast as the hard-to-handle star. For her cameo in *Pick a Star* she played brassy platinum blond Dagmar, a grotesquely temperamental actress. She sang "I Got It Bad" with a ridiculous Polish accent, gutterally gargling her "h's" and feuding with the director over her hot and sexy movements: "I'm giving you all the ch-hhhot I can give…ch-hhookay?"

She eventually teamed with Patsy Kelly for some comedy shorts. *At Sea Ashore*, which featured Lyda singing "Sweet and Hot," was followed with *Hill Tillies*. Lyda underwent an appendectomy in 1935 and while in the hospital met Hugh "Bud" Ernst, a radio announcer recovering from a car accident. They married, but reporters intimated that it was more like another accident. Coming back from a sea cruise in July of 1936, she wore dark glasses covering up a black eye dealt by Ernst. "You know how honeymoons are," Lyda told the newspaper men. "But everything is all right."

Lyda Roberti's health wasn't all right. It kept getting worse. She costarred with Joe E. Brown in *Wide Open Faces*—her last film. Her death at thirty-two was reported as a heart attack. At the time of her death, she was seeking an annulment of her marriage.

She left behind several memorable screen appearances, with *Million Dollar Legs* the best. As she said during one parody scene of sensuality, "I done all I can do—in public!"

BLOSSOM ROCK
Edith Blossom MacDonald, August 21, 1899–January 14, 1978

As "Grandmama" on *The Addams Family*, she had the coyness of a blossom but the face of a rock. Blossom Rock seemed a perfect name for the mysterious old sitcom actress. But, fans wanted to know, who was she, really? She told the show's publicity department in 1964, "Just say I'm Jeanette MacDonald's elder sister. Please add that I'm in pretty good shape for my age."

BLOSSOM ROCK, who played delightful comic support during the thirties and forties as Marie Blake long before becoming "Grandmama" to TV's *Addams Family*.

Born in Philadelphia, Blossom was indeed one of Jeanette's older sisters. She taught Jeanette her first songs, including "The Glory Hymn." When Blossom took dance classes, kid sister Jeanette tagged along. Blossom was originally the family's big star, appearing on Broadway as a chorus girl and forming a team in 1926 with her husband, Clarence Warren Rock. "Rock and Blossom" played the vaudeville circuit for years. She won good notices for her role in the comedy *Pursuit of Happiness* on stage in Philadelphia in 1935 and that year returned to Broadway as a streetwalker in *Dead End*, the show that featured the debut of the Dead End Kids.

When Blossom came to Hollywood to make films, the five-foot-four blue-eyed blond changed her name to Marie Blake. Her most notable role was Sally, the switchboard operator in the *Dr. Kildare* series. She was an amusing performer in a gaggle of minor comedies but it would be twenty years before she got a role that attracted special attention. That was playing the macabre mother of Morticia (Carolyn Jones), getting giggles and a few chills just by wandering around the Addams Family mansion cooking concoctions like "Eye of Newt" and grousing at the bizarre butler Lurch (Ted Cassidy) and the even more peculiar Uncle Fester (Jackie Coogan).

Ironically predating her popularity as a comical old crone, Blossom and her husband hosted a 1938 party with the theme: "Come as You Think You'll Look in Fifty Years." Showing her flair for the grotesque, Blossom wore a tombstone.

On the stone it read:

"As Blossom MacDonald she started life. As Blossom Rock she became a wife. For her movie career she was tagged Marie Blake. The studio told her to jump in the lake. P.S., She did!"

SELECTED BROADWAY APPEARANCES:
Dead End (1935), *But for the Grace of God* (1937)

SELECTED FILM APPEARANCES:
Love Finds Andy Hardy (1938), *Mannequin* (1938), *Calling Dr. Kildare* (1939), *Judge Hardy and Son* (1939), *Li'l Abner* (1940), *Caught in the Draft* (1941), *Dr. Kildare's Victory* (1941), *I Married a Witch* (1942), *The Major and the Minor* (1942), *Gildersleeve's Ghost* (1944), *Sensations of 1945* (1944), *Fun on a Weekend* (1947), *Girl From Manhattan* (1948), *Love Nest* (1951), *From the Terrace* (1960), *Snow White and the Three Stooges* (1961), *The Second Time Around* (1961), *The Best Man* (1964)

TELEVISION SERIES:
The Addams Family (1964–66)

COLLECTIBLES:
Various board games, card games, original soundtrack recordings and books bear Blossom's likeness in relation to *The Addams Family*

"SLAPSIE" MAXIE ROSENBLOOM

September 6, 1904–
March 6, 1976

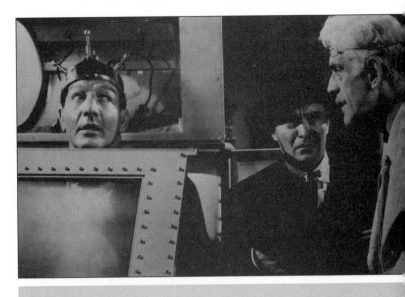

"SLAPSIE" MAXIE ROSENBLOOM, boxing champ whose second career was playing punch-drunk pugs and comic lugs, befuddles even Peter Lorre and Boris Karloff in *The Boogie Man Will Get You*.

A Runyonesque lug who often played punch-drunk pugs, Max Rosenbloom was once the light-heavyweight champion of the world. He wasn't a heavy puncher, often keeping his opponent off-balance with an openhanded cuffing jab. That's why Damon Runyon gave him his "slapsie" nickname.

A tough kid from New York whose street fighting led to a stretch in the Hawthorne Reform Home for Jewish Boys, he once slugged a teacher who tried to spank him. Rosenbloom's professional career lasted sixteen years and 289 fights. He won his first in 1923, and took the title by decision over Lou Scozza in 1930. He lost it to Bob Olin by decision in 1934, and quit in 1939 despite knocking out his final opponent and winning nineteen of his last twenty-one bouts. Boxing fans George Raft and Carole Lombard helped him get into show business, something he was attracted to as early as 1933 when he managed to get a part in the film *Mr. Broadway*.

Maxie tried vaudeville with Sid Fields as his straight man but had better luck in films; he didn't have too many lines to remember. As he once said, "I play a great big guy who's awful dumb." Carole Lombard used him in *Nothing Sacred*. With another of his pals, lifelong fight fan Shemp Howard, and Billy Gilbert, Maxie created a kind of Three Stooges team and the trio made three films together for Monogram in 1944.

Slapsie Maxie always had softheaded malaprops to mutter. In *The Boogie Man Will Get You*, mad doctor Boris Karloff is about to experiment. "Just relax," he tells Max. Max agrees, "I'll relapse." And then, while waiting for the anesthetic: "Am I unconscious yet?"

In later years he ran a local nightclub in Los Angeles and it was popular with stars and patrons for quite a while. The business failed in the sixties and his other investments were also unsuccessful. A marriage to a child psychologist had only lasted six years, leaving him on his own. Paget's disease dimmed the vitality of the aging ex-champ, who lived in a senior citizen's home in his last years. He was cheered by one last honor, his 1972 induction into the Boxing Hall of Fame.

BENNY RUBIN, versatile, ingratiating burlesque comedian who graduated to vaudeville, radio, and here, Anita Page's arms.

BENNY RUBIN
February 2, 1899–July 15, 1986

Once a vaudeville headliner, Benny Rubin is best remembered as a versatile character comedian: ethnic, blustery, or cute, depending on whether he was supporting the Three Stooges, Abbott and Costello, or Jack Benny.

Born in Boston, Rubin attended the Industrial School for Boys and learned house painting. A good dancer and a good boxer, he took fights when the prize money was worth it and show business jobs whenever he could get them. He got his first break thanks to Barbara Walters's father, Lou, who helped him get a booking with a Rhode Island revue in 1941. From there Benny made his way through small-time burlesque and big-time vaudeville as a dancer and comedian, and then on to radio.

A favorite with Jewish audiences, Rubin performed novelty tunes and routines with an ingratiating, Cantor-esque delivery. His tune "Laugh" offered bewildering philosophy: "If you want the moon to shining,/and the sun don't coming down,/throw away your frowning/and laugh, smile, clown./Life is full of sadness/and of gladness just as easy,/so puttin' on a camphor bag/and you will never sneezing./What's the use of crying/if you think you're gonna dying,/crying wouldn't help you any time./So wipe away the sneery,/commence to feeling cheery,/'cause the lobster is the wiseguy any minute/...so laughing while you're living,/and living while you're laughing— you'll be a long time dead if you live!"

Rubin played the Palace in New York in the thirties. He recalled, "I got belly laughs. [Jack] Benny used to stand in the wings and scream at my jokes…. He liked me even though I used bad language and I was a rough guy, loud and vulgar." Rubin teamed at various times with Jack Haley, Eddie Cantor, and ex-boxer Max Baer, and began making Jewish comedies in 1929 including a short that year, *The Delicatessen Kid*. Eventually he made fifty-five two-reelers, and appeared in more than one hundred fifty features.

SELECTED BROADWAY APPEARANCES:
5*Half a Widow* (1927), *Radio Carnival* (1932)

SELECTED FILM APPEARANCES:
Seven Minutes of Your Time (1928), *Naughty Baby* (1929), *Imperfect Ladies* (1929), *It's a Great Life* (1930), *Lord Byron of Broadway* (1930), *Sunny Skies* (1930), *Love in the Rough* (1930), *George White's Scandals* (1935), *Sunny* (1941), *Here Comes Mr. Jordan* (1941), *Broadway* (1942), *The Noose Hangs High* (1948), *Easy to Love* (1953), *Susan Slept Here* (1954), *The Tender Trap* (1955), *Will Success Spoil Rock Hunter?* (1957), *A Hole in the Head* (1959), *The Errand Boy* (1961), *The Patsy* (1964), *Looking For Love* (1964), *That Funny Feeling* (1965), *Thoroughly Modern Millie* (1967), *Airport* (1969), *Which Way to the Front?* (1970), *Won Ton Ton, The Dog Who Saved Hollywood* (1976), *Coma* (1978)

TELEVISION SERIES:
Stop Me If You've Heard This One (1948–49), *The Benny Rubin Show* (1949), *The Brighter Day* (1962)

COLLECTIBLES:
Self-published 1973 autobiography *Come Backstage With Me*

He invariably played a likeable ethnic character and was fun to have around. In one version of "Who's on First," Lou Costello paid him a tongue-in-cheek tribute, referring to the clean-up hitter in the routine as "Home Run Benny Rubin." His pals in the business always found small roles for him, though he supplemented his income with a dress shop in Hollywood. In 1949, he starred in his own TV variety show and in the fifties he added cartoon work to his credits, performing voices on the old *Dick Tracy* series. He was in the last appearance of the Marx Brothers together, the 1959 TV special *The Incredible Jewel Robbery*.

In the sixties the little fellow with the thick white hair had small roles in a few Jerry Lewis films, among others, comfortably filling the part of mildly excitable maitre d's, waiters, or businessmen.

CHARLIE RUGGLES
February 8, 1886–December 23, 1970

Charming and genial, Charlie Ruggles was beloved as a mildly befuddled and absentminded gent. Sometimes he was the puckish older fellow with a roving eye for the ladies.

Earlier in his career he was a mild-mannered husband or long-suffering employee. The comic highlight in either role would be the moment when he got up enough courage to get his way.

If I Had a Million, in which he had problems both as a husband and employee, established his identity for movie audiences back in 1932. He played the meek clerk in the china shop mortally afraid of

CHARLIE RUGGLES, mild-mannered, sometimes absentminded soul of propriety in a sixty-year show biz career.

breaking things and being charged for them. So, naturally, he nervously breaks things. The mousy little man would much prefer raising rabbits for a living, but his bossy wife won't stand for it. Suddenly getting a windfall gift of a million dollars, Ruggles has his revenge—a literally smashing visit to that china shop. Whatever the role, dapper or demure, Ruggles retained the common touch that made audiences identify with him. He once wrote over his name on a press agent's biography "always Charlie, NOT Charles."

Born in Los Angeles, he made his debut in a 1905 San Francisco stock company production of *Nathan Hale*. He performed with the Alcazar and Morosco stock companies until 1914 when he debuted on Broadway as Jack Scott in *Help Wanted*. Ruggles made a few silent films around that time, including *Reform Candidate*, *Heart Raiders* (directed by his brother Wesley), and *Peer Gynt*, but was best known on stage through the twenties. He noted, "At one brief period in my years in show business, I decided to write and direct my own play called *Fifty-Fifty* at the Alcazar Theatre, San Francisco. That was back in 1918—the play lasted one week. Needless to say, I never tried it again."

For a short time (1924–26) he toured vaudeville in his own comedy sketch, "Wives, etc." In thirties films Charlie's subtle gazes and wistful ways proved an interesting contrast to the dominating screwball and slapstick comedians. One of his first parts, minus his trademark little mustache, was in drag as *Charley's Aunt*. But after that he was more often part of an ensemble cast, his sly and quiet scene-stealing a challenge to W. C. Fields, Mary Boland (cast in over a dozen films as his nagging wife), and many other extroverted stars. He, Fields, and Boland were all in *If I Had a Million* and *Six of a Kind*. Charlie was the March Hare in *Alice in Wonderland* and was also featured in *Ruggles of Red Gap*, playing Egbert Floud. The title had nothing to do with Ruggles, himself. The movie was based on a 1914 *Saturday Evening Post* serial "Ruggles, Bunker and Merton" that was novelized the following year. He also had a starring role in *It Happened on Fifth Avenue* in the mid-forties.

Television viewers got to know Charlie when he starred in *The Ruggles*, about one mousy man's family. Charlie played "himself" and Erin O'Brien Moore was his TV "wife," Margaret. Now quite dated, it had a respectable three-season run at the time, and was followed by *The World of Mr. Sweeney* (about a genial small-town general store owner), which was shot live in New York on NBC. It was loosely based on his own 1934 film *The Friends of Mr. Sweeney*. Moving to New York was a big decision for Charlie. He had been declared the Honorary Mayor of San Fernando where he owned and operated the See-Are Kennels, along with orange and lemon groves.

Ruggles stayed in New York for Broadway work, winning a Tony Award for *The Pleasure of His Company* in 1958. In the sixties he returned home to 10829 Wilshire Boulevard, guest-starring on TV in roles calling for either the henpecked hubby or sly fox grandpa, well dressed, well spoken, but still amusingly bemused.

Ruggles won over a new generation of fans when he took on the only show business job he hadn't yet tried, lending his distinctively wry voice to the narration of the "Aesop's Fables" cartoons that were part of the *Rocky and Bullwinkle* TV series. He ended his career making a number of films for Disney.

SELECTED BROADWAY APPEARANCES:
Help Wanted (1914), *Canary Cottage* (1917), *The Passing Show of 1918* (1918), *Tumble In* (1929), *The Girl in the Limousine* (1920), *Ladies' Night* (1920), *The Demi-Virgin* (1921), *Battling Butler* (1923), *Rainbow* (1928), *Spring Is Here* (1929), *The Pleasure of His Company* (1958), *The Captains and the Kings* (1962), *Roar Like a Dove* (1964)

SELECTED FILM APPEARANCES:
Peer Gynt (1915), *The Heart Raider* (1923), *Gentlemen of the Press* (1929), *Charley's Aunt* (1930), *Young Man of Manhattan* (1930), *Husband's Holiday* (1932), *This Is the Night* (1932), *Trouble in Paradise* (1932), *If I Had a Million* (1932), *Alice in Wonderland* (1933), *Six of a Kind* (1934), *The Friends of Mr. Sweeney* (1934), *People Will Talk* (1935), *The Big Broadcast of 1936* (1935), *Ruggles of Red Gap* (1935), *Mind Your Own Business* (1936), *Wives Never Know* (1936), *Early to Bed* (1936), *Bringing Up Baby* (1938), *The Farmer's Daughter* (1940), *No Time for Comedy* (1940), *Go West Young Lady* (1941), *The Perfect Snob* (1941), *The Doughgirls* (1944), *Incendiary Blonde* (1945), *Bedside Manner* (1945), *My Brother Talks to Horses* (1946), *It Happened on Fifth Avenue* (1947), *Give My Regards to Broadway* (1948), *The Pleasure of His Company* (1961), *Son of Flubber* (1963), *The Ugly Dachshund* (1965), *Follow Me, Boys!* (1967)

TELEVISION SERIES:
The Ruggles (1949–52), *The World of Mr. Sweeney* (1954), *The Bullwinkle Show* (voice) (1961–62)

SIG RUMAN

Siegfried Albon Rumann, October 11, 1884–February 14, 1967

As a stereotypical, blustery German, Sig Ruman had some of his finest moments in Marx Brothers movies. He was Herman Gottlieb the diabolical impresario of *A Night at the Opera*, murderous Nazi Heinrich Stubel in *A Night in Casablanca* and the stuffy Dr. Leopold Steinberg in *A Day at the Races*. In the last he argues with Groucho Marx over the condition of his patient, Margaret Dumont. "She looks like the healthiest woman I ever met," Ruman announces. Groucho sizes him up and answers, "You look like you never *met* a healthy woman."

Ruman was so typecast as a German with an outrageous accent that he literally played the same role at either end of his long career. He was a suspicious Viennese doctor in Carole Lombard's *Nothing Sacred* and the Jerry Lewis remake, *Living It Up*. The bald Ruman lent his thick eyebrows, disapproving glare, guttural accent, and imposing height to other encounters with Jerry Lewis (*The Errand Boy*) as well as an entire gang of tormenting youths, the Bowery Boys (*Spy Chasers*), and the team of Allen and Rossi (*The Last of the Secret Agents*).

SIG RUMAN, the blustery German stereotype in comedies as well as dramas, here taking a bribe from POW William Holden in *Stalag 17*.

Ruman was born in Hamburg, Germany, and came to New York around 1924. He starred in German-language plays before being discovered by George Jessel. He was almost always the target for the star comedians, arrogantly standing in the way until he was knocked over by slapstick. Though he sometimes went beyond comic villainy into cruelty (he repeatedly beats Harpo Marx in *A Night in Casablanca*), he was such a cartoon, especially with his gooey, goose-like shouts of dismay and punctured dignity, most viewers were chuckling both before and after he was demolished.

Though he was the target of insults and slapstick, he was rarely allowed to use his exaggerated German accent to get a laugh on his own. Probably his only memorable line of comic dialogue was as Colonel Ehrhardt in Jack Benny's *To Be or Not to Be*, a stereotypical role that would set the standard for dozens of similar pompous and incompetent Nazis other actors would play for years to come. Asked for his opinion of ham actor Benny, Ruman remarks, "I saw him on the stage in Warsaw before the war. What he did to Shakespeare, we are doing now to Poland."

SELECTED BROADWAY APPEARANCES:
Fedora (1924), *The Channel Road* (1929), *Half Gods* (1929), *Grand Hotel* (1930), *Alien Corn* (1933), *Eight Bells* (1933), *Lily of the Valley* (1942), *Once There Was a Russian* (1961)

SELECTED FILM APPEARANCES:
The Farmer Takes a Wife (1935), *A Night at the Opera* (1935), *The Princess Comes Across* (1936), *A Day at the Races* (1937), *Nothing Sacred* (1937), *Never Say Die* (1939), *Ninotchka* (1939), *That Uncertain Feeling* (1941), *Love Crazy* (1941), *To Be or Not to Be* (1942), *They Came to Blow Up America* (1943), *The Hitler Gang* (1944), *The House of Frankenstein* (1944), *It Happened Tomorrow* (1944), *A Night in Casablanca* (1946), *Mother Wore Tights* (1947), *If You Knew Susie* (1948), *On the Riviera* (1951), *Stalag 17* (1953), *Ma and Pa Kettle on Vacation* (1953), *Living It Up* (1954), *The Spy Chasers* (1955), *The Wings of Eagles* (1957), *The Errand Boy* (1961), *Robin and the Seven Hoods* (1964), *The Fortune Cookie* (1966), *The Last of the Secret Agents?* (1966)

TELEVISION SERIES:
Life With Luigi (1952)

IRENE RYAN
Irene Noblette,
October 17, 1903–April 26, 1973

Best remembered by modern generations as the spry, high-strung Granny Clampett on *The Beverly Hillbillies*, Irene Ryan's show business career began at eleven when the El Paso-born girl sang "Pretty Baby" in an amateur contest—and won $3. In her teens Irene moved from bit parts and chorus work to become a headliner on Broadway. Irene Noblette married Tim Ryan in 1922, and with him as her straight man, the team of Ryan and Noblette took off: "We worked out a comedy act...very much like Burns and Allen, as a matter of fact...we bumped around and got into radio. We were pretty successful." The duo's name changed to the more friendly Tim and Irene.

IRENE RYAN, Granny Clampett on *The Beverly Hillbillies* and here getting Donna Douglas's goat.

After starring solo in 1932's *Carefree Carnival* show in San Francisco, Ryan won her first important role as a comic support player, spending two years guesting as a sad, hypochondriacal member of Bob Hope's radio company. Bob: "How are you tonight, Miss Ryan?" Irene: "I'm doing about as well as can be expected..." She played overseas World War II tours with Hope, and the character she honed with him later turned up on other shows and in films. Making the most of her indifferent looks, she appeared in several TV shows with Cliff ("Charlie Weaver") Arquette, portraying the doleful beauty, "Miss Mount Idy." Meanwhile, husband Tim served as a writer on a half dozen Bowery Boys movies in the fifties.

As Granny, Ryan was the most boisterously comical member of the Clampett Clan, and one of comedy's most memorable feisty old ladies, her abrupt, snappy delivery setting the tone for actresses like Estelle Getty to follow. "City women is spoiled rotten," she groused in one episode, "All they think about is smearin' themselves with beauty grease! Fancy smellin' renderin's! Why, if you was to hug one of 'em, she'd squirt out of your arms like a prune pit!"

Offstage she didn't look anything like her cantankerous, gray-haired character. The only similarity was her voice. She once said, "That's how most people recognize me, through my voice. I'd rather be known as 'The Body,' but I guess I'll have to be content with what I got."

Fans of *The Beverly Hillbillies* will be pleasantly surprised if they happen to catch one of her old movies, like *The Sarong Girl* (1943), jam-packed with dizzy dialogue between herself and her husband Tim Ryan (they're billed simply as The Ryans). Irene seems like a feistier version of Gracie Allen. In the film, Tim played a slow-burning detective trying to make sense of her antics. After flashing his badge he declares, "Dennis O'Brien, 79th Precinct. I'd like your name!"

Irene: "How do you know you would? I didn't even tell it to you. Maybe you wouldn't like it!"

Later, more typically silly and frisky dialogue written by Tim Ryan. Irene complains, "I have an awful headache every morning. See, I read with the light off."

"You read without light?"

"You see, I read to get sleepy, and if I read with the light on and fell asleep, why then the light would be on. This way–"

"The light is off. What do you read?"

"I don't know, it's so dark!"

In nightclubs and Las Vegas casinos, she'd come out as Granny, and then "striptease" to do songs and comedy as Irene Ryan, or "Renie" as she was known to her friends. Tim Ryan died in 1955, so without children, she decided to start the Irene Ryan Foundation in 1971, a million-dollar fund that provided scholarships to theater arts students around the country.

Her last role was on Broadway. She earned a Tony nomination in 1973 for *Pippin*, her debut on the Great White Way. Of her long career she said, "I've been bounced down, and I've had to come back with my own strength. You have to pull yourself up by yourself. Nobody can do it for you. You know the greatest influence in making me what I am? It's me." She signed to do a new TV pilot after the run of *Pippin*, but the seemingly indomitable but frail Ryan had a stroke during a performance of the show. She died a short time later.

Director Bob Fosse remembered her with fondness. He recalled the time he suggested she leave the stage just as the show ended to avoid being accidentally hurt in the hustle of moving scenery, stagehands, and actors. She said, "I've traveled three thousand miles, given up a beautiful home in California, left all my dear friends.... I really don't have to *work* anymore and all just to *hear* that sound. Please don't ask me to leave the wings until the last person has stopped applauding."

SELECTED FILM APPEARANCES:
Melody for Three (1941), *The Sarong Girl* (1943), *San Diego, I Love You* (1944), *Diary of a Chambermaid* (1945), *That's the Spirit* (1945), *Little Iodine* (1946), *The Skipper Surprised His Wife* (1950), *Meet Me After the Show* (1951), *Bonzo Goes to College* (1952), *Ricochet Romance* (1954), *Spring Reunion* (1957), *Don't Worry, We'll Think of a Title* (1966)

TELEVISION SERIES:
The Beverly Hillbillies (1962–71)

COLLECTIBLES:
Ryan can be heard on the Columbia album *The Beverly Hillbillies* and the cast recording of *Pippin* (Motown). She also wrote *Granny's Hillbilly Cookbook*.

AL ST. JOHN
September 10, 1892–January 21, 1963

AL ST. JOHN, in silents with Fatty Arbuckle (his uncle) and Buster Keaton and in Westerns as sidekick of cowboy stars.

Although Al St. John's uncle was Roscoe "Fatty" Arbuckle, that didn't help him break into show business. Fatty (Al's mother's brother) actually tried to keep the star-struck guy away from the cameras. Determined to make it in films, despite the wishes of his parents and his uncle, Al broke in the old fashioned way—he rode upside-down on his bicycle and did enough cycling stunts to leave Mack Sennett breathless. Sennett hired him after the audition and kept him as one of his acrobatic slapstick stooges despite the protests of his star, Arbuckle.

Lanky Al St. John became one of the most reliable stunt comics at Sennett's Keystone studio, but aside from bike stunts, unicycling, and trick driving, he evolved his own distinctive rube personality, complete with a few missing teeth, close-cropped hair to accent his ears, and a garish combination of plaids and checks for his shirt and pants. St. John was used as both a dupe and villain in supporting roles, did well in thrill comedies that relied on his agility, and in the twenties stripped away the yokel makeup to emerge as a passably sleek, tall comic leading man.

Al St. John remained close to his uncle Fatty and appeared with Arbuckle in a number of comedy shorts from 1917 onward. Afterward, St. John's comic persona changed again. Sporting a bushy beard and a large upturned cowboy hat, he became the grizzled sidekick "Fuzzy," opposite a variety of Western stars. He was "Fuzzy Q. Jones" in Fred Scott Westerns in 1937, then worked with Bob Steele, Buster Crabbe, and ultimately Lash La Rue. The feisty Fuzzy perfected little comic routines for everything from rolling cigarettes and chewing tobacco to scratching his head so hard his hat slipped over his eyes. He could be tough. From *Songs and Bullets* in 1938: "All right boys, I reckon you can take your hands down now, but don't try anything funny or I'll jump down your throats with my spurs on and rake you from tonsil to tonsil!"

In the fifties, billed as Fuzzy St. John, the sidekick made frequent rodeo appearances. The end for Fuzzy came after he had a heart attack between shows at a country fair in Georgia.

SELECTED FILM APPEARANCES:
Mabel's Strange Predicament (1914), *The Knockout* (1914), *Tillie's Punctured Romance* (1914), *The Butcher Boy* (1917), *The Bellboy* (1918), *Fast and Furious* (1921), *The Happy Pest* (1921), *Young and Dumb* (1923), *Pink Elephants* (1926), *Dance of Life* (1929), *Outcasts of Poker Flat* (1937), *Ranger's Round-Up* (1938), *Call of the Yukon* (1938), *Fuzzy Settles Down* (1944), *Frontier Revenge* (1948), *Frontier Phantom* (1952)

TELEVISION SERIES:
Lash of the West (1952–53)

213

S. Z. "CUDDLES" SAKALL, he of the teddy-bear jowls and fractured English, is so bewildered Edward Everett Horton shows some concern in *Thank Your Lucky Stars*.

S. Z. "CUDDLES" SAKALL
Eugene Gero, February 2, 1883– February 12, 1955

S. Z. "Cuddles" Sakall, a chubby-cheeked, white-haired, kindly old character actor, is probably best known for his minor role in *Casablanca*, playing one of the colorful employees at Rick's. One simple, sighing, sentimental expression on Cuddles face was enough to revolt Humphrey Bogart's, and give the film a little touch of comic relief. Sakall didn't get to show off his real trademark, though—a pair of teddy-bear jowls that he shook in comic confusion, as he slapped his cheeks and made a comment or two in fractured English. Sometimes his fellow actors would tease him and give his cheeks a tweak; one of the few times viewers could see someone blush in a black and white movie.

The jolly actor had grim beginnings, living in an old tenement across the street from a cemetery in Budapest. Named Eugene, he was called "Yani" by his family, but when he became a comic song writer at eighteen, he put the name Szoke Szakall on the sheet music. It literally means "Blond Beard" in Hungarian. He had one at the time.

A gag-writer for a Budapest comic, the aspiring performer appeared in German talkies. He came to America in the late thirties and changed Szoke to the catchier "S. Z." Soon a favorite in minor comic roles, he capitalized on his fleshy-faced grandfatherly appearance and earned the nickname "Cuddles."

One of Sakall's better roles was in the stellar *Thank Your Lucky Stars*. In one scene he and Edward Everett Horton are trying to get a reaction out of Eddie Cantor. "Vy don't you inzult him?" asks Sakall. "Why don't *you* insult him like we discussed?" retorts timorous Horton. Cries Sakall, "I vill tell you! Because you are more discussting than me!" More fractured English confusion and malaprops follow, as the confused Sakall gets excited: "Vat's dis animal it shouldn't happen to?" "A dog." "That's it!" Sakall gets so overwrought he even takes on Humphrey Bogart, who turned up in the all-star film as himself. Sakall cries, "If I talk to you, keep a civil tongue in my head…then you mind my busi-

SELECTED FILM APPEARANCES:
It's a Date (1940), *Spring Parade* (1940), *The Devil and Miss Jones* (1941), *Ball of Fire* (1942), *Yankee Doodle Dandy* (1942), *Casablanca* (1942), *Thank Your Lucky Stars* (1943), *Wonder Man* (1945), *Christmas in Connecticut* (1945), *The Time, the Place and the Girl* (1946), *April Showers* (1948), *In the Good Old Summertime* (1949), *Tea for Two* (1950), *Lullaby of Broadway* (1952), *Small Town Girl* (1953), *The Student Prince* (1954)

COLLECTIBLES:
Sakall's autobiography, *The Story of Cuddles: My Life Under Emperor Francis Joseph, Adolf Hitler and the Warner Brothers*

ness and I mind yours!" Mutters Bogie, pretending to be cowed, "Gee, I hope none of my movie fans hear about this."

Cuddles made films through the mid fifties. In 1954 he wrote his autobiography. It sold modestly, of course, but chances are that if it had been a blockbuster the modest supporting player would have been overwhelmed. Eyeing a bookstore full of people wanting his autograph, he'd probably utter a line from one of his movies: "The standing room is so crowded there's no place to sit down!"

NATALIE SCHAFER
November 5, 1900–
April 10, 1991

Known for playing a variety of tongue-in-cheek society matrons, the witty Natalie Schafer found lasting fame not from her many years on Broadway or her many films, but from the few high-profile seasons she spent as Lovey Howell on *Gilligan's Island*. On the show she presented her most perfect incarnation of a bored, self-preoccupied rich lady: "I really wouldn't mind being poor if it weren't for one thing…poverty."

Born in Red Bank, New Jersey, she was a student at the Merrill School on Long Island, New York. She was an

NATALIE SCHAFER, whose playing of wealthy matrons and society snobs (here serving tea to Jeanne Crain and Jean Peters in *Take Care of My Little Girl*) led to the role of Lovey Howell in *Gilligan's Island*.

understudy to actress Ina Clare and later worked for the Atlanta Stock Company. She found her way to Broadway and was cast in sophisticated romances and comedies like *The Nut Farm*, opposite Pat O'Brien, and *The Rhapsody*, which featured Louis Calhern, her husband from 1934 to 1942. *Lady in the Dark* in 1941 was a high point in her stage career.

She continued to appear on stage and beginning in 1941, in films, ultimately taking parts on television (teaching Lucy and Ethel some class in an episode of *I Love Lucy*). In 1964 she was cast as Mrs. Howell ("Lovey") to Jim Backus's Thurston Howell III. Asked if there was any similarity between herself and the lovably foolish, fashionably vain society lady, she said, "Yes. We both wear hats."

She went on to dramatic roles after that, successfully avoiding further typecasting. She starred in a touring version of the lesbian drama

The Killing of Sister George and played a madame in the film *The Day of the Locust*. She still insisted, "I'd rather do comedy than anything. Making people laugh is the most satisfying thing you can do. And comedy is a lot more difficult than drama."

She sought out good comedy parts, but her comic instincts led her to turn down inferior work. Sometimes, the good parts just didn't find *her*. Milton Berle told a story about the time Natalie called her agent, restless for something interesting to do:

"I'm going to show you what show business is today…two weeks later he calls and he says, 'I think I've got something for you, a movie of the week….' He sets up an appointment with the director of the picture. Now, let me preface it by saying the director is twenty-eight years old. He says, 'Sit down, Miss…' and he takes a peek at the paper. 'Miss Schafer. I suppose you're here to read for the part of Alicia. Miss Schafer, what have you done?' And without missing a beat she looked at him and said, 'You first.'"

VITO SCOTTI
January 26, 1918

Vito Scotti was creative in dealing with the two different stereo-typical sitcom characters he often played.

His variant on the "excitable Italian" was to concentrate more on the slow burn than the bluster. On the old *Andy's Gang* series, he'd play a pretentious expert trying to teach the kids how to cook or appreciate music—only to be interrupted by "Froggy the Gremlin." Scotti would absentmindedly repeat Froggy's wisecracks, glare, and frown in high dudgeon, and ultimately walk off in a helpless rage.

Scotti was also amusing as a soft-spoken eccentric, a diminutive Italian with an endearing laugh and his own mock-serious codes of manners and propriety. On an episode of *The Dick Van Dyke Show* he played Vito Giotto, a lovable, trustworthy little house painter—who happens to believe he should sign his work, even if it's the wall of an apartment. He was given to language miscues ("I promise you I'm gonna be quiet like a rat!") and confused logic ("You never wake up

Mama! Especially when she's sleeping!")

In the sixties he was often a variation on the then-popular José Jimenez type of foreigner, a bewildered little man who meant well but, with somewhat mournful demeanor and too-gentle personality, tended to get himself into trouble.

After replacing J. Carrol Naish for a season as the star of *Life With Luigi*, the San Francisco-born Scotti turned up on a variety of sitcoms, playing an eccentric professor in the first episode of *Get Smart*, Police Captain Formento on *The Flying Nun*, Gino Mancini on *To Rome With Love*, and Mr. Valasquez on *Barefoot in the Park*. Even in 1990, he was playing restrained variations of smiling Italians—a bistro owner in a ninety-minute *Columbo*. Dapper with his small mustache and jaunty step, Scotti had a very Chaplinesque way about him, overplaying his worries with a stern look that could not be taken seriously, broadly offering a toothy, good-natured smile of charm and guilelessness that few could resist.

VITO SCOTTI, dapper, jaunty "Continental," escorting Ingrid Bergman on a night out in *Cactus Flower*.

RETA SHAW
September 13, 1912–
January 8, 1982

SELECTED BROADWAY APPEARANCES:
Pinocchio (1939), *Steel* (1939)

SELECTED FILM APPEARANCES:
Cry of the City (1948), *Criss Cross* (1949), *Conquest of Space* (1955), *Where the Boys Are* (1960), *Two Weeks in Another Town* (1962), *The Pleasure Seekers* (1964), *What Did You Do in the War, Daddy?* (1966), *The Secret War of Harry Frigg* (1968), *How Sweet It Is* (1968), *Head* (1968), *Cactus Flower* (1969), *Chu Chu and the Philly Flash* (1981)

TELEVISION SERIES:
Mama Rosa (1950), *Life With Luigi* (1953), *The Flying Nun* (1968–69), *To Rome With Love* (1969–71), *Barefoot in the Park* (1970–71)

A large, domineering character comedienne who played no-nonsense housekeepers and glaring battle axes, Reta Shaw was born in South Paris, Maine, and grew up in a refined, educated atmosphere. She graduated from Leland Powers School of Theater in Boston.

A school teacher originally, Shaw worked as a recreational director during World War II with the Red Cross in Iceland, Belgium, and France. It was in 1947 that she came to Broadway with *It Takes Two*. Her theatrical career reached a peak with *The Pajama Game*. It was a role she repeated in the film version. She had the comic highlight playing against top banana Eddie Foy Jr., cheerfully goading him in a tune about infidelity, "I Would Trust Her." Her sister, Marguerite Shaw, an associate Dean of Students at American University, took the role with the national touring company.

After appearing as Dollie Tate in both the 1957 Broadway revival

RETA SHAW, amply-built comic battle axe of stage, screen, and television.

and the 1958 TV version of Mary Martin's *Annie Get Your Gun*, Shaw became best known for her work in television sitcoms, both one-shot roles (Frosty, the disapproving, white-haired tank of a maid trying to clean up after Oscar and Felix in *The Odd Couple*) and series (Aunt Lil on *Mr. Peepers*, Aunt Lavinia on *Ichabod and Me*, housekeeper Thelma on *The Tab Hunter Show*, and housekeeper Martha Grant on *The Ghost and Mrs. Muir*).

Shaw was so adept at glares, huffiness, foreboding expressions and resigned chagrin, few viewers could imagine that her real-life was different from her sitcom character. She *was* quite different—and unlike almost all her characters, she was married, and had a daughter, Kathryn Anne Forester.

SELECTED BROADWAY APPEARANCES:
It Takes Two (1947), *Gentlemen Prefer Blondes* (1949), *Picnic* (1953), *The Pajama Game* (1954), *Annie Get Your Gun* (1957)

SELECTED FILM APPEARANCES:
Picnic (1956), *The Pajama Game* (1957), *Polyanna* (1960), *Sanctuary* (1961), *Bachelor in Paradise* (1961), *Mary Poppins* (1964), *Escape to Witch Mountain* (1975)

TELEVISION SERIES:
Mr. Peepers (1954), *The Betty White Show* (1958), *The Ann Sothern Show* (1958–59), *The Tab Hunter Show* (1960–61), *Ichabod and Me* (1961–62), *Oh Those Bells* (1962), *The Cara Williams Show* (1964–65), *The Ghost and Mrs. Muir* (1968–70)

ALISON SKIPWORTH

Alison Groom, July 25, 1863–July 5, 1952

Remembered now as a battered but indomitable old wreck opposite W. C. Fields and Mae West, Alison Skipworth had some of the haughty bearing of Margaret Dumont, combined with the ragged earthiness and fallen dignity of Marie Dressler.

A veteran stage performer, Skipworth made her London stage debut in 1894 in *A Gaiety Girl*. She came to Broadway the following year in *The Artist's Model*, and began making films in 1915 but did her best work in thirties comedies with Fields.

In *If I Had a Million* she plays an old vaudevillian who receives a surprise gift of a million dollars—and proceeds to join her pal W. C.

Fields on a spree of vengeance, forcing road hogs into ditches and walls. In *Tillie and Gus* they play wary enemies, formerly married, dueling each other for an inheritance. Though W. C. Fields seemed to dominate her, the craggy, tough, plump Skipworth made a formidable foe. In the film, she was just as much of a charlatan as Fields, having made her living running a drinking and gambling den in the Orient. "I was a missionary in China," she would insist, "My object was to bring them in out of the darkness, to put more spirits into them, as it were, and relieve them of their material burdens."

Mae West was another adversary, but there were more sarcastic laughs offscreen than on. Egos collided during rehearsals of their scenes together. "You forget I've been an actress for forty years!" said Skipworth. "I'll keep your secret," muttered Mae.

ALISON SKIPWORTH, indomitable old pro who knew her way around a laugh, has a message for Sari Maritza in *A Lady's Profession*.

Skipworth had better lines when there wasn't a big name star like Fields or West around. In *The Princess Comes Across* she enunciated like Fields and sulked like West when she spied a concertina: "Very vulgar— a symbol of the lower classes. Put the thing on the floor and it crawls."

Late in her career, she replaced Marie Dressler in several brawling films with Polly Moran, including *Two Wise Maids* and *Ladies in Distress*. She came back home to New York in the forties, and had an apartment at 202 Riverside Drive. She appeared in a few Broadway productions before retiring later in the late decade.

SELECTED BROADWAY APPEARANCES:
The Torch Bearers (1922), *The Swan* (1923), *The Grand Duchess and the Waiter* (1925), *Buy Buy Baby* (1926), *Julie* (1927), *Spellbound* (1927), *Say When* (1928), *Button Button* (1929), *Marseilles* (1930), *When We Are Married* (1939), *First Stop to Heaven* (1941)

SELECTED FILM APPEARANCES:
Many silents in her early career. *Raffles* (1930), *The Night Angel* (1931), *If I Had a Million* (1932), *Tillie and Gus* (1933), *Alice in Wonderland* (1933), *Six of a Kind* (1934), *The Captain Hates the Sea* (1934), *Coming Out Party* (1934), *Doubting Thomas* (1935), *Shanghai* (1935), *The Gorgeous Hussy* (1936), *Satan Met a Lady* (1936), *The Princess Comes Across* (1936), *Two Wise Maids* (1937), *Ladies in Distress* (1938), *Wide Open Faces* (1938), *King of the Newsboys* (1938)

ARNOLD STANG, always looking stumped, stung, and forlorn as the comic underdog.

ARNOLD STANG
September 28, 1925

Like a cheap bed with a bad spring, Arnold Stang had a tough Brooklyn accent and a comical nasal twang. On radio and television he was the second banana to Milton Berle and Henry Morgan. In movies and on television Stang's feisty wise-cracking personality was offset by his slight build, pudgy jowls, almost non-existent chin, and the large owlish eyes that peered out from behind his horn-rimmed glasses. He was the stereotypical cab driver, store owner, or runt of the streetcorner litter—an amusing, nerdish underdog who stood up on his hindlegs to issue a (rarely heeded) complaint.

Born in Chelsea, Massachusetts, Stang wrote to the radio show *Let's Pretend* when he was nine asking for an audition. He joined the show and began his long radio career. He came to Broadway for *All in Favor* in 1942, and made his first film the same year, *Seven Days' Leave*. He did dozens of radio, film, and TV appearances, including one of his favorites, the role of the whining junkie Sparrow in the Sinatra movie *The Man With the Golden Arm*.

Kids identified strongly with the spunky little Stang. He wore his trademark chokingly-tight bow tie and black horn-rims for a series of TV commercials ("Chunky! Watta chunka chaw-klit!") and has been the voice of the character "Top Cat" for nearly thirty years of cartoon work, commercials, and record albums. For many fans who remember his sitcom guest spots and films, the puckishly cute Stang is even more lovable than his street-smart cartoon character.

SELECTED BROADWAY APPEARANCES:
All in Favor (1942), *You'll See Stars* (1943), *The Front Page* (1969)

SELECTED FILM APPEARANCES:
Seven Days' Leave (1942), *They've Got Me Covered* (1943), *So This is New York* (1948), *Dondi* (1961), *The Wonderful World of the Brothers Grimm* (1962), *It's a Mad, Mad, Mad, Mad World* (1963), *Second Fiddle to a Steel Guitar* (1965), *Skidoo* (1968), *Hello Down There* (1969), *The Gang That Couldn't Shoot Straight* (1971)

TELEVISION SERIES:
School House (1949), *Henry Morgan's Great Talent Hunt* (1951), *Doc Corkle* (1952), *The Milton Berle Show* (1953–55), *Top Cat* (voice) (1961–62), *Broadside* (1965)

COLLECTIBLES:
Waggish Tales (ABC Paramount), *Top Cat* (Colpix), *Favorite Funny Stories* (Peter Pan)

LARRY STORCH
January 8, 1923

LARRY STORCH as the acerbic and agonized Agarn on *F Troop.*

T hough best known as the alternately querulous, sarcastic, and agonizing Corporal Agarn of *F Troop*, Larry Storch enjoyed many support roles on stage and in films, and won praise for his stand-up act, a blend of storytelling and mimicry.

Born in New York City, Larry imitated the foreign accents of people he knew in his neighborhood. He joined the navy at seventeen and amused shipmates (including Tony Curtis) with his mimicry. Storch returned to New York to play clubs and even open his own nightspot for awhile. At twenty-three he was using his vocal talents on radio. He appeared on Frank Morgan's series and when Morgan misplaced his glasses during a rehearsal, Larry stepped in and read the part—in Morgan's voice. The impressive stunt won him a thirteen week contract.

Storch appeared in the Chicago revue *Red, White and Blue* in 1951 and that year replaced Jackie Gleason on TV for the summer run of *Cavalcade of the Stars*. In 1953 he had his own television series. Old buddy Tony Curtis got him his first movie, *The Prince Who Was a Thief*, and he often worked in Curtis films after that. Storch also appeared in several Broadway productions and played a Russian spy in *Who Was That Lady I Saw You With?* He also did the film version which reunited him with Curtis.

Back in the fifties, Storch had developed a penchant for character comedy, in both stand-up and revues. Dick Shawn recalled, "Most of the comics were doing standard jokes. Larry was one of the first ones to do characters." An excellent mimic, Storch invented the "Judy, Judy, Judy" line that would become the staple of everyone's Cary Grant imitation. In *Conversations With Cary Grant*, Grant himself acknowledged that it was Storch who created it during a night of ad-libbing.

Storch was a seasoned pro by the time he was chosen to play Forrest Tucker's daffy sidekick on

SELECTED BROADWAY APPEARANCES:
Red, White and Blue (1950), *The Littlest Revue* (1956), *Who Was that Lady I Saw You With?* (1958)

SELECTED FILM APPEARANCES:
The Prince Who Was a Thief (1951), *Who Was That Lady?* (1960), *40 Pounds of Trouble* (1963), *Captain Newman, M.D.* (1963), *Sex and the Single Girl* (1964), *Wild and Wonderful* (1964), *The Great Race* (1965), *That Funny Feeling* (1965), *The Monitors* (1969), *The Couple Takes a Wife* (1972), *The Happy Hooker Goes to Washington* (1977), *Without Warning* (1980), *Sweet Sixteen* (1981)

TELEVISION SERIES:
Cavalcade of Stars (1951–52), *The Larry Storch Show* (1953), *F Troop* (1965–67), *The Queen and I* (1969), *Ghost Busters* (1975–78)

COLLECTIBLES:
At the Bon Sior (Jubilee), *Epstein* (Lively Arts). Storch is also on the video *Miss Casino Comedy Show*

F Troop, bringing quite a bit of depth to the sitcom stooge character of crafty but gullible Randolph Agarn, a tough frontier soldier with a streak of hypochondria, a bully to underlings but prone to fawning over his superiors. Storch went on to appear as Tucker's feisty sidekick on the Saturday morning series *Ghost Busters* and would play similar roles in assorted sitcoms and movies.

His private life sometimes seemed like a sitcom. In 1972 he underwent a hip replacement operation. "I'd just had four hours surgery. They were going to move me from the operating table to my room. And they dropped me on the floor." When they scraped him up, they realized they had to operate again. Eventually Storch was back on his feet, performing in theatrical productions, including a 1990 West Coast version of *Oklahoma!* and the 1991 Off-Broadway comedy *Breaking Legs*. In the latter he was only around for the last half of the first act, but his scene-stealing routine as a very dumb crook was a highlight, his very entrance bringing hearty applause.

His stand-up act, still a mix of conversation, old fashioned stories, and mimicry, amused a *Variety* critic who found him as hilarious as ever, "mixing new material with tales he's been telling for decades."

A Storch classic concerns a delicate girl named Esther, a shy and frail and very sweet young thing. Telling the tale in dialect as Esther's Jewish granny, Storch says, "That goil must have come down from heaven on a moonbeam…she fell in love mit a truck driver…a bull in a China shoip! That big ape fell in love mit that girl. He proposed marriage…At de wedding ceremony, well, dat big bull backed into the canopy…when de rabbi gave him dat sacred glass of wine to drink, drank whole glass of wine, stomped on the glass, made by him such a racket that the poor delicate child had a miscarriage right there!"

ROBERT STRAUSS, whose specialty was gruff-voiced comic gangsters and even viscious thugs in dramatic parts.

ROBERT STRAUSS
Henry Robert Strauss,
November 8, 1913–February 20, 1975

Gruff-voiced and tough looking, Robert Strauss comically contrasted his foreboding face with dark-ringed eyes and his bulky build and a goofy good nature. The lovable bear was memorable as "Animal," the most dogfaced of soldiers in the prison camp comedy *Stalag 17* on Broadway and again in the film version. Frolicking toward the forbidden barracks of captured Russian women, or crying out in ridiculous agony "I'm blind—I'm bl-i-i-i-nd" because the cap of his hat fell over his eyes—he was standout comic relief.

Strauss grew up at 141 East 83rd Street in New York City. His father designed theatrical costumes. After graduating from James Monroe High School, young Strauss drifted through a variety of odd jobs from social director in the Catskills to bouncer in a Seattle bar. He was a singing waiter, a busboy, and a fund-raiser for Israel. He later organized fifteen actors to form "Santa's Helpers Inc." a group providing Santas for department stores.

His acting career foundered after a bit part on Broadway in 1937 in *Having Wonderful Time*. Seven years later, after a robbery at his costume jewelry business, he figured show biz was a better gamble. He recalled, "One day I saw a top-name comedian in action. I didn't think he was funny. So I went to an agent and I said, 'Look, that guy's making twenty-three hundred dollars a week and he ain't funny.' So the agent said, 'Okay, I'll give you a chance. I'm staging a benefit next week. What've you got that'll run twelve minutes?' I said: 'My watch.'"

Strauss put together and memorized an old vaudeville routine and slowly made his way upward. He was still a bartender when he got a role on Broadway in *Detective Story*. It was *Stalag 17* that really launched his career. Over the years, he played a variety of gruff servicemen and comic heavies, and in the short-lived play *Portofino* had the dual role of both priest and devil.

Happy to play "a clown—I was always clowning, even in school," Strauss appeared in several Martin and Lewis films (*Jumping Jacks, Sailor Beware*, and *Money From Home*) and with Marilyn Monroe in *The Seven Year Itch* as Kruhulick, the building janitor. He took sitcom roles from time to time, usually as a tough soldier or convict. The career of the powerfully-built Strauss ended when he suffered a debilitating stroke. Not long after, columnist Earl Wilson broke the news of his death. Of the ex-bartender turned comic, he wrote: "Bob, one of the fine people in the business, had requested that there be no services, and that his friends have a drink in his memory instead."

SELECTED BROADWAY APPEARANCES:
Having Wonderful Time (1937), *Helen Goes to Troy* (1944), *Down to Miami* (1944), *Nellie Bly* (1946), *Detective Story* (1949), *Twentieth Century* (1950), *Stalag 17* (1951), *Portofino* (1958)

SELECTED FILM APPEARANCES:
Sailor Beware (1951), *Jumping Jacks* (1952), *Stalag 17* (1953), *Here Come the Girls* (1953), *Money From Home* (1954), *The Atomic Kid* (1954), *The Seven Year Itch* (1955), *The Man With the Golden Arm* (1955), *Attack!* (1956), *Li'l Abner* (1959), *Wake Me When It's Over* (1960), *The Last Time I Saw Archie* (1961), *Girls! Girls! Girls!* (1962), *The Thrill of It All* (1963), *The Family Jewels* (1965), *Frankie and Johnny* (1966), *Dagmar's Hot Pants* (1971)

GRADY SUTTON
April 5, 1908

With his chubby jowls, dumpling body, apprehensive mild manner, and slow, drawling delivery, Grady Sutton served as a comic patsy in a variety of thirties comedies. The Tennessee-born actor came to California on vacation in 1924. A friend, director William Seiter, offered him some

GRADY SUTTON, apprehensive comic patsy in scores of screen comedies over fifty years, is being comforted after a robbery in *The Bank Dick* by David Oliver (left), William Alston, and Pierre Watkin.

film work and Grady's career began. He worked for Mack Sennett and appeared in many Hal Roach shorts, including *Pack Up Your Troubles* with Laurel and Hardy. Grady and Oliver Hardy became good friends.

Sutton was the hapless "Alabam" in an early thirties series of comedy shorts called *The Boy Friends*, and played a typically foppish fool, Charlie Van Rumple, in *My Man Godfrey*. The vacuous college boy was a convenient stooge for Carole Lombard in the film. In one sequence she tells partygoers that she's engaged to him. When congratulated, all Sutton can manage is a perplexed whine: "My mind's a little cloudy—I don't remember proposing."

In real life, Sutton was a little cloudy about the details of his career. He told Leonard Maltin, "People have asked me [how many films I've done] and I have no idea. Years ago, when I used to watch television, I was sitting up late one night and I though, 'Gee, that face looks familiar…why, it's me!' And I couldn't remember where I did it, or what studio, or anything. It's such a funny feeling."

The woebegone Sutton, whose career extended to fifties and sixties sitcoms (he was Jed Simmons, the handyman on the TV series of *The Egg and I* and Sturgis, the butler, in Phyllis Diller's *The Pruitts of Southampton*), retired in the early seventies. He's best remembered for his films with W. C. Fields. Fields liked the way Grady reacted—the

SELECTED FILM APPEARANCES:
The Freshman (1925), *Pack Up Your Troubles* (1932), *College Humor* (1933), *Alice Adams* (1935), *The Man on the Flying Trapeze* (1935), *My Man Godfrey* (1936), *Stage Door* (1937), *The Mad Miss Manton* (1938), *You Can't Cheat an Honest Man* (1939), *The Bank Dick* (1940), *Bedtime Story* (1941), *Whispering Ghosts* (1942), *The More the Merrier* (1943), *A Lady Takes a Chance* (1943), *A Royal Scandal* (1945), *Jiggs and Maggie in Court* (1948), *Living It Up* (1954), *White Christmas* (1954), *The Birds and the Bees* (1956), *Billy Rose's Jumbo* (1962), *My Fair Lady* (1964), *Paradise, Hawaiian Style* (1966), *I Love You Alice B. Toklas* (1968), *The Great Bank Robbery* (1969), *Myra Breckinridge* (1970), *Support Your Local Gunfighter* (1971)

TELEVISION SERIES:
The Egg and I (1951–52), *The Pruitts of Southampton* (1966–67)

wide eyes, the look of awe—and insisted over and over again on hiring him. He played a shiftless loafer in *The Man on the Flying Trapeze*, and was especially amusing in *The Bank Dick*, as Og Oggleby, the wishy-washy bank teller who agrees to some minor embezzling for Fields—only to lose his nerve and faint in a moment of crisis. Fields knew the man would cave in: "Og Oggleby? Sounds like a bubble in a bathtub."

MACK SWAIN
February 16, 1876–August 25, 1935

A big, good-natured bear of a man, Mack Swain was beloved by audiences not as a screen heavy, but as a jolly-built, harmlessly oafish clown. He was instantly identifiable: the toothy smile, the wide eyes, the dark limp noodle of hair that curved directly down his forehead, and the gross, thick black rectangle of mustache that extended far up the sides of his nose, making it seem as if he was breathing it in with every breath.

MACK SWAIN, the thick-mustached bear of a man who was constantly at odds with Chaplin's Little Tramp.

The ex-vaudevillian began making films for Mack Sennett in 1913. The following year he starred in his own *Ambrose* comedies. As Ambrose he was the big but bullied husband—often henpecked, but sometimes childlike, with a gleaming look in his roving eye as he chased after a girl far prettier than his wife. Tiny Chester Conklin was often a contrasting foil for Swain, but subsequently the big man ended up as the foil for other comics. He was the blustery cuckold opposite Mabel Normand (in *Mabel Lost and Won*) and lost many a screen battle to diminutive Charlie Chaplin.

It was Chaplin who washed away Swain's stereotyped "Ambrose" makeup and used him in a variety of guises, in *The Pilgrim*, *The Idle Class*, and *Pay Day*. He costarred in *The Gold Rush* as Big Jim McKay, balancing just the right amount of menace and forgivable gluttony, playing a starving prospector who deliriously believes poor Charlie to be a delectable chicken just waiting to be caught and cooked.

The Gold Rush was the high point for the aging Swain, coming ten years after he seemed to peak with his *Ambrose* film series. He appeared in several early talkies before his death in 1935.

SELECTED FILM APPEARANCES:
Laughing Gas (1914), *Ambrose's First Falsehood* (1914), *The Battle of Ambrose and Walrus* (1915), *The Idle Class* (1921), *Pay Day* (1922), *The Pilgrim* (1923), *The Gold Rush* (1925), *Finnegan's Ball* (1927), *The Beloved Rogue* (1927), *Gentlemen Prefer Blondes* (1928), *The Cohens and the Kellys in Atlantic City* (1929), *Finn and Hattie* (1931), *Lighthouse Love* (1932)

GEORGE TOBIAS, easygoing Warner second banana, doing an uncharacteristic song-and-dance turn with Olivia de Havilland (left) and Ida Lupino in *Thank Your Lucky Stars*.

GEORGE TOBIAS
July 14, 1901–February 27, 1980

George Tobias had a likable face and an easy-going personality. His most famous latter-day role, as Abner Kravitz on TV's *Bewitched*, was deceptively simple. All he did was watch in gentle amusement as his busybody wife, Gladys (Sandra Gould), spied on their neighbor, Samantha the witch. The weary-eyed husband would react to her snooping with a subtle barb, always delivered with amused detachment.

Gladys, amazed at catching Samantha performing witch magic: "I could cut my throat!" Abner: "I think I put a new blade in the razor this morning." Gladys, remorseful after her accusations are disproved: "Mrs. Stevens will probably never speak to me again." Abner: "I'll send her a letter of congratulations in the morning...."

Tobias was born on the East Side of New York and began his career at the Provincetown Playhouse. He had to take a lot of day jobs at the beginning, but they provided him with a unique opportunity: "When I worked in factories, on board ships, in foundries, I worked around people of every nationality and I learned their accents and mannerisms. I learned from life. The Stanislavsky method, you might say, without knowing about Stanislavsky."

Tobias specialized in ethnic characters, playing Corporal Lapinsky in *What Price Glory* and enjoying his best success as the Russian ballet master Boris Kolenkhov in *You Can't Take It With You*. He spent four months growing a long beard for the role, finding it quite uncomfortable during the hot New York summer. When rehearsals began, George S. Kaufman approached him and said, "I really only wanted a goatee. I should have told you."

He was soon typed for fall guy roles in films. Early he had been a capable dancer and utilized some Skeltonesque mannerisms. But over the years he played support parts requiring deadpan expressions and a wry, low key personality. Sometimes he was cast as the friendly thug or the inept cab driver, but whatever the role, he tended to react to almost everything with conciliatory resignation or amiable disinterest. He was one of the rare support players who stood out because he didn't stand out, the contrasting calm and unflappable one standing around amid comic chaos.

Tobias had a laid-back personality. Desiring only to keep busy and have new parts to play, he told the *New York Herald Tribune* in 1946, "the others can have the billing." In the fifties the lifelong bachelor slowed down, wanting to spend more time with his hobbies. He collected over five thousand classical records, was a Bach expert, and played the flute. Of acting, he ultimately remarked, "It's just a way of earning a living. My fun comes from living."

His success so late in life on *Bewitched* merely allowed him more money to spend on his hobbies. His lifestyle was so placed that the most excitement involving Tobias probably came *after* his death. He had died of cancer and his body was going to be routinely delivered for burial. But in an almost sitcom-like twist, as reported in the *New York Times*: "A car carrying his body from Cedars Sinai Medical Center to a morutary was stolen for a brief time before the thieves apparently realized their mistake and ran off, leaving the car."

SELECTED BROADWAY APPEARANCES:
What Price Glory (1924), *The International* (1928), *Sailors of Cattaro* (1934), *Paths of Glory* (1935), *Name Your Poison* (1936), *The Emperor Jones* (1936), *You Can't Take It With You* (1936), *Good Hunting* (1938), *Silk Stockings* (1958)

SELECTED FILM APPEARANCES:
Maisie (1939), *Ninotchka* (1939), *Music in My Heart* (1940), *City for Conquest* (1940), *The Bride Came C.O.D.* (1941), *Sergeant York* (1941), *My Sister Eileen* (1942), *Yankee Doodle Dandy* (1942), *This Is the Army* (1943), *Air Force* (1943), *Objective Burma* (1945), *Sinbad the Sailor* (1947), *The Judge Steps Out* (1949), *Ten Tall Men* (1951), *The Glenn Miller Story* (1954), *The Seven Little Foys* (1955), *Silk Stockings* (1957), *Marjorie Morningstar* (1958), *The Glass Bottom Boat* (1966), *The Phynx* (1970)

TELEVISION SERIES:
Hudson's Bay (1959–60), *Adventures in Paradise* (1960–61), *Bewitched* (1964–72)

ARTHUR TREACHER
Arthur T. Veary, July 23, 1894–December 16, 1975

The ultimate British gentleman's gentleman and butler, and then the ultimate parody of it, Arthur Treacher became popular in the *Jeeves* movie series. The butler seemed to have more class and breeding than his employee. He was an imposingly tall, world-weary, calmly efficient older gentleman whose jaundiced eye was usually looking down his nose at his antagonists.

Born in Brighton, Sussex, England, Treacher acted on the British stage through the twenties and Broadway in the early thirties, appearing in classics including *The School for Scandal* in 1931 and *Androcles and the Lion* in 1933, after which he came to Hollywood. In early film roles, he had the presence, but not the attitude. In Wheeler and Woolsey's *The Nitwits* (1935), he merely plays a rich fop who keeps getting knocked downstairs by

ARTHUR TREACHER, onetime valet to the stars on screen, here out of uniform.

227

a pushy Woolsey in one of the film's running gags.

It was in a film released around the same time, *Hollywood Party*, that Treacher discovered the key to his subsequent success. In one scene, Lupe Velez made conversation with him and mentioned that her boyfriend was as tall as he. Treacher added haughty comic disgust to his innocuous answer: "Really?" This delighted the director, who urged him to adopt that disdainful attitude throughout the film. Before long he was typecast as the butler who suffers his superiority in near-sullen silence, getting even not so much by what he says, but the way he says it.

The steady character comedian of the forties was thrust into the spotlight when he became the snooty announcer-stooge for Merv Griffin's syndicated sixties talk show. Treacher's curmudgeonly, officious sneer was now wholly a put-on. He said at the time, "I think that if some poor somebody wants to be exposed for eight minutes, they shouldn't be interrupted by an old man who's gone through it all." But, of course, a quick shot of Treacher's mordant gaze during the talk was enough to set the audience giggling.

He and Griffin released an entertaining album of British music hall comedy tunes, and, in a venture that was rather tasteful during its early years, he opened a chain of fast-food restaurants selling "Arthur Treacher's Fish and Chips." He looked back on his long career in films and noted, "In Hollywood success is relative. The closer the relative, the greater the success."

MARY TREEN
March 27, 1909–July 20, 1989

Round-cheeked coed Mary Treen seemed to be the best friend of every pretty teenage girl in thirties comedies. She never got the dreamboat; she could only sigh in disappointment or pout in comic frustration. As she aged, she played spunky office girls, plucky nurses, pesky career women, and good-natured spinsters.

Born in St. Louis, Treen grew up in Los Angeles where she began to appear in vaudeville productions, light opera, revues, and musical comedy. She developed an eccentric dance act with her partner Marjorie Barnett as "Treen and Barnett: Two Unsophisticated Vassar Co-Eds." They proved it with their highlight routine: tall Mary's dancing leg kicks that soared over the head of her five-foot-three partner.

In films, Treen worked with Bob Hope in *They Got Me Covered* and the Ritz Brothers in *Kentucky Moonshine*, and was almost a regular support player to Jerry Lewis, appearing in five of his films, notably as the WAC Sergeant in *Sad Sack*. She was also in three Elvis Presley films. In the sixties Treen was often a guest on Joey Bishop's sitcom. She took occasional TV roles in the seventies and, following the deaths of their respective husbands, the old vaudeville team of "Treen and Barnett" were back, sharing a house in Balboa, California.

MARY TREEN, leggy best friend of leading ladies, sizes up Joe Sawyer while Robert Lowery, Ralph Sanford, Phyllis Brooks, and Roger Pryor have a heated jailhouse discussion in *High Powered*.

SELECTED FILM APPEARANCES:
Happiness Ahead (1934), *Babbitt* (1934), *Don't Bet on Blondes* (1935), *The Case of the Lucky Legs* (1935), *Page Miss Glory* (1935), *Shipmates Forever* (1935), *A Night at the Ritz* (1935), *Life Begins at 20* (1936), *Coleen* (1936), *Ever Since Eve* (1937), *Second Honeymoon* (1937), *Sally, Irene and Mary* (1938), *Kentucky Moonshine* (1938), *First Love* (1939), *Kitty Foyle* (1940), *They All Kissed the Bride* (1942), *The Great Man's Lady* (1942), *They Got Me Covered* (1943), *So Proudly We Hail* (1943), *I Love a Soldier* (1944), *Casanova Brown* (1944), *It's a Wonderful Life* (1947), *Let's Live a Little* (1948), *Sailor Beware* (1952), *The Caddy* (1953), *Let's Do It Again* (1953), *Paradise Hawaiian Style* (1956), *The Birds and the Bees* (1956), *The Sad Sack* (1957), *Who's Minding the Store?* (1963), *The Strongest Man in the World* (1975)

TELEVISION SERIES:
The Joey Bishop Show (1964–65)

VERA VAGUE
Barbara Jo Allen, September 2, 1905–September 27, 1974

There are plenty of vague people in the world. Barbara Jo Allen discovered one at a PTA meeting she attended. The woman was called on to give a speech but was so flustered and confused, it came out funny. Years later, Barbara Jo remembered that woman and used her as the model for her own comic radio character, "Vera Vague."

Born in New York City, raised in upstate Goshen, she attended

SELECTED FILM APPEARANCES:
Village Barn Dance (1940), *Kiss the Boys Goodbye* (1941), *Design for Scandal* (1941), *Priorities on Parade* (1942), *Mrs. Wiggs of the Cabbage Patch* (1942), *Get Going* (1943), *Rosie the Riveter* (1943), *Henry Aldrich Plays Cupid* (1944), *Cowboy Canteen* (1944), *Girl Rush* (1944), *Lake Placid Serenade* (1944), *Earl Carroll Sketchbook* (1946), *Square Dance Katy* (1950), *The Opposite Sex* (1956), *Born to Be Loved* (1959)

COLLECTIBLES:
The Animal Convention, a children's book.

college at the Sorbonne in Paris, toured Europe, and appeared often on the London stage. She costarred in a thirties road company of *Wives and So Forth* with Charlie Ruggles and then began her radio career as Betty Holly on *One Man's Family*.

She first played Vera Vague on a 1939 *NBC Matinee* show. The Vague character was less a ditherer than a fussy dowager. When Barbara appeared in costume for the part, she wore a severe expression—and stereotype pince-nez. She became a hit on Bob Hope's show, trading barbs with Hope and costar Frances Langford. In a horse-racing sketch, Vera discusses her new vocation with Frances: "I'm going to be a jockey at Caliente." "You're going to be a jockey? Well, that's a switch—wearing pants instead of chasing them!" "Oh, Frances, you dear! I'll bet you were an adorable little baby. Really, it's a shame they didn't just leave you in the incubator!"

After enlivening the Hope show for a few seasons, and briefly starring in a series of comic film shorts, Barbara Jo became vaguely tired of her alter ego, Vera Vague. She married Bob Hope's producer Norman Morrell and became a housewife. She made few film appearances in the fifties. Her new hobby was taking courses at the University of California.

JOYCE VAN PATTEN
March 9, 1934

S omewhat stereotyped in the sixties and early seventies as everyone's nervously desperate single-too-long cousin, blond Joyce Van Patten played Peter Sellers's impatient fiancée in *I Love You Alice B. Toklas*, was a durable sketch player on *The Danny Kaye Show*, and regularly appeared on Broadway where her career first began.

Born in Queens, Joyce was only a subway ride away from Broadway and made the most of it. She and her brother Dick Van Patten (later the star of TV's *Eight is Enough*) were both child actors on Broadway. Tallulah Bankhead worked with Dick in *The Skin of Our Teeth* and recalled,

"The only child actor I ever liked was Dickie Van Patten, because he could read *The Racing Form*." Joyce only read her lines, which was enough to charm Walter Huston in *Love's Old Sweet Song* and Al Shean (of Gallagher and Shean) in *Popsy*.

She costarred with her brother Dick in both the radio and film versions of *Reg'lar Fellers*, toured in shows, and appeared on the stage through her teen years, including a 1948 summer theater turn in *The Second Man* opposite Turhan Bey. From 1950 to 1955 she was on the *Wendy Warren* radio series.

"I had a rough transitional period," she said. "I got very thin, very tall, and no one called me cute anymore." She was funny though, especially in thankless girlfriend or wife roles. On TV's *The Good Guys* she played Herb Edelman's wife and later played Mary Tyler Moore's secretary, Iris Chapman, on the short-lived *Mary Tyler Moore Comedy Hour* in 1979.

Van Patten's brand of comic intensity sustained her for years. She seemed to specialize in neurotics, whether seemingly self-possessed career women or tart-tongued housewives, who were on the edge of cracking. She got the most out of pretending to be cool and calm; her flashing bright eyes, crooked smile, and increasingly agitated voice giving her away. She was a Neil Simon favorite, appearing in his *I Ought to Be in Pictures*, *Brighton Beach Memoirs*, and *Jake's Women* (the version that didn't make it out of Los Angeles, being closed down and rewritten before becoming a Broadway hit).

JOYCE VAN PATTEN, tart-tongued, edgy blonde, costars in *Making It* with Kristoffer Tabori.

SELECTED BROADWAY APPEARANCES:
Love's Old Sweet Song (1940), *Popsy* (1941), *Tomorrow the World* (1943), *They Knew What They Wanted* (1949), *The Desk Set* (1955), *A Hole in the Head* (1957), *Spoon River Anthology* (1963), *Same Time Next Year* (1975), *I Ought to Be in Pictures* (1980), *Murder at the Howard Johnson's* (1979), *Brighton Beach Memoirs* (1983)

SELECTED FILM APPEARANCES:
The Goddess (1958), *I Love You Alice B. Toklas* (1968), *Something Big* (1971), *Thumb Tripping* (1972), *Mikey and Nicky* (1976), *Bad News Bears* (1976), *The Falcon and the Snowman* (1985), *St. Elmo's Fire* (1985), *Monkey Shines* (1988)

TELEVISION SERIES:
The Danny Kaye Show (1964–67), *The Good Guys* (1969–70), *The Don Rickles Show* (1972), *The Mary Tyler Moore Comedy Hour* (1979)

RAYMOND WALBURN, the genial, long-winded blowhard personified.

RAYMOND WALBURN
September 9, 1887–July 26, 1969

H e played jovial drunks, garrulous business-men, fuddy duddy bankers, and a variety of genially assinine and pompous old coots. Though usually a blustery blunder-er, Raymond Walburn had large eyes, a relaxed smile and an expansive, friendly manner that always made him a most welcome "nuisance."

He knew he was a nuisance. "You don't want an old fussbudget like me poking around here," he said in *Third Finger, Left Hand*. And in *Flowing Gold*, he admitted, "Well, to coin a phrase, there's no fool like an old fool." One of his best roles was as the fake Colonel Pettigrew in *Broadway Bill*, which helped type him for the rest of his career.

Walburn was born in Plymouth, Indiana. "I made my first professional appearance out on the Coast," he recalled. "That was in 1906, in Oak-land…. I was nineteen and was playing an old Ital-ian tamale peddler in *Soldier of Fortune*. While I was playing the role, we had the San Francisco earth-quake and fire. Didn't hurt me. Didn't hurt the theater. The whole cast helped take care of refugees."

After World War I he appeared in stage comedies in Mil-waukee and worked his way East to Broadway. He began making films in the thirties, but noted, "We were pretty 'hammy' on the screen in those days…we thought *The Count of Monte Cristo* a good job when we did it. That was 1934. Then I saw it again only four years afterward and it was ham."

Walburn played half-baked hams and blowhards for the next thirty years, his windy brand of intimidation and interruption working especially well against mild-mannered comedians from Harold Lloyd (*Professor Beware*, *Mad Wednesday*) to Eddie Bracken (*Hail the Conquering Hero*). In the late forties and early fifties he

SELECTED BROADWAY APPEARANCES:
The Awful Truth (1922), *The Show-Off* (1924), *If I Was Rich* (1926), *Take My Advice* (1927), *The Great Necker* (1928), *The House Beautiful* (1931), *Tell Her the Truth* (1932), *Man Bites Dog* (1933), *Another Love* (1934), *Park Avenue* (1946), *A Funny Thing Happened on the Way to the Forum* (1962), *A Very Rich Woman* (1965)

SELECTED FILM APPEARANCES:
The Laughing Lady (1929), *Lady by Choice* (1934), *Broadway Bill* (1934), *Thank a Million* (1935), *It's a Small World* (1935), *She Married Her Boss* (1935), *Red-heads on Parade* (1935), *The Great Ziegfeld* (1936), *Mr. Deeds Goes to Town* (1936), *Three Wise Guys* (1936), *Mr. Cinderella* (1936), *It Can't Last Forever* (1937), *Let's Get Married* (1937), *Professor Beware* (1938), *Start Cheer-ing* (1938), *It Could Happen to You* (1939), *Eternally Yours* (1939), *Third Finger, Left Hand* (1940), *Puddin'head* (1941), *Louisiana Purchase* (1941), *Let's Face It* (1943), *Dixie* (1943), *Hail the Conquering Hero* (1944), *Mad Wednesday* (1947), *Red, Hot and Blue* (1949), *Leave It to Henry* (1949), *Henry the Rainmaker* (1949), *Key to the City* (1950), *Father Makes Good* (1950), *Father's Wild Game* (1950), *Father Takes the Air* (1951), *Beautiful But Dangerous* (1953), *The Spoilers* (1955)

starred in a low budget series of "Henry" homespun comedies. Living in the Gramercy Park district in New York, still making Broadway appearances in his seventies, coming out of retirement to act in *A Funny Thing Happened on the Way to the Forum* for eighteen months, Walburn recalled, "I have appeared in some of the most flagrantly putrid films of this or any other era, but they have been in the minority, I believe, and it's only once in a while that I have to cringe while watching the Late Late Show. I think that's pretty good for a fellow who's made eighty-seven pictures...."

NANCY WALKER
Anna Myrtle Swoyer, May 10, 1921–March 25, 1992

NANCY WALKER, forever feisty but always lovable.

Nancy Walker wanted to be a serious singer— but when she sang for Broadway impresario George Abbott, he laughed instead. Then he signed her up for *Best Foot Forward*. At first compared to Bea Lillie and Fanny Brice, the sassy little (four-foot-eleven) lady soon earned praise for her own stylish approach to playing no-nonsense, smart-mouthed, Jewish mothers, man-hungry wallflowers, and a variety of eccentric maids.

Born in Philadelphia, Nancy traveled with her vaudevillian parents all across the country. Her acrobat father changed his name to Dewey Barto when he joined "The Three Bartos" and later was half of a comedy team called "Barto and Mann." Nancy didn't envision a comedy career, but after her "funny girl" role in *Best Foot Forward*, she played the cab driver in *On the Town*, securing her reputation as the one to pick for roles where an amusingly streetwise woman made for better comic contrast than a man. She went on to appear on stage in *Barefoot Boy With Cheek*, and even had a musical written for her, *Look Ma, I'm Dancin'*. Brooks Atkinson in the *New York Times* called her "the best slapstick comedienne of her generation."

Despite the praise, she admitted, "It took me about seven years to adjust to my stage personality. I was uncomfortable being funny. People expected me to be 'on' and I wasn't. I never am. But I kept at it, and learned to do comedy well." In films and on television there weren't many lead roles requiring a feisty, hardworking woman with an ironic sense of humor, but when she landed a supporting part, she made it work like a lead. She became familiar to viewers as Mildred, the wisecracking maid to Rock Hudson and Susan Saint James on *McMillan and Wife,* and then as Ida Morgenstern, Valerie Harper's good-hearted but slightly pushy mother on *Rhoda.*

Walker's light touch in playing working-class people earned her a

233

SELECTED BROADWAY APPEARANCES:
Best Foot Forward (1941), *On the Town* (1944), *Barefoot Boy With Cheek* (1947), *Look Ma, I'm Dancin'* (1948), *Along Fifth Avenue* (1949), *Phoenix '55* (1955), *Fallen Angels* (1956), *Wonderful Town* (1958), *The Girls Against the Boys* (1959), *Do Re Mi* (1960), *The Cherry Orchard* (1968), *The Cocktail Party* (1968)

SELECTED FILM APPEARANCES:
Best Foot Forward (1943), *Girl Crazy* (1943), *Broadway Rhythm* (1944), *Lucky Me* (1954), *Stand Up and Be Counted* (1972), *The World's Greatest Athlete* (1973), *Forty Carats* (1973), *Murder By Death* (1976), *Human Feelings* (1978)

TELEVISION SERIES:
Family Affair (1970–71), *McMillan and Wife* (1971–76), *Rhoda* (1974–78), *The Nancy Walker Show* (1976), *Blansky's Beauties* (1977), *True Colors* (1990)

different kind of fame in TV commercials. As Rosie, the coffee shop waitress, she spent over a decade dutifully cleaning up spills with Bounty paper towels, the "quicker picker-upper!" One of her most popular (and deceptively easy looking) roles in films was as the mute maid in *Murder by Death*. The comedy was all in Nancy's long-suffering shrugs and subtle expressions of weary woe.

A key supporting comedienne, Walker wasn't quite able to make the jump to solo star on TV. *The Nancy Walker Show* and *Blansky's Beauties* missed and a television movie, *Human Feelings*, nearly became a series, but was turned down. In that one, a switch on George Burns's *Oh God*, Nancy Walker played God, with Billy Crystal as her favorite angel. The versatile Walker slipped behind the movie camera to direct *Can't Stop the Music*, which featured a briefly popular, campy disco group, The Village People. It was yet another disaster for the plucky actress.

A quick "picker-upper" herself, Walker picked up her career in the eighties costarring with Eve Arden in a dinner theater production of *The Odd Couple* and resumed her identity as a salty, disapproving mother with *True Colors*, a sitcom about an interracial marriage, not long before her death in 1992.

RAY WALSTON
November 2, 1914

A pixie-ish actor with a devilish streak (or vice versa), Ray Walston had his most memorable roles in comic fantasies. He stole the show as the whimsical, knowing little devil Mr. Applegate in *Damn Yankees* (on stage, screen and television) and costarred with Bill Bixby as Uncle Martin, the stern, distant but magical man from Mars in *My Favorite Martian*. In the seventies and eighties he was well suited to playing comically flawed school principals, bosses, and businessmen. His piercing eyes, officious posture, and precise diction were humorously at odds with his high, resonant voice and slight build.

Born in New Orleans and raised in the French Quarter, Walston worked on stage at Houston's Civic Theater for six years and spent three at the Cleveland Playhouse. He recalled, "When I got to New York in 1945 I made ends meet by filling in as a linotype operator at the *New*

York Times." He subsequently earned
several awards as a promising newcomer in Tennessee Williams's *Summer and Smoke* and later appeared as
Luther Billis in the national company
of *South Pacific* and on London's West
End. *Damn Yankees* soon followed.
Back then, black humor was a rarity,
yet he pulled off one of the most
comically macabre songs of all time
in "Those Were the Days." The tune is
essentially mean-spirited and grim
("that glorious morn Jack the Ripper
was born—nyah ha ha ha! Those were
the good old days!") but it became
good nasty fun when sung by the
cheerfully demented Walston. He
once said his role model for the part
was José Ferrer. But as for his singing,
which he admitted was limited, he
said "you learn the song, then get out
and do it the best you can."

RAY WALSTON, whether as cheerful lecher early on or cantankerous
oldtimer on the contemporary
scene, he'll always be everybody's
favorite Martian.

TV audiences discovered him as
My Favorite Martian. Walston said at
the time, "The network conducted
one of its mysterious studies which showed that there are more adults
watching the show than children. To me, it proves a theory I have.
Wherever there is a home with a TV set and a child, that set will be
tuned to whatever show the kid wants." The program won a loyal following though, to Walston's chagrin, it had a much shorter run than
Bewitched and *I Dream of Jeannie*, two shows clearly influenced by the
supernatural comedy of his show. It remained popular in reruns for
decades. It was character comedy mostly, the frantic humor centering
around the magical Martian who delivered an occasional snippy one-
liner: "Earth's all right for a visit, but I wouldn't want to live here."

Walston replaced the ill Peter Sellers in *Kiss Me, Stupid* but would
have trouble finding roles quite as juicy as that or *My Favorite Martian*. He
appeared in dinner theater productions of everything from *The Odd Couple* to *Oliver* and continued to provide lively comic relief in films and on
TV, usually as a detached but easily perturbed type. He played Poopdeck
Pappy to Robin Williams's *Popeye* and guested on an episode of *The
Incredible Hulk* with "Martian" friend Bill Bixby. Repeating his role from
the hit movie, Walston was history teacher Mr. Hand in *Fast Times*,
which lasted on television from March to April of 1986, and he would
turn up frequently in thankless teen-oriented R-rated movie comedies.

In 1992, he became a regular as the judge on the quirky *Picket
Fences*. Most fans still remember him best for *My Favorite Martian*,
though Walston had deep reservations about the show. He recalled,
"The effects were more important than the actors and the writing. The

potential of the show was never realized." He resented how his character, a brilliant being able to read minds and create magic, was saddled with mundane sitcom plots: "I was attacked by a chimp on the ninth show. It went berserk and attached me and chewed my face up. I will remember that for the rest of my life."

CAROL WAYNE, curvaceous and wide-eyed, and personification of the air-headed bimbo, trying a bit of libido resuscitation on Vincent Price as an aged tycoon in *Scavenger Hunt*.

CAROL WAYNE
1942–January 13, 1985

Remembered as "The Matinee Lady" in over one hundred of Johnny Carson's "Art Fern Teatime Movie" sketches, Carol Wayne was one of television's most prominent "busty blond bimbo" comediennes this side of early TV's Dagmar. It was not an easy role to play. Only Goldie Hawn had previous TV success as a sexy-but-wholesome blond who had audiences giggling instead of merely panting.

While Hawn became a major star, Carol Wayne stayed a little too long on *The Tonight Show* playing the curvaceous "straight woman" to Carson, offering up wide-eyed stares and whispered inanities. In one sketch she said she worked for "Arthur Klutz's Dance School. I once had a fellow step on my foot." Carson, eyeing her chest: "He must've been awfully short." Carol's good nature and airy (some might argue "airheaded") tolerance to such wisecracks made her a fan favorite through the seventies.

She and her sister Nina, ages fifteen and sixteen, started in show business skating for an *Ice Capades* show. Two years later Carol suffered a fall that damaged her left knee and chilled her career. After working in *The Folies-Bergere* in Las Vegas Carol came to California to take minor roles in films. One of her best cameos of comic support is in *The Party*, as a pink-gowned dinner guest watching Peter Sellers fumble with a cooked chicken. A few years later, in 1971, her film career tapered off as she began her association with *The Tonight Show*.

Though she played sexy characters, in print interviews she always had more on her mind than sex. "I'm a vegetarian," the gentle actress said. "I eat no meat because I do not believe in killing animals. I'm not a crusader or a pusher though. I don't try to turn other people on to it."

Buxom Carol had a few chances at prime-time success but nothing seemed to click. A TV pilot with William Daniels, *Heaven on Earth*, in the late seventies never became a series. After hitting forty, she found herself trying to maintain her fame any way she could, appearing in several low budget comedies.

In January of 1985 the twice-married (to Burt Sugarman and Barry Feinstein) comedy star turned up at the Las Hadas Hotel in Mexico with a new man—but the relationship was rocky. "She didn't want to share a room with him," the hotel manager reported, "she went to the beach...he followed her." The man came back alone, checked out, and took a flight back to Los Angeles.

Carol Wayne's body was found floating in Santiago Bay the following afternoon. The man who had left Carol Wayne had been involved in a scandal years earlier. He was in the sixth-floor apartment of Art Linkletter's daughter Diane when she jumped to her death during an LSD experience. No charges were filed then, and none were filed in this case, which remains a mystery. In New York, ex-husband Feinstein said at the time, "She was too intelligent to walk into the ocean fully clothed in the middle of the night...it doesn't make any sense to me...she couldn't swim."

One of the last appearances Carol Wayne made was as a celebrity judge for a topless contest video called "Best Chest in the West." Introduced in the audience along with another celebrity judge, comedian Pat McCormick, she stood up and said, "Hi." McCormick pointed to her chest and smiled into the camera, saying "This lady will never drown."

SELECTED FILM APPEARANCES:
Gunn (1967), *The Party* (1968), *You Are What You Eat* (1968), *Savannah Smiles* (1982), *Heartbreakers* (1984), *Best Chest in the West* (1984)

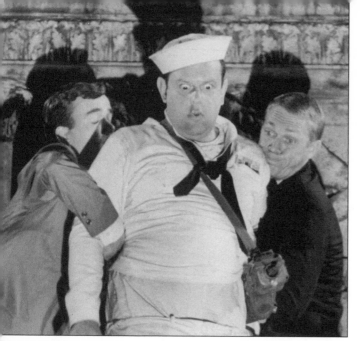

JACK WESTON, chubby, often sarcastically hyper pro who's worked with chimps, starred on Broadway, and played foil to the likes of Jim Hutton and Steve McQueen in *The Honeymoon Machine*.

JACK WESTON
Jack Weinstein, August 21, 1915

Jack Weston always did well as a friendly, chubby, pleasant neighbor-type but he occasionally played deceptively villainous characters. With an eager-to-please raspy delivery and a teddy bear look in his eye, he was often a comic side-kick ("Wormsey" on vintage TV's *Rod Brown of the Rocket Rangers*) and excitable costar (to Peggy Cass on *The Hathaways*, a sitcom about a couple and their family of chimps).

Born in Cleveland, young Jack became a theater usher, training in drama at the Cleveland Playhouse. He was the man of the house at twenty-five, when his Polish immigrant father was run over by a truck. After World War II, Jack resumed his acting studies, his classmates including Rod Steiger and Lee Marvin. He found a few roles on Broadway and got his first break playing (Wilbur Wormsey) Wormser to Cliff Robertson's Rod Brown on television. "I was the Phil Silvers of outer space," he recalled. He appeared in dozens of TV dramas that ironically contrasted his pudgy harmlessness with danger. He was a crybaby killer in the first episode of *Peter Gunn* and "The Artichoke King" in an *Untouchables* in 1959. Of *The Hathaways*, which children loved and critics didn't, he admitted, "I still hate chimps to this day."

In sixties film comedies, Weston was tabbed for roles requiring a tough New Yorker with enough vulnerability to bend like putty for the lead hero or heroine. One of his earliest screen roles was as a cab driver in *Please Don't Eat the Daisies*. He thrived in Hollywood but soon realized just how strange California could be.

In October of 1964 he made the newspapers; arrested after he picked up a flag that had accidentally toppled to the floor outside a "Goldwater for President" office. Two old women had called the police, insisting he had deliberately knocked it down and desecrated it. The publicity led NBC to drop him from an episode of *Dr. Kildare*. To prevent further blacklisting the hefty, hard-luck actor insisted on going through a trial to clear his name.

After that, he got the idea to "really shape up both physically and psychologically. I want to the gym every day for four years and lost eighty-five pounds...I went into analysis for seven years." Those were not particularly good years for him as an actor: "Nobody recognized me since I lost most of [the weight] from my face. Everyone thought I was ill." His wife, Marge Redmond, was doing better as Sister Jacqueline on *The Flying Nun*. She later became a star of Cool Whip commercials, leading Weston to remark, "She works five days a year and makes six figures!"

He made a comeback in stage comedies by Neil Simon and others. His chubby physique and excited, wide-eyed enthusiasm made him a perfect foil in *California Suite* and *The Ritz*, both featuring him in comic scenes of undress: "I guess I wear my underwear with dash and style and flare. Thank God, I've got nice legs."

The durable pro had one of his best parts in years as part of the ensemble cast in Alan Alda's film *The Four Seasons*. He received a Tony nomination for Woody Allen's *The Floating Light Bulb*. He said at the time, "I'm finally happy. After forty-five years in this business, I've received the best reviews I've ever had in my life. I'm finally accepted."

SELECTED BROADWAY APPEARANCES:
Season in the Sun (1950), *Bells Are Ringing* (1956), *Break a Leg* (1974), *The Ritz* (1975), *California Suite* (1976), *Cheaters* (1978), *The Floating Light Bulb* (1981)

SELECTED FILM APPEARANCES:
Please Don't Eat the Daisies (1960), *All in a Night's Work* (1961), *It's Only Money* (1962), *Palm Springs Weekend* (1963), *The Incredible Mr. Limpet* (1964), *Mirage* (1965), *Wait Until Dark* (1967), *The Thomas Crown Affair* (1968), *The April Fools* (1969), *Fuzz* (1972), *A New Leaf* (1972), *Gator* (1976), *The Ritz* (1976), *The Four Seasons* (1981), *High Road to China* (1983), *Ishtar* (1987), *Short Circuit 2* (1988)

TELEVISION SERIES:
Rod Brown of the Rocket Rangers (1953–54), *My Sister Eileen* (1960–61), *The Hathaways* (1961–62), *The Four Seasons* (1984)

JESSE WHITE
Jesse Wiedenfeld, January 3, 1918

Taciturn but capable of squinty good cheer, Jesse White could play a sneering Hollywood agent, a harried, cigar-chomping boss with a heart of at least brass, or a pushy salesman prone to a little shifty, risky business. For some, the stocky actor with the grim smile and nasal voice will always be best remembered as the lonely, seldom-used "Maytag Repairman" in twenty years of TV commercials.

White was born in Buffalo but grew up in Akron, Ohio, where at fifteen he was already finding work as a nightclub emcee. After graduat-

JESSE WHITE, who sneered his way through countless shifty-character roles, here being confronted by Alex Nicol and restrained by Horace McMahon in *Champ for a Day*.

ing from high school and appearing on local radio, he came to New York in 1942. He earned nine dollars a week on his day job as an elastic cutter for the Her Secret bra and corset company. (Years later he got a chance to utter the classic if feeble joke, "I'm in ladies underwear" as a lingerie salesman in a *Dick Van Dyke Show* episode.) The job had at least one bright side: he married the corset buyer for Constable's Department store.

White recalled his first Broadway roles as being "a sexy vacuum cleaner salesman" in *Sons and Soldiers* and "a horny Nazi lieutenant" in *The Moon Is Down*. He played Marvin Wilson, the male nurse, in 1,775 performances of *Harvey* during its four year run and later replaced Paul Douglas in *Born Yesterday*. He and Josephine Hull were the only ones to appear in both the original stage and film versions of *Harvey* (and later he even did it on TV with James Stewart and Helen Hayes).

In California, White played agent Irving La Salle in a touring production of *Will Success Spoil Rock Hunter*, and ended up playing similar agent parts in two long-running TV sitcoms. He was brassy agent Cagey Calhoun on *Private Secretary* and the equally pushy Jesse Leeds on *The Danny Thomas Show*. In the sixties, White was a favorite in sitcom-styled movies including *Looking for Love*, *Dear Brigitte*, and *The Spirit Is Willing*. It was in 1967 that he first became the lonely repairman in Maytag ads. (In 1989 sitcom actor Gordon Jump took over the role and White moved on to lucrative ads for other products).

White continued to appear in films and on television. (His daughter Carol played Big Rosie on *Laverne and Shirley*.) He always enjoyed stage work and appeared in summer stock productions of *The Odd Couple* and *Guys and Dolls* and took his old job of male nurse again when *Harvey* was revived. He said at the time, acknowledging his status as a famous character man and commercial spokesman, nobody knows by name, "As I look back over the years, little did I dream I would rise from obscurity to oblivion!"

SELECTED BROADWAY APPEARANCES:
The Moon Is Down (1942), *Sons and Soldiers* (1943), *My Dear Public* (1943), *Mrs. Kimball Presents* (1944), *Harvey* (1944), *The Cradle Will Rock* (1947), *Kelly* (1965), *Kiss Me Kate* (1965), *Harvey* (1970)

SELECTED FILM APPEARANCES:
Kiss of Death (1947), *Harvey* (1950), *Callaway Went Thataway* (1951), *Bedtime for Bonzo* (1951), *Francis Goes to the Races* (1951), *Million Dollar Mermaid* (1952), *Forever Female* (1954), *The Girl Rush* (1955), *Not as a Stranger* (1955), *Back From Eternity* (1956), *Marjorie Morningstar* (1958), *On the Double* (1961), *Sail a Crooked Ship* (1961), *It's Only Money* (1962), *It's a Mad, Mad, Mad, Mad World* (1963), *Looking for Love* (1964), *Pajama Party* (1964), *A House Is Not a Home* (1964), *Dear Brigitte* (1965), *The Spirit Is Willing* (1967), *The Reluctant Astronaut* (1967), *Bless the Beasts and Children* (1971), *The Cat From Outer Space* (1978)

TELEVISION SERIES:
Private Secretary (1953–57), *The Danny Thomas Show* (1955–57), *The Ann Sothern Show* (1960–61)

MARY WICKES
Mary Isabelle Wickenhauser, June 13, 1916

MARY WICKES, who always left 'em laughing—from *The Man Who Came to Dinner* to *Sister Act*.

T all Mary Wickes was no stereotyped man-chaser. She contrasted her gangling appearance with a stern, no-nonsense demeanor and scowls of chagrin. She was a formidable antagonist to Monty Woolley in *The Man Who Came to Dinner* and an even more formidable love interest in films opposite Shemp Howard, Lou Costello, and many others.

Born in St. Louis, a graduate of Washington University, Mary changed her mind about a career in law and took off for Stockbridge, Massachusetts, instead, appearing in a season of summer theater in 1934. She came to New York soon after. The aggressive actress paid a bellboy to point out Broadway producer Marc Connelly to her. She took care of the rest. He gave the plucky young girl a walk-on in his new show, *The Farmer Takes a Wife*.

She went on to other small roles in Broadway shows, ultimately playing Miss Preen, the nurse babysitting a blustery Sheridan Whiteside (Monty Woolley) in *The Man Who Came to Dinner*. Amid headshaking and glaring, she took plenty of insults: "My great Aunt Jennifer…she had been dead three days…looked better than you do now!" Wickes got even: "If Florence Nightingale had ever nursed you she would've married Jack the Ripper instead of founding the Red Cross!"

She played the role in the movie (and the 1972 TV version starring Orson Welles) and found many more comic roles in films. Though her dour scowls and sour jowls did not make her a typical leading lady, comedians were lovesick over the funny girl. She was Shemp Howard's lady friend in *Private Buckaroo*, lending the film its only laughs. In *Who Done It?* she was paired with Lou Costello. Realistic about accepting a less-than-perfect mate (and being less-than-perfect herself), she supports her bumbling boyfriend. When Lou handcuffs police detective William Bendix, she doesn't gush over his heroics. She grunts, "Got more nerve than I thought."

On a 1949 television production of *Studio One* Wickes played *Mary Poppins*. On subsequent series, though, she seemed typed as a domestic (*The Peter Lind Hayes Show* and *Bonino*) or a nurse (*Doc*). She received an Emmy nomination for her role as Maxfield on Gertrude Berg's *Mrs. G. Goes to College* and was Lloyd Nolan's wife, Melba Chegley, on *Julia*. Her long career as a plucky supporting player included the 1989–91 seasons of *The Father Dowling Mysteries* as the rectory housekeeper.

On stage in Los Angeles, Wickes won over critics as the eccentric Madame Arcati in a 1966 revival of *High Spirits*. In films, she played Sister Clarissa in both *The Trouble With Angels* and the sequel, *Where Angels Go,*

The Cat and the Canary (1935), *Accent on Youth* (1935), *Stage Door* (1936), *Father Maladry's Miracle* (1937), *The Man Who Came to Dinner* (1939), *Jackpot* (1944), *Town House* (1948), *Show Boat* (1952)

The Man Who Came to Dinner (1941), *Private Buckaroo* (1942), *Now Voyager* (1942), *Who Done It?* (1942), *My Kingdom for a Cook* (1943), *How About It?* (1943), *Happy Land* (1943), *Higher and Higher* (1943), *June Bride* (1944), *Anna Lucasta* (1949), *On Moonlight Bay* (1951), *I'll See You in My Dreams* (1951), *The Will Rogers Story* (1952), *Half a Hero* (1953), *Destry* (1954), *White Christmas* (1954), *Dance With Me Henry* (1956), *Don't Go Near the Water* (1957), *It Happened to Jane* (1959), *The Music Man* (1962), *How to Murder Your Wife* (1965), *The Trouble With Angels* (1966), *Where Angels Go, Trouble Follows* (1967), *The Spirit Is Willing* (1967), *Snowball Express* (1972), *Willa* (1979), *Touched by Love* (1980), *Postcards From the Edge* (1990), *Sister Act* (1992)

Inside U.S.A. With Chevrolet (1949–50), *The Peter Lind Hayes Show* (1950), *Bonino* (1953), *The Halls of Ivy* (1954–55), *Dennis the Menace* (1959–61), *Mrs. G. Goes to College* (1961–62), *Julia* (1966–71), *Doc* (1975–76), *The Father Dowling Mysteries* (1989–91)

Trouble Follows. For her many achievements, Washington University honored her with an honorary doctorate. She went on to get a master's degree in theater from UCLA, and appear in many more West Coast stage productions.

In her sixties, she was still more than capable of pulling off her trademark role of the earthy spinster, the woman less lovelorn than loved, lost, and now resolutely determined to get her fair share of love again. On an episode of *M*A*S*H* she played a senior officer in Korea with her eye on weak-chinned Major Frank Burns. After flirting ("You got your own place or do you live with your folks?"), she flat-out propositions him with the promise of a promotion.

It was another hard sell for Mary Wickes, but she was still trying. She had some strange choices (from Shemp Howard in films to Major Burns on TV) but when producers chose Mary Wickes, they got one of the few funny ladies in films who could hold her own against even the most disparate of comedy costars.

MARIE WILSON

Katherine Elizabeth White, August 19, 1916–November 23, 1972

Marie Wilson was one of the first "dumb blond" actresses to amuse audiences during the talkie era.

Her career began with a binge, if not a bang. Her father, an orange grove owner, died and left her $11,000. The sixteen-year-old took the money and her sister Marie's first name and headed for Hollywood. She bought a mink, a fancy car, and looked like a star. The only thing missing was movie roles.

When she ran out of money and began working in a department store, the "dumb" blond needed a smart idea to get ahead. One day her car conveniently ran out of gas in front of the home of a movie producer. Soon she was getting bit parts and extra work in a variety of films, and played Sam Spade's secretary in *Satan Met a Lady* (the Warren

William remake of *The Maltese Falcon).*

In 1938 she starred with James Cagney in *Boy Meets Girl.* Her best dumb-bunny line was actually delivered off-camera. In one scene she had to sit on Cagney's lap while he spoke a few lines. Afterward the impressionable starlet gushed to the surprised makeup woman, "Sitting on Jimmy's lap was like being on top of a flagpole!"

In the film, she did some standard airhead prattling, complete with airy punchlines. When one man interrupts her nonsense and complains, "I'm afraid I don't quite follow," Marie admits, "Nobody does." When it's discovered she's been involved with a married man someone tries to comfort her. "Nobody can blame you," he says. "His wife did," Marie cries. "She shot him."

Ken Murray picked Wilson for his *Blackouts of 1942* revue and bounced, tacky jokes off her breasts: "You look beautiful tonight. You're not in that dress too far? Ha ha...where were you born?" "Anaheim...in a grapefruit grove." "You were born in a grapefruit grove? Ha ha, that explains a couple of things...."

MARIE WILSON epitomized the dizzy blond scene stealers from the thirties to the fifties.

She was Murray's pretty stooge for seven years, both on stage and on radio. Then she got a chance to star in her own radio series, *My Friend Irma.* Analyzing her appeal, Wilson noted, "People like me because I'm dumb. It gives them a good feeling to be smarter than I am." Sometimes she could use a dumb line as a weapon. One night at the 18 Club in New York, emcee Jack White spotted Marie in the audience and coaxed her on stage. He suddenly thrust the microphone in front of her, and asked her to say a few words. She told the audience, "Don't drink your bathwater." Then she sat down, leaving White groping for a comeback. He was still groping when she left.

Wilson was always pretty clever when it counted. When insiders whispered that Betty Hutton would star in the film version of *My Friend Irma,* Marie rallied her fan club to her aid. The publicity over "another Irma" taking her place effectively stopped Hutton. Today the two *Irma* movies are viewed mostly because her comic support was a new comedy team called Martin and Lewis. The *My Friend Irma* television series hasn't been rerun often. Still, in the fifties Wilson played Irma for all it was worth. The curvy blond always tried to keep the humor on the sweet, Gracie Allen side: "Irma, do you like to travel?" "Oh yes, it's really the only way to get anyplace."

Wilson's career didn't flag too badly after her *Irma*

SELECTED FILM APPEARANCES:
Satan Met a Lady (1936), *Fools for Scandal* (1938), *The Sweepstakes Winner* (1939), *Boy Meets Girl* (1940), *Broadway* (1942), *The Young Widow* (1947), *Linda Be Good* (1948), *My Friend Irma* (1949), *My Friend Irma Goes West* (1950), *A Girl in Every Port* (1951), *Marry Me Again* (1954), *Mr. Hobbs Takes a Vacation* (1962)

MONTY WOOLLEY, irascible bearded actor who defined caustic superiority during twenty years on the screen, looks askance at Gracie Fields as Laird Cregar prepares to autograph a check in *Holy Matrimony*.

heyday. She kept busy in stock companies of *Born Yesterday* and *Gentlemen Prefer Blondes* and even found behind-the-scenes success in voiceovers (including the *Where's Huddles?* Saturday morning cartoon show). She appeared in an episode of *Love American Style* though ill with cancer. She died a short time later, leaving behind her husband and a son.

MONTY WOOLLEY
Edgar Montillion Woolley,
August 17, 1888–May 6, 1963

Monty Woolley's film credits were many, but the ex-professor from Yale will always be remembered best as *The Man Who Came to Dinner*, the arrogant, egocentric, irascible, over-enunciating critic who manipulates everyone around him—at least, everyone who allows it.

Woolley was born at the Bristol Hotel in New York. There wasn't anything too surprising about that. His father owned the place. Young Monty went to the best schools and was a friend of Cole Porter's at Yale. In fact years later Woolley played himself in the Porter film biography *Night and Day*.

Woolley was both an English and drama professor at Yale. He came to Broadway first as a director (*The New Yorkers* in 1930, *Jubilee* in 1935). As an actor he grew a beard (he once wrote an article on beards, "the historic trademark of genius") and seemed to specialize in swaggering parts that called for charismatic conceit. It was *The Man Who Came to Dinner* that secured his popularity.

In the notorious roman à clef, the character Sheridan Whiteside was critic and radio personality Alexander Woolcott, actress Lorraine Sheldon was Gertrude Lawrence, foppish Beverly Carlton was Noel Coward, and the comical Banjo was Harpo Marx. Woolley dominated with arch and acidic one-liners. He battled his nurse: "Take your clammy hands off my chair—you have the touch of a sex-starved cobra." He put off admiring visitors: "Stand back—don't get too close. I have several contagious diseases!" And he insulted his doctor: "Dr. Bradley is the greatest living argument for mercy killing."

Woolley managed to make rudeness amusing, if not lovable. It was a trait he carried with him in films both before and after *The Man Who Came to Dinner*. As a judge in Lubitsch's *Midnight*, he presides over a divorce proceeding: "It's permissible for a wife to be beaten, as long as

244

she's struck not more than nine times with an instrument not larger than a broomstick."

In real life, Woolley was similar to his film character. Arriving in Oklahoma City on tour, he told the gathered press, "All I ask is that you let me alone.If the

Secretary of War came to town you wouldn't pay any attention—you wouldn't even ask the President for his autograph. But let some lousy movie actor like me come along and you won't let me rest!"

SELECTED BROADWAY APPEARANCES:
On Your Toes (1936), *Knights of Song* (1938), *The Man Who Came to Dinner* (1939)

SELECTED FILM APPEARANCES:
Nothing Sacred (1937), *Arsene Lupin Returns* (1938), *Everybody Sing* (1938), *Young Doctor Kildare* (1938), *Girl of the Golden West* (1938), *Artists and Models Abroad* (1938), *Never Say Die* (1939), *Midnight* (1939), *Man About Town* (1939), *The Man Who Came to Dinner* (1941), *The Pied Piper* (1942), *Life Begins at 8:30* (1942), *Holy Matrimony* (1943), *Molly and Me* (1945), *Night and Day* (1946), *The Bishop's Wife* (1947), *Miss Tatlock's Millions* (1948), *As Young as You Feel* (1951), *Kismet* (1955)

AFTERWORD

Most of the comic support players in this collection were active primarily in films from 1930 to 1960. It was a distinctive age for them because it was a distinctive age for the major stars as well.

People wonder why there are no longer such memorable players as Edward Everett Horton, Arthur Treacher, Margaret Hamilton, or Margaret Dumont. Part of the reason is that there are no longer such identifiable stars as Cary Grant, Bela Lugosi, Humphrey Bogart, or Groucho Marx.

In the "golden era" of movies, most every star was bigger than life; charismatic and completely unique. A star wasn't a star unless he or she could be imitated and emulated: John Wayne, Bette Davis, Peter Lorre, James Cagney, Clark Gable, Charles Laughton, Edward G. Robinson, Lionel Barrymore, etc.

By the sixties, only a few stars were so distinctive. These included Kirk Douglas, Burt Lancaster, and Marlon Brando. Less quirky, more realistic "Everyman" stars, such as Paul Newman, James Garner, and Steve McQueen were the rule rather than the exception. And by the nineties, about the only modern movie stars that an impressionist could mimic were Jack Nicholson and Arnold Schwarzenegger. The majority were again the somewhat bland types who looked and spoke without exaggeration or much distinction: Michael J. Fox, Tom Cruise, Tom Hanks, and Kevin Costner.

And so it's been that the number of identifiable comic support players has dwindled, too. An eccentric comic costar would be distracting.

Fortunately, there's a bright side to this. It seems that some of the people who would have been supporting players in the thirties or forties are being given starring roles in movies and sitcoms today. The demand for unique and funny people is greater than ever.

And so the stereotypical fat man (John Candy) or fat woman (Roseanne Barr Arnold), little man (Rick Moranis), snide man (Dabney Coleman), ditsy girl (Teri Garr), or uptight woman (Jane Curtin) is not only given a bigger role than one might expect, but one with greater dimension, befitting these complex times. Ensemble shows like *Saturday Night Live* offer a different kind of comic support, with most of the players equally sharing the lines and the stage time, equally comfortable getting the laugh or just setting up a straight line for someone else.

These stars of today often admit that they've adapted techniques and styles of the past masters. The influence lives on. And so do the original comic support players, who continue to amuse and delight audiences old and new. While this page may close the book on the classic world of motion picture "comic support," the stars and their films remain immortal.

ORDER NOW!
Citadel Film Books

If you like this book, you'll love the award-winning Citadel Film Series. Each volume is packed with photos and behind-the-scenes insight about your favorite stars--from James Stewart to Moe Howard and The Three Stooges, Woody Allen to John Wayne. The Citadel Film Series is America's largest and oldest film book library.

With more than 150 titles--and more on the way!--Citadel Film Books make perfect gifts for a loved one, a friend, or best of all, yourself!

A complete listing of the Citadel Film Series appears below.
Ask for them at your bookstore.
Or to order direct from the publisher call 1-800-447-BOOK
and have your MasterCard or Visa ready.

STARS
Alan Ladd
Barbra Streisand: The First
    Decade; The Second
    Decade
Bela Lugosi
Bette Davis
Boris Karloff
The Bowery Boys
Buster Keaton
Carole Lombard
Cary Grant
Charles Bronson
Charlie Chaplin
Clark Gable
Clint Eastwood
Curly
Dustin Hoffman
Edward G. Robinson
Elizabeth Taylor
Elvis Presley
Errol Flynn
Frank Sinatra
Gary Cooper
Gene Kelly
Gina Lollobrigida
Gloria Swanson
Gregory Peck
Greta Garbo
Henry Fonda
Humphrey Bogart
Ingrid Bergman
Jack Lemmon
Jack Nicholson
James Cagney
James Dean: Behind the
    Scene
Jane Fonda
Jeanette MacDonald &
    Nelson Eddy
Joan Crawford

John Wayne Films
John Wayne Reference Book
John Wayne Scrapbook
Judy Garland
Katharine Hepburn
Kirk Douglas
Laurel & Hardy
Lauren Bacall
Laurence Olivier
Mae West
Marilyn Monroe
Marlene Dietrich
Marlon Brando
Marx Brothers
Moe Howard & the Three
    Stooges
Norma Shearer
Olivia de Havilland
Orson Welles
Paul Newman
Peter Lorre
Rita Hayworth
Robert De Niro
Robert Redford
Sean Connery
Sexbomb: Jayne Mansfield
Shirley MacLaine
Shirley Temple
The Sinatra Scrapbook
Spencer Tracy
Steve McQueen
Three Stooges Scrapbook
Warren Beatty
W.C. Fields
William Holden
William Powell
A Wonderful Life: James
    Stewart
DIRECTORS
Alfred Hitchcock
Cecil B. DeMille

Federico Fellini
Frank Capra
John Ford
John Huston
Woody Allen
GENRE
Bad Guys
Black Hollywood
Black Hollywood: From
    1970 to Today
Classics of the Gangster Film
Classics of the Horror Film
Divine Images: Jesus on
    Screen
Early Classics of Foreign
    Film
Great French Films
Great German Films
Great Romantic Films
Great Science Fiction Films
Harry Warren & the Holly-
    wood Musical
Hispanic Hollywood: The
    Latins in Motion Pictures
The Hollywood Western
The Incredible World of 007
The Jewish Image in Ameri-
    can Film
The Lavender Screen: The
    Gay and Lesbian Films
Martial Arts Movies
The Modern Horror Film
More Classics of Horror Film
Movie Psychos & Madmen
Our Huckleberry Friend:
    Johnny Mercer
Second Feature: "B" Films
They Sang! They Danced!
    They Romanced!: Holly-
    wood Musicals
Thrillers

The West That Never Was
Words and Shadows:
    Literature   on the Screen
DECADE
Classics of the Silent Screen
Films of the Twenties
Films of the Thirties
More Films of the 30's
Films of the Forties
Films of the Fifties
Lost Films of the 50's
Films of the Sixties
Films of the Seventies
Films of the Eighties
SPECIAL INTEREST
America on the Rerun
Bugsy screenplay
Comic Support
Dick Tracy
Favorite Families of TV
Film Flubs
Film Flubs: The Sequel
First Films
Forgotten Films to Remember
Gilligan, Maynard & Me
Hollywood Cheesecake
Hollywood's Hollywood
Howard Hughes in Holly-
    wood
More Character People
The Nightmare Never Ends:
    Freddy Krueger & "A Night-
    mare on Elm Street"
"Northern Exposure" Book
The "Quantum Leap" Book
Sex In the Movies
Sherlock Holmes
Son of Film Flubs
Those Glorious Glamour Years
Who Is That?: Familiar Faces
    and Forgotten Names
"You Ain't Heard Nothin' Yet!"

For a free full-color brochure describing the Citadel Film Series in depth, call 1-800-447-BOOK; or send your name and address to Citadel Film Books, Distribution Center 1399, 120 Enterprise Ave., Secaucus, NJ 07094.